AFTER THE WARS

International Lessons From the U.S. Wars in Iraq and Afghanistan

Edited by John A. Gentry and William M. Nolte

D0932606

July 2018

NATIONAL INTELLIGENCE UNIVERSITY

The goal of the NI Press is to publish high quality, valuable, and timely books on topics of concern to the Intelligence Community and the U.S. government. Books published by the NI Press undergo peer review by senior officials in the U.S. government as well as outside experts.

How to order this book: Everyone may download a free electronic copy of this book from our website at http://www.NI-U.edu. U.S. government employees may request a complimentary copy of this book by contacting us at: press@NI-U.edu. The general public may purchase a copy from the Government Printing Office (GPO) at http://bookstore.gpo.gov.

Editor, NI Press
National Intelligence University
Bethesda, Maryland

ISBN   978-1-932946-12-3
GPO Sales Stock Number   008-020-01650-1
Library of Congress Control Number   2018939634

For sale by the Superintendent of Documents, U.S. Government Publishing Office
Internet: bookstore.gpo.gov   Phone: toll free (866) 512-1800;   DC area (202) 512-1800
Fax: (202) 512-2104   Mail: Stop IDCC, Washington, DC 20402-0001
ISBN 978-1-932946-12-3

TABLE OF CONTENTS

List of Tables v

Foreword vii

Introduction 1
John A. Gentry and William M. Nolte

Chapter 1: Less Capable and Less Willing?
European Involvement in Combat Operations
After Iraq and Afghanistan 7
Peter Viggo Jakobsen

Chapter 2: The Country of Unrequited Dreams:
Lessons From Germany's Mission in Afghanistan 29
Patrick Keller

Chapter 3: What Did Russia Learn From the U.S. Wars
in Iraq and Afghanistan? 49
Stephen Blank

Chapter 4: Iran: Goals and Strategy "Steadfast," but Open
to Tactical Innovation 73
Thomas E. Dowling

Chapter 5: America's Wars and Turkish Attitudes:
A Slippery Slope 99
K.A. Beyoghlow

Chapter 6: How Pakistan Plays Its Double Game:
Lessons Learned Since 9/11 119
Stephen Tankel

Chapter 7: Chinese Views on the U.S. Wars on
Afghanistan and Iraq 133
David Lai

Chapter 8: Japan's Lessons in Iraq and Afghanistan 147
Michael W. David

Chapter 9: Perspectives of International Nongovernmental Organizations 165
Pauline H. Baker

Chapter 10: Learning by Insurgents 185
Lawrence E. Cline

Chapter 11: U.S. Intelligence Credibility in the Crosshairs: On the Post-War Defensive 201
Bowman H. Miller

Chapter 12: Conclusion: Lessons of the Lessons 217
John A. Gentry

Endnotes 231
    Introduction 231
    Chapter 1 231
    Chapter 2 239
    Chapter 3 244
    Chapter 4 251
    Chapter 5 265
    Chapter 6 270
    Chapter 7 278
    Chapter 8 294
    Chapter 9 299
    Chapter 10 303
    Chapter 11 310
    Chapter 12 313

Index 317

Contributors 339

LIST OF TABLES

Table 1: Overview of French, Italian, UK, and U.S.
Contributions to the Libya Intervention 11

Table 2: Overview of French, German, Italian, UK,
and U.S. Contributions to the Mali Intervention
(January–April 2013) 18

Table 3: Overview of French, German, Italian, UK, and
U.S. Military Contributions to Operation INHERENT RESOLVE
(August 2014–). 21

Table 4: Comparing the Four European Countries
Across Cases 25

FOREWORD

Providing decisionmakers with information that helps them to either avoid or successfully prosecute war is a core mission of intelligence professionals. In my 30-year intelligence career there were successes such as the Cold War, and failures such as 9/11 and Iraq WMD that led to the wars that followed. Formal examinations by experts followed both the successes and the failures in an attempt to develop appropriate responses to what could be learned from them. The responses were not uniform. After the Cold War the priority of some issues was lowered, and others were elevated. In the case of 9/11, the overseers of the Intelligence Community (IC) judged that its structure and approach to sharing information must be changed to respond appropriately to a new threat environment. The performance of the IC regarding Iraq WMD led experts to conclude that improvements in both collection posture and analytic rigor were essential to improving the IC's ability to counter the WMD threat writ large. In all the cases above, the examinations and the responses they engendered were appropriately focused on the internal workings of the U.S. government. They sought to improve performance, and most importantly to avoid war in the future.

But can we learn more of equally strategic import when we ask experts to examine how non-U.S. government entities view U.S. actions and what they have learned from them? This book answers that question with an emphatic yes. Drs. Gentry and Nolte have assembled a team of recognized experts and asked them to examine what non-U.S. government entities—adversaries and allies alike—have learned from the U.S. prosecution of wars in Afghanistan and Iraq. Over 11 thought-provoking chapters, this book takes the reader on an important journey through the lessons of the wars from very different perspectives. Like the internal examinations cited above, the lessons and responses are not uniform. We do not have to agree with the lessons and responses, but it is essential that we understand them and how they might shape future U.S. relationships with nation-states, international organizations, and insurgents. The book reminds us that we all learn from experience and are confident that we have indeed learned because we develop what we believe are appropriate responses to our experiences. We learn that a pot on a stove can burn us (experience), so we use some kind of protection when we touch it (response). That same kind of learning from experience and response formulation has happened across the world in regard to the U.S. wars in

Afghanistan and Iraq. This book presents what has been learned to date and challenges us to deal with the resulting responses to those lessons in the interests of national security.

As an intelligence professional I often struggled with the need to stay current on issues, while at the same time assessing and understanding their strategic importance. In providing a forum for the publication of this book, the National Intelligence Press has made a significant contribution to a strategic assessment of the lessons of the Afghanistan and Iraq wars even as they continue to be waged. In leading the creation of this manuscript, Drs. Gentry and Nolte have given all of us a gift—they have made us think and learn. I urge anyone charged with supporting the formulation of U.S. policy to read and internalize the lessons articulated here. I celebrate this groundbreaking work.

Maureen Baginski
Chair, National Intelligence University Board of Visitors
Former FBI Executive Assistant Director for Intelligence
Former NSA Director of Signals Intelligence

After the Wars: International Lessons From the U.S. Wars in Iraq and Afghanistan

INTRODUCTION

John A. Gentry and William M. Nolte

The wars the United States fought in Iraq (2003–11) and in Afghanistan since September 11, 2001, have generated much commentary and analysis. Studies of lessons have begun even as both wars really are not finished. Conflict has resumed in Iraq in different ways and continues in Afghanistan. Nevertheless, one major U.S. international experience did end in Iraq in 2011, and the largest part of the international effort in Afghanistan appears to be over. Hence, it is reasonable to begin the process of assessing lessons, recognizing that assessments will be tentative or conditional.

The U.S. military has formal "lessons-learned" processes, which focus mainly on assessing the experiences of U.S. military forces and, to a lesser extent, other U.S. government agencies and their processes. Department of Defense research assets already have examined aspects of the wars.[1] American scholars also have assessed U.S. performance in the wars.[2] Undoubtedly there will be many more such studies.

This book takes a different approach. It examines the perspectives of actors other than the U.S. government—states and nonstate actors—on the wars in which the United States participated, and assesses the extent to which these actors learned lessons that have implications for their long-term foreign, security, and other important policies, and for their major future actions. Eventually and perhaps indirectly, many of these lessons may affect U.S. policymaking and national interests. Some of these implications already are evident and seem significant, meaning it is important for U.S. decisionmakers and for scholars—preferably sooner than later—to understand, take account of, and in some cases prepare for manifestations of these lessons. Other ramifications of these learning processes undoubtedly will not be apparent for some time to come.

This book therefore has several target audiences. We hope that insights and understanding of the perceptions and lessons of others will help U.S. government decisionmakers to add variables to the already complicated mix of factors that enter senior-level strategic decisionmaking. The book should be useful for parts of the bureaucracy, including defense planners and foreign aid managers. These chapters discuss a wide variety of strategic-, operational-, and tactical-level issues that should help identify the important intelligence issues of future military operations. In early 2010, Major General Michael Flynn (USA), who then was in Afghanistan and who later as Lieutenant General Flynn was director of the Defense Intelligence Agency, penned (with two colleagues) a scathing critique of U.S. intelligence performance in Afghanistan. Flynn wrote:

> Eight years into the war in Afghanistan, the U.S. intelligence community is only marginally relevant to the overall strategy. Having focused the overwhelming majority of its collection efforts and analytic brainpower on insurgent groups, the vast intelligence apparatus is unable to answer fundamental questions about the environment in which U.S. and allied forces operate and the people they seek to persuade.[3]

We hope this book will help avoid a recurrence of this kind of "irrelevance" by identifying strategically important issues for U.S. intelligence to examine before, and consistently during, conflicts and non-violent missions the U.S. government may consider or actually undertake. These same issues are also important for other governments to address, although perhaps in different ways and for different reasons.

We hope, too, that scholars and analysts of the wars will find the book beneficial. The various perspectives of participants and interested observers enable a comparative perspective rare in histories and political analyses of wars.

The United States displayed much of its military material strength, used new technologies, employed new military doctrines, operated unilaterally and with a variety of allies and coalition partners, and fought the states of Iraq (2003) and Afghanistan (2001) and a variety of nonstate actors. U.S. strategies in both countries changed repeatedly since 2001 and have been widely criticized for inconsistency even within the United States. The citizenry and political leaders of the United States also have demonstrated various types and degrees of support for, and opposition to, both wars, which have in different ways both influenced and reflected the foreign and domestic policies of the administrations of Presidents George W. Bush and Barack Obama.

With a withdrawal from Afghanistan of most U.S. and coalition troops certain, and a messy and long-term, if low-level, military commitment appearing likely as of this writing in early 2016, the United States seems to be on the verge of ending its originally intended involvement in both wars with its initial goals only partially achieved. This result has led, and is likely to continue to lead, many countries and nonstate actors—U.S. friends, potential enemies, and neutral observers—to ask major, related questions: How could the world's "superpower" have achieved so little at such great cost? Why and how did the United States fail to achieve its goals? Were there systematic problems of leadership, military strategy and doctrine, political will, or other failures? What did the United States and its coalition partners do well? Given American strategies, operating practices, and operational problems and successes, what have potential American enemies learned about how to fight militarily and engage politically the United States in the future? What have U.S. friends and more neutral third parties learned about dealing with Washington? How will major states react to the perceived lessons of other states and nonstate actors in other international and domestic situations?

The countries, nonstate actors, and functional subjects chosen for discussion in this book are ones the editors expected to be important in coming years in various aspects of international relations. We expected that key actors had already asked themselves questions similar to those above and reached at least some tentative conclusions. We therefore gave chapter authors a broad mandate: provide your best assessment of how foreign actors see lessons of the wars in ways important *to those actors*, and analyze how those lessons will affect their future foreign and security policies and actions. We invited chapter contributors to think about, at least:

- Lessons useful for designing strategies to attack the United States or U.S. interests.
- Perceptions of the will (or lack thereof) of the United States and its coalition partners to stick with their commitments in open-ended, costly wars. What vulnerabilities are created by a shortage of national will combined with significant casualty aversion? Do important actors see these as vulnerabilities they intend to exploit? If so, how? For what expected strategic purposes?
- The U.S. controversy over counterinsurgency doctrine and operations, and lessons for the conduct of irregular warfare.
- The role of airpower.
- The role of military land power.
- Perceptions of America's friends and allies about the United States in general.
- Command and control and cyber issues.

- Information operations.
- The strategic effectiveness of special operations forces in counterterrorist roles.
- Political/technology issues, perhaps including the military and political ramifications of drone warfare.
- Implications for international organizations, especially United Nations system agencies, and nongovernmental organizations (NGOs).
- Coalition operations—including their advantages, disadvantages, and operational challenges.
- Implications for international intelligence sharing.
- Implications for humanitarian interventions and their participants, including NGOs, international organizations, and "weak actors"—both states and nonstate actors.

All of these issues, and more, are addressed in various ways in the chapters that follow.

The authors of these chapters are all experts in their fields—scholars and practitioners with a wealth of knowledge and unique insights. For this reason, the editors encouraged creativity in answering the core questions: what have actors learned, and what are the implications of those lessons for the future? The result is an eclectic set of high-quality chapters that reflect the divergent lessons important states and nonstate actors have learned, as well as the insights of the authors. All of the chapters were peer-reviewed by at least one specialist in the same area.

Contributors wrote their chapters independently. Their considerable freedom to identify important lessons for their identified group(s) means that the focus and style of the chapters differ somewhat. The unifying theme of the chapters is lessons, broadly defined, of the wars. And, of course, even a large book could not capture all of the lessons of all of the parties that participated or were interested in long and complicated wars. This book therefore is not a comprehensive examination of the wars. There are appreciable gaps in coverage in this volume, and there are modest differences in judgment among the contributing authors. We appreciate those differences and view them as useful contributions to the early part of the process of understanding important and very complex events.

Eight country-focused chapters look at states that are major international players and that were either participants in one or both of the wars or were interested observers known to study keenly the lessons of other states' wars. These include three chapters on states allied to the United States—a NATO-focused chapter that discusses the United Kingdom, France, Italy, and Germany, and separate chapters on Germany and Japan. These countries' lessons focus heavily on alliance and domestic political factors. A chapter on Turkey covers conflicting pressures—recognition of the importance of membership in NATO but also many domestic political and regional concerns about the purpose and conduct of the Iraq war. Chapters on Russia and China cover lessons those important countries learned largely vicariously; these chapters make clear that Russian and Chinese analysts have studied the wars closely and that senior political and military leaders of both countries have acted on those lessons to alter policies, military and other government capacities, and operations in ways designed to help achieve both domestic and international objectives. The chapter on Pakistan largely addresses internal lessons and consequences of the war in Afghanistan. And, the chapter on Iran addresses lessons of a country with which the United States and its coalition partners fought low-level proxy wars in both Iraq and Afghanistan and which, by virtually all accounts, has become a stronger regional power as a result of the wars.

Two chapters address the lessons of nonstate actors of very different sorts. One, on nongovernmental organizations (NGOs), discusses how major international humanitarian NGOs operated in complex environments that were difficult for them in several important ways: the wars were dangerous and many of their people were killed; changing U.S. and coalition contracting rules and operational doctrine threatened the neutrality they value; and the nature of the counterinsurgency wars had significant ramifications for the ways they organize and fund themselves. States in recent years have delegated to these organizations growing responsibilities for a wide variety of security-related activities. NGOs, in turn, have agendas that often differ from those of their state sponsors, and they have not been completely happy with their roles in coalition operations in either war. Their altered perspectives promise to be important for military personnel, foreign aid agencies, and policymakers for years to come.

Another chapter addresses the very different lessons of three violent nonstate groups the United States fought in various ways during and after the conventional phases of both wars: al-Qaida in Iraq; the Taliban of Afghanistan; and the Islamic State of Iraq and the Levant (ISIL). The Taliban and ISIL learned important lessons that helped them overcome significant setbacks they, and especially al-Qaida in Iraq, experienced, and arguably to thrive. Indeed, as in virtually all counterinsurgent wars, learning by weak actors is essential for their survival. Some of the lessons ISIL, in particular, has learned are already clear—and are in part reflected in newspaper headlines and political/military strategies of many states around the world.

A chapter discusses intelligence sharing. Although it is inherently difficult to do in an unclassified forum, this chapter discusses some implications of aspects of the wars on intelligence sharing by the United States with several major allies.

The final chapter summarizes recurrent themes and assembles issues the editors think especially worthy of additional consideration. The explicit objective of this collection was to see the American involvement in Iraq and Afghanistan from a range of international perspectives. Had we focused only on the views of American observers, we would have expected a range of analytical approaches and views. With this broader perspective, a wider range of relevant issues and judgments seems natural, and we have expanded the scope of analysis even further in the final chapter. Not all of the perspectives view U.S. conduct of the wars favorably—for a variety of reasons. We ask readers, even in disagreement with aspects of one chapter or another, to reflect on the significance of the wide range of views of major international actors presented here and the insights of knowledgeable analysts.

CHAPTER 1
Less Capable and Less Willing? European Involvement in Combat Operations After Iraq and Afghanistan

Peter Viggo Jakobsen

There is near consensus among decisionmakers and analysts on both sides of the Atlantic that the Afghanistan and Iraq wars have contributed to make the European NATO allies less capable and less willing to use force. U.S. Secretary of Defense Robert Gates made headlines with his complaint that too many European members were unwilling and unable to conduct strike missions as part of the NATO air campaign against Libya in 2011.[1] Many European and American analysts agreed with him, characterizing the European NATO contributions to the Libya campaign as underwhelming.[2] Similar assessments have been made of the European contributions to the subsequent combat operations in Mali and Iraq, and they are nicely summed up by Camille Grand, a leading French military expert, who judged in the wake of the Mali intervention that "we are moving toward a Europe that is a combination of the unable and the unwilling."[3] Across the Atlantic a RAND report agreed, concluding in 2013 that "three of the most capable forces in NATO—the British, French, and German armies—are making themselves less capable of shouldering security burdens by accepting budget cuts that make them smaller, less ready, and less able to sustain forces abroad."[4]

This chapter takes issue with the prevailing argument that the wars in Afghanistan and Iraq have accelerated a process that will make the Western European NATO members increasingly less capable and less willing to engage in combat operations. This argument is problematic because it ignores that the lessons learned from Afghanistan and Iraq differ markedly across Europe, and that a nation's willingness to spend on defense and use force is shaped by factors other than recent operational experience. Europe's future ability and willingness to engage in combat will also depend on national threat assessments, national views of the military instrument, and U.S. policy. Whether the

Western European NATO members will indeed become less capable and less willing to engage in combat will therefore be determined by the interaction of all these factors, and the operational experience in Afghanistan and Iraq will carry increasingly less weight as new operational experiences come into play. Europe's future ability and willingness to fight are therefore much harder to predict than most analyses currently assume.

This chapter will demonstrate how these four explanatory factors shaped the willingness of Western Europe's four largest military powers, France, Germany, Italy, and the United Kingdom, to provide combat contributions to the interventions undertaken in Libya (2011), Mali (2013), and Iraq/Syria (2014–). These four countries were chosen because they are the only Western European ones left with a capability to act as lead nations in out-of-area operations. Since the other European NATO members take their cues from these countries (using their action or inaction as a guide for their own actions), the actions of the "big European four" constitute a good indicator of the overall European ability and willingness to fight.

The argument has three parts. Part one presents the four determinants shaping the European capability and willingness to fight: threat, national views of force, recent operational experience, and the need to maintain a good relationship with Washington owing to Europe's growing security dependence on the United States. Part two analyzes how these four factors influenced the willingness of Western Europe's four largest military powers, France, Germany, Italy and the United Kingdom, to provide combat contributions to the interventions in Libya, Mali, and Iraq/Syria. The final part compares the three cases and discusses their implications for future transatlantic combat cooperation.

The Four Determinants of the European Combat Contributions

Perceptions of the military instrument play a fundamental role in shaping a nation's willingness and ability to use force. If the use of force is perceived as essentially "bad," as is the case in Germany, where the legacies of two world wars and the Holocaust have given the use for force for purposes other than national survival a bad name, the willingness to engage in combat is low. Conversely, if use of force is viewed positively in terms of both national identity and as an instrument of policy, as is the case in France and the United Kingdom, the willingness to engage in combat operations will be high.

The perceived utility and legitimacy of the military instrument is also influenced by recent operational experience. Recent failures tend to generate "never again" sentiments and reluctance to engage in new combat operations, whereas successes tend to create a greater preparedness to use force.

As indicated above, the Afghanistan and Iraq wars have resulted in a greater reluctance to engage in combat operations with ground forces on both sides of the Atlantic. This fear of being embroiled in another quagmire ruled out any use of ground forces in Libya in 2011, and this reluctance has also shaped the "no boots on the ground approach" to the management of the civil wars in Iraq and Syria.

A third determinant is the perception of threat. Europe's reduced willingness and capability to fight are the logical result of a reduced sense of threat. Since the collapse of the Soviet Union, Europe has not faced any existential military threat, and this remains the case today despite Russia's annexation of the Crimean Peninsula and subsequent destabilization of Eastern Ukraine. Although 70 percent of the Poles participating in a Pew poll (April–May 2015) regarded Russia as "a major military threat to neighboring countries," the average percentage of respondents taking this view in France, Germany, Italy, Spain, and the United Kingdom was a mere 47 percent, and most European NATO allies are not sufficiently worried by events in the Ukraine to increase their defense spending.[5] A 2015 Eurobarometer poll indicated that Europeans worry primarily about terrorism, economic and financial crises, poverty, organized crime, and corruption. War was only perceived as a threat by 11 percent—the ninth most worrisome threat when threats to European security were ranked.[6] Moreover, the majority of the respondents did not regard their national armed forces as the most relevant provider of national security. The police (68 percent) and the juridical system (61 percent) were regarded as more important security providers than the armed forces (46 percent). Even if these perceptions are not shared fully by European decisionmakers, this obviously makes it harder for them to mobilize and sustain domestic support for combat operations.[7]

This reduced sense of threat does not stem solely from an absence of existential military threats. It is also caused by the belief that the United States will come to the rescue of its European allies if a military threat appears on the horizon. Thus, a majority of Europeans (67 percent) believes that the United States will use force to protect a NATO ally from Russian attack.[8] This belief is hardly surprising, considering that the United States has come to the rescue of its European allies repeatedly since World War I, most recently in response to the Ukraine conflict erupting in 2014. Since the establishment of NATO after World War II, the Europeans have become increasingly dependent upon the United States for both national defense and power projection, and this has turned the alliance into a quid-pro-quo bargain in which the Europeans provide support for U.S.-led or desired operations away from home in exchange for U.S. protection against threats to their national security.

Maintaining a good relationship with Washington has therefore become a principal determinant of the defense and security policies pursued by most European nations. None of the European nations contributing forces to Afghanistan or Iraq were driven primarily by a sense of threat. The primary driver was an interest in maintaining a good relationship with the United States and keeping it engaged in NATO. The motivations for keeping the United States engaged varied. Some NATO members, particularly the new ones to the east, wanted U.S. assistance in keeping the Russians in check; other members wanted support for managing conflicts and other threats to their security occurring on Europe's doorstep or further afield; and then there were the "believers," Denmark and the United Kingdom, who wanted to assist the United States in doing the "right" thing, and who regarded their "special" relationships with the United States as a force multiplier enabling them to punch above their weight on the international scene.[9]

This interest in keeping the United States "in" gives the European nations a strong incentive to accept or contribute to combat operations that they either oppose or perceive no direct interest in. This mechanism has been visible in all NATO operations involving major use of force, and these cases also demonstrate how the United States played the "NATO survival is at risk" card to pressure reluctant European allies to take part.[10]

European Combat in Libya, Mali, and Iraq/Syria

These case studies demonstrate that the legacies of Afghanistan and Iraq do not have the direct and negative impact on the European willingness to fight that many assume, and that the lessons from these wars vary greatly across the four nations studied.

The Overthrow of the Qadhafi Regime in Libya 2011

In early 2011 the wave of popular protests sweeping the Arab world triggered an armed rebellion in Libya. To prevent the Qadhafi regime from massacring civilians in rebel-held areas, the UN Security Council authorized the imposition of a no-fly zone on March 17, which was swiftly imposed by a small coalition of the willing led by France, the United Kingdom, and the United States. On March 31, NATO assumed command of the coalition's efforts, which it led until the Qadhafi regime had been defeated and rebel forces had taken control of the country. When that happened, the United States reduced its involvement significantly, leaving most of the strike missions to its allies and refusing to insert special forces on the ground. NATO's operation lasted 223 days and involved some 260 military aircraft flying 26,500 sorties and dropping 7,600 precision-guided munitions, as well as 21 naval ships hailing 3,100 vessels.[11]

On the one hand, the operation highlighted Europe's dependence on American capabilities and its reluctance to fight. The United States played a dominant role in suppressing Libya's air defenses and providing intelligence, surveillance, and reconnaissance (ISR); targeting personnel; air-to-air refueling; and the satellite communications used by the special forces on the ground.[12] Only six European nations were willing to carry out strike missions (Belgium, Denmark, France, Norway, Italy, and the United Kingdom), and less than half of NATO's members provided military contributions to the operation. Germany not only abstained from the vote authorizing the use of force in the UN Security Council, it, together with Turkey, also opposed NATO's takeover of the mission.

On the other hand, the British and the French displayed a greater willingness to use force than the United States. It was a joint British-French push for a no-fly zone in the UN Security Council, supported by the Arab League, that induced an internally divided Obama administration to support military

Table 1: Overview of French, Italian, UK, and U.S. Contributions to the Libya Intervention				
Contributions	France	Italy	United Kingdom	United States
Manned Aircraft	60	59	37	104
Sorties	5,600	2,113	3,220	7,225
Smart munitions dropped	1,200	710	1,420	1,026 — (as of Aug. 22, 2011)
Ships + submarines	27	18	16	16
Personnel	4,200	3,500 + 4,800 staff on Italian bases	3,200	8,500

Sources: Gregory Alegi, "The Italian Experience: Pivotal and Underestimated," in *Precision and Purpose: Airpower in the Libyan Civil War*, ed. Karl P. Mueller (Santa Monica: RAND, 2015), 206, 220–31; Karine Blandel, "Harmattan en chiffres," email to author, June 6, 2012; House of Commons Defence Committee, *Operations in Libya* (House of Commons Paper 950, February 8, 2012), 45–46; Deborah C. Kidwell, "The U.S. Experience: Operational," in *Precision and Purpose*, ed. Mueller,121, 139; Tom Kington, "Italy Gives Bombing Stats for Libya Campaign," *DefenseNews*, December 14, 2011; Tim Ripley, "UK, France Detail Sorties Mounted, Ordnance Expended," *Jane's Defence Weekly*, November 2, 2011, 5.

intervention only 48 hours before the vote authorizing the use of force.[13] The United Kingdom and France also made major contributions to the air and naval operations and put special forces on the ground. Italy also became a major force contributor once it realized that France, the United Kingdom, and the United States were determined to overthrow the Qadhafi regime.

Our four explanatory factors demonstrate why France took the lead both diplomatically and militarily among the European contributors. France regards itself as a military power and takes great pride in its military ability to act unilaterally on the international scene. In addition to its 40 military interventions in former African colonies since 1960,[14] France has been an active contributor to UN and NATO missions and regards its ability and willingness to use force as a precondition for maintaining its great power status and international influence, and as a way of legitimating its permanent seat on the UN Security Council.[15]

Against this background, the French preparedness to use force was not surprising, and the legacies of Iraq and Afghanistan bolstered it. France stayed out of the Iraq war, opposing it vigorously, and it was not exhausted by Afghanistan, which it left in 2010. Instead, Afghanistan served as a wake-up call for the French army, inducing it to alter its training so that its soldiers once again were prepared for high-intensity warfighting—a move that suited its warrior ethos. Unlike its British counterpart, the French military consequently returned from Afghanistan with its head held high.[16]

The decision to intervene appears to have been driven more by opportunity than threat, i.e., a political need to get on the right side of history by supporting the "Arab Spring" revolts sweeping the region with popular movements pressing for greater personal and political freedoms, and an (erroneous) assumption that Qadhafi's forces would be defeated easily and quickly. For French President Nicolas Sarkozy, it was more about showing leadership and enhancing France's international prestige than protecting France's national security.[17]

The importance of the United States in the French calculus is demonstrated by France's reluctant acceptance of the NATO handover. Paris initially opposed this, fearing that it would impose too many restraints on the conduct of the mission and send the wrong signal to the Muslim world. But it had no choice other than to accept it when the United States, the United Kingdom, Italy, and other members made NATO command a prerequisite for their participation in the operation.[18] Paris was aware that France could not conduct the operation and achieve its objectives without allied participation. France effectively used the United States and NATO as force multipliers enabling it to act as a great power, and President Sarkozy was no doubt thrilled by President

Barack Obama's decision to "lead from behind" as it magnified the role played by Paris. France thus came away from the operation with a more positive view of NATO and its utility in French grand strategy.

The United Kingdom also perceives itself as a great power and takes great pride in its military history. Its forces have been engaged in military operations away from home on a continuous basis since World War II, and it has consciously used its military instrument to retain its great power status on the international scene.[19] It is therefore in keeping with its positive view of the military instrument that it teamed up with Paris to obtain a UN resolution to intervene and played a key role in the prosecution of the military campaign. Prime Minister David Cameron was reportedly determined to avoid another Srebrenica, and the humanitarian argument also played a key role in generating the huge majority of members of Parliament voting in favor of the intervention (557 to 13) and the many commentators welcoming it.[20]

It is somewhat surprising, however, that it did not make the largest European combat contribution. Since World War II, the United Kingdom has made it a priority to make the largest contributions to the U.S.-led military operations. This was the case in Korea, Kuwait, Bosnia, Kosovo, Afghanistan, and Iraq.[21] The reason it failed to do so in the Libya campaign can be in part explained by the American reluctance to intervene. But it was also a reflection of the perceived lack of threat to British interests and the negative fallout from Iraq and Afghanistan. The wars in Afghanistan and Iraq were highly unpopular, and the British public was perceived as unlikely to stomach another war.[22] Moreover, the defense staff and defense secretary failed to see the strategic wisdom of engaging in another open-ended military commitment at a time when the armed forces were struggling as a result of budget cuts and the commitment in Afghanistan.[23] The negative experiences from Iraq and Afghanistan were clearly visible as the British contribution was explicitly designed to be everything that Iraq and Afghanistan were not. In the words of Prime Minister Cameron, "We set limited goals and stuck to them. We worked with allies. We went through the United Nations. We had the support of the people. We didn't presume to tell people what sort of government they should have."[24]

The special relationship with the United States also played a key role. Despite the close partnership with France in the run-up to the UN vote, the United Kingdom still preferred to plan the military operation together with the United States without allowing the French to take part.[25]

Judging from the interaction among our four explanatory factors, the arguments in favor of non-intervention generated by the operational experiences in Iraq and Afghanistan and the absence of a direct threat to British interests were overruled by the British view of itself as a great martial power, its longstanding habit of fighting alongside the United States, a strong desire to prevent another Srebrenica, and a belief that the intervention would be doable at acceptable costs because it did not involve combat troops or a commitment to state building.

Italy's perception of the military instrument is very different from that of the French and the British. Its disastrous World War II experience generated a deep and lasting mistrust of the military instrument in Italian society. The Italian Constitution adopted in 1947 renounces war as an instrument of aggression and as a means for the settlement of international disputes.[26] Italy's involvement in Iraq and Afghanistan was highly unpopular, and the outcomes of these wars and the resulting 88 Italian fatalities, the greatest loss of lives experienced by the Italian armed forces since World War II, did nothing to increase public support for the use of force. In a 2013 poll, 86 percent of Italians opposed the use of force to secure peace in the world, 83 percent believed that the use of force does nothing but exacerbate the problems, and 60 percent opposed making contributions to international missions with Italian soldiers.[27]

This perception stands in sharp contrast to a broad political consensus that contributing to international missions enhances Italy's international status and influence, and that such missions help to maintain a good relationship with the United States. There is also broad consensus among Italian decisionmakers that the United States underpins the security of Europe, the Mediterranean, and the Middle East.[28] Italian decisionmakers have therefore used their armed forces actively as a foreign policy tool since the end of the Cold War to enhance Italy's standing and influence in the EU, NATO, the UN, and in Washington. Italy has been a major contributor to EU, NATO, UN, and U.S.-led missions and took the lead in launching and conducting military operations close to its borders (in Albania in 1997 and in Lebanon in 2006). The priority attributed to maintaining a strong relationship with the United States was demonstrated by the willingness of different Italian governments to defy public opinion and maintain Italian forces in Iraq and Afghanistan. The conservative government led by Silvio Berlusconi maintained some 3,000 troops in Iraq despite losing 19 Italians in a single attack early in the mission.[29] In Afghanistan, Italian governments also defied public resistance to become the fourth largest troop contributor in 2009 with over 4,000 troops.[30] Since Italy's support for NATO's Kosovo campaign almost brought the government down, Italian decisionmakers have portrayed all international missions, including the ones involving combat such as Afghanistan and Iraq, as peace missions, employed caveats to reduce the risk of casualties, and limited public information about controversial contributions to a minimum in order to circumvent the strong public opposition to the use of force.[31]

The UN authorization of the use of force against Libya presented a dilemma for Italy because an overthrow of the Qadhafi regime would threaten important economic interests as well as an agreement significantly reducing the inflow of illegal immigrants from Libya.[32] The intervention only enjoyed support from 29 percent of the public, and Prime Minister Berlusconi displayed little desire to abandon the Libyan leader Muammar Qadhafi, with whom he had built a personal relationship.[33] The lack of determined American leadership made it difficult for Italy to assess whether the Libyan regime would fall and how far the military operation would go. Italy consequently sat on the fence diplomatically until the UN resolution had been passed and France, the United Kingdom, and the United States signaled their determination to overthrow the regime. Italy then jumped on the bandwagon to become a major force contributor, as Table 1 demonstrates.

Italy's considerable involvement in strike missions is remarkable considering the strong public aversion to the use of force, and the fact that Italy in previous air campaigns, with the exception of the Kosovo air campaign, had refrained from conducting such operations. Before the Libya air campaign, Italian fighter bombers operating in Afghanistan were not allowed to carry out strike missions. This caveat was only lifted after the conclusion of the Libya intervention.[34] Press reports portraying Italy as a half-hearted ally unwilling to conduct strike missions may have contributed to the political decision to gradually deepen the Italian involvement in strike missions. However, the desire to establish a good relationship with the new Libyan regime in order to protect Italy's significant economic interests and to influence the conduct of the air campaign probably carried greater weight.[35] Italy was thus relatively quick to recognize the rebels as the legitimate representatives of Libya (April 4) and to put advisors on the ground to support them. Italy's interest in influencing the conduct of the mission and avoiding being sidelined by France and the United Kingdom was clear in its strong insistence that the operation be given NATO command when the United States decided to scale down its involvement.[36] To limit public opposition to the war, the Italian government told the public very little about the contributions made by Italian forces, and information about the munitions dropped was only released after the end of the mission.[37]

Germans view the military instrument in much the same way as Italians, but Germany's even more disastrous World War II experience has helped to create an even stronger political and public aversion to the use of force for purposes other than territorial self-defense.[38] In the course of the 1990s international, and especially American, pressure combined with the positive operational experience generated by Germany's participation in NATO's Bosnia missions led to a greater involvement in international peace operations. This evolution culminated in the 1999 Kosovo campaign, when German Minister of Foreign Affairs Joschka Fischer justified the German air force's first-ever strike missions with his "nie wieder Auschwitz" (Auschwitz never again) argument.[39] This controversial decision was first and foremost shaped by the German desire to do the "right humanitarian thing" and its interest in maintaining a good relationship with Washington and keeping NATO alive.[40]

Afghanistan and Iraq reversed this trend. Most Germans now believe that the German government made the right call opposing the 2003 invasion of Iraq and perceive NATO's Afghanistan operation as a costly failure.[41] Not only were peace and stability not achieved, but 54 German soldiers were killed and German soldiers were responsible for the killing of Afghan civilians (up to 154 in a single German-ordered airstrike in 2009). German decisionmakers found themselves caught in the crossfire between an increasingly hostile public (by 2010, 70 percent wanted German troops withdrawn) and ungrateful allies that kept criticizing Berlin for its unwillingness to engage in combat even though Germany was the third-largest troop contributor and third-largest aid donor for civilian reconstruction.[42]

Berlin's approach to the conflict in Libya was shaped by this reading of Afghanistan and Iraq, which amplified its aversion to the use of force, the American reluctance to become involved, and the absence of a direct threat to German interests. The German government was determined not to get militarily involved and believed that the United States shared this view. Washington's last-minute change of heart took Berlin by surprise, and it meant that the German debate in Parliament was based on the erroneous assumption that the United States would oppose the imposition of a no-fly zone. When Berlin learned of this development, it had little time to consult Parliament, and this difficulty appears to have reinforced the misgivings that the principal decisionmakers (Chancellor Angela Merkel, Foreign Minister Guido Westerwelle, and Minister of Defense Thomas de Maizière) shared about the use of force in general, about intervening in Libya in particular, and about how it would be received by the electorate (88 percent of the German public opposed German involvement in an intervention in Libya on March 16).[43] If the United States had immediately informed the German government about its change of heart concerning the UN resolution and put pressure on it to vote in favor and subsequently make a symbolic non-combat contribution, the German government might have acquiesced, as such a policy would have been in keeping with past practice. Judging from the domestic controversy that the decision to abstain created in Germany, the government would probably have been able to obtain a mandate from Parliament for such a policy. The importance attributed to the views of allies and not least the United States is clear from Chancellor Merkel's personal assurance to British Prime Minister Cameron that Germany would not allow the resolution to fail,[44] and the supportive steps taken in the wake of the abstention. Germany played a pro-American role in the various international forums managing Libya conflict, sent AWACS crews to Afghanistan to free up personnel for the Libya operation, and allowed 103 German officers in NATO billets to support the Libya mission.[45] In order to deflect American pressure for military contributions, Berlin also pledged to deploy peacekeepers in Libya if it proved necessary after the fighting was over.[46]

The German non-participation in the intervention was over determined. All four explanatory factors pushed German decisionmakers toward this course of action. Early and consistent American pressure might have persuaded the German government to vote in favor of the UN resolution and provide non-combat support. The American change of heart late in the game caught German decisionmakers on the wrong foot and made it next to impossible for them politically to alter course. At the same time, the strong domestic and international criticism triggered by the German policy subsequently convinced many German decisionmakers and opinion leaders that the decisions to abstain and stay out of the mission were mistaken. The Libya war ignited a domestic debate on how and whether Germany should play a greater role in international crisis management.[47] Although the Libya war did not lessen Germany's aversion to the use of force, it did convince many decisionmakers that the political costs of completely opting out of allied interventions were too high.[48]

France's Intervention in Mali

In January 2013, France intervened unilaterally in Mali to halt an offensive initiated by jihadists in the northern part of the country against the government-controlled south. Within a matter of days, a combination of French airpower and special forces had succeeded in halting the jihadist offensive. By April, the jihadists had been pushed out of northern Mali, their military capacities were significantly degraded, and the surviving hardcore elements dispersed into ungoverned areas of neighboring countries. The combat operation was primarily conducted by 4,000 French and 2,000 Chadian troops. Six French and 38 Chadian soldiers lost their lives in the operation.[49] These forces were supported by a 4,300-strong African force led by Nigeria, the Malian army, and a number of Western countries providing airlift, refueling, and ISR.[50] The United States once again played a critical role, providing 75 percent of the military airlift, transporting 75 percent the personnel and materials moved during the first three weeks of the operation, 30 percent of the aerial refueling, and a considerable but unspecified portion of the ISR.[51]

The decision was eased by France's positive view of the military instrument and the recent success in Libya, which was perceived and portrayed as a great triumph by the French government. As pointed out by French analysts, Libya strengthened French decisionmakers' belief in the utility of force,[52] and in this particular instance, the French military regarded the jihadist march on the capital as an opportunity to "break the back" of their organizations.[53] The decision to intervene was supported by 75 percent of the French public,[54] and there was broad agreement among French analysts that the decision would strengthen President François Hollande's domestic popularity provided that the intervention did not turn into a quagmire.[55]

The French decision to intervene was first and foremost threat-driven. President Hollande and his advisors were concerned that the jihadist offensive in a worst case scenario could lead to the collapse of the Malian state and

Table 2: Overview of French, German, Italian, UK, and U.S. Contributions to the Mali Intervention (January–April 2013)				
France	Germany	Italy	United Kingdom	United States
14 aircraft, 20 helicopters, 15 ISR assets, 5 C-135FRs (air refueling), 24 transport planes, 1 command and amphibious assault ship	3 Transall transport planes, 1 A310 MRTT (air refueling)	2 C-130 transport planes, 1 KC-767A (air refueling)	2 C-17, R-1 Sentinel, 1 Roll-on-Roll-off Ferry	3 C-17 and 2 C-130 transport planes, 3 KC-135 (air refueling) tankers, U-28 light ISR aircraft, Navy EP-3 Signal Intelligence aircraft, 1 E-8C Joint Stars plane, 1 Global Hawk, 2 Predators
6000 troops	Up to 330 troops providing non-combat support	Up to 24 trainers	Up to 240 trainers	100 trainers

Sources: Auswärtiges Amt, "Large Majority in the Bundestag Approves Bundeswehr Deployment in Mali," February 28, 2013, http://www.auswaertiges-amt.de/EN/Aussenpolitik/Laender/Aktuelle_Artikel/Mali/130228-Mali-Bundestag-Mandate.html; Gros, *Libya and Mali Operations*, 9–11; Claire Mills, Arabella Lang and Jon Lunn, "The crisis in Mali: current military action and upholding humanitarian law," *House of Commons Library Briefing*, SN06531, March 11, 2013, 9.

a subsequent destabilization of the entire Sahel region. This would not only threaten the 5,000 French nationals living in Mali but also France's supply of uranium from neighboring Niger.[56] This threat perception was reinforced by the interim government of Mali, members of the Economic Community of West African States (ECOWAS), and President of Niger Mahamadou Issoufou, who all called on Paris to intervene militarily.[57]

The United States did not encourage France to intervene. France was disappointed that the United States did not consider the jihadists a direct threat to American and Western interests, and Paris had to criticize Washington publicly to persuade it to become engaged.[58] Though U.S. support had been necessary for the launch and conduct of the Libya air campaign, Paris could have carried out the Mali operation without it. It would, however, have made the operation slower and far riskier since it would have been impossible for the French forces to maintain the high operational tempo and the element of surprise that played a major role in their quick defeat and rollback of the jihadi forces.[59] It would also have strained the relationship between Washington and Paris. Instead, the Mali operation had the opposite effect, paving the way for closer diplomatic and military cooperation between the two countries.[60]

The British decision to quickly support the French intervention was in keeping with its positive view of military force and its great power status. But the decision not to provide combat contributions or put troops on the ground also reflected the public and military combat fatigue created by Iraq and Afghanistan, the lack of a direct threat to British interests and national security, the absence of American leadership, and the strain on the British forces generated by their 7,000-strong commitment in Afghanistan. Prime Minister Cameron's strong rhetorical support was in keeping with Britain's martial great power tradition. He welcomed the French intervention to stop Mali being overtaken by an al-Qaida–backed group of rebels and was the first to provide air- and sea-lift and ISR support. But he was equally quick to stress that British forces would not be given a combat role. "No combat," "no mission creep," and "no quagmire" became standard phrases the British government used in the course of the intervention in its efforts to reassure anxious members of Parliament that Mali would not turn into a new Iraq or Afghanistan.[61] But the British failure to offer combat contributions also reflected the limited involvement of the United States, and the fact that British decisionmakers do not attach the same importance to their bilateral relationship with France as is given to its "special relationship" with the United States. Cameron undoubtedly would have offered combat contributions if the intervention had been led by the United States. He was certainly quick to do so when the United States was contemplating airstrikes to punish the Syrian regime for its use of chemical weapons in August 2013.

The American and British noninvolvement in the combat operations all but guaranteed that Italy and Germany would stay out as well. Like the United Kingdom, Italy was quick to offer airlift, refueling, and trainers for the Malian army, legitimizing its involvement with the need to prevent the establishment of a terrorist state posing a direct threat to Italy and the Mediterranean and to show solidarity with France. Although the jihadists were characterized as a threat to national security to legitimate the Italian involvement, the actions taken by Rome did not signal any urgency or acute concern belying its characterization of the conflict as a direct threat to national security. Thus, the Italian government was also at pains to emphasize that Italian forces would not be employed in a combat mode and stressed the point repeatedly in order to obtain parliamentary support for the deployment.[62] The message to the Italian public was clear: the operation would not be a new Afghanistan or a new Iraq.

The story was the same in Germany. The government justified the mission as self-defense in order to prevent the establishment of a terrorist state in Mali, which would be a threat to Western (but not German) security.[63] Berlin did not feel directly threatened, and its emphasis was not on warfighting but on helping the Africans themselves to re-establish security, start a political process, and hold elections. The operation would not be a new Afghanistan: German soldiers would not engage in combat but would train Malian and African troops, provide paramedics, airlift, and air-to-air refueling. The mission was supported by a vast majority in the Bundestag, whereas the public was more skeptical: 45 percent of the German population supported the mission, with 36 percent against. Only 6 percent supported making combat contributions.[64]

The U.S.-led Intervention Against ISIL

In August 2014, the United States launched airstrikes in Iraq against ISIL and started forming a broad international coalition aimed at "degrading and defeating" the organization in Iraq and Syria. Some 60 nations and organizations make up the coalition, but only 12 countries have been willing to conduct strike missions as part of the U.S.-led air campaign, and until September 2015 none of the European countries involved were willing to strike targets in Syria, limiting their strike missions to Iraq. Then France, and subsequently the United Kingdom, decided to expand their strike missions to Syria as well.[65] The military campaign has been dominated by the United States, which has made the largest contributions and determined the strategy by its refusal to deploy ground troops and its insistence that ISIL can be degraded and defeated by the combination of coalition airpower and the training of local security forces.

	France	Germany	Italy	United Kingdom	United States
Table 3: Overview of French, German, Italian, UK, and U.S. Military Contributions to Operation INHERENT RESOLVE (August 2014–)					
Aircraft	17 (Sep 2015)	0	7	29	23 different types of aircraft in unspecified quantities
Strike missions	215 (Sep 18, 2015)	0	0	251 (Sep 8, 2015)	5,239 (Sep 8, 2015)
Munitions dropped	Classified, but 334 targets have been struck	0	0	375 (Aug 4, 2015)	5,600 (Sep 8, 2015)
Troops (max strength)	800	100	500	900	4,850 troops

Sources: Chris Cole, "UK Increases Drone Missions in Syria," August 12, 2015, http://dronewars.net/2015/08/12/uk-increases-drone-missions-in-syria/; Rebecca Frette, "Chammal," email from the French Embassy in Copenhagen to author, September 18, 2015; Laura Hawkins, "GR4: Tornado By Numbers," August 4, 2015, http://forces.tv/36366546; Claire Mills and Ben Smith, "ISIS/Daesh: the military response in Iraq and Syria," *House of Commons Library Briefing Paper* No. 06995, September 8, 2015, 9, 21, 26–27; David Cenciotti, "This Is How Italian Tornado Jets and Predator Drones Will Contribute to the War on ISIS," *The Aviationist*, November 17, 2014.

France was the first country to join the United States in conducting air-strikes against ISIL in Iraq. The decision was first and foremost legitimated by the "mortal" and "direct" threat that ISIL posed to Europe and French national security. But French decisionmakers also stressed France's respon-sibility as a "great power" with a permanent seat on the UN Security Council and a longstanding presence in the Middle East.[66] The decision was eased by France's positive view of force buoyed by its recent operational successes in Libya and Mali as well as the intervention in the Central African Republic in December 2013 to stop massacres in the capital.[67] The French decision to go to war and the accompanying domestic debate reflected strong determination and self-confidence, and it enjoyed strong popular and political support.[68]

Unlike the other European countries joining the air campaign, France did not use international law as an excuse for restricting its airstrikes to Iraq. On the contrary, French Foreign Minister Laurent Fabius kept France's options open by arguing that a legal case could be made for bombing in Syria as well. Instead, the restriction was justified on the grounds that France "could not be everywhere."[69] Yet it seems more likely that the restriction was determined by the lack of reliable partners on the ground in Syria, Russian and Iranian opposition, and the "Iraq first" strategy adopted by the United States.[70]

France also joined the campaign to cement the closer relationship that it had established with Washington during the campaigns in Libya and Mali, and as a result of the French willingness to support the airstrikes that President Obama had threatened to punish the Syrian regime for its use of chemical weapons in August 2013. France was the only country to offer direct military support for such strikes. In keeping with its recent operational experience, France agreed with the "light footprint" approach adopted by the United States, thereby ruling out the deployment of combat forces.

The United Kingdom was a far more reluctant participant in this operation than France. The reason for this was not just to be found in the unhappy Iraq and Afghanistan experiences. It was primarily a result of the humiliating and historic defeat that the Prime Minister Cameron had suffered in the House of Commons in August 2013 when he asked for support to join the United States in carrying out airstrikes against the Syrian regime for its use of chemical weapons. Although not constitutionally obliged to ask permission from the House of Commons, Cameron had done so to avoid accusations of pushing another "Iraq" in the face of strong international opposition. Following his unprecedented defeat, the first ever in British history, Cameron made clear that the United Kingdom would not use force.[71] To avoid another defeat when the United States asked for contributions to the campaign against ISIL, Cameron therefore decided to "lead from behind" in order to be sure that Parliament and the public were behind him when he took the country to war.

That the United Kingdom would do so was a foregone conclusion, however. To have stayed out of a major U.S. air campaign that other allies, including Australia and France, had already joined would have been unthinkable for the British, who have been the United States' most reliable and closest comrades in arms since World War II. Given the brutality displayed by ISIL, its beheading of a British citizen, and the direct threat it was perceived to pose to the stability of the Middle East and British security, it was an easy sell. A large

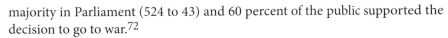

majority in Parliament (524 to 43) and 60 percent of the public supported the decision to go to war.[72]

That the United Kingdom did not take part from day one was unusual, however, and so was the relatively modest size of the British contribution. In Iraq, Afghanistan, and most other U.S.-led post-World War II campaigns, the British contributions had dwarfed all others.[73] Not so this time as the British were content to simply match the French contribution.[74] As had been the case in the run-up to the Libya intervention, the British debate was strongly influenced by its experiences in Afghanistan and Iraq. The British Army chief warned the government not to make the same mistakes again, and the Royal Air Force warned of possible overstretch.[75] To avoid the problems of legitimacy and legality generated by the Iraq war, British aircraft were only allowed to bomb in Iraq and Prime Minister Cameron promised to let Parliament vote on a possible future extension of the mission to Syria. Finally, the use of British combat troops was ruled out with reference to the lessons learned in Iraq and Afghanistan.[76]

The size of the British contribution and the restriction of the air campaign to Iraq gave rise to criticism from military analysts and officers, and the British government has struggled to convince the critics that it was meeting its responsibilities as a great power and a reliable U.S. ally. In February 2015, the Commons Defence Select Committee described the British contribution as "strikingly modest" and demanded that the government do more.[77] This view was shared by 56 percent of the British public who wanted the government to step up its airstrikes.[78] In early July, the British government used a terrorist attack linked to ISIL killing 30 Britons to make the case for extending airstrikes to Syria provided that the government could muster the necessary support in Parliament.[79] Sixty-seven percent of the British public supported this proposal,[80] and the government obtained parliamentary support requested in a vote on December 2, 2015.[81] The French extension of its airstrikes to Syria strengthened the government's case, as most British decisionmakers continue to regard it as unacceptable to be second to the French in a U.S.-led campaign.[82]

Although Italy was quick to join the U.S.-led coalition against ISIL, Rome did not provide aircraft for the air campaign until November 2014 and limited its contribution to surveillance and refueling. In addition, Rome also sent trainers and military equipment to Iraq and has played an active role in the coalition efforts to cut off ISIL's access to financing and funding.[83] This contribution is in keeping with the expectation generated by our analytical framework; Rome balanced Italy's security interest in maintaining a good relationship with the United States with the domestic need to respect the public's strong aversion to the use of force. The decision to refrain from carrying out airstrikes reflected that the civil war and the growing influence of ISIL in Libya were perceived as a greater and more direct threat to Italian security than the ISIL presence in Iraq and Syria. Italy has borne the brunt of the problems generated by the massive outflow of migrants from Libya with little support from the European Union. It spent $130 million on Operation MARE NOSTRUM (September 2013–October 2014), saving over 100,000 migrants, and has offered to commit 5,000 peacekeepers to Libya if the UN succeeds in brokering a peace agreement.[84] The leading role played by Italy in the efforts to manage the Libyan conflict has enabled it to withstand U.S. pressures for doing more in Iraq and Syria.

Germany's categorical refusal to make any contribution to the air campaign against ISIL underlined its aversion to the use of force, its lessons learned from Iraq, Afghanistan, and Libya (where the use of force in the German perspective did more harm than good), and the absence of a direct threat to German national security.[85] At the time when the air campaign was launched, the German government was more focused on the armed conflict initiated by the Russian annexation of Crimea and its destabilization of Eastern Ukraine. This conflict posed a far more direct threat to Germany, necessitating a fundamental reorientation of its policy toward Russia and the imposition of economic sanctions, which imposed considerable costs on the German economy.[86]

Its decision to train and arm the Kurdish forces in Iraq reflected its interest in maintaining a good relationship with Washington and the lesson learned from the Libya campaign that complete noninvolvement could be too costly. The German policy is therefore both logical and predictable. Three of our four explanatory factors suggested non-participation in combat, whereas the Libya experience and the need to show solidarity with the United States ensured that non-combat contributions would be made.

The most striking thing about this case is the persisting gap between American and German perceptions and expectations. Although American decisionmakers expected far more than arms supplies, humanitarian assistance, and 100 personnel, the German government believed that it had gone out of its way to show solidarity with the United States and support the fight against ISIL.[87] Its decisions to arm and train Kurdish forces in northern Iraq were controversial domestically and regarded as an important break with past practice. Sixty percent of the German public opposed the decision to send $80 million worth of arms to the Kurds, and the deployment of trainers was viewed as unconstitutional by some legal experts and politicians, because it lacked an international mandate.[88]

It was the first time that Germany supplied arms to a war zone and the first military deployment without an international mandate since World War II. To obtain parliamentary support, the training mission was designed as strictly non-combat. As German Foreign Minister Frank-Walter Steinmeier pointed out in his speech to Parliament, the mission was very different from the one in Afghanistan. The focus was on non-combat skills and the trainers would not go out on missions with the troops they were training. To further enhance the legitimacy of the mission, Steinmeier also characterized the Kurdish Peshmerga as a "defensive army."[89] The strategy worked as the German Parliament approved the mission with a large majority (457 to 79).

Implications for Future Transatlantic Combat Cooperation

The Afghanistan and Iraq wars do not have the direct and negative impact on the European NATO members' capacity and willingness to fight that conventional wisdom assumes. The comparative analysis undertaken here demonstrates that the European willingness to engage in combat is determined by the interaction of four factors and that their relative importance and

Table 4: Comparing the Four European Countries Across Cases

	Libya		Mali		Iraq/Syria	
France	Combat		Combat		Combat	
	+ Force	+ Op. exp.	+ Force	+ Op. exp.	+ Force	+ Op. exp.
	– Threat	– U.S.	+ Threat	– U.S.	+ Threat	+ U.S.
Germany	Non-participation		Non-combat		Non-combat	
	– Force	– Op. exp.	– Force	– Op. exp.	– Force	– Op. exp.
	– Threat	– U.S.	– Threat	– U.S.	– Threat	+ U.S.
Italy	Combat		Non-combat		Non-combat	
	– Force	– Op. exp.	+ Force	– Op. exp.	– Force	– Op. exp.
	+ Threat	+ U.S.	– Threat	– U.S.	– Threat	+ U.S.
United Kingdom	Combat		Non-combat		Combat	
	+ Force	– Op. exp.	+ Force	– Op. exp.	+ Force	– Op. exp.
	– Threat	+ U.S.	– Threat	– U.S.	+ Threat	+ U.S.
+ = presence of an explanatory factor; – = absence of an explanatory factor						

interaction varies markedly from nation to nation. These four factors—recent operational experience, sense of threat, view of the military instrument, and security dependence on the United States—not only account for the national variations between Italy, Germany, France, and the United Kingdom. They also account for the different behaviors displayed by the four countries in the three interventions examined.

The case studies demonstrate clearly that Germany is no warrior nation. Its deep public and political aversion to the use of force has been reinforced by the wars in Iraq, Afghanistan, and Libya. A direct threat to German security as well as human suffering on a massive scale (as in Kosovo in 1999) and strong American pressure will therefore be required to persuade German governments to make combat contributions. These conditions were not met in any of our cases. The mistaken belief that the United States would oppose use of force played a key role in the German decision not to participate at all. The high political costs of this decision all but guarantee German non-combat contributions to future transatlantic combat operations.

A deep public aversion to the use of force makes Italy a reluctant warrior. This reluctance was reinforced by the experience in Iraq and Afghanistan, which is why it will take a direct threat to national security and U.S. pressure to induce Italian decisionmakers to use force. These conditions were only met in Libya, where the Italian government used force in order to protect its economic interests in Libya and to limit the future flow of immigrants.

The United Kingdom is a warrior nation that can be expected to make combat contributions to all U.S.-led operations. Its warrior identity and its "special relationship" with the United States make British governments favorably disposed to respond positively to American requests for military contributions. Though the negative Iraq and Afghanistan experiences have made it harder for British governments to mobilize parliamentary and public support for combat operations, the domestic criticism that the British government has faced for doing too little in the campaign against ISIL suggests that the skepticism created by Iraq and Afghanistan is likely to be temporary provided that the ISIL operation does not turn bad and serve to reinforce it.

France is Europe's most willing warrior. Its positive view of force has been reinforced by the positive experiences from Libya and Mali, and it put pressure on the United States to involve itself in both of these cases. As a result, France does not have to feel directly threatened in order to use force. The decision to use force against Libya was motivated more by opportunity than threat—underlining the French perception of force as an effective policy instrument.

Taken together, these findings suggest that the future of transatlantic combat cooperation is brighter than the conventional wisdom focusing on Iraq and Afghanistan assumes. Although Iraq and Afghanistan have reinforced Germany's traditional reluctance to use force, this analysis does not rule out German combat participation in future operations provided that the United States takes the lead and German decisionmakers perceive a threat to national security. This would no doubt be the case if the conflict in the Ukraine escalated and engulfed the entire country, or if Russia launched an attack on the Baltic countries.

British decisionmakers still want to make combat contributions to U.S.-led operations as the ISIL case demonstrates, and France has emerged as a new and enthusiastic supporter of transatlantic combat cooperation. It has begun to put pressure on the United States to support French-led combat operations, and the emerging relationship between Paris and Washington will create new opportunities for cooperation that did not exist before.

The operational experience in Afghanistan and Iraq does not appear to have had a major impact on Italian decisionmakers. In the 1990s Italian governments were prepared to participate in combat operations if the United States took the lead and they perceived national interests to be at stake.[90] They did so again when these conditions applied in Libya in 2011, and nothing suggests that they would not be willing to do so again in the future.

This analysis in short suggests it unlikely that Iraq and Afghanistan have made the Europeans more unlikely to use force than they have been since the end of the Cold War. Recent developments on Europe's eastern and southern fronts also suggest it unlikely that they will be less capable. The conflict in the Ukraine and the growing flow of refugees caused and accelerated by the civil wars on its southern doorstep appear to have stopped the decline in European defense spending. Although most European NATO members are unlikely to meet the 2 percent spending target set by NATO in the foreseeable future, they appear to have realized that they need to maintain their spending at existing levels and perhaps even spend some more in order to tackle the non-existential threats facing them from the east and the south.

Acknowledgments

I would like to thank the editors, an anonymous reviewer, and my colleagues in the International Relations Department at the University of Southern Denmark for useful comments on an earlier draft.

CHAPTER 2
The Country of Unrequited Dreams: Lessons From Germany's Mission in Afghanistan

Patrick Keller

Germany's contribution to the international effort in Afghanistan after 9/11 was unplanned, unexpected, and unlike anything the Federal Republic had ever experienced.[1] For more than 13 years, Germany has been engaged in stabilizing the post-Taliban country through military, economic, and diplomatic means—all while balancing the expectations of its allies and partners with the constraints of domestic political expediency.[2] In the course of the Afghanistan mission, Berlin went through five different governments, spent almost 9 billion euros ($10.1 billion) on the military effort alone, and faced the first high-intensity ground warfare of its armed forces since World War II.[3] Fifty-four German soldiers died in Afghanistan, more than half of the sum total of mission casualties the German armed force—the Bundeswehr—has suffered since its inception. For the Federal Republic's military, it was the longest, most costly, and most consequential mission ever. The broader political and strategic repercussions for Germany's role in the world, its approach to international crisis management, and its bureaucratic and interagency processes reverberate to this day and will continue to do so.[4]

Given the unique relevance of the Afghanistan experience for the German body politic, German leaders have shown surprisingly little interest in evaluating their efforts and drawing lessons from that analysis. There are no major speeches, commissions, or party platforms on the subject. The only public government documents of note are the annual *Fortschrittsberichte Afghanistan* (Progress Reports Afghanistan) compiled by the Foreign Office since 2010.[5] Often ridiculed for touting the international community's efforts while downplaying the fragility of reported "progress," these reports focus on the situation in Afghanistan, not on assessment of German policy. Similarly, the Ministry of International Development and Cooperation has produced a few publications on Afghanistan that focus solely on questions of effective development aid.[6] The military, of paramount importance to the German effort, receives brief (and highly critical) mention. Even though the Ministry of Defense has conducted and even commissioned several studies on "lessons learned" from Afghanistan, the results are not available for a public debate since they have been classified.

On the other hand, the political leadership's reluctance to ascertain what parts of Germany's Afghanistan strategy did and did not work (and why) might not be so surprising after all. Clearly, a majority of the German public in 2014 considered "Afghanistan" to be, if not a failure, then hardly a "success" either.[7] No one in office has an interest in drawing attention to mistakes and misperceptions of the German government. This tendency to stonewall has been exacerbated by the fact that five of the major German parties—Christian-Democratic Union, Christian-Social Union, Social Democratic Party, Free Democratic Party ("Liberals") (FDP), and Alliance 90/Greens[8]—consistently voted in favor of the German mission in Afghanistan. At various times, these parties were in governing coalitions responsible for executing the mission.[9] Moreover, German political elites—as with most Western leaders today—display absolutely no desire to repeat any time soon an extended effort of nation-building under conditions of counterinsurgency in a land as vast, remote, and hard as Afghanistan. Discussing lessons learned from this effort, and especially from the military operations, is thus unattractive for two further reasons: public musings about what to do better "next time" are simply deemed unnecessary and—even worse in electoral terms—might give the unpopular impression that there *will be* a next time.

However, there is little doubt among German experts on international security that there will indeed be a next time. That is, there will be a situation when Germany will decide to use military force outside NATO territory because of its own interests, or because it is called upon by its allies, or both. History from the Balkans to Afghanistan to crisis management on the African continent shows that these missions tend to happen with great urgency but little warning. They also tend to be more complicated and time-consuming than initially expected. And while the Afghanistan mission developed from unique circumstances in the wake of the terrorist attacks of 9/11, there is reason to assume that the combination of failing states, regional instability, and international terrorism will require large-scale international interventions in the years ahead.

If "another Afghanistan" is a likely scenario, even if it is in a transmuted form, then it is the duty of German strategists to prepare. Because preparation starts with reflection upon experience, this chapter will sketch 10 lessons that can be derived from Germany's Afghanistan mission. Maybe the lessons should rather be called observations, because they are not designed as definite answers to the many contradictions characterizing German Afghanistan policy but as impulses for further research, thinking, and debate about Germany's contribution to international crisis management.[10] To place this analysis in the proper context, it might first be useful to recapitulate the storyline of Germany's involvement in Afghanistan and to recall the key political players, decisions, and events that shaped the German re-encounter with war.

Overview: Political-Military Storyline[11]

The Schröder Years: Solidarity and Minimalism

After 9/11, Chancellor Gerhard Schröder (1998–2005), a Social Democrat, declared Germany's "unlimited solidarity" with the United States.[12] Accordingly, he sought to join in the common response of NATO allies by contributing to Operation ENDURING FREEDOM (OEF) in Afghanistan. On November 16, 2001, Schröder put his chancellorship on the line by linking the vote in the Bundestag (Federal Parliament) about the Afghanistan mission with a vote of confidence in his government. He won narrowly, underlining the reservations in his left-of-center Red-Green coalition about fighting terror with military means. In another vote on December 22, 2001, the Bundestag decided to contribute troops to the new International Security Assistance Force (ISAF).[13] This first mandate allowed for deployment of 1,200 German soldiers to Afghanistan and specified many open and secret caveats about the regional and military limits of the commitment, including very restrictive rules of engagement and the focus on the comparatively stable northern region of the country.[14] It also cemented the strong German preference for ISAF over OEF.

The German preference for a civilian over a military approach was also evident at the Petersberg Conference from November 27 to December 5, 2001, in the former German capital of Bonn. Here, both Afghans and the international community worked from a United Nations (UN) initiative to define the political process for Afghanistan's future. The Petersberg Declaration became a cornerstone of Afghanistan's political transformation, and Germany, as the host country, became strongly associated with that process.

In terms of the rationale behind its military contribution, the Bundestag's mandate identified a clear purpose of the mission from the beginning until the end of ISAF: help the Afghan government create a safe and secure environment for the reconstruction efforts undertaken by Afghans and the international community. (Only in 2010 was this amended to explicitly include the protection of Afghanistan's civilian population as a purpose of the German military engagement.)

It remained unclear, however, what exactly this (military) assistance should look like. When Defense Minister Peter Struck, a Social Democrat, explained in December 2002 that "German security is also to be defended at the Hindu Kush," he hinted at a strategic narrative that went beyond mere support in reconstruction but also included German security interests in fighting terrorism.[15] Since then, Struck's comment has often been quoted (usually derisively) in German public debate, but received hardly any traction in its strategic and military implications. This indicates that the German rationale behind supporting ISAF was mostly grounded in NATO solidarity rather than an analysis of more immediate national interests. This became even more pronounced after Chancellor Schröder strongly opposed President George W. Bush's war in Iraq in 2003 in a campaign that was rife with anti-American overtones and led to a worrisome alliance between Berlin and Moscow.[16] In order to counteract that rift, German solidarity with the United States in Afghanistan was crucial to balancing international and domestic opinion. By the end of Schröder's tenure, almost 3,000 German soldiers were stationed in Afghanistan.

The Merkel Years: War in a Time of Peace

In the 2005 elections, Angela Merkel defeated Gerhard Schröder more narrowly than most polls had expected. This forced her Christian-Democratic Union into a coalition with the Social Democrats, hence ensuring much continuity in Germany's Afghanistan policy. The slow increase of German troops continued, as did the very muted communication of German reasons, ambitions, and interests regarding the mission. In 2006, the Merkel government published a new defense white paper, the first such document since 1994. It strongly reflected the German attitude toward Afghanistan by emphasizing the German version of NATO's comprehensive approach, *Vernetzte Sicherheit* (networked security). This interplay between civilian and military means to stabilize fragile states in strategically important regions was seen as key to German policy.

Her success in the 2009 elections allowed Merkel to change her coalition partner from the Social Democrats to the center-right FDP. While this gave her more leeway in domestic and economic policy, it hardly affected German Afghanistan policy—the mission had long receded to background noise in German politics.

This changed on September 4, 2009, when Taliban insurgents near Kunduz City captured two fuel tankers that were subsequently stuck in a riverbed and looted. The commanding ISAF officer in the area, German Colonel Georg Klein, called an airstrike on the tankers, which was conducted by two American F-15E fighter jets, killing up to 142 people, including at least 90 civilians.[17] Defense Minister Franz Josef Jung, a Christian Democrat, initially commended Col Klein's leadership against the Taliban threat and denied that there had been any civilian casualties. When several reports by NATO, the Bundeswehr, and independent media came to a different conclusion, Jung resigned (by now he had been appointed minister of labor). New Defense Minister Karl-Theodor zu Guttenberg, of the Bavarian Christian Social Union, fired both his assistant secretary, Peter Wichert, and the highest-ranking Bundeswehr soldier, Inspector General Wolfgang Schneiderhan, over allegations of covering up and keeping from the ministers what really happened in Kunduz.

The tragic Kunduz incident shattered many of the comfortable German misconceptions about the Afghanistan mission. It forced Chancellor Merkel, who always preferred to keep German military contributions quiet and below the radar of intense public debate, to give a speech in the Bundestag, justifying and explaining the mission of the German Bundeswehr—the first such speech in her 4 years as chancellor.[18] Apparently, Germany was not just involved in technical assistance but in fighting insurgents as well. The young, dashing, and extremely popular zu Guttenberg understood this as an opportunity to change the German narrative about Afghanistan. He was the first leading German politician to not only speak of the mission as a "non-international armed conflict within the perimeters of international law" but also introduce the term "war" into German public discourse over Afghanistan by acknowledging "war-like conditions" on the ground.[19] He reinforced the message that German soldiers were fighting for noble goals in Afghanistan and that they needed all the necessary support, including heavy weaponry and less restrictive rules of engagement. Moreover, zu Guttenberg initiated a far-reaching reform of the Bundeswehr that aimed at making the armed forces leaner, more deployable, and more effective in fighting insurgents. This change in leadership corresponded with renewed American interest in the Afghanistan mission, leading to a (small) surge of German forces between 2009 and 2011 as well. When zu Guttenberg had to resign in 2011 over allegations of plagiarism in his Ph.D. dissertation and Thomas de Maizière, a much less flashy, bureaucratic type of public servant, became defense minister, much of the steam of the previous months was lost.

The 2013 elections confirmed Merkel as chancellor. She received the best result yet for her Christian Democratic party, but since the FDP failed to clear the 5-percent hurdle and dropped out of the Bundestag, Merkel had to forge a grand coalition with the Social Democrats again. At this point, the international coalition had already been looking for an exit from Afghanistan. France, Canada, and the Netherlands had ended their combat missions and withdrawn most or all of their forces. Under President Barack Obama, the United States was also winding down its mission, seeking to hand over responsibility for the security situation to the Afghan military and police. The German government fell gratefully in line with this policy but took care to honor its commitments to the Regional Command North until the formal end of ISAF in 2014. Moreover, de Maizière was the first NATO defense minister to promise a concrete number of soldiers to the follow-up mission called RESOLUTE SUPPORT. As of June 2015, Germany provided about 850 troops to RESOLUTE SUPPORT and was the third largest contributor, behind Georgia (885) and the United States (6,834).[20]

Ten Lessons Learned (or Observations Made)

1. Afghanistan reflects Germany's identity crisis about its role in international security affairs.

At the beginning of the Afghanistan mission, the Federal Republic of Germany had been a sovereign country for merely a decade. During the Cold War, both West Germany and—to a much larger extent—East Germany had been subject to Allied control. Even the Bonn government, for all the shrewdness and confidence of its political leaders, was not a true actor in international strategic affairs. Tucked away under the wing of U.S. power, its politicians could focus on the economy, human rights, and international development rather than the hard power questions of international order. That had to change with reunification, with many partners and NATO allies pushing Germany to take on international burdens commensurate with its size and wealth.

The Afghanistan mission was the first major test for Germany's new role. To be sure, Germany had participated in NATO's air campaign against Serbia during the Kosovo War in 1999, but in terms of scale, risk, and duration, the Afghanistan mission was fundamentally more challenging. Opinions on whether Germany passed or failed this test are as divided as they are on Germany's overall performance in international security since reunification.

Basically, there are two opposing camps. First, some believe that Germany has come a long way in a short amount of time. In all major crises since reunification, Germany has played an increasingly active and constructive role: from Kuwait to Bosnia to Kosovo to Afghanistan. As ISAF's third largest troop contributor and lead nation in the Regional Command North, Germany had indeed grown into a well-respected role as one of the key purveyors of global order.

This success story has numerous detractors both in Germany and abroad. This second camp contends that what Germany has done was always too little and too late. Still hiding behind the horrors of Nazism and a supposedly pacifist public, German leaders have always sought as little (military) burden as possible without losing face with allies, especially the United States. The logic of Alliance solidarity at minimal cost precluded German policy from having decisive impact on the critical situation in the crisis region. Moreover, in crises since Afghanistan, most notably in Libya, Syria, and Ukraine, the German government was always quick to rule out any military participation. The learning curve was thus hardly trending consistently toward more engagement, but rather the opposite.[21]

Interestingly, both camps use Afghanistan as a case in point for their assessment of Germany's role in international security affairs. ISAF is seen, with some justification, as an example of both increased German commitment to international stability and German unwillingness to shoulder such commitments. However, given the effects of the financial and debt crises since 2008, which highlight Germany's relative power vis-a-vis other (especially European) states, it is hard to argue that Germany has increased its commitments to international security accordingly. In any event, the debate about whether Germany is taking on enough responsibility in international security continues with intensity in Germany itself.[22] Afghanistan is the dark mirror reflecting the origins and consequences of that debate.

2. Germany's political class struggles with the use of military force.

This second observation is closely related to the first. But where the first focuses on the tension between Germany and its international environment, the second points to a tension between Germany's political leadership and the military as an instrument of politics. The Afghanistan experience is full of examples revealing how uncomfortable German politicians are with the use of force. This was most evident in the description of the Bundeswehr's task as a stabilizing mission, protecting the development of Afghan society and infrastructure.[23] Pictures of German soldiers painting schools and drilling wells accompanied and supported the image of the Bundeswehr as a kind of technical assistance unit with (decorative) guns.

At least until 2010, when facts on the ground and especially the Kunduz incident forced members of the Bundestag to accept and adapt to a different reality, Afghanistan was not portrayed as a military mission in the genuine sense of the word. Limited to the originally rather quiet north, Germans left the fighting (and dying) to their British, American, Dutch, and Canadian allies, among others. It allowed German policymakers to downplay the dangers of the mission, to uphold the (in practical terms) rather absurd distinction between ISAF and OEF (with ISAF understood as laudable civilian reconstruction, and OEF portrayed as questionable killing of alleged terrorists), to ignore any serious thinking about counterinsurgency, and to refrain from using the terms "war," "fighting," or "casualty" when discussing Bundeswehr operations in the "non-international armed conflict" in Afghanistan.[24] Starting in 2010, some of these affectations were overcome, also thanks to a re-energized U.S. effort to turn the deteriorating security situation around. Defense Minister zu Guttenberg introduced the term "war" into Germany's public conversation about Afghanistan, and the rules of engagement were adjusted.[25] The Bundeswehr engaged in its heaviest battles ever and performed admirably. However, these changes were made too late in the mission. As had happened in other Western countries, German society had grown weary of the Afghanistan effort, and German troop levels started dropping consistently from 2011 onward.

The overall impression from the Afghanistan mission is how far the German attitude toward the use of force still is from normalization. More than four decades of re-education of the German people have been utterly successful: the use of military force is not accepted as a "normal" tool of statecraft among the German public and their political leaders.[26] It is a point of contention whether Afghanistan has deepened this reservation or whether it has helped to increase understanding that the German military can be a force for good in international affairs. The generally perceived lack of success in Afghanistan has probably reinforced the belief that the military is not the right instrument for this sort of crisis management. Yet the ease with which a charismatic, thoughtful, and argumentative leader such as Karl-Theodor zu Guttenberg could rally public support behind a militarization of Germany's Afghanistan policy should give pause to advocates as well as skeptics of a stronger German role in international security affairs.

3. German public opinion on the use of force is fickle and receptive to determined leadership.

The political elite's reluctance to use force in international affairs mirrors a general German sentiment. The use of force is not just an ultima ratio in the sense that it is the most extreme measure at the government's disposal but also in the sense that it is the last option to be drawn—if at all. Some observers have argued that there is a "pacifist streak" in Germany, a consequence of two lost World Wars and four decades of stifled strategic culture.[27]

And yet, despite its increasingly war-like nature and mounting number of casualties, the Afghanistan mission has been supported for almost 15 years by all major political parties except the socialist Die Linke. What is more, there has been not a single significant public protest against Germany's military effort in Afghanistan. In fact, the mission has received surprisingly respectable public support, especially given the lackluster political advertising for it.[28] At the outset in 2001, hardly anyone in the German strategic community would have expected such acquiescence on the part of the public.

The public reaction to the use of force thus remains a puzzle to German strategists. Two observations, however, are widely agreed upon. First, most Germans favor using force for humanitarian reasons (to prevent genocide or similar violence), but interest-driven missions (for instance to secure a steady supply of oil or to ensure free and open trade routes) generate skepticism.[29] Second, most Germans do not really care about foreign and security policy or about the state and purpose of the armed forces. This lack of interest, strong feelings, and deep knowledge was captured by former Federal President Horst Köhler's attesting the German public's *wohlwollendes Desinteresse* ("benevolent ignorance") of the Bundeswehr.[30]

As a consequence, it seems highly likely that German public opinion will follow strong and caring leaders if they make a coherent and consistent argument for why they feel compelled to use force in a given international crisis. If decisionmakers explain their choice to the public, address concerns, and keep emphasizing their reasons they will most probably gain a window of time to pursue a policy of force.[31] If they are able to phrase their reasons in the language of humanitarian intervention, public support will be particularly strong. The political communication of the Afghanistan mission surely will be studied for a long time by German strategists—and will be condemned for its lack of enthusiasm, clarity, and consistency.

4. Shifting goals and purposes ruin the credibility and effectiveness of a mission.

A key reason for the dwindling public support in Germany for the Afghanistan mission was widespread confusion about the aim of the effort. Was it to uproot al-Qaida and defeat them in the country that served as the main training ground for the 9/11 attacks? Was it to topple the Taliban regime that allowed international terrorist groups to operate on Afghan soil? Was it to establish democratic structures and a government that served both Western security interests and liberal ideals? Was that possible without widening the political and military efforts to include Afghanistan's neighbors, especially Pakistan? Were women's rights, universal schooling, free speech and religious freedom, political self-determination, and modernized infrastructures essential to the mission's success? Or could the scope of the mission be limited to the stabilization of Kabul and an Afghan government that upheld not more than a sheen of accountability—as long as it prevented international terrorism from taking root again? Or maybe not even that; the West could, after all, fight terrorists in Afghanistan with a strategy of maintenance bombing and drone strikes, leaving the Afghan people victimized and to their own devices. Or could it not?

Thinking about these various approaches, three observations stand out. First, the goals are more interrelated than they might appear at first glance. The fight against terrorists, for instance, requires a broader effort than a campaign of seek and destroy. The best provision against a terrorist resurgence is a strengthened society in terms of representative and fair political structures as well as in terms of economic development. This is why the liberal agenda of nation-building in Afghanistan was so hard to separate from the more narrow security agenda of the anti-terror coalition.

Second, exactly because the various explanations of what the international forces were doing in Afghanistan were part of the same continuum, public discourse could emphasize different aspects at different times. The same political leader could at one point stress the necessity of enforcing human rights in Afghanistan and the primacy of fighting back insurgents at another. Naturally, the public at large perceived such different accentuations as inconsistent and dubious. In fact, they hampered the effectiveness of the mission because they questioned and re-cast priorities on the ground. In the context of the coalition effort, this problem became even more pronounced because different states emphasized different priorities at the same time. In an age of instant global communication, the sometimes contradictory discourses in the United States, France, and Germany, for example, contributed to the confusion and uncertainty in the German public and chipped away at public support.

Third, a particularly German dilemma is evident: Of the many purposes of the mission, those that are hardest to achieve are the ones that are most likely to receive strong public support in Germany. Do-good tasks such as nation-building, getting children into schools, and pushing for women's equality—even if they require the exertion of the Bundeswehr—are what catch the imagination of the German public. More limited military operations such as fighting al-Qaida cells or defending certain territory against insurgents will be met with reservations. This drives German politicians to stress the liberal development aspects of the mission, which in turn creates false expectations among the German public and thus generates disillusionment and resentment when the reality of the situation on the ground becomes impossible to ignore.

Political communication is therefore one of the few areas where an undisputed lesson can be drawn from the Afghanistan experience: at the very beginning of a mission, political leaders should provide a clear rationale and

a definite goal. They should not just mention it once but repeatedly, and stick with it. At least in internal communication with military commanders and civilian officers, the goal should be broken down into a timeline identifying several verifiable milestones. This focuses resources and bureaucratic attention, avoids mission creep, and simplifies public diplomacy.[32] This should not prevent learning and adaptation, however. To the contrary, the more pronounced the rationale and the goals at the beginning of a mission are, the easier it will be to convince the public of certain necessary adjustments because trust in the truthfulness, seriousness, and competence of the leaders will be more firmly established.

5. The comprehensive approach has become the default attitude toward international crisis management—its flaws and limitations notwithstanding.

After re-unification, Germany first experienced crisis management in the Balkans. Those missions gave rise to what NATO calls CIMIC (or **CI**vil-**MI**litary **C**ooperation), the necessity for civilian and military cooperation in stabilization efforts, which the U.S. military calls "civil affairs." Obviously, the combined task of peacekeeping (or even peace enforcement) and nation-building required the right mix of military and civilian (mostly diplomatic and development aid) measures. Given the different cultures of both domains and the fact that in German coalition governments this usually involves ministries led by different parties, CIMIC proved difficult to implement.

When CIMIC needed to be projected on the much vaster canvas of Afghanistan, these first impressions were confirmed. And yet, the cooperation between civilian and military efforts was essential for the overall success of the mission. Therefore, the "comprehensive approach" (sometimes, in small variations, called the whole-of-government approach or, especially in Germany, *Vernetzte Sicherheit* [networked security]) became key to ISAF's strategy. Germany's 2006 white paper on defense, for instance, elevated networked security to a guiding principle of German security policy in general.

There are many interpretations of what the comprehensive approach actually means, but two elements are always central: (1) the coordination of civilian and military measures of crisis management on the ground in the crisis region, and (2) the coordination and cooperation of bureaucracies in the capital at home. In Germany, these twin tasks are closely associated with Afghanistan but have become accepted common sense for all German crisis management operations today, as the most recent White Book—published in July 2016—reiterates.

Therefore, it is even more important to look at the flaws of the comprehensive approach and think about possible remedies. Even if the flaws are here to stay, it is crucial for the political leadership to be aware of them and manage expectations accordingly. The most prominent difficulty is the coordination of the many actors on the ground. Although everyone is in favor of coordination in the abstract, the crucial question of who coordinates whom is certain to create frictions. In dangerous environments, the central coordinating role tends to drift toward the military. Civilian nongovernmental organizations in particular, however, have to keep their distance from the military in order to maintain credibility and effectiveness with the local population.

Obviously, there can be no master solution. The right mix of force and development, military and civilian measures, and leadership is often unclear and situational. Take the crown jewel of the comprehensive approach in Afghanistan, the Provincial Reconstruction Teams (PRTs), which unified military, diplomatic, and development expertise in small units under ISAF command. Germany led two PRTs, in Kunduz (2003–13) and Feyzabad (2004–12). Although those teams implemented several projects and achieved some improvement of the Afghan infrastructure, they can hardly be called a best-practice model for the comprehensive approach. After all, until 2010, Berlin had not even approved a coherent conceptualization of what the PRTs were supposed to do and how they were to be organized.[33] Their successes were a matter of improvisation and, maybe because of that, remain fragile at best.

The same holds true for the inter-ministerial process in Berlin. Competition between different agencies, exacerbated by political fights between the coalition parties, remains strong and often destructive. The prime example of the comprehensive approach in action in Berlin was the *Staatssekretärrunde* (a regular meeting of deputy ministers from the foreign office and from the defense, development cooperation, finance, and other ministries). It was initiated because of the situation in Afghanistan and demonstrated initial changes in bureaucratic mindsets. Today, it is not meeting anymore, at least not on issues of security and stabilization. In international crisis management, the German ministries are still far from conducting common analyses, not to mention common planning and action.

As an ironic consequence, it was the German military that received most of the criticism for the lack of success in Afghanistan. In the public mind, the mission became identified not with the whole of government but with the Bundeswehr, exactly because that was the only German institution that contributed its considerable share to the overall success of ISAF. This reflects less on the strength of Germany's military commitment than on the weakness of the other components of the German comprehensive approach. The Bundeswehr, for instance, deployed more cooks to Afghanistan than the Foreign

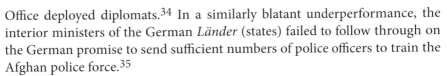

Office deployed diplomats.[34] In a similarly blatant underperformance, the interior ministers of the German *Länder* (states) failed to follow through on the German promise to send sufficient numbers of police officers to train the Afghan police force.[35]

There is a familiar lesson here about the future of the comprehensive approach: efficient civilian-military cooperation and a unified government at home are sensible and rather self-evident ideas, but their implementation requires strong leadership from the top, steady and focused, in order to overcome bureaucratic inertia and inevitable systemic frictions. Conceivably, the political leadership has internalized this lesson. It is not guaranteed, however, that lessons learned will be heeded once another crisis generates its own political pressures.

6. The scope and intensity of Germany's commitment to the ISAF mission was in large part dependent on U.S. leadership.

Without the Bush administration's decision to invade Afghanistan and eradicate the al-Qaida terrorist threat, the Bundeswehr would not have been sent there. From the beginning, the German effort was designed and explained as a contribution to an international mission, led by the United States and mandated by the UN Security Council. It was (in small part) assistance to the United States under Article 5 of the NATO Treaty and (in large part) a commitment to stabilize a war-torn country in the aftermath of regime change. German leaders saw hardly any genuine, direct national interests at stake in Afghanistan; the mission gained its strategic importance through Germany's alliance with the United States.

Accordingly, when the United States in 2003 shifted its focus from Afghanistan to Iraq, Germany's Afghanistan policy drifted as well. Between the end of 2002 and the fall of 2005, the Schröder government reduced the number of Bundeswehr soldiers in Afghanistan from 2,500 to 2,250. This trend was stopped by the end of 2006, after the United States changed course with starting the surge in Iraq.[36] And when the United States finally turned attention back to the deteriorating security situation in Afghanistan and increased troop levels between January 2007 and May 2008 from about 26,000 to about 35,000, Germany followed suit. By the end of 2008, the Bundestag mandate allowed for 4,500 German soldiers in Afghanistan, exactly twice the number of 2004. This was not an isolated incident, as the short-lived "Obama surge" demonstrated: the rise in U.S. troop levels (from roughly 45,000 in May 2009 to roughly 100,000 in September 2010) was met by a German increase to 5,350 in January 2011. Also not coincidentally, the drawdown of U.S. troops starting that same year was reflected in German deployments, with only 4,900 troops by December 2011 and 4,400 in 2012.

It is striking that U.S. leadership on Afghanistan also affected the quality—or at least intensity—of German strategic thinking about the mission. The very first progress report on Afghanistan by the German government, published in 2010, was a direct reaction to the increased U.S. (and German) effort to change the dynamics on the ground. The overdue revision of the German administration's "Afghanistan Concept" in 2006 should also be seen in the context of renewed American attention to Afghanistan around that time. And that Minister of Defense Karl-Theodor zu Guttenberg, in office from 2009 to 2011, could have such an impact on the level of public debate about Afghanistan is also due in no small part to the shifting international attitude around that time, led by the United States.

These observations allow for three conclusions. First, since Germany is lacking a certain national interest-driven strategic assertiveness, one of its key interests in joining military missions abroad is its standing within NATO and its desire to maintain a reliable security alliance with the United States. Therefore, the best way to keep Germany out of foreign entanglements is to portray any decision about the use of force as irrelevant to the cohesion of NATO in general and to Germany's credibility as an ally in particular. Alternatively, if political leaders want Germany to participate in a given mission, they need to play the card of "Alliance solidarity."

Second, German leaders learned that U.S. security policy, at least in part, depends on the mood swings of electoral politics and public opinion as well as on the strategic preferences of individual presidents. It might thus be dangerous or unnecessary for Germany to commit to long-term deployments in any given crisis as the U.S. leadership is likely to determine (and reverse) course based on factors other than the situation on the ground.

Third, in the beginning and early years of the Afghanistan intervention, the United States could probably have assembled a far more potent international coalition if it had pressed for it. But the Bush administration's reluctance to allow NATO allies to join the mission at all and the doctrine of the light footprint have prevented such a stronger international presence, which might have had a significant impact on the overall development of the security situation.

7. The Afghanistan mission propelled the transformation of the German armed forces. (Or, at least, it uncovered their deficiencies.)

Afghanistan was the first substantial and prolonged fighting mission for the Bundeswehr since its inception. Initially, the mission was not expected to involve heavy combat, which made the German learning curve particularly steep.

One of the first things German military strategists had to acknowledge was that the Bundeswehr lacked some of the key capabilities required for this type of mission, e.g., the German armed forces had no strategic airlift of their own, relying on allies or rented Russian planes to get them to the theater. Tactical airlift also was in short supply and often was not fully operational. In combat, German troops—constrained anyway by strict rules of engagement—did not possess sufficient firepower. (Major reinforcements arrived only in 2010 when, over the concerns of advocates of the light footprint, the 155-mm Howitzer 2000 was brought into action.)

In general, the Bundeswehr was neither designed nor equipped for force projection out of area. Even at the beginning of the 21st century, it was still very much the Bundeswehr of the Cold War, ready to defend the homeland against an invasion from the Soviet army. The best indicator of this outdated posture is the fact that, for structural reasons, only 7,000 of the 250,000 German soldiers in 2010 were able to deploy out of the NATO area at any given time.[37] In that sense, even the rather limited engagement in Afghanistan stretched German forces to the maximum.

Both military and, after some time, political leaders understood this situation to be untenable and pushed for further adjustments in the reforms of the German armed forces that had been underway since reunification. In the 1990s, these reforms were mostly driven by the incorporation of the East German forces into the Bundeswehr and the downsizing of the overall number of troops according to the logic of the "peace dividend." Now, they were driven by the combat experience in Afghanistan and, after the financial and debt crises took effect since 2008, by austerity.

Begun under Defense Minister zu Guttenberg and then conceptualized and implemented under Defense Minister Thomas de Maizière, a *Neuausrichtung* ("re-orientation") of the armed forces took hold. It aimed at greater deployability, leaner and more effective forces, and a more efficient procurement process. Among the measures taken were the controversial suspension (and effective end) of conscription, a reduction to 185,000 soldiers by 2017 (10,000 of whom should be able to deploy simultaneously), and an increased effort at creating synergies with European partners ("pooling and sharing" of capabilities).[38]

Today, after the end of ISAF and under Defense Minister Ursula von der Leyen, this process of re-orientation is continuing. A new generation of career officers with combat experience is also likely to ensure that the lessons of Afghanistan will in the future be applied to Germany's force posture. Recent geostrategic developments, especially Russia's aggression in Ukraine, however, have led all NATO allies to re-emphasize Article 5 and territorial defense vis-a-vis crisis management and stability projection out of area. The 2016 German White Book explains how this tension leads to force planning that must do both. It must, for instance, recreate a substantial tank force for territorial defense and reassurance of allies in Eastern Europe while also creating a more agile and deployable force for crisis management abroad.

It is also noteworthy that the Afghanistan experience has affected not just the transformation of the Bundeswehr but also the political process of mandating deployment. In a groundbreaking 1994 decision, the German Constitutional Court affirmed the powers of the Bundestag to decide upon any engagement of the Bundeswehr abroad, coining the term *Parlamentsarmee* (parliamentary army). With its at least annual parliamentary debates about the extension and nature of the ISAF mandate and especially the complicated decisionmaking over the legitimacy of German soldiers serving in integrated structures such as AWACS,[39] the Afghanistan mission illustrated how cumbersome and perhaps unreliable this parliamentary prerogative is in practice—as commendable as it might be in democratic theory.

The discussion over whether, and how, to make this process flexible by giving the administration more leeway through anticipatory resolutions and parliamentary rights to re-call deployed troops has been going on for more than 10 years. It heightened in intensity after Germany's opting-out of NATO's mission in Libya, Operation UNIFIED PROTECTOR, creating concern over Germany's reliability in cooperative and, especially, integrated military structures. It culminated in July 2015, when a multi-party commission headed by former Defense Minister Volker Rühe recommended only minor changes to the established rules of the 1990s.[40]

However, the key problems experienced in Afghanistan and other missions remain unsolved. How reliable are the German government's commitments, especially in situations requiring quick decisions, if they are dependent on a vote in the Bundestag first? Even worse, the current system provides strong incentives for the administration to always and automatically aim for the lowest common denominator instead of asking for courageous and necessary commitments.

8. With Afghanistan, the German understanding of "defense" was broadened to "security."

Afghanistan was Germany's first military mission of the 21st century, and it established a new way of thinking about the relationship between defense and security. In the past, especially during the Cold War, the purpose of the Bundeswehr was primarily to defend German territory against possible invasion. With the changing international landscape after the dissolution of the Soviet

Union, new threats and concerns arose. With the attacks of 9/11, the nexus of international terrorism, failing states, and weapons of mass destruction gained particular relevance. Defense, thus, had to be interpreted in a broader sense. Meaningful defense had to address certain threats before they reached the homeland—otherwise, it would be too late to prevent them creating destruction at home. This is why the discourse of "prevention" and "stabilization" became so successful in the 2000s. In essence, it shifted Western understanding of defense toward the more encompassing concept of security.[41]

This holds true for all NATO allies, including Germany. It is debatable, however, how deeply the new concept took root in Germany. After all, the German people never fully accepted Peter Struck's phrase that "German security had also to be defended at the Hindu Kush"—arguably the most succinct expression of the new understanding by a German leader.

One of the reasons for the reluctance to embrace the new understanding of security is the fact that it makes it very hard to define success. The more narrow understanding of defense is comparatively easy: as long as territorial integrity remains inviolate (or, in case of attack, can be re-established reasonably soon), defense policy succeeds. Security, by contrast, is rather vague and, in essence, impossible to achieve. It aims at perfect conditions of stability, conducive to all interests of the state. Every threat, even every risk, is by definition an impediment to security. The dangerous consequences of a very broad understanding of security are constant alert and overstretch of forces and resources.

On the other hand, the limited understanding of territorial defense is not sufficient anymore in the face of the complex interconnectedness of today's international security situation. Hence, the tension between "defense" and "security" is here to stay. Germany, like all Western nations, has not yet found a perfect solution to this puzzle, but its Afghanistan experience stands at the beginning of its understanding and experience of it.

9. Ambitious goals of nation-building in remote, complex, and non-Western countries are impossible to sustain at the level of engagement the West is prepared to invest.

The international community, including Germany, has achieved impressive results in supporting the Afghan people's desire to build a better future for themselves. Massive improvements in infrastructure, medical care, and education facilities are accompanied by substantial political progress in terms of democratic elections, accountability, and inclusiveness. These are the foundations for the emerging economic prosperity and sustainability.[42]

At the same time, all these improvements remain as fragile as the overall security situation in Afghanistan. As of 2016, the end of ISAF and the limitations of the RESOLUTE SUPPORT mission do not bode well for the future of Afghanistan as the Ashraf Ghani government faced severe challenges in maintaining current levels of stability on its own.[43] The leading powers of the West display little appetite for further substantial engagement in Afghanistan. This is due to a mix of domestic preferences after the financial and economic crisis and of international assessments attributing rather little strategic value to Afghanistan as long as it does not again turn into a home base for international terrorism. Leaders and publics alike seem to be ready to write off some of the achievements in nation-building in Afghanistan as long as a modicum of stability remains intact. At least they are not willing to invest the resources—as, for example, the United States did with the Marshall Plan after World War II—needed for a decisive change in outcome.

The lesson German decisionmakers seem to have drawn from this is to downsize all ambition regarding further commitments to nation-building in both rhetoric and practice. Fearful of first setting, and then failing to achieve, too ambitious goals, they settle for the other extreme of underselling the impact decisive German and Western action could have on many of the struggling, failing, and festering states around the world. Even in situations directly pertaining to German and European Union security interests, as in Libya, Syria, and Ukraine, German leaders emphasize the need for restraint and a low level of ambition. In their desire to not repeat the Afghanistan experience they run the danger of failing to sufficiently support agents of democratic stability in other, truly very different, crises.

10. Whatever the lessons from Afghanistan are, Germany's next significant military mission will probably be very different.

However useful the discussion of past missions is for learning more about best practices and about problems to be addressed on the strategic, political, and military levels, one must also eschew the fallacy of uncritically projecting the circumstances and lessons of the last war onto the next. This holds especially true for Afghanistan, as it seems to be a very special case in most regards. Its origin, tied to the unique 9/11 attacks, as well as its particular political and geographical conditions, do not make it a likely model for future scenarios of German warfare.

For instance, war in Afghanistan did not involve a great power as an adversary. It took place in a land-locked country and thus gave hardly any relevance to maritime forces. It had a strong focus on nation-building and human security. And it was mandated by the UN which, especially for Germany, strongly affects the legitimacy of the use of force in a domestic political context. Virtually none of these conditions are likely to apply to the next significant military engagement of Germany. Recent trends in international security, from Chinese assertiveness in the Asia-Pacific to Russian revisionism in the post-Soviet space to the violent dissolution of order and competition for hegemony in the Middle East, all point to a future that will hold different tasks for Germany and its armed forces than Afghanistan did.

CHAPTER 3
What Did Russia Learn From the U.S. Wars in Iraq and Afghanistan?

Stephen Blank

Studying other governments and contemporary war enjoys (or at least should enjoy) a prominent place in military establishments. Russia historically has devoted enormous attention to such studies and habitually cites other governments' wars, or more generally the lessons of contemporary wars, in its military literature. Nevertheless, some Russian analysts believe that Moscow has learned little, either out of willful rejection or incapability, from U.S. wars in Iraq and Afghanistan, especially the former.[1] This author can attest from past experiences that the Russian military spurned learning from the United States in the 1990s and 2000s.[2] But Operation DESERT STORM in 1991 and NATO's Kosovo war in 1999 clearly had a profound impact. Likewise, Russian military reforms since 2008 consciously involved learning from foreign sources, and perhaps Russian tactics and operations in Ukraine since 2014 reflect this learning.[3] But no two cultures learn in the same way or learn the same lessons from the same events. In the United States a veritable library of works on insurgency and counterinsurgency continues to proliferate, triggered by American experiences in the wars in Iraq and Afghanistan. But those are not the lessons Russia has learned from those wars.

This does not denote Russia's failure to grasp that these were insurgency or counterinsurgency wars, although it may use different terms for that phenomenon. Having been an empire throughout its history, Russia possesses a rich and long history of these operations in service of imperial management.[4] Moreover, Russia's bitter experience in Afghanistan enabled Russian leaders to grasp events there after 2001. In addition, Russia has been fighting a jihadist insurgency in Chechnya, and now the North Caucasus, since 1994. Neither is Russia above learning from terrorist forces like HAMAS and Hizballah. Reports from Ukraine indicate that Russian forces there have employed the terrorist tactic of placing artillery next to or among civilian installations and institutions to impede enemy counter-fire or to create propaganda spectacles in case of return fire on those artillery positions.[5]

Nevertheless, Russian military and political leaders were unable to see, and arguably still cannot see, insurgency and counterinsurgency as the primary forms of contemporary war or as the main threats to Russia. Instead, it appears that for them the Iraq war highlights continuing trends toward high-precision, long-range strike technology, informatization of warfare, and the importance of land power, i.e., rather different lessons.[6] Moreover, for a long time after the fall of the Soviet Union, Russia, by its own admission, could not draw usable conclusions about the major strategic trends of modern war, let alone implement a coherent strategy to meet whatever trends it did discern. The 2003 so-called "white paper" on Russian defense advocated preparing for every kind of conceivable war, e.g., the canonical theater war in Europe that Moscow believed (and still believes) is the most likely threat, insurgency at home, and a Russian counterinsurgency campaign against that threat. Defense Minister Sergei Ivanov stated then that:

> Military preparedness, operational planning, and maintenance need to be as flexible as possible because in recent years no single type of armed conflict has dominated. The Russian armed forces will be prepared for regular and anti-guerrilla warfare, the struggle against different types of terrorism, and peacekeeping operations.[7]

This statement reflected more than a felt need; it also showed a deep strategic confusion and inability to settle upon the fundamental nature of modern war and of the ensuing threats to Russia. Russian military leaders had perceptions but could not forge a truly strategic assessment or response to what they saw. In 2003, the then Chief of the General Staff General (ret.) V.L. Manilov, who then was First Deputy Chairman of the Federation Council Defense and Security Committee, told an interviewer:

> Let's take, for example, the possible development of the geopolitical and military-strategic situation around Russia. We don't even have precisely specified definitions of national interests and national security, and there isn't even the methodology itself of coming up with decisions concerning Russia's fate. But without this it's impossible to ensure the country's progressive development…. It also should be noted that a systems analysis and the monitoring of the geostrategic situation around Russia requires the consolidation of all national resources and the involvement of state and public structures and organizations. At the same time, one has a clear sense of the shortage of intellectual potential in the centers where this problem should be handled in a qualified manner.[8]

Because Russian planners could not develop or adequately define a truly credible hierarchy of threats or Russia's national interests, they inevitably saw (and still see) threats everywhere while often lacking the conceptual means for categorizing them coherently. Lacking a priority form of war or threat for which they had to train their troops, they had to perform traditional tasks and priority missions like defending Russia's territorial boundaries, perceived as Soviet territorial boundaries; preventing and deterring attacks on Russia; and maintaining strategic stability. They also had to participate directly in achieving Russia's economic and political goals and conducting peacetime operations, including peace operations sanctioned by the United Nations or Commonwealth of Independent States (CIS). Consequently, coherent planning and policymaking were bedeviled by multiple threats that still haunt senior military leaders, although less than before. In 2003, the then Deputy Chief of the General Staff General Yuri Baluyevsky said:

> In order to conduct joint maneuvers [with NATO], you have to determine who your enemy actually is. *We still do not know* (emphasis added). After the Warsaw Pact disappeared, there was confusion in the general staffs of the world's armies. But who was the enemy? Well, no enemy emerged. Therefore the first question is: Against whom will we fight? ... But the campaign against terrorism does not require massive armies. And NATO's massive armies have not disappeared at all. No one says "We do not need divisions, we do not need ships, we do not need hundreds of thousands of aircraft and tanks..." The Russian military are accused of still thinking in World War II categories. Although we incidentally realized long before the Americans that the mad race to produce thousands and thousands of nuclear warheads should be stopped![9]

Thus, the General Staff and the Ministry of Defense at that time either had abdicated or could not execute their critical task of forecasting the nature or character of today's wars.

However, that is no longer the case. Even in 2003 Russian leaders perceived a major lesson of contemporary war to be that "there has been a steady trend toward broadening the use of armed forces" and that "conflicts are spreading to larger areas, including the sphere of Russia's vital interests."[10] Since then numerous official statements have noted the growing tendency to use force in interstate relations, generally have ascribed that tendency to the United States, and explicitly have regarded this as grounds for concern about Russian security.[11] Thus, one key lesson of U.S. wars in Iraq and Afghanistan is the steady, if not increasing, perception that Washington is far too "trigger-happy" regarding the resolution of major issues in world politics and has therefore launched several wars in the Middle East that it did not know how to terminate. Those wars have morphed into protracted conflicts between Islam and the West or within Islamic communities that involve Russia (as in the North

Caucasus), place its vital interests at risk, and could spread more deeply into Russia or its immediate neighborhood (Central Asia).

This critique applies to Iraq and to NATO's 2011 operation in Libya, the latter apparently having decisively influenced President Vladimir Putin's growing anti-Americanism. Afghanistan, for obvious reasons, is regarded differently. But Russian concerns about Afghanistan have risen as their belief in the success of U.S. strategy has diminished. By 2011 Russian spokesmen were warning about the course of the war in Afghanistan. Russia's Presidential Representative in Afghanistan Zamir Kabulov told a press conference in May 2011 that the Afghan situation was constantly deteriorating.[12] Russia's Ambassador to Afghanistan Andrei Avetisyan warned in 2013 that NATO was abandoning Afghanistan in the middle of the war against terrorism with predictably tragic results.[13]

Avetisyan also warned that the Afghan armed forces were not ready to replace NATO.[14] And an official of Russia's Ministry of Foreign Affairs, writing in the ministry's journal *International Affairs*, proclaimed that the Taliban would sooner or later take over Afghanistan, and said that unnamed American intelligence reports concurred that the Afghan government could not govern the country and would steadily lose influence until it is confined to separate cities.[15] Avetisyan's remarks reflected other pessimistic Russian opinions.[16] Consequently there was, and is, a widespread expectation of a future civil war outside of U.S. military control and a gathering number of critiques of what numerous critics have long felt is a misconceived U.S. strategy.[17] This assessment has driven Russian thinking about security threats in Central Asia.

Russia's General Staff expected the Afghan situation to deteriorate as NATO and the United States left, and Kabulov expected Islamists to grow in number and expand operations to, if not beyond, the borders with Tajikistan and Turkmenistan by the spring of 2015.[18] Indeed, they had already gotten to that border by the end of 2014.[19] And some analysts assert that the Taliban is already [in late 2015] present and active in northern Tajikistan.[20] Specifically, Chief of the General Staff General Valery Gerasimov reported to foreign defense attachés:

> In the light of the political decision adopted by the US leadership to withdraw the contingent of American troops from Afghanistan by the end of 2014, we predict with a high degree of probability a significant deterioration in the situation in that country with the transfer of real control of particular regions to terrorist groupings. In the context of the severe deterioration in the situation in Iraq and Syria as well as the stepping up of the activities of the terrorist grouping ISIL [Islamic State

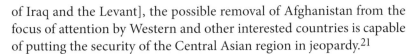

of Iraq and the Levant], the possible removal of Afghanistan from the focus of attention by Western and other interested countries is capable of putting the security of the Central Asian region in jeopardy.[21]

Presidential Representative in Afghanistan Kabulov has recently gone even further. He claims that about 100 ISIL fighters have been deployed from Syria and Iraq to Afghanistan to prepare an attack on Central Asia. He warned that:

A "spillover" into Central Asia is inevitable, especially considering that all the foundations are there. They have created two beachheads in Afghanistan: one on the border of Tajikistan, and the other of Turkmenistan. There they have concentrated fairly large forces. Let's say on the Tajikistan beachhead there are 4-5000 fighters concentrated. And on the beachhead opposite Turkmenistan [there are] 2500 fighters. They have deployed camps for two-month preparation courses for fighters. We know of three such camps, and there may be more. They are training 50 fighters in every course, so if you take at least three camps that we know about, that's 150 fighters every two months. What's interesting is that they are mostly natives of Central Asia.[22]

Similarly, Kabulov believes Western countries are unlikely to repeat military operations in Afghanistan, and the director of Russia's Federal Drug Control Service, Viktor Ivanov, has repeatedly blasted NATO for its ongoing unpreparedness to fight Afghan heroin.[23]

A Turkish source reports that at a meeting of the intelligence chiefs of the Shanghai Cooperation Organization in 2014, member states expressed fear that in the short term the Taliban and ISIL can form an even stronger bond as the West withdraws from Afghanistan and that this bond will place all Central Asian governments at greater risk. Turkmenistan has reportedly begun taking measures to strengthen border security.[24] This meeting's communiqué openly alluded to concerns about Central Asian terrorists' participation in the fighting in Syria and Iraq.[25] These concerns are understandable. There is abundant evidence that Central Asians (and Azeris) are looking to join ISIL and that some members of ISIL are considering extending their operations to Tajikistan and Turkmenistan, if not to other Central Asian countries.[26]

President Putin, at the December 2014 summit of the Collective Security Treaty Organization (CSTO), warned the representatives of the Russian and other armies there that they must prepare to take "preventive actions" in the light of a forthcoming threat to Central Asia from Afghanistan. Putin said:

The CSTO should continue focusing its attention on enhancing its close cooperation with Afghanistan, especially in view of the greater risk to regional security posed by the withdrawal of International

Forces. We are all interested in a flourishing, happy and neutral Afghanistan. We proceed from the notion that the Afghan leadership will work to stabilize the situation in the country. At the same time, the current situation causes concern. Militant groups of the Islamic State are attempting to include certain Afghan provinces in the so-called Islamic Caliphate. Terrorist and extremist groups are already spreading their activity to Central Asia. In these circumstances, the CSTO states should be ready to take adequate preventive measures. In particular, we need to continue focusing on the Tajik-Afghan border and on providing Tajikistan with financial and material aid to modernize its armed forces.[27]

Similarly, Defense Minister Sergei Shoigu stated that Russian and Tajik defense forces must be ready for any scenario, including the most negative one. Bolstering the combat potential of those forces, and the capacities of the base in Tajikistan that houses the Russian army's 201st Division, therefore is essential.[28] Kabulov even raised the possibility of so-called precautionary moves on the Russo-Kazakh border or the Caspian Sea or fighting the terrorists on the Amu Darya rather than on the Volga.[29]

Yet despite these warnings of doom and gloom Moscow still insists that NATO must bear primary responsibility for the situation in Afghanistan, thus reflecting its ambivalence since it also "finds it inexpedient to send border guards to reinforce the Tajik-Afghan border."[30] Kabulov also reported that Russia would not send troops into Afghanistan.[31] Thus, apparently, the greatest lesson Moscow has learned from U.S. wars in Iraq and Afghanistan is that the United States is a kind of rogue elephant that acts unilaterally and is too prone to resort to violence. For all its power and tactical proficiency, which Russia respects and admires, Washington does not know how to bring these wars to positive strategic conclusions. Therefore, although America has failed to curb its ways and represents a growing threat to Russia, its power is steadily diminishing, which opens possibilities for Russian advances, e.g., in Ukraine. Such conclusions could only come from a study of foreign, albeit unspecified, wars.

Strategic Lessons for Domestic Security

Since 2003, the leadership's ability to define the contemporary strategic environment, to identify the lessons of contemporary wars in general (not just Iraq and Afghanistan), and to codify a threat perception based on those processes has visibly grown. But Russian perceptions and the lessons learned are miles apart from U.S. writings. Nonetheless Moscow's lessons from U.S. military engagement in the Middle East, including Libya and perhaps other

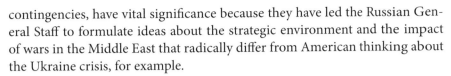

contingencies, have vital significance because they have led the Russian General Staff to formulate ideas about the strategic environment and the impact of wars in the Middle East that radically differ from American thinking about the Ukraine crisis, for example.

On November 17, 2011, Chief of the General Staff General Nikolai Makarov told the Defense Ministry's Public Chamber that:

> The possibility of local armed conflicts virtually along the entire perimeter of the border has grown dramatically .... I cannot rule out that, in certain circumstances, local and regional armed conflicts could grow into a large-scale war, possibly even with nuclear weapons.[32]

Makarov further warned that the cause for such wars in the CIS lies in NATO's advancement to the borders of the CIS and Russia.[33] Makarov echoed previous statements by his predecessor Baluyevsky that while Russia faced no direct threat of aggression, "[given] the existence of nuclear weapons, any localized armed conflict—let alone a regional conflict—could lead the international community to the brink of a global war."[34] Makarov thus postulated the possibility of a seamless transition from local wars like those in Iraq after 2003, or now [in late 2015] in Ukraine, all the way up to a theater or even strategic nuclear war This is clearly another lesson from U.S. wars in the Middle East: they could extend (since Russia regards its strategic frontiers as the Soviet frontiers) from a local war in one of those states or closer to home in Ukraine all the way up to major theater war, possibly involving use of nuclear weapons.

This wider lens of global competition now informs Moscow's approach to all regional crises in areas it views as strategic to its interests. Director of the Security Council Nikolai Patrushev stated:

> Over the past two decades, 95 percent of conflicts affecting global and regional security started as domestic ones .... Threats and conflicts inside certain countries quickly go the regional and also global level. This is particularly noticeable in the case of North Africa and the Middle East, in particular, in Libya, and now in Syria.[35]

Implicit in these and other statements is Moscow's abiding belief that the United States and its allies have frequently employed coercive tactics and policy, if not direct force, against objectionable governments, including proliferators like North Korea and Iran, or have exploited domestic crises to force regime change upon them. From Moscow's standpoint these policies aggravate difficult issues, thereby generating intractable crises if not prolonged wars that negatively affect international security and Russia. U.S. policies also jeopardize its interests because they enlarge the scope of U.S. dominance and implicitly, if not explicitly, put Russia's own objectionable behavior under the microscope of potential international pressure. Russian interests also suffer because these objectionable or rogue states are, not coincidentally, Russia's partners against U.S. power. Therefore, any potential international intervention in a state must be subjected exclusively to the oversight of the UN Security Council, where Russia has a veto.[36]

Simultaneously, the increasing emphasis on the use, or threat of use, of force in Russia's neighborhood has apparently marched in conjunction with Moscow's growing disposition to threaten others with force if it thinks it can do so with impunity. Moscow, demanding equal status with Washington, believes it can emulate U.S. actions without cost. This is a somewhat perverse form of learning from U.S. wars. Moscow's operation in Ukraine is only the latest and probably not the last example of this trend.

Lessons for Domestic Security

Moscow has also learned that contemporary wars could threaten its domestic system. Here Moscow has learned from U.S. experiences with counterterrorism and counterinsurgency operations, but probably has learned more from its own experiences in Chechnya. NATO's 2011 Libyan intervention led General Makarov to warn that the Russian army must be prepared for a Libyan or similar scenario.[37] But beyond such warnings there is also the great danger that Russian security forces—the army, the Ministry of Interior's forces (VVMVD), and the Federal Security Service (FSB), and other paramilitary forces—might be employed if domestic protests became too serious. Moscow has long prepared for that scenario. Already in 2005–06, the Ministry of Defense formed Special Designation Forces from Spetsnaz brigades under the minister's direct control. These units have air, marine, and ground components and conduct peace support and counterterrorist operations.[38] Since the defense minister answers only to the president, essentially this also means putting all Russia under threat of counterterrorist or other so-called operations without any parliamentary accountability or scrutiny.

Since then matters have, if anything, grown worse. An April 2009 press report outlined quite clearly the threat the authorities perceive. It stated:

> The Russian intelligence community is seriously worried about latent social processes capable of leading to the beginning of civil wars and conflicts on [Russian Federation] territory that can end up in a disruption of territorial integrity and the appearance of a large number of new sovereign powers. Data of an information "leak," the statistics and massive number of antigovernment actions, and official statements and appeals of the opposition attest to this.[39]

This report proceeded to say that these agencies expected massive protests in the Moscow area, industrial areas of the South Urals and Western Siberia, and in the Far East while ethnic tension among the Muslims of the North Caucasus and Volga-Ural areas was not excluded. But despite the threat of this unrest, the government characteristically used strong-arm methods to meet this threat by strengthening the VVMVD along with other paramilitary forces, thereby repeating the efforts of past regimes.[40]

This report, and other articles, outlined the ways in which the internal armed forces were being strengthened as of 2009. Presumably this process has continued without letup. Special intelligence and commando subunits designed to conduct preventive elimination of opposition leaders were being established in the VVMVD. These forces received new models of weapons and equipment, including armored, artillery, naval, and air defense systems. Some 5.5 billion rubles were allocated in 2008 for these forces' modernization. Apart from the already permitted "corporate forces" of Gazprom and Transneft that monitor pipeline safety, the Ministry of Interior (MVD) set up an *Olimpstroi* (Olympics Construction) Army and even the Fisheries Inspectorate created a special armed subunit called Piranha.[41] We may assume that these trends are ongoing.

Since then, more information has emerged about the extent of the domestic reconstruction of the MVD and its forces, the VVMVD, into a force intended to suppress any manifestation of dissent. As of 2003, there were 98 special-purpose police detachments (OMONs) in Russia whose mission was state security. By comparison, in 1988, 19 OMONs existed in 14 Russian regions and three union republics. By 2007, there were 121 OMON units composed of 20,000 men and another 87 police special designation detachments (OMSNs) with permanent staffing of over 5,200 people operating with the internal affairs organs, making a grand total of 208 special purpose or designated units with some 25,000 well-trained and drilled soldiers. The OMSNs have grown from being originally an anti-crime and anti-terrorist force to a force charged with stopping "extremist" criminal activity. All these units train together and have been centralized within the MVD to fight "organized crime, terrorism, and extremism." From 2005 to 2006, the budgets of these units almost doubled. By 2009, they were also working with aircraft assets, specifically the MVD's Aviation Center, which has nine special purpose air detachments throughout Russia. Seven more such units are to be created. Furthermore, the MVD has developed a concept for rapidly airlifting its forces to troubled areas from other regions when necessary. These forces are also receiving large-scale deliveries of new armored vehicles with computers in some cases and C3 (command, control, communications) capabilities.

These forces are separate from the regular VVMVD.[42] As the journalist and expert on Russian security service, Irina Bogoran observed, "On a parallel basis with the OMON empire, a multi-level internal security troop machine is being developed—with its own special forces, aircraft, armored equipment, situational crisis centers, and so forth."[43] When one considers this huge expansion of the domestic *Silovye Struktury* (power organs), it becomes clear why Russia announced in 2008 that it would increase funding for the MVD by 50 percent in 2010 and where the government believes the true threat to Russian security lies.[44]

These moves suggest a regime that is all too prepared to believe it is under siege and to react in forceful, coercive ways. They also suggest a regime deeply prone to over-inflated threat assessments and even hysteria. Although that is not the image Moscow wants to present abroad, it is the reality. Thus, we can say that the most important, though surely not the only, lesson Moscow has learned from U.S. wars relates to the likelihood that Washington will touch off a protracted local or regional conflict in its strategic neighborhood that endangers Russia's domestic stability and vital foreign interests. Those lessons relate to the nature of the strategic environment and the danger that a regional or local war, in Russian terminology, will morph into a theater-sized conventional or even potentially nuclear war given the threats that such wars could pose to vital Russian interests.

Chechnya, Georgia, and the Character of Contemporary War

Apparently Russia has incorporated the military lessons it learned from recent U.S. wars and engagements mainly into its decisions about force structure, operational concepts, and strategic perspectives.[45] The reforms of force structures have been extensively traced in works by Roger McDermott, Keir Giles, and Rod Thornton and need not be repeated here.[46] But there are other important lessons from Russia's, and to a lesser degree America's, wars that possess great contemporary relevance. Certainly the major reforms launched after 2008 reflected not just the study of contemporary wars up to that point but also the experience of other military organizations, even including the Swiss model.[47] Therefore, the decisive learning experiences for Russia concerning such basic questions as the nature of the correct force structure and technology for the armed forces were only partly learned from U.S. experience. By far the most important experiences for Russia in this context of learning are the second Chechen war from 1999 to 2007, when Moscow declared Chechnya to be pacified, and the 2008 war in Georgia. These wars not only graphically highlighted the Red Army's defects but also impelled the post-2008 innovations regarding information warfare (IW), force structure, and military armament, and led to discernible improvement in the armed forces.[48]

The reforms of 2008–12 aimed to generate an army that could credibly fight the kinds of war Moscow saw in Georgia, Iraq, and elsewhere in the Middle East, including the Israel-Hizballah war of 2006. The need for a force capable of rapidly projecting power to Russia's peripheries had become overwhelmingly obvious in Chechnya and Georgia, and those wars, plus U.S. experience in the Middle East, warned of what happens when such forces are unavailable or badly led and equipped. But the demand for such forces does not mean a belief that current and future wars will be insurgencies. Rather, those forces must be able to conduct small-scale theater operations like wars in Georgia, seize and hold ground in conventional wars as before, and exploit high-tech, precision-strike capabilities.[49]

Contemporary wars have also demonstrated the need for a would-be great power to compete in the domain of precision-strike, high-tech weapons. Putin and the military leadership have consistently reiterated the need for this. To give but one example, Putin in September 2013 urged paying priority attention to "the development of high-precision weapons not only of long-range but also of tactical strike zone. An analysis of recent military conflicts shows that its role and scale are constantly growing. Therefore, a systematic effort is needed to coordinate all components of high-precision weapons."[50] Nor is there doubt of Russia's careful study of U.S. conventional and precision-strike capabilities as displayed in Kosovo, Iraq, and Afghanistan.[51]

Similarly, extensive American use of unmanned aerial vehicles (UAVs) has taught Russians the importance those weapons have for reconnaissance and strike operations. Indeed, they have learned from the United States that both these capabilities assigned to UAVs apply equally to maritime and land warfare. Russian analysts grasp that UAVs have become one of the most important categories of weapons for ships of the main classes, even for aircraft carriers.[52] One possibility is to deploy UAVs onboard ships that provide air support and thus make them independent of support from coastal aircraft. The UAV provides accurate target detection and conducts reconnaissance while evading the enemy's anti-air assets, which supports anti-ship activities all the way up to attacks on carriers and carrier battle groups (including attacks using long- and medium-range anti-ship missiles based on surface ships, submarines, naval aviation aircraft, and perhaps coastal batteries). UAVs also provide reconnaissance support for combating enemy light forces operating in littoral areas or conducting landing operations. Third, UAVs can detect enemy aviation groups at distances beginning at 600–700 kilometers and can help integrate the combined arms anti-air operation.[53]

Russian Views on Information Warfare and Network Centric Warfare

Control of precision weapons and UAVs requires high-quality information technology that is also capable of waging IW. But Moscow's concept of IW fundamentally differs from the American concept. Indeed, Moscow's embrace of information technology points in two different but unopposed directions. Russia's concept of IW includes taking down, corrupting, and disrupting networks, but it goes well beyond that. It includes shaping mass political consciousness and a comprehensive attack on an entire state and society, as Russia tried in Estonia in 2007. It has refined its efforts since then to reach the abilities we have seen in 2014–16 in Ukraine. Although these developments owe much to Russian efforts to control the narrative in Chechnya, Western sources also have influenced Russian thinking.[54]

Indeed, such ideas evidently are "in the air" as a result of America's recent wars. In a 2002 Russo-American conference on terrorism, Oleg Stepanov of Russia's Ministry of Interior approvingly quoted a top, though unnamed, Pentagon official, who said that, "We are approaching a level of development where no one is a soldier but everyone is a participant in military actions. The task now is not to destroy living forces, but rather to undermine the goals, views, and outlooks of the population—to destroy the society."[55] Similarly, some Russians apparently believe recent U.S. handbooks on warfare provide justifications for using precision-guided munitions (PGMs) to target the popular will.[56] However, if popular will and morale are legitimate targets and PGMs are not usable, e.g., to target the domestic population or desirable for other reasons, then IW becomes a fully legitimated Russian weapon not just to take down networks as in the typical U.S. understanding of the term, but rather, in Moscow's concept, to influence mass political consciousness. As Defense Minister Sergei Ivanov observed in 2007:

> The development of information technology has resulted in information itself turning into a certain kind of weapon. It is a weapon that allows us to carry out would-be military actions in practically any theater of war and most importantly, without using military power. That is why we have to take all the necessary steps to develop, improve, and, if necessary—and it already seems to be necessary—develop new multi-purpose automatic control systems, so that in the future we do not find ourselves left with nothing.[57]

This mode of thinking derives from the experience and lessons of Chechnya as well as Russia's overall perception of U.S. efforts, and not just in Iraq and Afghanistan.

The second (or other) branch of military thinking comprises Russia's adaptation of the U.S. concept of network-centric warfare (NCW). By 2008, authoritative Russian military writers were publishing detailed analyses of NCW and effects-based operations (EBO), as they understood them.[58] There is also good reason to argue that the recent defense reform aims to create an army capable of conducting NCW and EBO in future wars.[59] Other writers focused on the advent of IW in all its operational and political forms, e.g., creating the basis for public information and political support as well as protecting critical civilian and defense infrastructures, and again accused Washington of waging IW against Russia, in this case on behalf of Georgia in 2008.[60] Since the Georgia war, these themes and Russian interest in NCW have been amplified in the security literature and in political statements. Russian commentary on NCW, as Russians view the concept, traces its evolution to the Israeli-Syrian air battles of 1982 and to Operation DESERT STORM in 1991, which led military thinkers to see the advent of high-technology warfare demonstrated in these conflicts evolving by the first decade of this century into NCW.[61] But there is no inherent contradiction between these two concepts of war.

Even as NCW became a prominent concept, Russian writers were rediscovering an obscure émigré theorist and tsarist officer named Yevgeny Messner (1891–1974), who formulated the concept of global "insurrection (or rebel)-type warfare" (*Vsemirnaya Myatezhnaya Voina*). This concept involves popular movements, irregular formations, and communities organized around values where psychology, agitation, and propaganda would equal if not surpass the importance of weapons. Thus, "if high-technology and net centric wars are demolishing the concept of classic warfare 'from above,' then insurrection-type warfare is doing the same job from below."[62]

Thus, since 2000, high-tech and IW technologies and techniques have come to the fore of Russian thinking, but probably as much due to Russian experience as to the study of U.S. experience. Or perhaps more precisely, the United States taught everyone the necessity and utility of high-tech weaponry, but Russia learned as much if not more from its own experiences regarding force structure, the nature of contemporary war, and the intricacies of IW as defined by Russian writers, not theorists in the United States.

Defense Minister Sergei Shoigu and other members of the Russian military-political leadership have clearly come to regard the threat to cyber security that comprises foreign efforts to reshape the political consciousness of Russian society as equaling the threat from weapons of mass destruction. Indeed, Shoigu thinks that even without conventional or nuclear weapons, information or cyber weapons alone could seriously damage any metropolis or society.[63] Chief of the General Staff Makarov likewise observed in early

2012 that land and sea have ceased to be the main theaters of war and that the focus has shifted into the aerospace and information spheres, including cyber security. Moreover, wise use of "asymmetric action, [and of] the initial period of hostilities has begun to exercise a decisive effect on the way a war is waged and on its outcome."[64] Both kinds of IW can be used then. In this context it is hardly remarkable that then-President Dmitry Medvedev in 2011 tasked the armed forces to develop measures "to destroy the information and control assets of an [anti-ballistic missile] system as part of a campaign emphasizing the information-technical aspect of IW."[65] Russian definitions of the two aspects of IW are notable because they openly talk of a long campaign that is carried on in peacetime to undertake what amounts to—at a minimum—an information/intelligence preparation of the battlespace (IPB) that can long precede the actual manifestation of overt conflict (as was the case in Estonia in 2007, Georgia, and Ukraine). Here the distinction between peace and war has been effaced, indicating that for Moscow "war is peace," in Orwell's words, and is being waged continually, even now.

Indeed, these leadership, doctrinal, and expert statements define a two-part strategic role for IW and information operations (IO) in the future:

> First, IO can be used to undermine the leadership and decrease the morale of the citizens of a target country. The operational ways of such actions would be, as was displayed in 2007 and 2008, attacks on government, media, and financial websites aimed at limiting a government's ability to control its resources and communicate with the population.[66]

The events of 2007–08 cited here are Russia's attacks on Estonia and Georgia. Given this long-term and implicitly cumulative and steadily reinforcing nature of IW, some analysts have likened its effects to the tightening vise of a naval blockade. The destruction or degradation of an enemy's means of communication and weapons systems represents the information-technical aspect of Russian IW concepts, and the attacks on the enemy country's media and population represent the information-psychological component.[67]

Although some Western writers see IW and IO in this light, for the most part this kind of conceptualization is fundamentally alien to U.S. and Western writing on IW and IO, which focuses on the technical and not the psychological aspect.[68] Whereas American writing on IW and IO definitely underrates or omits the information-psychological aspect and concentrates almost exclusively on the information-technical aspect of "cyber war," Russian writers explicitly and fully incorporate the information-psychological aspect into their assessments.[69] Moreover, Russia employed both aspects of IW and IO in its strategic activities since its war with Chechnya in 1994–96. Thus, IW and IO have featured prominently in Russian operations at home, in the wars

with Chechnya since 1994, in the domestic consolidation of the Putin regime, against Estonia in 2007 and Georgia in 2008, and against other CIS targets at various times in the last several years.

This Russian way of thinking and of employing information technologies in warfare denotes an autochthonous approach that is informed by Western practice and writing but diverges from it, representing a creative adaptation or updating of these phenomena in Soviet strategic and military-political thinking. As Colonel Richard Zoller's analysis of Russian thinking about IW concerning the general process that Russians call *informatization* observed:

> More than any other nation-state, Russia uses the cognitive domain of cyber as much as the technical domain. Where Western definitions of cyberspace focus on technical aspects of information technology, "informatization" takes on a much broader definition. "Informatization" can be broadly defined as applying modern information technologies into all fields of both social and economic development, including intensive exploitation and a broad use of information resources. What this means is that Russia uses cyberspace more to disrupt an adversary's information than to steal or destroy it.[70]

Thus, for Russia, IW and IO are fully legitimated weapons of internal political as well as foreign military-political contestation. IW and IO are weapons of internal and/or external political struggles within or between political entities (not only states) and can be used as parts of public, governmental, civic, and private strategies. Accordingly, it goes without saying that in Russian thinking, in all wars and in any society in peacetime or at war, the struggle to influence and shape "the information space" is ongoing. Moreover, recent Russian writing about IW notes that conflict over information space has been waged throughout history between states to expand their political zones, control raw material resources, etc. Meanwhile, today IW is being waged constantly both between and within states for all kinds of purposes, not least the "possibility of manipulating moods and behaviors of large masses of people."[71] Indeed, Vladimir Karyakin argues that the advent of information and network technologies, coupled with advances in psychology regarding the study of human behavior and the control of people's motivations, "make it possible to exert a specified effect on large social groups but [also] to also reshape the consciousness of entire peoples."[72] This kind of thinking links current Russian writings about IW and IO to the Leninist tradition of using indoctrinated communist party cadres as a political surrogate for armies, e.g., "a fifth column."[73]

Therefore, we can argue that at least in the efforts to influence a society's "information space," for Russia there is no distinction between war and peace, and some would also argue that there is also no distinction among war, peace, and the use of social technology for criminal purposes. This is a new phase in a process of "neither war nor peace" and is a direct continuation of the Leninist tradition of a constant state of siege within and between states, societies, and blocs. Similarly, there is no hard and fast Russian definition between war and peace (unlike U.S. thinking). Conflict in this environment is constant, and one major target, especially in domestic political arenas or among populations at war with each other, is the mentality of the "home front."[74] According to Karyakin:

> The mental sphere, a people's identity, and its national and cultural identity have already become battlegrounds. The first step in this direction is the discrediting of and then the destruction of a nation's traditional values. And in order for external aggression to be perceived painlessly to the mass consciousness, it must be perceived as movement along the path of progress.[75]

Karyakin then outlined a systematic campaign of IW against a nation's mental perspectives.[76]

Patrushev alleges the United States waged such a war against post-war Germany and Japan to destroy these societies' earlier martial spirits and *to enforce an irreversible outcome* unlike that of shooting wars. Information and network attacks were duly directed against their mental space and led to a replacement of earlier national values by those of liberalism. He further argues: "In this case, the mass consciousness does not recognize the fact of implantation of the enemy's mental viruses."[77] Today, therefore, Patrushev argues that such warfare assumes the following form:

> The aggressor puts multiple social structures into play in the information and network war. First, and foremost, this includes the mass media and religious organizations, cultural institutions, nongovernmental foundations, and social movements, several of which are funded from abroad. In their totality they wage what is called a "distributed attack" by inflicting numerous pinpoint destructive actions against a country's social system under the banner of "development of democracies and civil society" and "observance of human rights."[78]

Karyakin also sees such tactics in the alleged Western manipulation of the Arab Spring. He observes that information and network confrontation of states encompasses a struggle to establish control over territory through global information and surveillance systems; encouraging separatist and terrorist movements; engaging enemies in low-intensity conflicts and organizing agitation of the masses; economic warfare including embargoes and sanctions; ideological warfare as described here; and network strikes accomplished by organizing hacker attacks and introducing various computer viruses into computers, communication systems, and databases.[79] In this context it is noteworthy that the Putin regime's attacks on Estonia and Georgia, as well as its targeting of domestic reformers, all follow Karyakin's (and others') script concerning both the targets and methods of waging IW and IO.

Therefore, the following observations apply to Russia with particular force. First, the expansion of the "theaters" of military operations from purely battle-field phenomena to the totality of states' physical and socio-political networks can be construed as a direct evolution from the Leninist theory of political struggle. Just as Lenin expanded "the state of siege" within Russian social democracy into a global one that reached its apogee in the Cold War and comprised struggles within states as well as between blocs on a global scale, information technology has vastly expanded the opportunities for almost anyone to conduct such operations in depth as well as in both real time and over time. Anyone can target anyone else, or anything, for as long as they want and do so more often than not with "plausible deniability."

Moreover, in this context, information technology and the uses to which it can be put can replace the strategic and political role played by indigenous communist parties, which historically functioned very much as a surrogate for combat power to affect the political balance of power in targeted countries. Russian leaders, even before Putin's remarks above, openly viewed information technology as a non-military means by which they can achieve military, strategic, or political goals. One need not organize a ramified "organizational weapon" like a communist party to gain leverage over, if not control, a nation's policies if information weapons can be used adroitly for those purposes.

Thus, the use of IW at home and abroad becomes a conscious securitizing move to enhance the power and stability of the Russian state and its security services. Since actors make "securitizing moves" not just to place an item on a political agenda, but also to claim that their agency alone has the capability either to define or resolve the problem or to implement the appropriate solution, this Russian process is consciously intended to regain state control over multiple domestic processes after the much freer and uncontrolled experience of the 1990s. Consequently IW and IO are legitimate weapons of domestic and/or international struggles for political power. These lessons were first learned and employed in the second Chechnya war of 1999–2007.[80]

Because the Russian government believes it is under attack from a linked ensemble of foreign governments and democracy promoters who have joined with domestic reformers, IW and IO in Russia are critical instruments of what might be called a domestic counterinsurgency strategy. But this is not what Westerners typically recognize as counterinsurgency. At the same time in foreign contexts, information weapons and information-based strategies are deployed cumulatively over time—not just to disable an adversary's military machine, but also to demoralize and subvert it from within and isolate it from other networks abroad that could support it.

Although Russian theorists have discussed what they call the information-strike operation against enemy forces, and although this aspect was evident in the 2008 war with Georgia, most uses of information weapons in actual operations have aimed at the domestic "nerves of government" or of society, not combat forces or military command and control. Indeed, the "information-psychological" aspect that covers the use of the press and the media broadly conceived against a target's information space is a key category among many in the Russian definition of IO and IW.[81]

A discussion by the journalist Aleksandr' Gorbenko of the overall national military plan devised in 2013 links this discussion of IW to its domestic as well as external military contexts. He emphasizes the connection for Russian leaders between IW *a la Russe* and what can only be described as an embryonic "whole of government" operation and mass mobilization plan:

> Preparations to repulse aggression [that] are using only military methods are preparations from the war of past centuries. The times of the declaration of war and the noble settlement of scores between states on the battlefield passed long ago .... In modern conditions it is impossible to resolve the task of the defense of the state by means of armed forces alone. The popularity of non-military methods of aggression and military influence on all segments of the state including purely civilian ones demands measures in response from all state structures and all of society.[82]

Gorbenko points out that this plan of mass mobilization began in the Zapad-2013 exercises involving the Ministry of Transport, the Ministry of Energy, and the regional government of Nizhny Novgorod Oblast. The new national state defense management center called for in the new defense plan therefore is essentially a center for the administration of all regional power structures and all 49 ministries and departments that take part in implementing Russia's defense plan.[83]

As Gorbenko observes, the model for this is not a U.S. wartime organization, but is instead Stalin's conduct of World War II:

> Something similar was created by I.V. Stalin on the initiative of L.P. Beria in the early days of the Great Patriotic War. The State Defense Committee was an emergency organ of administration which possessed the full range of power in the USSR in wartime. The State Defense Committee issued direct instructions to the Council of Ministers, all the organs of central power, and all city defense committees

which held all civilian and military power at local levels in their hands. Essentially the State Defense Committee made it possible to mobilize the whole country for the attainment of victory. But it did not duplicate the leadership of the armed forces. *In the same way a structure is now being created that is capable of administering the whole country (and not just the armed forces) in wartime. And the defense minister who must ensure the country's readiness for any war may have broader powers than any simple defense minister. So, are we preparing for war? Generally speaking, yes. Being prepared for war is better than being unprepared* (emphasis added).[84]

Once again, the origins of this concept of wartime mobilization date back to the National Security Strategy of 2009 that began the task of organizing such a structure. And that impetus was driven by the experiences of Russia's, not America's, recent wars.[85] Indeed, Director of the Security Council Patrushev recently observed that Russia's 2014 defense doctrine was essentially a reflection of the predominance of internal and informational threats more than the threat of war from outside.[86]

Lessons of the Second Chechen War, 1999–2007

So if we are to grasp what lessons Moscow learned from recent wars we must revisit what it learned from the Second Chechen war that Putin led from 1999 to 2007. In the first Chechen war, many officers, political figures, and commentators repeatedly expressed their belief (not unlike many in the United States regarding the U.S. war in Vietnam) that the war was lost because the government failed to ensure that public opinion supported the armed forces. Some, such as General M.A. Gareyev, the grand old man of Russian military thinking, and military historian Alexander Kirov, came close to utilizing a variant of the old German stab-in-the-back theory about the lack of state (and public) support for the armed forces in 1994–96.[87] These critics insisted that public opinion line up uncritically behind the government and Moscow's actions in the second war that began in 1999. Thus their demands reflected the government's learning of this lesson and how to implement it. Therefore, in this context, IW and IO at home were critical parts of Russian strategy and reflected the government's understanding that *in counterinsurgency wars domestic public opinion, not the hearts and minds of the enemy, is the critical center of gravity.*

Any discussion of Russian strategy must reflect the fact that Moscow, unlike Washington in so many past cases, instinctively grasped the far-reaching and fundamentally political challenge posed by Chechnya in 1999 and shaped its strategy to prevent a recurrence of this kind of secession and to bring about the concomitant strengthening of the edifice of state power. First, in 1999

Moscow clearly recogized that the terrorists sought the breakup of the Russian state. President Putin even invoked a domino theory of the conflict.[88] He still believes (probably correctly) that Russia's territorial integrity is at stake in the North Caucasus.[89] Furthermore, since there is evidence of the spread of Islamist agitation into Russia's Tatar and Bashkir provinces along the Volga and in the Ural Mountains, many elites follow Putin in holding to something like a domino theory of the conflict.[90] Accepting the secession of either locale or of the entire North Caucasus region would then generate pressure for similar religious or possibly ethnic insurgencies in the Volga-Ural areas in Russia's heartland.[91] Russia's elite fully understands and accepts this point and understands that secession would also trigger demands for a change of the government in Moscow.[92] Given recent signs of the presence of this version of the Islamist ideology in Bashkiria and Tartarstan, even though they are currently at peace, this is not a trivial threat or an inaccurate threat perception.[93]

Russia's success in Chechnya after 1999 also possesses considerable comparative importance for other governments that are analyzing counterinsurgency practice and the relatively new field of IW and/or media warfare. First, Moscow dispensed with, and could not build, "flexible forces" with which to wage this war. And it certainly did not have the funds to launch massive economic development programs in Chechnya in 1999. Indeed, it cannot even afford its recently proclaimed strategy for the North Caucasus.[94] Instead, it concentrated on achieving a "cumulative point of overwhelming superiority of force."[95] Second, rather than appeal to Chechens' "hearts and minds," it waged a systematic campaign to capture Russian hearts and minds, recognizing that target as the true center of gravity. It made public support the lubricant of the armed forces, and, using media campaigns to seize that public support, isolated the insurgents from overall Russian domestic and foreign support, framing the war as a terrorist campaign. IW was both a surrogate for missing combat power and a strategic weapon in its own right that was designed for a critical front, if not *the* critical front, in the conflict. The government thus framed Russia's reaction as a counterterrorist operation against fundamentalists bent on destroying Russia rather than as a war, seeking thereby to "control the narrative."[96]

Russia's effective insulation of the theater and of the Russian media space demonstrates just how important to any victorious war strategy are the control of the media and the "narrative" or "framing" of the war. In a recent analysis of Chinese lessons learned from studying the Gulf Wars, Dean Cheng writes:

> Just as advances in information technology allow one side to apply psychological pressure without having to first defeat the other side's military, it also significantly improves the ability to influence public

opinion of both sides and of neutrals. Consequently, the media's role has advanced from being a strategic supplement focusing on battlefield reports, to a type of "combat multiplier" that can help affect and decide the outcomes of conflicts. In this view, public opinion is now a distinct, second battlefield, almost independent of the physical one.[97]

Similarly, Max Manwaring of the U.S. Army War College's Strategic Studies Institute, a leading American student of insurgencies and of counterinsurgency, writes:

> Lastly, it must be emphasized that this kind of war is fought against enemies who are firmly embedded in the population and cannot present a traditional strategic or operational target. No conventional act of force can ever be decisive. Winning a trial of military strength will not deliver the will of the people. Fundamentally gaining the will of the people is the only effective objective of any use of force in modern conflict. The reality of contemporary conflict and a new paradigm is that information—not firepower—is the currency upon which war is conducted. The new instruments of power are intelligence, public diplomacy, the media, time, and flexiblity. These are the basic tools of power that can ultimately capture the will of the people.[98]

Moscow's successful concentration upon winning the will of the Russian people and bludgeoning the Chechens into surrender demonstrates its grasp a decade ago of at least some of Manwaring's and Cheng's insights.

From 1999 to 2007, Moscow learned from its abysmal failure in the media, or information war, aspect of the first Chechen war and devised the successful strategies outlined here. It sealed off the area from virtually all journalists and seized control of the "narrative" to portray the Chechen rebels as foreign Wahhabi terrorists who aimed to seize Russian territory. Crucially, the Russian media and information campaign concentrated on cementing the support of the Russian people.[99] As Mazx Manwaring of the US Army War College has written:

> As far as the military was concerned, the goal of the robust state-controlled media campaign served three inter-related purposes. First, it helped to isolate the region politically as a precondition for military operations; second, it rendered the public at home deaf to the suffering of the Chechen state and its inhabitants; and finally it prepared the Russian families to accept war casualties.[100]

In turn, this IPB allowed Moscow to use the unrestricted and overwhelming force that media criticism had precluded during the first Chechen war.[101] Moscow established information centers in Dagestan and North Ossetia on

Chechnya's borders, supplied journalists with videos and briefing material, and provided official escorts for journalists to specific locations. This allowed the government to control tightly the information that came out of the theater.[102]

Here we see the sophisticated integration of an unrelenting deep intelligence penetration, subversion (of the Chechen regime in 1996–99), and media portrayal of the area as run by Muslim terrorists.[103] And beyond the benefits this suppression of the media provided to the armed forces, it played a major role in habituating the Russian population to accept overall media censorship, to acknowledge that they were living in a state of siege, and to provide unlimited support for the government that used this media policy as a major part of its overall campaign to impose an authoritarian state. This strategy vested Putin with virtually unlimited and even dictatorial powers at least as proscribed by law as well as custom, accorded with at least some theorists' view of the necessity for strong centralized rule in an emergency situation, and facilitated and justified Putin's accumulation of powers even after the emergency.[104]

Strategy of Securitization

Thus, this strategy of securitization of the media, i.e., invoking security as a preeminent criterion for defining the purview of state activity, was materially boosted by the Chechen attacks of 1999 and served a major "state-building" purpose as well. It also showed that, for the Russian authorities, Russian public opinion was a crucial center of gravity that had to be reinforced against all external efforts to penetrate and thereby (in the government's estimation) weaken it. Beyond these considerations it was also true that already in 2000 the government made several moves to control the dissemination of news both on television and through the Internet and that it facilitated, if it did not actually launch, a steadily mounting campaign to expand its control over information technology even before the color revolutions of 2003–05 in Georgia, Ukraine, and Kyrgyzstan.[105]

"Securitization" of the media and of information channels began quite early and deliberately in Putin's tenure. For example, in July 2000 a conference of the Security Council under Sergei Ivanov charged that religious organizations' activities "are taking on a more radical, politicized character and represent a real threat to state security" because of the internal political situation in parts of Russia and the penetration into Russia of foreign extremist organizations.[106] Because the Chechen attack on Dagestan in 1999 that precipitated the war that year supposedly confirmed this threat and its linkage with international terrorism, the Security Council recommended actions enhancing the effectiveness of state organs of authority to regulate "the mutual relations of the state and religious associations, and the activities of foreign religious organizations" inside Russia.[107] Since then these recommendations have been put into effect, and the members of religious organizations and the media have been subjected to much more intrusive police regulation, surveillance, and monitoring than was ever the case under President Boris Yeltsin.[108] Meanwhile, the Russian Orthodox Church and other religious associations have been effectively taken over by the state. These examples validate the observations found in a 2006 study of Russian domestic politics, namely:

> The securitization approach illuminates one of the overarching self-conceptualizations of the Putin government. If the Yeltsin regime defined itself in terms of democratization; then much that has been done since that time is defined in terms of security. Analysis of discourse, which is central to the methodological approach employed here, reveals repeatedly the power of the key signifier "security" and the frequency of its adoption by the forces seeking hegemony within Russia's political elite.[109]

Accordingly, the regime aims to securitize ever more aspects of politics; subject them to centralized and unlimited official regulation based on their connection to officially defined canons of Russian security; remove them from active public debate; subordinate them to discourses and actions rationalized by security considerations; and/or take control of them by figures and institutions associated with the preservation of security, usually defined as hard, or military-police, security. This does not mean that debate over security has ceased. Instead, the debate has generally, though not always, been rendered opaque, and it occurs between or among bureaucratic factions who generally endeavor to hide their maneuvers and rationales from the public. This process is at best a mixed blessing and more often than not, considerably worse than that. The securitization of ever more realms of politics creates many dangers for democratization and for state development, and certainly not only in Russia.[110] Moreover, the foregoing analysis clearly links the lessons learned from Chechnya to the preparations for ongoing information operations supporting Moscow's operations in Ukraine. This reasoning establishes a direct line from Russian operations in Chechnya to those in Ukraine based on lessons applied and learned dating back to 1999–2000.

Conclusions

Moscow undoubtedly has learned much from the past generation of American wars. But it has not learned what Americans learned, and it has finally begun to apply its lessons innovatively. Its operations in Ukraine and its concept of contemporary war, outlined in official articles and statements since 2013, clearly are inspired by U.S. use of high-tech and IW. Russia's experiments in force structure also owe something to these wars. But the primary point of reference for Russian learning remains the Russian wars in Chechnya and Georgia. And, U.S. actions are refracted through a very insular Russian prism. Yet Washington appears either unable or unwilling to fully grasp the implications of that point.

Although this conclusion concerning how Russia learns from our actions should not have surprised the U.S. government, it clearly has. And it suggests that Washington equally was caught up in blinkered ethnocentrism and did not learn enough about the evolving character of contemporary war and how others might assess that evolution. But since the United States has systematically eviscerated its abilities to learn from Russia, if not others, U.S. surprise and confusion remain self-induced. Moscow's lessons are harsh, but as Russian writers tell us, Russia lives in a harsh geopolitical environment that they believe is worsening.[111] But thanks to U.S. failure to monitor what Moscow is learning and has learned, it is not only Russia's strategic environment that is deteriorating, but Washington's as well. Worse yet, international security as a whole now appears increasingly endangered. Ultimately there can be no greater indictment of the U.S. failure to learn than this outcome. The price the United States and its friends must now pay is large, growing, and long-term to boot.

CHAPTER 4
Iran: Goals and Strategy "Steadfast," but Open to Tactical Innovation

Thomas E. Dowling

Although the U.S. role and presence in the Middle East has changed significantly since 2001, Iranian decisionmaking remains consistently opposed to U.S. interests and policies in the region. Since the 1979 Revolution, policy has been dictated by a small elite—now led by Supreme Leader Ayatollah Ali Khamenei—whose perceptions are shaped by geography, history, and a belief that the United States is implacably opposed to the Iranian regime. Roughly a dozen men in the military and security apparatus oversee military strategy. These men form a tight-knit group sharing fundamental beliefs shaped by their experiences during the revolution and, more importantly, their service in the Iran-Iraq War (1980–88). Unable to match U.S. military capabilities, Iran's leaders have settled on what they view as a successful strategy of employing asymmetric techniques to keep stronger forces hesitant to confront Iran and then enmeshing them in costly defensive warfare if they do. Strategy has changed very little—if at all—in the face of encounters with U.S. forces over the last 15 years. Absent significant changes in Tehran's leadership, Iran is unlikely to alter a strategy that already has brought success in Iraq. However, continuing Iranian efforts ranging from the introduction of unmanned aerial vehicles (UAVs) to ever-increasing efforts in the field of cyber warfare suggest a willingness to innovate at the operational and tactical levels.

Leadership View: U.S. "Failures" Strengthen Iranian Resolve

Since consolidating power after the 1979 Revolution, the Iranian regime consistently has opposed U.S. interests and policies in the Middle East. Although the recent nuclear agreement apparently removes the primary reason for direct conflict, Tehran has repeatedly and emphatically denied that the nuclear arrangement will lead to any change in its attitudes toward the United States. In the words of Supreme Leader Khamenei, "Our policies toward the arrogant government of the United States will not be changed at all."[1] Iran thus will continue to be a dedicated antagonist seeking every opportunity to obstruct U.S. policies, damage and weaken U.S. ties to other nations, and supplant U.S. influence with its own.

Scholar Saeid Golkar's analysis of the Islamic Revolutionary Guard Corps' (IRGC's) view of the United States provides an excellent summation of the strategic perspective of the ruling elite. This view assumes a dualistic world in which a "domination axis" of Western states that have long exploited the world faces a "resistance axis" of their historic victims.[2] "The system of world domination (*Nezam-e Solteh-e Jahani*) is inherently unstable, requiring war and exploitation."[3] The result is a strategic confrontation between evil (*jebeh Batel*)—the United States—and the good (*jebeh-e Hagh*)—Iran. By this logic, both continuing perceived U.S. efforts to destroy the Iranian regime and Iranian efforts to defeat them are inevitable and enduring.[4] At the same time, Iran considers "any threat against its security as jeopardizing the security of the entire region."[5]

Iranian analyses all view U.S. intervention in Iraq as a failure.[6] In the words of then-Foreign Minister Hoshyar Zebari, "They [the Americans] succeeded in freeing the Iraqi people from the tyranny of that regime… [but there were] many, many failures and mistakes. The occupation was a curse, it didn't work."[7] This failure is ascribed not to specific U.S. or allied operational or tactical actions, which appear to draw little interest in open literature. Instead, Iran attributes U.S. failure to two fundamental and, from its perspective, enduring flaws in U.S. strategy.

First, Iranian commentators and officials argue the United States entered Iraq with little to no real understanding of the country or the Middle East as a whole. One Iranian analyst argues that the failure of the U.S. occupation was preceded by the failure of what he styles U.S. "coercive diplomacy" against Iraq.[8] Iranian commentators are equally critical of U.S. policy in Afghanistan,[9] which they argue reflected no learning from Iraq events, a view perhaps best summarized by the title of one critique, "US Troops Surge in Afghanistan, Repetition of Mistake Committed in Iraq."[10]

Foreign Minister Mohammad Javad Zarif, for example, argues that "military intervention and crude efforts aimed at the social engineering of Middle Eastern societies are reflective of the depth of illusions in the policymaking of the U.S. and some other Western powers vis-a-vis the region."[11] Zarif goes on to argue that:

> What was referred to as the "Greater Middle East Initiative," and was aimed at the engineering of Middle Eastern societies along social and political lines with the ultimate goal of exporting "democracy" had provided the theoretical framework for military interventions. This "initiative" prompted intense resistance in the region, and only managed to entail more extensive instability.

Those who devised this plan were incapable of understanding that democracy can neither be imposed on a nation through brute force, nor can it take root in a society under the rule of an occupying military. The damage done to Iraq and the region while attempts were being made to enforce this illusory scheme has been so extensive and deep that years of endeavors to undo it have had little effect.

The objective of these policies, that were formed based on utter ignorance toward the innate dynamism of the region, was to impose on it a model completely alien to the region and in contradiction to the traditions, cultures and ways of life of native societies.[12]

By this logic, the United States created the conditions for its own failure. Ayatollah Khamenei, for example, has claimed that "occupiers who interfere in Iraq's affairs through their military and security might" are the main cause of Iraq's problems and are the "... main obstacle in the way of the Iraqi nation's progress and prosperity."[13] In this analysis, the explanation for U.S. failure is not specific actions committed (or omitted) during the occupation but rather that, by invading, the United States trapped itself in inevitable failure regardless of its subsequent actions.

Other Iranian commentators implicitly suggest specific U.S. mistakes without identifying them. For example, Kayhan Barzegar argues that U.S. "strategy failed because the United States has been unable to control the crisis in post-invasion Iraq, where conflict continues to rage after more than seven years," without identifying what U.S. actions or shortcomings produced this failure.[14]

Second, a broader critique claims that the United States fails to understand that geopolitical changes have created new conditions that make it impossible for U.S. efforts to succeed. In Foreign Minister Zarif's words:

The world is now moving toward a state of mutual interdependence. Contrary to the situation in the past, the pursuit of go-it-alone policies by former hegemons or current powers has led to a state of impasse and paralysis.

As an inevitable consequence of globalization and the ensuing rise of collective action and cooperative approaches, the idea of seeking or imposing zero-sum games has lost its luster. Still, some actors cling to their old habits and habitually pursue their own interests at the expense of others. The insistence of some major powers on playing zero-sum games with win-lose outcomes has usually led to lose-lose outcomes for all the players involved.[15]

Building on this logic, Zarif argues that these changed circumstances require the United States (and presumably other major powers) to form multinational coalitions:

> The much-challenged position of the United States in the world today, notwithstanding its preponderance of military power, is a glaring case in point. The actual situation in various parts of the world where the United States is directly involved, most notably in the greater Middle East and in Iran's immediate neighborhood, points to Washington's reluctant but unmistakable turn to the path of coalition building with other global powers and even regional actors.[16]

However, given the Iranian conviction that U.S. aims are inherently self-defeating, coalition building is not seen as raising the chances of U.S. success. In fact, a number of Iranian commentators see U.S. efforts to create an emerging coalition against the Islamic State of Iraq and the Levant (ISIL) as simply another U.S. effort to tighten its regional grip. In a 2014 article, Hossein Amir-Abdollahian, deputy foreign minister for Arab and African affairs, claims that "what brings the Americans into such scenes is pursuit of their covert goals in these countries."[17]

Iraqi allies of Iran echo these allegations. In October, 2015, the leader of the Iraqi Popular Mobilization Forces claimed that some members of the U.S.-led coalition try to contain ISIL, but not to really destroy it.[18]

This latter argument dovetails with Iranian accusations that the United States created or sponsors ISIL and other Sunni extremist groups. These claims are discussed in the Information Operations section of this chapter.

Key Geostrategic Factors

Foreign and defense policymaking in this large, complex nation is in the hands of a relatively small elite who operate in and through a web of personal alliances, friendships, and rivalries poorly understood abroad. An Iranian study explains that, since the Revolution, this elite consistently has held that "the dominant world order and power arrangement are hierarchically organized to the disadvantage of Iran, the Muslim World, and the developing world in general, it is unjust both in terms of a revolutionary reading of Islam as well as the current conception of Iran's national interests, and hence, it must be changed."[19]

This common strategic view is shaped by five broad factors.[20] First, there is geography. Iran is surrounded by unstable neighbors and nonstate actors (e.g., al-Qaida, the Kurdish Workers Party [PKK], and People's Mujahedin of Iran [MKO]) and is further threatened by what it views as the illegitimate and extremely menacing presence of U.S. and other Western military forces. Iran rejects the claim that it is a "threat" to the security of regional states, viewing its own continuing buildup of conventional military capability as essential to deterring foreign aggression against itself and the region.[21] Interestingly, some Iranian analysts claim that the ruling elite actually views the U.S. presence (and economic sanctions) as surmountable security challenges that will create a stronger and more independent Iran.[22]

Second, the historical experience of Sunni oppression created a Shia self-description as "The oppressed of the Earth" and the expectation of an inevitable time of retribution and justice. Since the 1979 Revolution, the regime has seen itself as the instrument of that justice against all presumed oppressors, including the United States. This role allows Tehran to assert the legitimacy of its actions and refusal to compromise its self-assigned responsibilities to the world's Shia and now, increasingly, to the oppressed anywhere.

Iranian secular nationalism is a third shaping factor. At various times, mostly in the pre-Islamic period, Iranian power reached deeply, albeit only temporarily, into the Middle East. This history provides the leadership a sense, probably widely shared by the general public, that Iran is rightfully a Middle East, and, indeed, a great power. Hence, leaders believe that Iran is returning to its legitimate Middle East and global roles.

The fourth factor is the regime's revolutionary ideology, or what some Iranian commentators term the religious nature of the regime.[23] Though its only real allies—Hizballah and, to an apparently lesser extent, some Iraqi Shia groups—have embraced Iran's ideology, most notably allegiance to Supreme Leader Khamenei, even these groups have not sought to replicate the Iranian political system. Beyond them, Tehran's attempts to spread its model of a Shia theological state generally have proven a dismal failure. The creation of a Shia clerical state has never drawn any broad support or interest for reasons ranging from intense Sunni aversion to a Shia model for anything, especially one so heavily influenced by exclusively Iranian concepts and forms; competing Sunni models from the Taliban to ISIL; and irritation with often heavy-handed Iranian assertions of the incontestable superiority of its theocratic oligarchy.

Despite this failure, Tehran persists in the belief that its revolution inspired the Arab Spring. For example, in 2014 Supreme Leader Khamenei claimed that for more than 30 years, "the imperialists have been trying to contain the influence of the Islamic Revolution to the borders of Iran, but finally the Islamic Awakening bore fruits and created great waves across the region."[24]

One Iranian analyst argues that the Arab Spring further shifted the regional power balance to Iran's benefit by "first, the removal of U.S. allies and the intense isolation of the Zionist Regime and second, the prevalence of Islamic nature in the Middle East movements."[25]

What Iranians term "the Imposed War" with Iraq, the fifth critical shaping factor, has left a legacy of resentment, a quest for self-sufficiency, and fear of how vulnerable Iran can find itself. The term "imposed" reflects the claim that Saddam attacked Iran in 1980 at U.S. (and probably other enemies') urging. A Western scholar summarized this Iranian argument as "during the Imposed War, the young Islamic Republic was not just fighting Iraq but also the Western powers, particularly the United States, which felt threatened by the emergence of a state that refused to serve U.S. interests."[26] The post-war Iranian narrative of the war's outcome ignores the fact that Ayatollah Khomeini was compelled to accept peace because Iran was facing total defeat, and instead focuses on asserting that "[t]he resistance and victory of the Iranian nation in the imposed war proved to the world that attacking the Islamic Republic is costly."[27]

The war also demonstrated that Iran had few, if any, friends and so could not depend on foreign military support, leading to intense, continuing Iranian efforts to develop the greatest possible domestic military industrial capacity. Lastly, the war cemented the foundations of power for both the IRGC as an institution and its network of war veteran officers throughout government and society. Over time, this network gained vast influence in shaping—and suppressing—political activity and an ever expanding grip on key economic sectors with the IRGC now controlling up to an estimated 70 percent of the economy. This network also will have a major, if not decisive, voice in the selection of the next Supreme Leader.

Tehran Believes Path to Iranian Preeminence Now Assured … And Continued Conflict With the United States Is a Certainty

Taken together, these five factors shape Iranian leaders' worldview, providing context for their policies and inspiring their confidence that Iran is on an irresistible, upward course. However, since the United States is the most powerful obstacle to Tehran's ambitions, despite its troubles in both Iraq and Afghanistan, they also provide the ideological underpinnings for continued antagonism toward the United States.

Iranian leaders appear to believe Iran is in the best strategic position it has enjoyed since the overthrow of the Shah. In late 2015, Brigadier General Gholamreza Jalali of Iran's Civil Defense Organization bragged that "today, the Islamic Iran's pride and might has made the world's biggest materialistic and military powers kneel down before the Islamic Republic's might."[28]

The regime's attitude is a product of historical factors that inspire it with both fear of the consequences of engaging in full-spectrum conflict with the United States and confidence that it can obtain its aims by inflicting damage below the threshold for triggering a crushing U.S. response. At the same time, the regime views the American presence in the Gulf, if not the entire Middle East, as inherently illegitimate and thus inevitably doomed to failure.

From that perspective, Iran's task (and opportunity) is to accelerate this impending U.S. failure. The near total withdrawal of U.S. ground forces from Iraq and Afghanistan encourages Tehran's belief that it is moving toward its goal of becoming the Gulf's and, in time, the Middle East's dominant power. Events in Syria are the latest source of Iranian confidence. For example, IRGC commander Brig. Gen. Amir Ali Hajizadeh claimed that "86 countries stood and said the Syrian government should be changed and Bashar Assad should go, but they failed because Iran had a different point of view, and they were eventually defeated."[29] Such boasts, of course, sidestep the issue of just how much of Asad's Syria actually survives.

The View From Tehran: Lessons Learned From Iraq, Afghanistan, and Syria

Three factors strongly suggest that Iran will oppose future U.S. operations outside Iran with the methods it used in Iraq, Afghanistan, Syria, and Yemen—essentially Iranian leadership and support while proxy forces provide most of the manpower. First, from Tehran's perspective, these methods have proven highly successful in thwarting U.S. and coalition policies and inflicting severe casualties at an acceptable cost to Iran.[30]

Second, Iranian and Iranian-controlled third-party assets are readily available, most likely drawn from Lebanese Hizballah and/or Iraqi militia personnel and probably deployed as complete units of varying size.[31] Mercenaries also will appear, again probably as complete units to facilitate Iranian control of their actions. These forces have sufficient experience to quickly gear up to effective levels on the ground. The Qods Force (QF)—the special operations component of the IRGC—will provide battlefield coordination and, as necessary, operational command, as well as provide training, technical advice, equipment, and logistics support. Non-Iranians will provide the bulk of combat manpower. If possible, these will be local forces from either pre-existing pro-Iranian organizations or Iranian-created ones. However, if local forces initially are insufficient or non-existent, Qods Force intervention will provide a framework into which locally raised forces can be integrated.

Third, the IRGC's tight leadership elite "owns" this so far successful approach. In fact, one analysis suggests "that future IRGC QF commanders operating in Iraq are likely to be those serving in Base Ramezan/Ramadan [which manages Iranian involvement in Iraq, and is discussed below] today."[32] This pattern suggests that absent massive failure, the IRGC is highly unlikely to see reason to alter what it sees as an established, successful approach.

Given the perceived successes of IRGC-led operations in Iraq and Syria, Iran is very likely to remain willing to accept a continuing loss of senior and middle-grade officers and a limited number of lower-ranking personnel.[33] However, Iran's consistent use of non-Iranian forces to provide the bulk of the combat manpower strongly suggests that Tehran is unwilling to sustain large-scale casualties of its own personnel. In the case of the Qods Force, this wariness of heavy casualties may reflect concern that high casualties would quickly erode the force's relatively small overall strength. The apparent reluctance to risk high losses for the IRGC and the Artesh (the regular Armed Forces of Iran) probably reflects concerns about public reaction to heavy losses in causes that, outside the elite, enjoy little popular support.[34] Indeed, unconfirmed press reports suggest that even senior IRGC officers already have attempted to avoid service in Syria.[35]

Iran and its allies have so far fielded largely infantry forces with some supporting units. Descriptions of Hizballah's force structure and the training both Iran and Hizballah have provided Iraqi Shia forces reinforce this impression of an infantry focus. Operationally, in addition to ordinary infantry units, Hizballah forces reportedly incorporate three specialized contingents. A 2010 study by Canadian scholar Martin Rudner identifies these as "A Martyrs contingent (for individuals willing to lead suicide operations); a Commando contingent (elite fighters who have distinguished themselves in guerrilla warfare, some trained in Iran); and Rocket launching contingents (which also operate a range of heavy weapons including mortars)."[36]

A similar structure can be expected with other Iranian-allied groups. In Iraq, the Iranians provided three levels of training, which are well described in a 2008 study by the U.S. Military Academy's Center for Combating Terrorism. All recruits went through a "Basic Paramilitary Skills and Weapons Course. Potential leaders also took advanced courses covering such topics as Logistics and Support, Weapons Employment, Engineering/Explosives, Tactics and Information Operations."[37] Those intended to become organizers of larger forces attended courses on conventional weapons such as machine guns and AK-47s, and took individual "master trainer courses" in one of four areas: explosively formed penetrators, projectile weapons (e.g., mortars and rockets), conventional weapons such as machine guns and AK-47s, and Tactics and Guerrilla Warfare.[38]

The Iranians are likely to make some technological innovations, such as the UAVs already in use in Syria and, Iraq and reportedly used by HAMAS. However, the forces likely to appear in future operations should be essentially variants of the mostly infantry formations already deployed. This relatively conservative approach does not necessarily mean future Iranian operations will be unable to duplicate past successes.

Although Iran has demonstrated some tactical innovations, most notably its improvised explosive devices (IEDs), its successes in the region do not owe to innovative strategies or novel operational techniques. Rather, Iranian success to date rests on the exploitation of strategic opportunities provided by its opponents, especially the introduction of sizeable U.S. or allied forces for prolonged periods of time. This allows Tehran to apply its asymmetric approach to erode and hamstring those forces.

Who Will Do the Fighting?

Iran can draw on three types of forces to challenge the United States and its interests: Iranian state organizations, allied non-Iranian forces, and apparently increasingly, foreign Shia mercenaries fighting under IRGC direction and control.

Iranian State Organizations

The Artesh

Iran's largest military resource, the regular armed forces (usually denoted collectively as the Artesh, the Farsi term for army) are organized and deployed to perform their primary task of defending the territory of Iran. The Artesh's primary responsibilities include deterring, defending against, and defeating foreign aggressors. Although nominally a professional military, clerical leaders within the regime ensure Islamic ideological indoctrination within the ranks. To maintain absolute control over the military, officers in the Artesh are promoted on the basis of loyalty to the regime and political reliability rather than merit or effectiveness.[39]

The appearance of sizeable Artesh units outside Iranian borders seems unlikely. Sustained operations would impose logistics demands difficult to meet even at relatively short distances from Iran's borders due to a lack of transportation resources and infrastructure. The Artesh thus appears not to have a significant, continuing role in Iraq and Afghanistan and no apparent role in Syria. On rare occasions when ISIL advances threatened critical damage to the Iraqi state, individual Artesh units have briefly deployed just across the Iranian border. In early 2015, artillery units were sent to support Iraqi government forces, although press sources are unclear about whether these were Artesh or IRGC units.[40] A clearer example appears to be the deployment of tanks into Iraqi Kurdistan in late August 2015. Photos published by Kurdish sources led to the apparent identification of the tanks as being from the Artesh's 81st Armored Division.[41] In any case, this deployment involved only relatively shallow cross-border movements for apparently limited periods.

Officially admitted Iranian battle deaths in Iraq and Syria include a small number of relatively low-ranking individuals who appear to be from Artesh units. Iranian government admissions of the death of Artesh personnel in Syria suggest that individual Artesh specialists and, perhaps, small units, are used to fill specific needs. However, absent direct U.S. invasion of Iran, there seems little prospect of U.S. forces encountering Artesh units en masse. A key reason is that the primary Iranian instrument of aggressive action, the IRGC, has sufficient resources to operate without significant Artesh help.

The Revolutionary Guard Corps (IRGC)

Unlike the Artesh, the IRGC is completely a product of the Iranian Revolution. Michael McBride explains:

> It was formed out of several militias that emerged during the Islamic revolution in order to act as a counterweight to the Artesh and protect the newly formed Islamist regime against a military coup. Particularly since the end of the Iran-Iraq War, the IRGC has positioned itself as the pre-eminent service within Iran's military apparatus reaffirming itself as the "guardians of the revolution" responsible for maintaining internal stability as well as "exporting the revolution."[42]

IRGC veteran officers, both serving and retired, constitute an interlocking, self-promoting elite who have given the IRGC ever increasing influence over state institutions and especially, as many commentators have noted, the national economy.[43] One thorough study identified what it terms the "IRGC Command Network (IRGC-CN)" to refer to a group of ten individuals who have formed a cohesive faction since the Iran-Iraq War.[44] "Members of the IRGC-CN have publicly demonstrated their political unity during points of potential conflict or crisis, and endured these inflection points while advancing to dominate nearly all of the key command and staff positions within the IRGC."[45] Another Western analyst suggests that "experience in the Iran-Iraq war and personal bonds with Iraqi insurgents are crucial components to getting promoted within the IRGC."[46]

Although officially distinct organizations, the relationship between the Artesh and the IRGC is symbiotic. For example, the head of the Operations Directorate of the Armed Forces General Staff, which is responsible for overseeing the military affairs of both the IRGC and the Artesh, is a member of the

IRGC-CN. While obviously committed to the territorial defense of Iran, the IRGC's primary purpose remains the protection of the current regime and what it defines as the ideology of the 1979 Revolution through the prevention and suppression of internal dissent. The IRGC is especially concerned to thwart what it defines as the threat of "Soft War," a combination of cultural inroads that would undermine loyalty to the Islamic Republic.[47]

This means that while still essentially a military organization, the IRGC has many other interests than active combat, especially at a distance from Iran's borders. As a result, the IRGC ground forces created the Qods Force, which is trained and organized for external foreign operations. The existence of the Qods Force means that, as with the Artesh, absent U.S. direct invasion, it is unlikely that U.S. forces would encounter non-Qods Force IRGC ground units. Although, again as with the Artesh, individual main IRGC members and small groups may be integrated under Qods Force control in special situations.

The Qods (Jerusalem) Special Operations Forces of the IRGC

Since its emergence, which coincided with Iranian efforts to foster the growth of Hizballah in the early 1980s, the Qods Force has been Iran's main instrument of foreign intervention. Organized into regional commands, it has provided training, supply, planning assistance, operational advice and, on occasion, battlefield direction to a variety of allied forces.[48] While the close relationship with Hizballah continues, this extensive support also has been extended to the Iraqi government, a variety of Iraqi Shia militias, the Syrian government, and some other Syrian groups. It also supported, in apparently more limited forms, groups in Afghanistan including the Taliban. Moreover, Iran has provided similar support to groups far from its immediate region.

In 1996, for example, NATO troops raided a "clandestine paramilitary training center" near Sarajevo described as a "joint Bosnian government-Iranian facility;" Admiral Leighton Smith, commander of NATO forces in Bosnia, said the camp contained a wide range of munitions and explosives, booby-trapped toys, and models of buildings that were apparently being used to prepare attacks.[49] In another example of distant presence, press reports claim that IRGC had established a clandestine weapons facility in Sudan.[50]

This provision of arms and training were and remain fundamental elements of the Qods Force's international activities but not its sole function. The Qods Force has been implicated in a wide range of terrorist attacks throughout the world.[51]

Qods Force operations are marked by thorough organization of its allies and the support they receive. In Iraq, in 2007, U.S. forces identified the

"Ramazan (Ramadan) Corps as a sophisticated command structure coordinating military, intelligence, terrorist, diplomatic, religious, ideological, propaganda, and economic operations. This Corps is responsible for most of the Qods Force operations in Iraq."[52] The Ramazan Corps encompassed three subordinate organizations responsible, respectively, for operations in northern, central, and southern Iraq. All three subordinate headquarters were located in Iranian towns near the Iraqi border.

The Iranian role in Iraq was well known and openly discussed by U.S. officials who first complained of Iranian meddling soon after the U.S. invasion.[53] Coalition officers began to publicly discuss Iranian support for Shia militants in 2005.[54] Typical was then-Secretary of Defense Robert Gates's 2008 remarks that "I think that there is some sense of an increased level of supply of [Iranian] weapons and support to these groups [what were termed 'special groups' of Shiite militants]."[55] Iran responded with denials of its role.[56] Over time, Iranian denials turned into open declarations of Tehran's role and especially that of the Qods Force. By 2015 several Iranian figures, including Vice-Speaker of the Majles Mohammad Hassan Aboutorabifard, claimed that Iranian forces saved Iraq from ISIL conquest.[57]

In Afghanistan, Tehran's support extended to the often intensely anti-Shia Taliban, something repeatedly noted by U.S. commanders.[58] In 2008, for example, the then-chief of U.S. operations, Lieutenant General Carter Ham, said there was "some clear evidence" of continuing Iranian provision of "weapons and material" to the Taliban, albeit not "at the same level sent into Iraq."[59] General Ham noted that there was "no indication Iran is providing the high-powered roadside bombs it has given to insurgents in Iraq."[60] Iran also apparently provided 107 mm artillery rockets.[61]

According to press reporting, the Qods Force has established a similar comprehensive command and control center in Syria. This command center reportedly includes "a multinational array of officers: the heads of the Syrian military, a Hezbollah commander, and a coordinator of Iraqi Shiite militias, which [QF commander Qassem] Suleimani mobilized and brought to the fight."[62] Using a centralized headquarters implies the existence of a robust command and control network. Open sources indicate that Hizballah has had such networks, established with Iranian-provided equipment and advice, for some years.[63]

Ansar Al Mahdi Corps

This is another IRGC unit with apparently some special operations capability. Much less well known than the Qods Force, its main task is the security of government leaders and, according to some sources, protection of Iran's nuclear program. It also is reportedly tasked with counterintelligence and

covert operations outside Iran's borders.[64] Evidence that it operates abroad is the inclusion of 2 of its members among 31 Iranian personnel reportedly killed in northern Syria in October 2015.[65]

The Basij

Although designated as one of Iran's three defense organizations (the Artesh and the IRGC being the other two), the Basij is harder to categorize. Unlike the other two, the completely volunteer Basij (Sazmane Basij-e Mostaz'afin, literally "The Organization for Mobilization of the Oppressed") is probably best described as a "pro-regime militia."[66] Encompassing a variety of subordinate organizations among which the Women's and Student Basij branches are prominent, it functions as a mass militia primarily for internal security and defense. As one author has observed, the Basij is "extensively integrated in economic, social, cultural, and civil spheres." It claims an ability to mobilize up to one million men.[67]

Open sources suggest the Basij personnel, most of whom apparently are part-time or reservist members, are trained to a lower standard than are IRGC forces. However, Basij personnel have participated in simulated ambushes on enemy armored columns and helicopters in exercises reportedly focused on urban combat because Basij personnel are tasked with a major role in internal defense of urban areas.[68] Some plainly have skills valued in foreign operations. One press account suggests that Basij personnel provide propaganda and mass mobilization support in Syria and perhaps elsewhere. The reported death of three Basij members in northern Syria in October 2015 confirm a Basij role of some type. This may include work as advisors in urban warfare and security operations.

The Ministry of Intelligence and Security (MOIS)

This civilian agency is heavily involved in past terrorism and murder against both dissidents in Iran and opponents abroad.[69] MOIS performance has been steady and unswerving since its establishment after the Revolution. MOIS is focused on internal affairs and concentrates on protecting the current Islamic system. This goal has been implemented through covert operations inside and outside of the country although, since the creation of the Qods Force in 1990, MOIS has mostly concentrated on monitoring and assassinating Iranian dissidents inside and outside of the country.[70] In post-invasion Iraq, MOIS reportedly "deployed many agents to Iraq to influence Iraqi elected officials and to train Iraqi rebel groups."[71]

Iran also has intelligence networks in other Middle Eastern countries, chiefly in Shia-majority countries and in countries with unpopular Sunni rulers. For instance, in 2010 and 2011 two Iranian networks were exposed in Kuwait and Bahrain.[72]

Because the Qods Force is responsible for collecting intelligence in foreign countries, the responsibilities of MOIS and the Qods Force clearly overlap. Therefore, the two organizations must collaborate closely. The Qods Force is believed to coordinate with MOIS through foreign embassies, charities, and cultural centers in targeted countries.[73] It is assumed that the Qods Force reports its intelligence-gathering activities and their results to MOIS.[74]

At the same time, bureaucratic rivalries between MOIS and the IRGC probably mean that the IRGC heavily limits, if not excludes, any significant MOIS role in ongoing foreign combat. This rivalry is likely to intensify with the Supreme Leader's recent decision to increase the role of the IRGC's own intelligence branch in the suppression of dissent.[75] This expanded role overlaps with MOIS responsibilities in ways certain to increase infighting and further constrain MOIS foreign operations in areas where the Qods Force is dominant.

Non-Iranian Forces

Often termed proxy forces, these are of two types: allied and mercenary. Allied forces are those of non-Iranian, sub-state organizations. In Iraq, U.S. officials referred to these Iranian proteges as "special groups," which they defined as "militia extremists funded, and armed by external sources, specifically by Iranian Revolutionary Guard Corps Qods Force."[76] These groups all appear to have some degree, however slight, of independent existence.

Hizballah is the clearest case. Although heavily dependent on Iranian support and clearly willing to go far in assisting Iranian ambitions, it remains a Lebanese organization whose decisions are tempered by both Lebanese politics and the demands of its Lebanese support base. As a result, Hizballah attempts to maintain some, albeit limited, freedom of action. Its 2013 decision to withdraw some of its fighters from Syria gave a fair picture of that freedom.[77] Hizballah's initial decision to pull back was in response to Lebanese Shia concerns over mounting losses for the sake of Asad. However, a few weeks later, Hizballah leader Nasrallah reversed the decision and declared that Hizballah "is in Syria for the long haul," underlining the limits of Hizballah independence.[78] In 2015, Hizballah losses again rose, with the potential of eroding its Lebanese support base, a concern reflected in Hizballah's reported decision to list "traffic accident" as the cause of death on death certificates of its fighters killed in Syria.[79]

Another significant allied force is the Iraqi Al-Hashd al-Shaabi (Popular Mobilization Forces[80]), a group of Shia militia organizations now providing fighters in Syria.[81] Some are openly funded and equipped by Tehran and directed by its local supporters in Iraq, under the supervision of the IRGC.[82]

For example, the Asa'ib al-Haqq, which split from Muqtada Sadr's forces, is reportedly directly funded by Iran. Perhaps the most important such militia is the Kataib Hizballah, which fought against the United States in Iraq. Foreign observers believe it displays discipline and cohesion superior to that of other Iraqi fighters, including Iraqi Security Forces. At present, these Iraqi militias appear to have far less autonomy than Hizballah.

Iranian-created Syrian paramilitary National Defense Forces (NDF) appear to be a hybrid organizational form. Although they are nominally Syrian government troops, IRGC officials have described the formation of this force as "their most significant contribution to the defense of President Bashar al-Assad."[83] In May 2014, General Hossein Hamedani, who was killed in early October 2015 near Aleppo, announced that "Iran had trained and organized 70,000 Syrians into 128 NDF battalions."[84] In October 2015, IRGC commander-in-chief Mohammad Ali Jafari claimed "the NDF now has 100,000 fighters."[85]

Mercenaries

Recruited from Afghan Shia and Pakistanis, also presumably Shia, mercenaries are a new factor likely to become a fixture of future Qods Force-led Iranian interventions.[86] In Syria, these mercenary forces are organized into two brigades. Unlike Hizballah and Iraqi Shia militia units, which are fielded as complete units by existing political organizations, these mercenaries reportedly are recruited as individuals and only formed into Iranian-controlled units after their arrival in Syria.

The Fatimiyun Brigade is composed of Afghans only and fights under the auspices of Hezbollah Afghanistan.[87] According to an Iranian news source, the number of Afghans fighting for the Assad regime is between 10,000 and 20,000, while other news sources put the number of Afghans at between 10,000 and 12,000.[88] An American scholar who studies the group describes it as "a foreign legion of sorts for Iran," apparently under Qods Force command, with "Quds Force aides and commanders that are going with them to the front, not always Afghan."[89] Press reports suggest the Afghans are recruited individually from refugees living in Iran.

The Pakistanis were originally integrated with other units but now serve in their own distinct unit known as Zaynabiyun Brigade.[90] It is unclear whether the Pakistanis are recruited in Pakistan or Iran. For both the Afghans and the Pakistanis, the principal inducements seem to be high pay (reportedly $500 a month) with the promise of a passport and residency in Iran if and when the fighter returns.

How Iran Might Fight the United States

Although Iran plainly now has a substantial body of experience in confronting U.S. forces, its long, close ties to Hizballah make it likely that Tehran also draws lessons from Hizballah's experience against Israel. U.S. and Israeli forces and tactics and procedures differ significantly; however, Israeli operations against Hizballah provide Iran with a wealth of experience in the problems of confronting a high-tech, firepower-heavy, modern military. Given pervasive Iranian influence and advice, Hizballah's performance suggests methods the Iranians themselves might employ against U.S. forces. At the same time, Hizballah's extensive role in training Iranian-allied groups in Iraq, Syria, and perhaps elsewhere suggests that Iran wants these newer groups to replicate Hizballah organizational structure and tactical methods. For example, IRGC Brigadier General Hossein Hamadani, former commander of Mohammad Rasulollah Corps for Greater Tehran, has claimed that "Iran has built a "second Hezbollah in Syria."[91] Since, as noted above, Iranian practice has been to have these allied groups provide the bulk of the combat manpower, an understanding of their likely composition and methods is critical to predicting future Iranian challenges.

Iranian commentary invariably emphasizes the defensive nature of Tehran's war planning. To demonstrate their defensive capabilities, the Iranians highly publicize their large military exercises, usually with a few photos of participating forces and/or their equipment.[92] These exercises—the majority of which appear to be naval—are invariably reported as completely successful, often emphasizing the claimed use of asymmetric tactics. However, these reports provide few details of actual operations. The methods and tactics of offensive operations are never discussed.

Iran and its allies confront the problem of neutralizing the mobility and firepower of conventional U.S. (or Israeli) forces that they cannot hope to match now or in the immediate future. In response, the Iranians and their allies have embraced the concept of asymmetric warfare, especially at sea. The optimum outcome from Tehran's point of view would be the ability to readily destroy superior weapons through lower cost, lower capability asymmetric weapons and methods. Iranian propaganda works hard to create the impression that Iran already has achieved this capacity. Current evidence suggests that, in fact, Iran is a long way from achieving this aim. However, such boasting serves the broader aims of Iran's asymmetric doctrine—inducing its opponents to reduce their use and reliance on certain weapons or tactics. This reduction might be the product of fielded Iranian weapons and tactics such as the use of anti-armor landmines and IEDs to curtail aggressive patrolling or the use of specific transport routes. Even better from Tehran's viewpoint would be an opponent's decision to voluntarily remove a major system from the battlefield. Iranian efforts to harass U.S. naval forces in the Gulf and constant claims of being able to sink aircraft carriers at will are perhaps the plainest example of this sort of attempt to get the United States to decide that the use of carriers or other large warships in the Gulf has become too risky.

Iranian asymmetric warfare therefore seeks through tactics and, where possible, infrastructure to reduce their opponents' freedom of maneuver while, if possible, consistently inflicting heavy casualties. The clearest example of this approach to land combat is the Iranians' well-publicized strategy of "mosaic defense" for Iran itself. It is based on small units—Basij forces reportedly would play a major role in this defense, especially in urban areas—tasked with defending geographically limited sectors. The aim is to tangle an invader in an interlocking system of localized defenses that impose high casualties while sharply restricting maneuver.[93]

Hizballah's resistance to Israel's 1982–2000 occupation of southern Lebanon is an early example of this approach. Ambushes, landmines, and explosive traps steadily reduced the Israeli army's ability to move where it wished by imposing steadily increasing costs. Eventually, the Israelis were forced to rely mainly on static strong points, including one whose conquest was captured in a widely circulated Hizballah video.

U.S. and coalition forces in Iraq faced the same problems once they transitioned from a powerful, fast-moving invasion force to one largely tied to attempts to control specific areas. This required creation and support of a multitude of bases, each a ready target for attack that required vulnerable convoy routes for supply. By imposing ever greater defensive requirements on U.S. and coalition forces, the Iranians and their allies steadily reduced the capability gap between their almost exclusively infantry forces and coalition forces. Although never completely successful, the Iranian effort went far toward imposing its own operational tempo on the battlefield. Iran and its allies, especially Hizballah, which fights largely independently, can be expected to try to impose such operational dominance in any future conflict. Achieving this dominance is a slow process requiring the Iranians and their allies first to endure a possibly lengthy period of being outmatched and then a probably longer period of more even struggle before, if ever, achieving dominance.

This process could be shortened if combat occurred in areas where Iran has allies already present and/or if the Iranians had time to prepare the battlefield with defensive works and redundant communications. In Iraq and, to a lesser extent, Afghanistan the Qods Force had an established presence with local allies. After the U.S. invasion of Iraq, the Iranians increased or found new local allies relatively quickly but still had to expand and strengthen their presence and support networks. This extended the period of relative Iranian weakness. In Syria, the Iranians appear to have avoided much of this problem by bringing in allied Iraqi Shia militia and mercenary forces to shortcut the transition. A similar pattern of reliance on third-party forces as at least an interim measure probably will appear in future Iranian interventions.

Israeli experience in Lebanon and Gaza suggests that future conflicts in places where Iranian or allied forces have had time to prepare defensive structures would be grim, slow, and costly. The Iranians appear eager to integrate field fortifications into their defensive methods. For example, Iranian press coverage of recent maneuvers gave prominent coverage to what were termed "pop up" positions featuring individual mortars and recoilless rifles protected by a supposedly new Iranian "multi-cellular wall" fortification system.[94]

Seemingly far more elaborate and extensive is the robust network of bunkers, tunnels and defensive positions used by Hizballah and, apparently to a lesser extent, by HAMAS. North Korean experts reportedly assist in these construction efforts and provide various forms of training, thus providing Iran with another source of valuable experience.[95] Such positions offer relatively secure bases for staging attacks, recovering from operations, and channeling enemy forces into prepared kill zones. When supplemented with IEDs, landmines, and buildings prepared for demolition onto advancing troops, these defensive positions impose high casualties and, at a minimum, frustrate enemy operational plans. Also, a period of preparation would allow the development of redundant communications likely to survive and function against high-tech opponents.

Besides the conflict variants discussed above, in which the United States would oppose an Iranian-led and -advised force conducting operations more complex than simple guerrilla warfare but below the level of full-spectrum warfare, there are two other situations in which U.S. and Iranian ground forces could engage in direct combat.

The first situation is special operations attacks by Iranian and/or Iranian-controlled forces against U.S. command, basing, transport, supply, infrastructure, or symbolic targets. Such attacks could be standalone efforts or part of a broader campaign. In the latter case, such attacks need not be confined to the conflict area. Given past Iranian attacks, any future attack will be conducted in ways to conceal Iranian involvement and maximize deniability. One example is the 2007 attack on a U.S. advisory office in Karbala, Iraq. The attack, which initially killed one U.S. soldier and saw four more kidnapped and shortly thereafter murdered, was a classic special operations force attack. False uniforms, vehicle markings, and identification documents were used to cross the security perimeter. The attack was brief, well-focused, and cost free to the attacking force. Although U.S. officials avoided a direct charge of Iranian involvement, they emphasized close Iranian ties to local, anti-U.S. groups.[96]

Future special operations attacks will almost surely be variants of this pattern adjusted to cope with whatever enhanced security procedures exist at the time of attack. The choice of future targets will be guided by Iranian perceptions of opportunity and the operational or symbolic value of the target(s).

The second and more remote possibility is an overt Iranian invasion of a friendly state and a corresponding U.S. response. This seems unlikely for three reasons. First, Iran has achieved its aims so far with covert or semi-covert methods and, as noted, apparently has high confidence that those methods will continue to meet its policy objectives. Second, and probably more importantly, Iran lacks both the logistics capability to project and sustain sizeable conventional forces outside its borders and the airpower necessary to protect such forces. Engaging in a conventional invasion would expose an Iranian force to the full weight of a U.S. response best suited to America's arsenal and tactics. A third constraint is the fact that many of Iran's neighbors possess equal or superior conventional military forces.

Developing Cyber Operations

Beyond physical combat, Iran also has the option of attempting cyber warfare with or without simultaneous violent action. One analysis speculates that we may be seeing "a process in which cyber war replaces classical terrorism as the main tool in Iran's doctrine of asymmetrical warfare."[97] Iran has made no secret of its interest in cyber warfare. Brigadier General Gholamreza Jalali, head of Iran's Passive Defense Organization, which is charged with protecting Iran's cyber systems, has declared that Iran plans "to fight our enemies with abundant power in cyberspace and internet warfare."[98]

Iranian attempts to develop a cyber warfare capability apparently began after 2001. The IRGC reportedly was the first to propose, in 2005, the development of what has come to be known as the Iranian Cyber Army, initially as means of preventing and suppressing internal dissent.[99] However, some Western observers trace Iranian efforts back to the 2002 creation of the Ashiyane hacking collective, which also operates a cyber security firm.[100] In 2010 came reports of Iranian computers being infected with what came to be known as Stuxnet.[101] In the words of one Western expert, "Stuxnet was kind of an awakening for them in cyber security matters ... so the country decided that building the national cyber capability was just the next natural step."[102]

In March 2012, Supreme Leader Khamenei announced creation a new Supreme Council of Cyberspace to oversee the defense of the Islamic Republic's computer networks and develop ways of infiltrating or attacking the computer networks of its enemies.[103] In early-2013, an IRGC general publicly claimed Iran had the "fourth biggest cyber power among the world's cyber armies."[104]

The Iranian Cyber Army is supposedly the key force in these efforts. Although it is plainly linked to the government, open sources are unclear on the size and composition of this Cyber Army or the degree to which it is integrated into the IRGC. The IRGC is known to recruit hackers directly, reportedly threatening jail for those unwilling to participate. A senior Basij officer boasted that "Basiji teachers, students, and clerics are attacking enemy sites."[105] Hacker recruitment apparently is not restricted to Iranians, with some sources suggesting Iran employs foreign hackers, some of whom are criminals. Although not confirming these latter allegations, it is worth noting the Passive Defense Organization's Jalali's statement that "We welcome the presence of those hackers who are willing to work for the goals of the Islamic Republic with good will and revolutionary activities."[106] Current Iranian hackers are described as seeming to "prefer to operate as individuals or small groups with plausibly deniable links to the state," but "acknowledge their relationship with state and security entities from time to time."[107]

Speaking at a 2015 conference, Andretta Towner, a senior intelligence analyst at CrowdStrike, which is a provider of security technology, said that "Iran's budget for cyber security reportedly increased 1,200 percent between 2012 and 2015."[108] Iranian capabilities have impressed experts such as Google's Eric Schmidt, who believes that "the Iranians are unusually talented [at cyber warfare] for some reason we don't fully understand."[109] An April 2015 study found "evidence that they are developing sophisticated software to probe U.S. systems for vulnerabilities, inject malware, and gain control. Their attacks are designed to blend into normal traffic and use compromised third-party systems for obfuscation."[110] Israeli analysts believe Iranian cyber-attacks during Israel's 2014 Operation Protective Edge against HAMAS forces in Gaza showed Iran "is capable of conducting an extensive military cyber operation against a range of targets using a wide spectrum of methods."[111] Other analysts have identified Iranian use of malware[112] and botnets, at least some of the latter reportedly can be rented by non-Iranian individuals or groups.[113]

Why Cyber?

As other portions of the chapter show, asymmetric warfare is Iran's only option in confronting the United States. Cyber is thus an obvious choice. An Israeli analysis identifies four major attractions of cyber warfare for Iran: asymmetry, outsourcing, deniability, and use of cyber as a conventional force multiplier. Outsourcing is perhaps the most intriguing motive with the

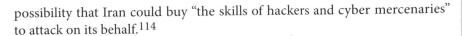

possibility that Iran could buy "the skills of hackers and cyber mercenaries" to attack on its behalf.[114]

What Sort of Cyber Conflict?

Gen. Mohammad Aqakishi, the commander of the information technology and communication department of the Artesh General Staff, has claimed that "we are fully prepared to fight cyber warfare."[115] To do so, Iran can draw not only on its own cyber systems but systems in the United States, Canada, and Europe wittingly or unwittingly under Iranian control.[116]

A model of what Iran might attempt occurred during Israel's Operation Protective Edge against HAMAS forces in Gaza in 2014. A senior officer in Israel's C4I Corps noted that during the campaign Iranian elements launched a widespread cyber offensive against Israeli targets, including efforts to damage security and financial networks.[117] Israeli analysts saw these attacks, which were reportedly "relatively easily" defeated by Israeli cyber defenses, as demonstrating that "Iran is investing heavily in the development of effective offensive capabilities against infrastructure systems."[118]

Iran already has been accused of conducting a number of cyberattacks including on Saudi Aramco and RasGas, a Qatari natural gas firm.[119] Iran reportedly also has attacked a variety of U.S. firms, including a complex attack mounted against the Sands Casino Corporation.[120] In late 2014, the cybersecurity firm Cylance published what appears to be the most comprehensive open-source analysis of Iranian hacking to date.[121] Terming the Iranian activity as "Operation Cleaver," from a term found throughout the hacking codes used, the report identified 16 countries that Iran attacked, usually in multiple economic sectors including institutions of higher education and airlines.[122] This detailed report includes a comparative time line for cyberattacks against and by Iran.[123]

Aggressive cyberattacks against websites and infrastructure, the primary concern, are not Iran's only cyber warfare options. One is using social media accounts to create the impression of massive support for, or opposition to, Iranian and foreign policies, respectively, something Iran reportedly has been doing for some time.

Information Operations

Until ISIL is destroyed, it and similar groups of Sunni extremists will be the core theme for Iranian information operations in the Middle East. Iranians are careful to always label such groups as Takfiri, rather than Sunni. Takfir is the declaring of another Muslim to be a Kafir (plural Kufr), a non-believer. Although it is an old concept, the authority to make such a declaration—the closest Christian analogy would be deeming a fellow Christian an apostate or, for Catholics, a heretic—has normally rested only with respected, senior Islamic clerics because apostasy is traditionally a capital offense under Islamic law. In the 1950s, the Egyptian Sunni extremist Said Qutb provided an altered version that justified designating and destroying any fellow Muslims whom extremists—with or without any clerical education—deemed Kufr. Those Sunni extremists who follow Qutb's approach are deemed Takfiris by their opponents. The Iranian distinction recognizes that although all Takfiri extremists are Sunni, they represent only a tiny portion of all Sunnis. This distinction allows Tehran to advance an interlocked series of arguments that dismiss U.S. efforts while building a case that Iran is the main and most principled defender of the interests of all Muslims. By structuring its narrative in this way, Tehran seeks to present itself as standing above sectarian rivalries.

First, Tehran rejects any suggestion that the current and apparently intensifying Shia-Sunni divide is the result of historical forces within the Muslim world or that Iran's own actions contribute to the problem. Instead, as Majles speaker Larijani claims, the "Presence of foreign elements in the region who aimed at damaging Muslims' coexistence was the main cause of the present tensions in the Middle East region."124 In Ayatollah Khamenei's words, "The hands that sow discord among Shiites and Sunnis are linked to the spy services of the enemies of Islam." Completely ignoring the historical reality that Islam, like Christianity, has suffered from sectarian conflicts for over a thousand years, he holds these external forces solely responsible for what he terms "the imposed, intentional and wicked problem of kindling differences among the Muslim Ummah and (Islam's) religious sects." He further claims that "The (so-called) Shiism linked to the UK's MI6 is not real Shiite Islam."125 Without ever defining what is this supposed MI6 version, Ayatollah Ahmad Khatami, a member of the Assembly of Experts, warns that "[f]ollowers of different Islamic sects should be vigilant towards enemies' divisive plots" and that "those who provoke discord among Muslims are agents of enemies."126 Mohammad Javad Koulivand, a Majles member, asserts that "One of the most important plots hatched by the West against the Muslim world is sowing discord among Muslims."127

Having asserted that current tensions are the product of foreign manipulation, the Iranian narrative then argues that this alleged manipulation has two aims—to permit and justify Western/Israeli domination of Muslim countries while simultaneously fostering Islamophobia to weaken Muslim influence globally. In the words of the Final Statement of an Islamic Unity Conference that concluded in Tehran on December 30, 2015, "Present violence and terrorism faced by the World of Islam are within preplanned plots to tarnish the image of Islam and pave the way for intervention of the enemies in the domestic affairs of Muslims."[128]

The United States, the United Kingdom, and Israel inevitably head the list of supposed plotters. Member of the Majles National Security and Foreign Policy Commission Mohammad Esmayeeli claimed in July 2013 that "Depriving the countries of the region from tranquility is the goal of the U.S. and Israel."[129] By Tehran's narrative, the chosen weapon for achieving those aims is ISIL, which is portrayed as strictly the creation of the West.

The assertions of Western sponsorship of ISIL range from the December 2014 claim by Alaeddin Boroujerdi, Chairman of the Majles National Security and Foreign Policy Commission, that "the Americans have played the biggest role in the creation of Takfiri groups"[130] to the charge of the Supreme Leader's senior advisor Ali Akbar Velayati that Takfiri extremists are the "hirelings of the aliens and pave the way for the implementation of the U.S. and Israeli plots in the Muslim states."[131] Other examples include Ayatollah Ahmad Khatami's claims that ISIL was "created and supported by the U.S. and UK."[132] Ayatollah Abbas Vaez Tabasi blamed the "West for creating and sponsoring the Islamic State of Iraq and the Levant Takfiri terrorists."[133] And, Deputy Armed Forces Chief of Staff Brigadier General Massoud Jazayeri in November 2014 charged that, "In a criminal move, U.S. and the so-called coalition forces have sent fresh arms for the surrounded terrorists of ISIL in Jalula (Iraq)."[134] More recent iterations of this argument came in December 2015 with the claim of "President Obama's landmark contribution to placing the U.S. Air Force at the service of ISIL and Al-Qaeda in Iraq, Syria and Yemen."[135] And, on January 12, 2016, the Iranian Mehr News Agency reported that it is "generally believed that Saudi Arabia, Turkey, Qatar along with Western countries, especially the US, sponsor terrorism, training, arming and funding the terrorist groups, including ISIL."[136]

While continuing to claim U.S. and allied efforts against ISIL are weak, irrelevant, and doomed to fail because the United States and its allies do not understand Middle Eastern realities, Tehran's ISIL narrative adds another explanation—the United States has no interest in destroying its creature ISIL. In the words of Khamenei's representative in the Supreme National Security Council Ali Shamkhani, "The U.S. does not intend to destroy ISIL, but rather it seeks to benefit from terrorism as political and propagandist instrument to legitimize its long-term presence in the Middle East and Muslim countries."[137]

Other senior officials echo this line. Amir Abdollahian, Deputy Foreign Minister for Arab and African Affairs, states "we believe the U.S. lacks sincerity (in its anti-terror bid) as some of these terrorist groups are simultaneously supported by the US."[138] Majles speaker Larijani dismissed what he called "the fake US-led coalition."[139] Acknowledgements of U.S. strikes on ISIL are rare. One exception was National Security and Foreign Policy Commission Chairman Boroujerdi's December 2014 remark that "the coalition is ineffective and inefficient because they fire missiles at these Takfiri groups at most."[140]

Geopolitically, the presumed American aim is therefore reassertion of U.S. dominance of the Middle East through what the aforementioned Final Statement claims is "Zionist terrorism and American plots whose final objective is to dominate Muslims following their redrawing the World of Islam and carry out the plot 'managed chaos' for shaping the so-called New Middle East."[141]

From the religious/cultural perspective, this alleged U.S./Western/Israeli strategy seeks to further weaken the Islamic world by creating Islamophobia outside the region in reaction to the atrocities of ISIL and other Sunni extremists. Larijani, for example, has "lamented that currently some Westerners are instrumentally taking advantage of terrorists like the ISIL to distort the real image of Islam and spread Islamophobia while the thoughts of terrorists don't match any strand of Islam whether Shia or Sunni."[142] In 2015, then-Foreign Minister Ali Akbar Salehi offered another variant of this argument, claiming that "Western efforts to promote Islamophobia and campaign against Islamic values [are] an indication of the West's failure in achieving its goals."[143]

Discrediting Western opposition to ISIL/Sunni extremist forces allows Iran to claim to be the sole effective and legitimate answer to extremist outrages and the main and most principled defender of the interests of all Muslims. This approach requires Tehran to downplay the Shia dimension of its claims. Iran's current role in Syria thus offers Iran the opportunity to claim it is acting effectively on behalf of the entire international community and burnishes Iranian claims of a legitimate role in the entire Middle East. Tehran's narrative therefore probably will continue to stress that solutions to regional problems can only come from regional states.

Lastly, outside the Middle East, Iran will increasingly claim to be a defender of all oppressed people, regardless of faith or location. In January 2015, President Rouhani said, "The Islamic Republic of Iran as a Muslim world power under the leadership of Supreme Leader (of the Islamic Revolution) supports any nation which fights terrorism, violence and extremism."[144] This approach probably will be reinforced by both practical steps to expand and strengthen ties outside the Middle East—such as those already established with Venezuela and its recent overtures to Cuba—and rhetorical emphasis on claims to a revolutionary integrity and ethical purity opposed to the corrupt and oppressive United States and its friends.[145]

To bolster these claims and strengthen Iranian access globally, we can expect an increase in Iranian non-military (especially medical) assistance and commercial outreach to non-Western countries. Here Iran probably will focus on countries that believe their assistance from the West is insufficient. Medical missions in particular offer potentially significant increases in influence at very little real cost.

Conclusions

Convinced that the United States is determined to destroy its clerical regime, Iran will remain committed to reducing and ultimately eliminating a U.S. role in the Middle East. At the same time, despite much bluster, Iran recognizes that its actions must remain below the level at which they would provoke a direct, devastating U.S. response. However, Tehran appears confident that U.S. efforts in the region are inherently doomed to fail and believes it can accelerate that failure and subsequent U.S. withdrawal by an asymmetric approach.

At sea, this approach is intended to frighten the United States into reducing the number, type, and operations of naval vessels it deploys within the Gulf before any conflict. On land, it seeks to deprive U.S. and coalition forces of battlefield initiative and the ability to use superior forces effectively while inflicting steady, heavy casualties through the use of Iran-led forces composed overwhelmingly of its non-Iranian allies. As its actions in Syria now demonstrate, Tehran sees this approach as a proven formula for success that requires no significant changes in the Iranian organizations or individuals responsible for its execution.

Iran also remains intensely interested in cyber warfare, which offers both attractions and substantial risks. Iran will continue to explore cyber warfare possibilities and preparations for its eventual use. However, as with direct conflict, Iran will be hesitant to go too far lest it lose the cloak of deniability and so risk severe retaliation—a caution likely reinforced by its Stuxnet experience.

Whether engaged in direct conflict with the United States or not, Iran will continue its information efforts to damage U.S. influence, raise questions about U.S. intentions, and present itself as the most principled champion of both the Islamic world and, increasingly, the disadvantaged everywhere. Such efforts, which have met with only limited success so far, will continue indefinitely not only to damage the United States but also to win friends and so reverse Iran's near total lack of allies.

CHAPTER 5
America's Wars and Turkish Attitudes: A Slippery Slope

K.A. Beyoghlow

The American-led wars in Afghanistan, Iraq, and Syria have hardened Turkish public attitudes against U.S. policies in the Middle East region resulting in potentially enduring friction that is likely to adversely affect Turkey-United States relations in the long run. This trend occurred despite the unique and close strategic and operational relationships that Turkey enjoyed—and continues to enjoy, albeit at a much reduced level—with the United States throughout much of the Cold War. This essay explores the changing nature of Turkey-United States relations within the framework of domestic, regional, and international dynamics and stresses the need for Turkey and the United States to recalibrate their relations in light of growing antiwar and anti-American sentiments in Turkey.

As a result of the increasing U.S. reluctance to remain militarily engaged in the Middle East and North Africa region, Turkey has been left to fend for itself, particularly following the Arab popular uprisings in 2011 that led to entrenched authoritarian rulers in several Arab countries being jettisoned from office. Turkey also aligned itself with Qatar in support of the Islamists—including the Muslim Brotherhood and other non-mainstream groups—who gained new legitimacy in the Middle East and North Africa through the ballot box. The 2011 Arab popular uprisings forced a realignment within America's other Gulf allies into two camps, with Qatar—and Turkey—championing the uprising's main goals of liberation and free will, and with Saudi Arabia and the United Arab Emirates selectively siding with the status quo of dictatorial regimes as a hedge against the potential spread of political Islam and violent extremist Islamic threats to their own political survival. There are increasing indications that new alignments are still evolving as a result of the war in Yemen, a rising Iranian military influence in Iraq and Syria, and increasing Russian military involvement in Syria. Such developments are most likely to continue to impact Turkey-United States relations both positively and negatively. Also, increased Russian military involvement in the Syrian imbroglio since September 2015 and the shooting down of a Russian jet fighter by the Turkish armed forces on November 25, 2015, posed yet another challenge to Turkey-United States relations. Moreover, the July 15, 2016, failed coup in Turkey, which the conspiracy theory-prone Turkish public believes was indirectly supported by the United States, has heightened anti-Americanism there and has accentuated tensions between the two NATO allies.

Turkey's Domestic Imperative

From a geostrategic perspective, Turkey has been a pivotal state for the West and, in particular, for the United States in terms of regional security and stability. Unlike its position on the losing side during the Great War, when it sided with Germany and Austria-Hungary against the Allies, Turkey declared its neutrality during World War II in order to safeguard its territorial integrity in line with the strategy of Mustafa Kemal Ataturk, founder of the Republic in 1923, who declared from the beginning that Turkey needed to pursue a foreign policy based on peace and not war. Ataturk coined the phrase "Peace at home; peace abroad" following the loss of key Ottoman territories in the Balkans, the Middle East, and North Africa, and in the Caucasus after Turkey's defeat in World War I; he also was concerned about further shrinkage of Turkish territory. As a result, he set out to mend fences with the Allied powers after their failed Gallipoli expedition in 1915, and more importantly, after his military victory against the Greeks in Western Anatolia in 1922. In short, Ataturk wanted to avoid overseas entanglements and conflicts as a hedge against losing more territories to more powerful regional (e.g., Russia) and international (e.g., Great Britain) adversaries.

This strategic approach and Ataturk's personal vendetta against old Ottoman and Islamic tendencies resulted in Turkey's state of economic and political isolation during the interwar period between World War I and II, especially from the Islamic world. The Turkish economy under Ataturk was so constrained that much of Turkey remained backward, rural, and overwhelmingly dependent on foreign aid. This centrally controlled economic system lasted until the first limited opening in the late 1980s under Prime Minister Turgut Ozal, but did not reach its full potential until the advent to power of the moderate Islamic Justice and Development Party (the AKP) in 2002.

Following the death of Ataturk in 1938 and with the advent of the Cold War following the defeat of the Axis powers, Turkey found itself in the West's corner after joining NATO, benefiting from the Marshall Plan, and fighting against communism in the Korean War on behalf of the United Nations-led coalition. As a result of the Truman Doctrine of containment, Turkey, Iran, and Iraq (before the 1958 revolution that toppled the monarchy of King Faisal II) became the first line of defense against communist (Soviet) penetration into the greater Middle East.

The Turkish military benefited from the post-World War II American strategy as a result of having aligned its strategic vision and doctrine closely with that of the United States. In part, Ankara's motivation had been as a hedge against domestic communist agitation sponsored by the Soviet Union, but more importantly, it was a response to the country's dire economic straits stemming from successive military-backed regimes following a series of coups that institutionalized military rule at every level of government and brought little economic benefit. In short, Turkey under the military's rule (1923–2002) achieved domestic security at the expense of national prosperity, and the Turkish military was more or less seen by the Turkish public as serving primarily U.S. regional interests. The Turkish military reigned supreme in Turkey until dramatic changes in electoral politics and Turkish public opinion turned the tide in favor of civil society and the AKP in 2002. This trend toward democratization and political reform in Turkey forced the Kemalist (that is, featuring adherence strictly to the secularist teachings of Ataturk) military to become increasingly politically marginalized following the consistently spectacular AKP successes at the ballot box beginning in 2002. The AKP also dramatically reversed the economic malaise of Turkey and brought about an average annual growth rate of 7.5–8.0 percent.[1] The marginalization of Turkey's military since 2002 also meant that the United States and its ally, Israel, could no longer count on as close a relationship with Turkey's military as before. Nor could Turkish support for America's wars any longer be taken for granted.

Before 2002, the Turkish military was seen by the public as having a stabilizing *political* effect on the country, especially given the corrupt and at times violent nature of Turkish civilian politics since the early 1950s. Hence, as an institution, the Turkish military enjoyed a great deal of public trust as a "corrective institution" and one that always eventually went back to the barracks following "corrective coups." This attitude changed dramatically when Turgut Ozal became economic minister, and later prime minster, under the Turkish military junta that came to power in 1981. Despite enjoying a high level of domestic trust as political "fixers," the Turkish military was also known for violating human and civil rights. Its involvement in politics did not endear it to Western publics, including many members of the U.S. Congress whose powerful anti-Turkish constituencies—Greek and Armenian—did not hesitate to use such human and civil rights abuses to keep alive the memories of the Armenians and Greeks killed or displaced between 1914 and 1919–22, respectively. In 2006 and 2007, the AKP accused the military of attempting to overthrow the duly elected government of Prime Minister Erdogan by force and in response jailed hundreds of middle- to high-ranking officers from all the services on conspiracy charges. The officers were subjected to humiliating court procedures and long prison sentences that demoralized large segments of the military. Scores of officers resigned in protest, and ever since, the old pro-U.S. Turkish military has been purged by the AKP leadership. The alleged conspiracies were code-named Ergonekon and Sledgehammer, respectively.[2]

Turkey's Iraq War Perspectives

It is no secret that Turkey-United States relations have been going through several bumps in the road since 2002.[3] What are the root causes of these bumps? To address these issues systematically it is important to analyze the domestic determinants of Turkish foreign policy since at least the first Gulf War (1990–91), which started when then-Iraqi strongman Saddam Hussein ordered the invasion/occupation of Kuwait on August 2, 1990. Barely a year in office as president of Turkey, Turgut Ozal saw fit to side fully with the United States and its coalition partners against the Iraqi invasion of Kuwait, seizing the moment to "redefine Turkey's role in regional and global politics and positioning it as a long-term strategic ally of the United States."[4] Ozal's decision included providing U.S. access to Incirlik Air Base, a key military installation close to the Syrian border. Ozal also provided the U.S.-led coalition with overflight rights of Turkish territory and participated in the UN-sponsored sanctions against the Iraqi regime.[5]

Turkish public opinion, however, was another story. There was a great deal of domestic opposition to involvement in the war from a number of quarters, including Islamist parties and groups, secular and leftist parties, and groups that had been outlawed following the military coup of 1980 but had continued to function unofficially since then. The Islamists viewed the war as one against Islam, while secular opposition groups argued that support for the war was contrary to Turkey's Kemalist tradition of non-interference in the internal affairs of neighboring states. Both sides also argued that any change in the status quo in Iraq produced by force would increase domestic, regional, and international tensions by (1) exacerbating sectarian conflicts in Iraq and elsewhere among Sunnis, Kurds, and Shias; (2) upsetting the balance of power in the Gulf following the recently concluded Iran-Iraq War, which ended more or less in a draw; and (3) accelerating an unwanted arms race in the region. Debates at that time in Turkey even included conspiratorial allegations that the ultimate objective of the United States was to lay the groundwork for a weakened Iraqi regime in Baghdad that would eventually pave the way for the emergence of a Kurdish enclave in the north. Such an eventuality would threaten Turkey's territorial integrity, given the ongoing and deadly war against the Kurdish Workers Party (PKK) insurgency in the southeastern part of Anatolia, and the longstanding Kemalist policy of not recognizing autonomous rights of ethnic minorities within Turkish borders.

Some of these concerns—such as the rise of Kurdish and Shia power within Iraq—materialized when both these communities rose in rebellion against Baghdad in 1991, even though both were put down brutally by the Iraqi regime.[6] Economic factors provided Turkey with yet another reason to avoid participation in the coalition against Iraq—the same factors that would come to play an important role in the very narrow Turkish parliamentary vote denying U.S. military access to Turkish territory in the invasion of Iraq in 2003. This will be discussed in more detail below, but for now, it is important to note the existence of strong economic ties between Iraq and Turkey on the eve of the first Gulf War. During the Iran-Iraq War (1980–88), the Turkish and Iraqi economies had become increasingly intertwined. In a quest to tip the balance against Iran, Western economic and military aid to Iraq had been channeled in part through Turkish private firms and official institutional military-to-military channels. According to a noted scholar on Turkey, the country faced a "loss of $8 billion in cross-border trade with Iraq" as a result of the first Gulf War and official Turkish support for the anti-Saddam coalition in 1990–91.[7] This loss was duly noted by the Turkish public and their representatives in parliament when the United States invaded Iraq in 2003.

The invasion of Iraq in 2003 was preceded by several important developments in Turkey's domestic political dynamics. Foremost among these was the civil war between the PKK and the Turkish military after the sudden death of the pro-U.S. President Turgut Ozal on April 17, 1993. Ozal's death from natural causes left behind a vacuum of political power, if not political uncertainty. Ozal's premiership was marked by a semblance of stability, economic recovery, and return to civilian control over the military and the government. The following nine or so years, however, often referred to in Turkey as the "Lost Decade," marked a return to political bickering between Turkey's political parties, economic stagnation, and a dramatic rise in casualties and political violence between the military and the PKK. This domestic turmoil paved the way for rising Islamic populism, and in particular, for the emergence of a new conservative Islamic party—Rafah or Welfare—under Necmettin Erbakan, which eventually metamorphosed into the current ruling AKP Party.[8] Rafah promised a return to stability, Ozal's economic vision, and rapprochement with Turkey's Muslim neighbors in the Middle East, North Africa, the Caucasus, and Central Asia. Rafah owes its rise to two important factors: (1) the traditionally corrupt and politically inept ideological parties left and right of the center; and (2) the tolerant policies of Ozal, whose brother Korkut was an active member of the Islamic Tarikat (Islamic brotherhoods that flourished under Ottoman rule and survived clandestinely during much of the Kemalist secular political predominance, 1923–2002) and was the chair of the Islamic wing of Ozal's Motherland Party.

When the invasion of Iraq by U.S. forces was underway in 2003, the Turkish economy was beginning to rebound somewhat due to the vision of the new AKP leadership following its solid success in the 2002 parliamentary elections. This was due to two factors: (1) the enlistment of Kemal Dervis, a former World Bank economist, as the first AKP finance minister, who helped open up the economy and introduced economic and fiscal reforms aimed at a broad economic liberalization and encouraging foreign direct investments; and (2) the coming of age of moderate Islamist politics which began under Ozal but gained momentum during the Lost Decade of the 1990s and culminated with the rise of the AKP and its maverick leader, Tayyip Erdogan.[9] This time, however, unlike during the first Gulf War, Turkish public opinion was more assertive and more anti-war, raising questions about the potential impact of the war on Turkey's changing economy and political structure.

Although the Turkish public was not enamored of Saddam Hussein's violent and erratic behavior against his people, he was viewed by Turks in general as providing stability in the region as a whole—something coveted in Turkey. Moreover, the continuing cross-border trade with Iraq during most of the 1990s and Saddam Hussein's anti-Kurdish position, especially against the PKK in northern Iraq, suited Turkey just fine. Turkey drew a distinction between Saddam's domestic and foreign policies in line with Ataturk's original tradition of not interfering in the internal affairs of neighboring states as articulated by Kemal Ataturk's original slogan of "Peace at Home; Peace Abroad." This policy/strategy framework would later be fully endorsed with some modifications by the AKP and its future foreign policy architect Ahmet Davutoğlu.[10] This focus signaled a new independence from the United States in managing and resolving simmering and frozen regional conflicts in the Middle East and beyond because it offered a new sense of neutrality and transparency and differed dramatically from America's interests-driven objectives worldwide. This approach was welcomed in many states in the Middle East and elsewhere, at least rhetorically. It was later put to the test during the Israeli-Palestinian clashes in Gaza in 2004, 2008, and 2014 and during the Israeli-Hizballah war in Lebanon in 2006. Moreover, Turkey's unsuccessful attempts to reconcile strategic differences between Israel and the Palestinians, Syria and Israel, Armenia and Azerbaijan, and Iran and the United States disappointed the AKP government of Tayyip Erdogan and highlighted the major mismatch between Turkey's new idealism and long-standing regional and global political realities.

It is no surprise, then, that the fissures between the United States and Turkey that began to appear in 1991 and again following the 2003 invasion of Iraq endure to this day. Basically, Turkey differed from the United States over the nature, character, and conduct of the 2003 war in Iraq. Its parliament responded to the invasion by refusing to allow American troops to access or transit Turkish territory to attack Iraq. The AKP urged its members to vote for the resolution because, like its predecessor government under former Prime Minister Ozal, the AKP wanted to ingratiate itself with the United States as a hedge against military intervention in politics. Moreover, given the Turkish military's lukewarm position on the issue, the parliamentary debates that ensued highlighted the deep political divisions between the different political parties and groups.[11] Ironically, the ambivalent military position was a major departure from the past when the Kemalist secular military and bureaucratic officials were largely insulated from public opinion and foreign policy was conducted with little or no public deliberations. With the AKP accession to power in 2002 and the maturing views of the Turkish public vis-a-vis the military, Turkish public opinion became more assertive and more skeptical as the wars in Iraq and later in Syria dragged on.[12]

Turkey expressed doubts about America's futile efforts to democratize Iraq and Syria, often attributing to the United States a lack of understanding of the cultural, religious, and national-ethnographic nature and character of local societies and political dynamics. Turks also complained about the lack of a long-term U.S. commitment toward regime stabilization and reconstruction. They objected most to the lack of a "Plan B" to stabilize Iraq and to empower the Sunni and Turkmen minorities in post-Saddam Iraq. Turkish officials and the public initially viewed U.S. military preparations and subsequent attacks on Iraq as an attack on an Islamic state without credible justification.

The Abu Ghraib incident in Iraq in 2003–04 in which Iraqi detainees, including women and teenagers, were abused and humiliated physically and psychologically by U.S. personnel, did not help matters in the Muslim world, including in Turkey. One popular movie playing in Turkey at the time featured American soldiers raiding a Turkish wedding and shooting the groom and guests—just for the fun of it.[13]

Tensions between the United States and Turkey were exacerbated in 2011 by the demise of the Libyan regime of Muammar al-Qadhafi, when NATO- and U.S.-backed airstrikes provided key support to Libyan rebels. Turkey did not support the airstrikes at first, given its adherence to the "zero problem with neighbors" strategy but also—as with the case of Iraq in 1990 and 2003—because Turkish firms were deeply entrenched in lucrative business and trade deals in Libya. Therefore, the U.S.-led NATO attacks had—as also was the case in the U.S.-led invasion of Iraq in 2003—a negative impact on Turkey's economy. Events such as these created an atmosphere of ill will in Turkey toward the United States despite the fact that Turkey remained a key player in NATO and has continued to have a close military and intelligence relationship with the United States. Ironically, immediately after Qadhafi and his clan disappeared from the scene, Turkish firms and businessmen returned in full force to Libya despite serious security risks for Turkish contractors in Libya because of the ensuing civil war.

Despite Turkey-United States differences on how best to address the fall-out from regime change in Iraq and its aftermath, particularly the emergence of a semi-autonomous independent Kurdish enclave in northern Iraq led by Masoud al-Barazani—an old Kurdish rebel and now strongman in northern Iraq—Ankara turned a blind eye to the lucrative cross-border trade, especially in oil and construction materials, between Turkish entrepreneurs and their Kurdish counterparts in northern Iraq. Turkey ignored demands by the central government in Baghdad that it halt such unsanctioned transactions. This tactical economic move may have been carried out by Turkey to pressure the Shia-led government in Baghdad into making political concessions to the Sunni and Turkmen minorities and to shield the latter from the ongoing Iraqi Shia militias' violent onslaughts. Nevertheless, Turkish businessmen continued as an important conduit to market unsanctioned Iraqi oil on behalf of the Kurdish Regional Government in Irbil, northern Iraq.

Turkey's Syrian War Perspectives

With the rise of violent extremist group the Islamic State of Iraq and the Levant (ISIL) in Iraq and Syria in June 2014, relations between Turkey and the United States were again directly affected by Turkey's continued refusal to allow U.S.-led airstrikes against ISIL from Turkish bases or airspace. This would, however, change in July 2015, when Turkey and the United States finalized an agreement giving the latter unfettered use of Turkish territory, including the famed Incirlik Airbase, to attack ISIL and the PKK militia in Syria and Iraq.[14]

Nevertheless, from the beginning, Turkey's approach to the Syrian crisis and subsequent civil war differed markedly from that of the United States. Before the Arab popular uprisings in 2011, and the one in Syria in particular, Turkey sought to develop an independent political and diplomatic strategy vis-a-vis the Syrian regime of President Bashar al-Asad. It was based on Prime Minister Davutoğlu's dictum of "zero problem with neighbors." Davutoğlu made over 60 cordial visits to Damascus to woo President Asad away from his close ties to Iran and Hizballah in Lebanon at the regional level, and from Russia at the international level. In return, Turkey offered to help Syria in its bid to recover the Golan Heights—a key sticking point in previous negotiations between Israel and Syria—which Israel has occupied since 1967. Turkey attempted similar moves between Israel and the Palestinians in the Occupied Territories without success. At the same time, Prime Minister Erdogan and his family established a close relationship with Asad and his family, and Turkish firms flourished in the Aleppo region of Syria under several joint venture arrangements made between 2002 and 2011.

One of Turkey's largest and most successful Islamic trade organizations and a key original supporter of the AKP, the Confederation of Turkish Businessmen and Industrialists (known by its acronym, TUSKON) invested heavily in these factories and firms in Syria with the blessings and support of the AKP leadership before the outbreak of the civil war. It is also worth noting that Turkey and Iran had similar commercial ties—albeit at a much reduced level—despite the UN and U.S. sanctions against the Tehran regime. Many TUSKON members originated in Anatolia and formed a new rising and youthful class of business-savvy and hard-working entrepreneurs. They were appropriately referred to as the Anatolian Tigers. The latter group are adherents of Fetullah Gulen, an Islamic thinker and preacher who has lived in seclusion in the United States since the late 1990s as a result of his opposition to the old Kemalist secularist military institutions. Gulen was aligned with the AKP until about 2 years ago, when he and Prime Minister Erdogan had a major political fallout. The AKP-led government has since asked the United States to extradite Gulen to stand trial in Turkey under trumped-up corruption charges that also included allegations that Gulen used Turkish governmental security and judicial institutions to set up a shadow government in Turkey. The United States has refused Turkey's request—another source of recent tensions between the two NATO allies. More recently, the Erdogan government has renewed calls for Gulen's extradition from the United States to Turkey to stand trial for his alleged involvement in the failed July 15, 2016, coup. The United States has responded by informing Turkey that it must provide concrete evidence of Gulen's involvement in the coup and has urged it to follow legal procedures in U.S. courts to affect Gulen's extradition.[15]

As the situation inside Syria began to deteriorate in 2011, Turkey continued to advise Asad to bring about much needed economic and political reforms. Those efforts, however, were to no avail as Asad simply refused, equating such pleas with Turkish desires to weaken his grip on power since the Baath regime that he had inherited from his father in June 2000 was a family-run authoritarian regime.[16] By 2012, Turkish strategy toward Syria began to shift in the direction of regime change and to support for the moderate non-ideological and non-dogmatic Free Syrian Army (FSA), whose members had broken with Asad. There have been several splits within the FSA since then, while new groups affiliated with al-Qaida (including al-Nusra), ISIL, Kurdish militias, and many smaller Islamist militias, are now also part of Syria's continuing quagmire.

The United States welcomed the new support in Turkey for regime change in Damascus, and the two allies' interests converged. However, as the civil war in Syria dragged on and a clear outcome became increasingly elusive, fissures in the Turkish-American alliance began to surface. This development was exacerbated by the huge influx of Syrian refugees into Turkey, estimated in late 2015 to be about 2 million, which created a major humanitarian and financial burden on Turkey. By 2013, Turkey started calling for a no-fly zone inside Syria to create a secure and militarily enforced safehaven to allow Syrian refugees to return to their homeland. The United States was cool to the safehaven idea for two reasons: (1) it did not want to be directly involved in yet another war following the high cost of its involvement in the wars in Afghanistan and Iraq; and (2) Russia—a key Syrian ally—was opposed to any direct American military intervention to topple Asad, its only remaining regional ally. Russia was mindful of U.S. and NATO unilateral action in Libya, which Russia opposed.[17] For the United States, Syria is and continues to be merely a limited war, whereas for Turkey the Syrian quagmire threatens to destabilize Turkey and its broader regional interests and even territorial integrity. In short, American involvement in Syria has limited strategic objectives, namely to defeat ISIL, while for Turkey, Syria and its spillover effect, as well as its unintended negative Kurdish consequences, are limitless. Turkey also believes that Syria has a direct effect on its economy, and the conflict could, if left unresolved, threaten the economic prosperity that the current AKP regime under President Erdogan has spearheaded since 2002.

Syria too has had an impact on America's most important ally in the Middle East, Israel. Israeli policymakers are weary of the spillover effect of the chaos and anarchy of neighboring Syria particularly since Hizballah—Israel's main adversary in Lebanon—and the rising, soon-to-be nuclear-armed Iran actively bolstered the Asad regime since the start of the Syrian civil war in late 2011. Although on the surface it appears that Israel is least affected by the civil war in neighboring Syria, it continues to be concerned about the proliferation of sophisticated weapons to Hizballah, the establishment of a stronger Iran-Hizballah axis in Lebanon, and spillover military or quasi-military operations into Israel. Israel also faces yet another challenge shared closely by the United States, namely the rise of ISIL violence in the region and elsewhere. For the time being, however, the ISIL threats to Israel are contained within Iraq and Syria. Israel, which fought a major war against the Iran and Syria-sponsored Shia Hizballah militia in Lebanon in 2006, is carefully watching developments in Syria. Israel originally had preferred the continuity if not certainty that Syria provided under the dictatorial rule of the Asad clan, but now that rule is in jeopardy. The security outcome in Syria and Lebanon is becoming unclear for Israeli security, especially as Hizballah gains from being battle-hardened in Syria and by deploying increasingly sophisticated Iranian weapons and missiles closer to Israel. Ever since Hizballah's military involvement in Syria in 2013, Israel has been floating the idea of a repeat of the costly 2006 war with Hizballah. Another major Israeli attack on Hizballah in Lebanon will most certainly have a ripple effect throughout the region and could further test the already troubled United States-Turkey relations—especially if Israel puts pressure on Hizballah by attacking Lebanese infrastructure and other targets as it did in 2006. Turkey and Lebanon have had cordial relations since the AKP came to power in 2002.

Although the United States and Turkey agreed in principle, at least in the initial stages of the Syrian civil war, that Asad must go, neither knows who would replace him, given the fluidity and shifting alliances among Syria's warring factions. Moreover, to Turks, the United States is becoming increasingly ambivalent about the ultimate fate of Asad as the war in Syria drags on and as Asad gains back territory with military backing from Russia, Iran, Iraq, and Hizballah. At one extreme stands the secular Free Syrian Army, made up of defectors and rebels from within Syria's armed forces; at the other extreme are pro–al-Qaida al-Nusra militiamen and the ISIL fighters. In the middle are Syrian Kurdish militias, some of which were aligned with Turkey's old nemesis, the PKK, which the United States and Turkey consider to be a terrorist organization. Others, such as the Syrian Kurdish Democratic Union Party (PYD), are also aligned with the PKK, but a small minority of Kurds are sympathetic to the Kurdish Regional Government of Masoud al-Barazani in northern Iraq, which in turn is sympathetic to Turkey. The PYD was given a free hand by Asad, who allowed it to operate unchallenged as retaliation for Turkish and U.S. support for the Syrian political and military opposition. The PYD has been seeking autonomy in Syrian towns and villages such as Qamishli, Kobani, and Afsin, beginning in October 2014—ironically with U.S. air support. Turkey has resented U.S. support for the PYD and has sought to set up Sunni rival areas inside Syria, especially around Aleppo, to counter the growing PYD rise. Turkey simply does not want the insurgent PYD-PKK anti-Turkish Kurds to have a free hand inside Syria because it fears that such a presence could ultimately lead to more tangible demands for cultural and ethnic rights for the Kurds inside Turkey. Turkey has consistently resisted the emergence of a Kurdish entity in the region, much less inside Turkey's southeastern provinces ever since the nation's founding in 1923.

The Kurdish problem in Turkey smacks right into the issue of national identity and Turkish nationalism. The Kurds fared rather well under the Ottoman Empire by being left alone to practice their religious and cultural beliefs, like other minorities, but the founder of modern Turkey, Ataturk, set out in 1923 to build a new national identity based solely on the idea of "Turkishness."

The latter concepts simply replaced the more culturally tolerant multi-cultural, multiethnic, and multireligious aspects of the Ottoman Empire. It rejected minority rights for Greeks, Armenians, Alawis, and Kurds, by establishing one national identity based on a state-driven secularism, unity of purpose, and modern patriotism.[18]

In short, unlike the case for the United States, it is the Kurdish problem that is the primary driver for Turkey's policy toward Syria. Turkey will not tolerate the rise of a competing Kurdish national entity in Syria and Iraq so close to its predominantly Kurdish southeastern provinces for fear this might lead to calls for Kurdish autonomy and ultimate secession. In other words, Turkey fears dismemberment first and foremost when it comes to Greek and Kurdish demands for the return of lost rights and territories. This is the crux of the Armenian problem for Turkey. Unlike successive presidential administrations in Washington, the U.S. Congress has been more sympathetic toward minority rights in Turkey, including for the Armenian, Kurdish, and Greek communities. These congressional concerns have been a source of contention between the two NATO allies.[19]

The rising tensions between Washington and Moscow over energy problems in Europe, Ukraine, and President Vladimir Putin's unwavering support for Asad have also complicated bilateral Turkey-United States relations. Turkish officials have been displeased by what they viewed as a lukewarm U.S. response to the Turkish request for a Syrian no-fly safehaven, and a general U.S. lack of concern for Turkish security interests as a result of the Syrian crisis. Ankara responded by allowing ISIL fighters, potential ISIL recruits, and arms from different countries to transit its borders into Syria while at the same time turning a blind eye to atrocities committed by ISIL against Western and other civilian targets in areas controlled by ISIL in Syria and Iraq. This did not sit well with the United States, then busy building a coalition against ISIL, which it viewed as a national security threat second only to al-Qaida and its worldwide affiliates. The bottom line is that Turkey's seeming support for ISIL is a hedge against rising Kurdish nationalism and a mechanism to maintain as much control and influence in Syria as possible should Asad fall. However, Turkey is also becoming increasingly worried about the potential unintended consequence of its support for ISIL—namely the entrenchment of ISIL sleeper cells inside Turkey, a major long-term security concern.[20] The ISIL-led attack on Istanbul Ataturk Airport on June 29, 2016, which killed 42 and injured 230, provoked Turkey into escalating its military attacks on ISIL's enclaves in Syria and elsewhere. This emerging anxiety has developed despite the fact that, as early as the January 2011 popular Arab uprisings, Turkey under then-Prime Minister Erdogan had embarked on a risky strategy of wooing Sunni Arab rebels like the Muslim Brotherhood in Egypt, Al Nahda in Tunisia, and

HAMAS in Gaza, hoping to lead a new front of moderate Islamic states under Turkish tutelage. In Syria, Turkish-supported rebels have sometimes turned on Turkey as the latter came under pressure from the United States and other NATO allies to do more to combat violent extremism (i.e., ISIL and al-Qaida Syrian affiliate, Jabhat al-Nusra).

The Turkish-Muslim Brotherhood rapprochement in Egypt and elsewhere has been due both to ideological and practical reasons. From an ideological perspective, Turkey shares with the Muslim Brotherhood a conservative, non-extremist approach to governance, unlike other Salafi or al-Qaida-affiliated groups such as ISIL, Jabhat Al Nusra, al-Qaida in the Maghreb, al-Qaida in the Arabian Peninsula, or Ansar Al Shariah in Libya (the alleged murderers of the U.S. Ambassador to Libya, Chris Stevens, in Benghazi in 2012). On the practical side, President Erdogan believes that the Muslim Brotherhood—like himself—was elected in a free and fair election and hence reflects the general will of the people. Incidentally, Turkey felt the same way about the Al-Nahda Islamist party that won similar parliamentary elections in Tunisia following Tunisia's uprising in 2011. At the beginning, Turkey's stance put it at odds with the status quo Arab Gulf states, namely Saudi Arabia and the United Arab Emirates, which favored repressive continuity rather than anarchy following the overthrow of dictatorial regimes in many Arab countries. Only Qatar sided with the Turkish approach, this despite a significant improvement of relations between Turkey and all the Arab Gulf states before the Arab popular uprisings. Turkey, however, continued to downplay the nuclear rise of Iran whenever Arab Gulf states raised the issue of Iran's growing power and influence of in the region. This is in keeping with Turkey's strategy of "zero problems with neighbors," but it also keeps Turkey's important economic ties with Iran, especially oil and gas, on track.

A noted scholar on Turkey put the issue of Turkey-Arab Gulf states as follows: "Turkey's approach to Saudi Arabia goes beyond the need to contain Iran. Turkey considers the Gulf countries and particularly Qatar and Saudi Arabia as major financial investors in the Turkish economy."[21] Significantly, as of this writing, Turkish relations with Arab Gulf states appear to once again be in flux because of the ongoing conflicts in Syria, Iraq, and Yemen. There are new indications that Saudi Arabia is reassessing its relationship with Turkey from one of antagonism following the Arab popular uprisings to one of more understanding, especially on the Muslim Brotherhood issue. Significantly, Saudi Arabia's Foreign Minister, the late Prince Saud, stated in early 2015 that not all Muslim Brotherhood members were bad.[22]

In the meantime, Turkey faces a serious strategic military dilemma, namely that it is constrained from executing large-scale military operations in Syria without "full and unconditional" NATO or U.S. political and military support.

Indeed, Turkey is at a crossroads, and its ability to project force on its own inside Syria and elsewhere is limited at best. This is attributable to three factors. First, the Turkish military was originally structured to protect the Kemalist secular legacy which, among other things, called for disassociating Turkey from its Ottoman cultural, religious, and military past and, hence, from venturing out of Turkey's heartland. Today, the Turkish military sees no strategic value for Turkey in getting more deeply involved in Syria and has, in fact, opposed sending significant forces into that country. Secondly, ever since World War II, the Turkish army—with the exception of the Korean War—has only fought against either domestic insurgencies or extreme ideologically driven militias, or has been engaged in primarily humanitarian efforts, as in Afghanistan. Thirdly, Turkish military doctrine and training remain primarily defensive. The Turkish military has been bottled up and purged by the AKP since 2003, although it continues to project an image of strength and professionalism—at least within NATO's framework. As a result of U.S. reluctance to meet its repeated requests for a U.S.-led NATO no-fly zone and a safehaven for Syrian refugees inside Syria, Turkey has been forced to establish a semi no-transit zone west of the Euphrates River for Syrian Kurdish fighters belonging to the Democratic Union Party (PYD). The PYD, which is aligned with the Kurdish Workers Party (PKK), is supported by the United States in its quest to defeat ISIL, but Turkey views this relationship with great suspicion and alarm. Any territorial gains made by the PYD in Syria with U.S. help are considered by Turkey as benefiting the PKK and its strategic objective of carving an independent Kurdish enclave in the predominantly Kurdish southeastern region of Turkey. Ironically, the PKK is considered by the United States as a terrorist organization. Moreover, in a move to press the European Union (EU) for more political and financial concessions as a result of the Syrian refugee crisis of 2015–16, Turkey turned a blind eye to the smuggling of hundreds of thousands of Syrian and other political and economic refugees through Turkish territory to Western Europe. In return, Turkey agreed to rein in human traffickers and smugglers and to take back refugees returned for illegally entering EU states via Turkey.

Turkey's course reversal on ISIL and the Kurds was prompted by increased ISIL militancy and by violent attacks inside Turkey, according to the media.[23] However, additional press reports indicate that although Turkey agreed to provide more tangible support to the U.S.-led coalition against ISIL in Syria, it is not clear what Turkey would get in return. So far, Turkey seems to want to degrade both ISIL and the Syrian Kurds, as well as the latter's PKK supporters. A White House press statement issued following the signing of the new Turkey-United States agreement on July 23, 2015, affirmed that Turkey had the right to defend itself against Kurdish terrorism and separatists while

NATO has called on Turkey not to use excessive force against the Kurds. The flareup of hostilities at this writing between Turkey, the PKK, and the Kurds in the southeastern provinces means that the ceasefire declared by jailed PKK leader Abdallah Ocalan in 2013, which laid the foundation for a broader peace process between the Kurds and the AKP-led government, is in jeopardy. President Erdogan had promised to introduce constitutional reforms giving Kurds more rights, but his efforts stalled in parliament because of determined opposition from the Kemalist Republican People's Party (CHP, Kemal Ataturk's old Republican Party) and the right-wing nationalist National Movement Party (MHP). These parties are vehemently opposed to giving Kurds or other minorities autonomy or political rights, which is in keeping with Ataturk's original denial of recognizing ethnic minorities. Ataturk believed that such recognition would foster factionalism at the expense of national unity. The June 2015 general election weakened Erdogan's grip on power and deprived him of his ability, or perhaps will, to fulfill his promises under the 2013 peace agreement with Kurdish PKK leader Abdullah Ocalan. The AKP in November of the same year recovered from its June electoral slump, but this did not translate into improved any political fortunes for Kurdish nationalism. Turkishness preempts Kurdishness to this writing.

There may be another reason why President Erdogan decided to unleash his army against the PKK and the Kurds at this critical juncture. Tactical and operational intelligence exchanges between Turkcy and the United States have been instrumental in the fight against PKK operatives in the remote areas of northern Iraq for many years, and the new agreement will most certainly intensify this cooperation.[24] No sooner had the July 2015 Turkey-United States agreement been announced than Turkey began intensive air bombardment of PKK positions in the remote areas of northern Iraq, inside Syria, and in its own southeastern provinces. This was despite U.S. reluctance to give assurances to Turkey on the establishment of a Syrian refugee safehaven, which would have alleviated some of the financial and logistical pressures emanating from the Syrian refugee problem in Turkey.[25]

Turkish and Russian Perspectives: The U.S. Dilemma

Russia's direct military intervention in Syria starting in late September 2015 posed serious challenges to Turkey-United States relations. First, Turkey, as a member of NATO, expected full and unconditional support from both its NATO and U.S. allies if it found itself drawn into a sudden and unexpected military confrontation with Russian forces operating along its border with

Syria. However, such a development could embroil NATO and the United States in an unwanted or accidental war with Russia given the ongoing tensions over Ukraine. In an effort to make its air effort in Syria more effective, Russia has repeatedly violated Turkish airspace along its border with Syria since September 2015, and Russian aircraft have even carried out scores of bombing missions against pro-Turkish militia targets nearby.[26]

The shooting down of one of the Russian SU-24 jets on November 25, 2015, by a Turkish F-16 aircraft was exactly what the United States and NATO had wanted to avoid, namely a wider and more serious military confrontation with Russia. But, at the same time, the incident was viewed as a test by Turkey as to how far its NATO allies, especially the United States, were willing to go in supporting the Turkish political position on Syria, namely the removal of President Asad from power and the bolstering of pro-Turkish militias against PKK and other operatives should a political settlement to the Syrian crisis materialize in the future. Turkish officials and public have continuously been unhappy about what they perceive as an American strategic and policy vacuum in the region as a whole and, specifically, about America's reluctance to commit to a firmer, clear, and predictable strategy vis-a-vis Asad and his future.

The November 25 incident could not have come at a worse time for Turkey, given its declining economic growth rate and its domestic political uncertainties, despite the new mandate handed to the AKP on November 1, 2015, by the Turkish electorate. Turkey's economic ties to Russia are very strong, as Turkey is one of Russia's biggest trade partners, and the country relies on Russia to meet three-fifths of its needs in natural gas. This is in addition to the lucrative business generated in Turkey by Russian tourists and by light industry investors. Any cutoff or reduction in Turkey-Russia economic relations will most likely contribute to more domestic political problems for Turkey—an unwelcome prospect for the United States, given its increasing military operations against ISIL in Syria and Iraq.[27]

Recent media reports indicate that the United States is urging Turkey to temporarily halt Turkish air missions in Syria in a quest to ease tensions with Russia and avoid getting Turkey—and by proxy NATO—entangled in a military showdown with Russia. This is despite the fact that Turkey has become somewhat more focused against IS since Russia opted for a more active military role in Syria. In the meantime, Turkey is eager to keep its military options in Syria open especially against the PKK, and to a lesser extent, Syrian Kurdish insurgents. Ironically, the latter are viewed by the United States-led coalition as critical elements in the ultimate defeat if not destruction of ISIL.[28]

A Persistent Anti-American Turkish Style

Turkey-United States relations and the linkage between the wars in Iraq and Syria and Turkey's attitudes toward the United States continue to be affected by domestic determinants of Turkish foreign policy. Foremost among these is the increasing role of public opinion in the making of Turkish policy in regard to the U.S.-led wars in the Middle East and beyond. Results of surveys conducted by the Pew Research Center in Washington, DC, between 2002 and 2013 reveal consistently negative Turkish public attitudes toward U.S. policies in the Middle East and elsewhere.[29] Even so, a common attitude in Turkey is captured by a cartoon that says "Yankee go home, but take me with you." Turks may dislike U.S. policies but, like others around the world, they admire U.S. technological, business, educational, and scientific achievements. Most financially able Turks prefer their children to be educated in the United States. When asked what Turks admire most about the United States, most mentioned American ideals such as freedom of speech; free and fair elections; representative government; a depoliticized and independent judiciary; the rule of law (equality under the law); and constitutional liberalism (protecting human and civil rights). The problem arises in the mind of Turks as well as of others when there is a mismatch between ideals and reality, such as what happened at the U.S. detention facility at Abu Ghraib; the death of innocent civilians in Gaza at the hands of America's ally, Israel; or in Afghanistan and elsewhere because of collateral damage to civilian lives and property caused by U.S. combat operations.

A glance at Turkish public attitudes reveals some other interesting data.[30] For example, 87 percent of Turks oppose the use of drones by the United States to kill terrorists. When asked whether the United States takes into account Turkey's interests when making decisions affecting Turkey, 75 percent said no. Also, 49 percent of Turks say the United States is more of an enemy compared to 14 percent who say it is a partner and 37 percent who hold no opinion. These percentages will most likely shift more against the United States in the aftermath of the July 2016 failed coup in which the conspiracy theory-prone Turkish public believes the United States may have been involved. Turks who are most favorable toward the United States fall in the 18–29 age group, which is in line with youth everywhere under the age of 30, who often hold positive views of the United States. Such positive attitudes could be attributed to social media, technological influences, and the Internet, in which the United States remains in the lead.[31] Although the United States gets largely favorable attitudes from Turkey's youth, Pew found in 2013 that 70 percent of Turks overall had unfavorable views of the United States, exceeded only by the Palestinians in the Occupied Territories with 79 percent;

Egypt 81 percent; and Jordan 85 percent. Pew found that anti-Americanism was also prevalent in other countries in 2008 when it reported that "it [anti-Americanism] runs broader and deeper than ever before. And it's getting worse."[32] However, the report went on to state that "people [abroad] did not let their distaste for U.S. policies affect their views of the American people even though American policies and power fuel apparent resentment for U.S. throughout the world." The Bush administration seemed to have caused these resentment to surface faster and more noticeably than has its successor Obama administration.[33]

Indeed, the U.S.-led fight against al-Qaida and later ISIL was viewed by the Turkish general public as a fight against Muslims. As a result, both the Bush and Obama administrations rated low in Turkish public opinion, with President Obama's approval rating in Turkey dropping from 34 percent in 2009 to 20 percent in 2013 (others were undecided). This data suggests that fighting terrorists has "proven no match for the Cold War as a unifying force," according to Pew Research data.[34] When asked whether the reelection of President Obama in 2012 was viewed favorably or unfavorably by Turks, 25 percent were favorable and 27 percent unfavorable (others were undecided). President Bush's ratings in Turkey had been dramatically lower than those for President Obama. This is a clear indication that the Turkish public was dissatisfied with how the Bush administration handled the Iraq War and the fight against terrorism. Surprisingly, the Pew Turkish data in recent years revealed that although Turks do not look favorably upon the United States, they also do not look favorably upon other "foreign powers" including the Arabs, Israelis, or Western Europeans. In short, Turks have trust issues with the rest of the world, not just with the United States. Turks also oppose extremist groups and their tactics, with 85 percent having negative views of al-Qaida and its affiliates. However, despite the Turkish public's aversion to outside powers and groups, most still want to be part of the European Union and/or NATO.[35] This outlook is primarily related to their overall sense of insecurity or quest to be included in trading blocs for economic or financial gains.

Conclusion

There is no doubt that the U.S.-led wars in Iraq and Syria and the U.S. War on Terror (against al-Qaida and ISIL) have had a major impact on Turkey's domestic, regional, and international dynamics. As a result, Turkey today finds itself at a crossroads in its relationships with the United States and the world at large. Turks have clearly become more suspicious and more distrustful of outside powers and feel more alienated despite their continued dependence on these powers for their economic, political, and social survival. As far as Turkey-United States relations are concerned, both countries will most certainly continue to muddle through as long as the protracted and unending internal wars in Iraq and Syria continue to sputter and as long as the Palestinian-Israeli conflict remains unsolved. Iran's rise and its ultimate quest to be a regional hegemon will most likely also complicate Turkey-United States relations and could lead to more misunderstandings between Turkey and the United States on one hand and Turkey and Russia on the other. Prime Minister Davutoğlu's concept of strategic depth and "zero problems with neighbors" has been nothing but problematic. Even if Turkey's strategic interests are based on non-intervention and "zero problems with neighbors," its policy will increasingly be driven by vital national security interests based on economic and trade considerations, first with its joint nemeses Iran and Russia and, second, by its uneasy relations with the United States and NATO, given the multiple strategic objectives being pursued individually by the NATO states.

Thus, Turkey's current difficulties stem from a serious mismatch between its strategy and its domestic and regional policies. Turkey will continue to face difficulties staying above the current Sunni-Shia fray, especially in the Gulf, while having to increasingly confront its own conflicting Kurdish, Islamic, and national identity challenges. In terms of the bilateral Turkey-United States relations, the partnership will remain at best tactically ad hoc for the near-term, given the multi-faceted, rapidly evolving, and uncertain nature and character of war in Syria, Iraq, Afghanistan, and elsewhere where Turkey has vital national security interests.[36] Until the United States and Turkey recalibrate their strategic objectives in the Middle East and North Africa, and agree on mutually acceptable outcomes, their relationship will most likely remain on a slippery slope for the foreseeable future. Turkish public opinion is unlikely to shift in a more positive American direction given the July 15, 2016, failed coup.

It is tempting for the United States at this critical juncture to abandon Turkey and its faulty dictatorial direction of mass purges, arrests, and violations of human and civil rights, but both allies need one another more than ever. The United States must help moderate the excesses of the Erdogan regime, while Turkey must help the United States eliminate the scourge of terrorism, including defeating ISIL, and illegal immigration into Europe and beyond. In the words of a keen observer of the relationship, "In a region where Americans have no true friends, the United States-Turkey tie is too important to cut."[37]

Acknowledgments

The author is indebted to Drs. Norman Cigar and Hakan Tasci for reviewing and providing valuable comments and suggestions on earlier drafts of this chapter.

CHAPTER 6
How Pakistan Plays Its Double Game: Lessons Learned Since 9/11

Stephen Tankel

Ask a casual observer what has changed with regard to Pakistan's approach to militancy and she or he would be forgiven for saying, "not much." Pakistan has used nonstate militants as a proxy force against India since the first Kashmir war following Partition.[1] By the 1970s, the Pakistani government was providing military training to an Afghan Islamist vanguard for incursions into Afghanistan.[2] The policy of supporting nonstate proxies to achieve geopolitical objectives accelerated in the 1980s when Pakistan hosted, equipped, and helped to direct the Afghan mujahideen for their fight against the Soviet Union. In the 1990s, the Pakistani military oversaw the creation of a full-blown militant infrastructure to support asymmetric warfare against India and, after 1994, in support of the Taliban in Afghanistan. Fast-forward to today, and the militant infrastructure still exists. Pakistan-supported militants continue to wage jihad in Afghanistan and against India. Some of the sectarian groups, which formed with state support in the 1980s to wage jihad against the Shia, remain active as well. Yet this broad continuity masks critical changes. This chapter identifies several key developments regarding the nature of militancy in Pakistan and lessons learned by the security establishment since the attacks of 9/11. Exploring how Pakistani decisionmakers adapted yields important insights for U.S. analysts, policymakers, and practitioners seeking to understand events in the region and plan for the future. Before turning to these developments and lessons learned, this chapter begins with a brief overview of inflection points related to Pakistani militancy.

Riding the Tiger

President Pervez Musharraf's decision to assist the United States in its war against al-Qaida and the Taliban after 9/11 was predicated on the calculation that if Pakistan refused then the United States would form an alliance with India. Musharraf believed this could result in Pakistan being declared a terrorist state and enable India to "gain a golden opportunity with regard to Kashmir."[3] He also feared the United States might target Pakistan's nuclear arsenal, which provided parity with India. This nuclear capability also raised the costs of a conventional response by India to a terrorist attack, thereby enabling Pakistan's use of Islamist militants as tools of foreign policy against India. Islamabad agreed to provide access to Pakistani facilities and intelligence for the U.S.-led military campaign in Afghanistan, withdraw diplomatic and material support for the Taliban government, prevent Pakistanis from crossing into Afghanistan to fight alongside the Taliban movement, and pursue al-Qaida members who fled into Pakistan.[4] In return, the United States lifted the sanctions applied to Pakistan after its nuclear tests in 1998 and the military coup that brought Musharraf to power as well as agreeing to provide economic and security assistance.[5]

Despite Islamabad's agreements on Afghanistan, Pakistan's policy was a "[y]es-but approach," according to Pakistani Foreign Minister Abdul Sattar.[6] In practice this meant that Pakistan would "unequivocally accept all U.S. demands, but then we would express our private reservations to the U.S. and we would not necessarily agree with all the details."[7] The practice of doing enough to stave off American pressure while keeping its options open on militancy is one that Islamabad would employ repeatedly in the years to come. Pakistani decisionmakers never took action against state-allied groups that they could not walk back if necessary. And once Pakistan began cooperating with American counterterrorism efforts, the costs for the United States of using coercion increased and leverage declined. Once the invasion of Afghanistan began, Pakistan provided Taliban leaders and members safehaven.[8] Pakistan did the same for other Afghan militants, including the Haqqani Network, which had a long history of operating on both sides of the Durand Line.[9] Decisionmakers in Islamabad believed the United States would not stay long in the region and so preserving the Taliban in some form made sense for the day when American forces departed.

Taliban who remained in Afghanistan and their leaders in Pakistan were attempting to return to civilian life. In exchange, they promised to disarm and recognize the new Afghanistan government.[10] The idea of any type of reconciliation was anathema to American officials who continued pushing the fight long after the Taliban had collapsed. U.S. forces in Afghanistan sought intelligence from established and would-be warlords who seized the opportunity to settle scores, arrogate power, and enrich themselves. Local strongmen served up tribal or business rivals as "terrorists" and created "actionable intelligence" out of thin air for profit. American troops lacked knowledge of the complex tribal dynamics and became unwitting enforcers for competing power brokers. Fabricated intelligence led U.S. forces to execute overly aggressive raids to capture or kill Taliban members and tribal leaders who had switched sides to support the government. Local Afghan forces allied with America also routinely tortured the men they captured. Together, the raids by

U.S. troops and behavior of their Afghan allies angered the local population.[11] Afghanistan's newly installed government compounded the problem. The United States and other outside powers had promoted a centralized system of government that simultaneously contradicted the Afghan tradition of decentralization *and* lacked the resources to govern the country. As a result, Hamid Karzai, who led Afghanistan, was forced to rely on many of the same warlords with whom the United States was working, creating a situation in which the government was competing with these warlords for power and funds.[12] This contributed to endemic corruption that further alienated the population and ripened conditions for the Taliban's return.[13] It also contributed to a growing schism between Kabul and Washington, leading each side to cozy up even closer to local power brokers.

After their attempts at reconciliation were rebuffed, Taliban leaders began laying the groundwork for the insurgency that continued to rage at the time of writing.[14] They took advantage of the growing anger among local Afghans and the safehaven on offer in Pakistan. U.S. officials believed the Taliban had been defeated on the battlefield. While American forces hunted down "dead-enders" in Afghanistan, the focus of Washington's engagements with Pakistan was mainly on al-Qaida. The United States sought and received Pakistani cooperation with hunting down al-Qaida members and foreign fighters.[15] In addition to cooperating to capture al-Qaida operatives in Pakistan's cities, Islamabad initiated Operation al-Mizan, a military incursion into the South Waziristan agency of the Federally Administered Tribal Areas (FATA) in 2002. This and subsequent military operations targeted al-Qaida and other foreign fighters, while conspicuously avoiding areas where the Taliban and Haqqani Network were known to operate. This practice has remained in place ever since, despite the growth of an insurgency composed of Pakistani militants with ties to the Taliban and Haqqani Network. During numerous operations in the FATA since 2002, the security forces have repeatedly refrained from targeting militants who eschewed attacks in Pakistan and focused on fighting in Afghanistan. At the time of writing, evidence indicated that even during Zarb-e-Azb, the much vaunted and long-awaited operation in North Waziristan launched in 2014, Pakistani forces once again spared the Haqqani Network.[16]

From their base in Pakistan, the Taliban began an assassination campaign in Afghanistan in spring 2003 and announced a leadership council that summer.[17] Training camps for Taliban fighters were operating in Pakistan by this time, and the movement began a recruitment drive, which included dispatching Mullah Dadullah, the Taliban's senior military commander, to *madaris*, or religious schools, in Baluchistan and Karachi. He was reportedly accompanied by Pakistani authorities.[18] Significant recruiting efforts directed toward

Pakistani volunteers increased in 2004, and by 2005 these recruits were playing an important role in the Afghan insurgency.[19] The overriding primacy the United States gave to al-Qaida allowed the Taliban-led insurgency space to regenerate, while concerns about U.S. staying power in the region contributed to Islamabad's decision to increase significantly its active support for the Taliban and Haqqani Network from roughly 2005 onward.[20] It is also worth noting that India's economic and diplomatic footprint in Afghanistan was growing, which likely heightened Pakistani anxiety about Indian encirclement.[21] In addition, the United States and India agreed in summer 2005 on a framework for a civilian nuclear deal, and this may have reinforced Musharraf's decision to increase support for the Taliban-led insurgency. Islamabad's interests in Afghanistan include rolling back Indian influence and promoting a government friendlier to Pakistan's interests. Supporting the Taliban and Haqqani Network is also viewed as a way of maintaining influence once they inevitably migrate most of their infrastructure back across the border.

Attacks against coalition forces in Afghanistan jumped to over 5,000 in 2006, more than a three-fold increase from the previous year.[22] While Pakistani authorities had arrested only a handful of senior Taliban officials before 2006, U.S. pressure following the insurgent escalation in Afghanistan resulted in superficial crackdowns afterward.[23] In several instances, these crackdowns were used as a way to deter Taliban leaders from negotiating directly with the Afghan government or to punish those who did.[24] One Pakistani intelligence officer admitted the arrests served two purposes: "we punish people who want to betray Pakistan, and can at the same time secure the trust of the United States."[25] This anecdote illustrates the degree to which Pakistan's ability to manage its relations with various militant groups and with the United States were often intertwined.

By 2008, the Afghan insurgency was going from strength to strength. The U.S. troop surge in 2009 temporarily blunted the Taliban's momentum but failed to decisively alter the ground reality in Kabul's favor. When he announced the surge, U.S. President Barack Obama also made clear his intention to withdraw U.S. combat forces by 2014. The Pakistani military attempted to position itself as the lead facilitator for any political settlement that might eventuate in Afghanistan.[26] After attempts at an autonomous diplomatic approach failed—in part because the Pakistani military acted as an effective spoiler—Washington acceded to a more prominent role for Pakistan in any subsequent peace process.[27]

Meanwhile, Mohammad Ashraf Ghani's election as President of Afghanistan in September 2014 provided a boost to the peace process. Ghani went out on a limb to improve relations with Pakistan—a move that was deeply unpopular with many Afghans—and to jumpstart negotiations with the Taliban. Afghan government and Taliban officials met in Murree, Pakistan, in summer 2015, but prospects for peace dimmed for two reasons. First, the Taliban confirmed Mullah Muhammad Omar's death. The Taliban leader had reportedly died in 2013 in Karachi, thus rendering illegitimate the statements issued in his name endorsing negotiations. The fact that Mullah Omar reportedly died in Pakistan also further soured many Afghan leaders on Ghani's efforts to improve cross-border relations. Second, the Taliban and Haqqani Network launched a spate of high-profile cross-border attacks after the new Taliban leader, Mullah Akhtar Mansoor, was announced.[28] These attacks further damaged relations between Islamabad and Kabul.

The cooperation Pakistan agreed to provide the United States after 9/11 did not include action against militants fighting in Indian-administered Kashmir or attacking India, except to keep them from traveling to Afghanistan to support the Taliban.[29] At the time, Musharraf claimed to have saved Pakistan's Kashmir policy from American interference and signaled that support for the insurgency there would continue.[30] In December 2001, militants belonging to the Pakistani Jaish-e-Mohammad (JeM) attacked the Indian Parliament in New Delhi. India and then Pakistan mobilized for war. In response to U.S. pressure and to avert a possible conventional conflict with India, Musharraf banned numerous militant groups including JeM and the even more powerful Lashkar-e-Tayyiba (LeT).[31] However, officers from Pakistan's Directorate General for Inter-Services Intelligence (ISI), whose S-Directorate handles the militant portfolio, forewarned many of these organizations about the ban and facilitated their re-emergence under new names thereafter.[32]

Following the launch of the peace process with India in early 2004, known as the Composite Dialogue, and accompanying back-channel negotiations, militants were directed to wage a controlled jihad in Kashmir for which state support ebbed and flowed.[33] Kashmir-centric militant groups were curtailed further in response to international pressure the following year, and militant activity declined significantly over the next several years.[34] The aim was to rein in militant groups and hold their members in reserve, either to be demobilized or reengaged, depending on regional developments. By 2008, though, the peace process was foundering, as were Musharraf's prospects for retaining power. He resigned his position as chief of army staff in November 2007 and the presidency in summer 2008. In contrast to Musharraf, who had pushed to advance the peace process with India, Ashfaq Parvez Kayani, who succeeded him as chief of army staff, took a tougher line on Pakistan's neighbor to the east.[35]

In November 2008, Lashkar-e-Tayyiba launched a coordinated, 10-person assault in Mumbai, India, that killed 166 people.[36] Subsequent investigations revealed the complicity of at least several ISI officers, and raised questions about whether the operation was sanctioned—in principle, even if not in scope—at the highest levels.[37] Pakistan once again reined in the Lashkar-e-Tayyiba after the Mumbai attacks, though the group may have contributed to several bombings against India from 2010 onward.[38] Lashkar-e-Tayyiba also appears to have spearheaded the increase in militant violence along the Line of Control and in Indian-administered Kashmir since 2013.[39] In summer 2015, the group launched its first successful, unilateral terrorist operation against India (outside Indian-administered Kashmir) since the Mumbai attacks.[40]

The Tiger Bites Back

Despite ongoing support for Afghanistan- and India-centric militants, the Pakistani state's relations with the militant community were strained to varying degrees after 9/11. Most of the established Pakistani militant groups were formed in Punjab province during or soon after the anti-Soviet jihad in Afghanistan. The overwhelming majority of these Punjabi organizations followed the Deobandi school of thought, as do the Taliban and Haqqani Network. Lashkar-e-Tayyiba is the only major Punjabi group that adheres to the Ahl-e-Hadith school of thought. Lashkar-e-Tayyiba therefore has no natural allies in Pakistan and has remained more reliable and obedient to the security establishment than the other Punjabi organizations. Conversely, the Deobandi groups splintered to different degrees as a result of internal disputes over whether to remain loyal to, or wage jihad against, the Pakistani state after 9/11. The fact that militants from these organizations quickly became involved in attacks inside Pakistan should have signaled to the security establishment that there were significant risks involved with its selective approach to militancy. Instead, the regime went to great lengths to preserve its jihadist assets for use against India.

Pakistan's sectarian groups—Sipah-i-Sahaba Pakistan (SSP) and its offshoot Lashkar-e-Jhangvi (LJ)—had less utility vis-a-vis India. SSP was tolerated for domestic political purposes and has carried on its activities under a string of new names.[41] In addition to its political usefulness, SSP has roots in society and sectarian support that includes those in the lower ranks of the police and bureaucracy.[42] LJ offered less domestic utility, and instead became a convenient scapegoat for the anti-U.S. and anti-Pakistani violence in which some militants from other Deobandi groups began to engage following 9/11.[43] Crackdowns on LJ led to its fragmentation and drove many of its members to deepen their ties with al-Qaida and later to begin launching attacks against the state.[44]

Pakistani security forces clashed with militants in the FATA during Operation al-Mizan in 2002. More clashes followed during subsequent campaigns in the tribal areas and contributed to the rise of pro-Taliban, anti-state Pashtun militants. After two assassination attempts against President Musharraf in December 2003, the authorities detained more than a thousand individuals associated with Pakistani Deobandi militant organizations.[45] Some of those who escaped the crackdown remained in Punjab, but others took shelter in the FATA.[46] This strengthened the ties between Pakistani militants from the settled areas and FATA-based pro-Taliban tribal militants.[47] The Musharraf regime failed to commit fully to counterinsurgency efforts in the FATA or to engage in any meaningful counterterrorism activities, and as a result, military incursions into the FATA were poorly resourced. Instead, the Pakistan army signed a series of failed peace deals with pro-Taliban militants, enabling them to extend their writ in the northwest frontier.[48]

On July 10, 2007, Pakistani commandos launched an assault against Lal Masjid (Red Mosque) in Islamabad. Among those killed in the raid were militants who had been holed up in the basement of Lal Masjid since spring in anticipation of a clash.[49] Many more viewed the raid as the latest in a series of betrayals. The Pashtun-led proto-insurgency in FATA erupted into a full-blown insurgency following the raid, and the fight soon came to Pakistan's heartland, Punjab province; to its capital, Islamabad; and to its economic center, Karachi. By this time, the Talibanization that had begun in South Waziristan in 2004 had spread to other agencies in the FATA and was expanding into frontier areas such as Bannu, Tank, Kohat, Lakki Marwat, Dera Ismail Khan, Swat, and Buner. In December, militants who shared the aim of establishing "local spheres of sharia" in Pakistan's western frontier united to form the Tehrik-e Taliban Pakistan (TTP, or Pakistani Taliban).[50] It was intended to serve as a vehicle for various actors to coordinate their activities against both coalition forces in Afghanistan *and* the Pakistani Army.[51] Different ideological camps quickly emerged. One camp prioritized the fight against the state, the other focused mainly on fighting in Afghanistan.[52] In short, the TTP is not a unified actor, and the security establishment did not treat it as one. Keeping in mind its umbrella-like nature, I use the name "TTP" throughout this chapter to refer to the collective group of factions who prioritized jihad against the Pakistani state. I do this both for ease of reference, and because the TTP, despite its internally diffuse nature, ultimately became the face of the insurgency in Pakistan.

In 2009, following a military incursion (Operation Rah-e-Haq, or Path of Truth) into Swat, Pakistan reached yet another peace agreement. This one was with Tehreek-e-Nafaz-e-Shariat-e-Mohammadi (TNSM), better known as the Swat Taliban. The agreement, which was the first one codified by the government and not the army, institutionalized sharia in Malakand Division and the Kohistan district of Hazara Division.[53] Emboldened, the TNSM—along with other militants operating in the area—began to occupy areas of Swat before expanding to the districts of Shangla and Buner. The proximity of these districts to Islamabad helped catalyze Pakistani public opinion against these militants and paved the way for a major military offensive, Operation Rah-e-Rast, in May 2009 in Swat. The military launched another major campaign against the TTP in South Waziristan—Operation Rah-e-Nijat—the following month. Punjabi militants provided power projection capabilities for an escalation of high-profile terrorist attacks against sensitive targets in cities such as Islamabad, Lahore, and Rawalpindi, intended to punish the state for these incursions.[54] On one hand, these incursions achieved a degree of success in the frontier. On the other hand, they also served as an object lesson in the potentially high costs of such operations.

Blurring Militant Boundaries

Historically, militants in Pakistan had been motivated either by pan-Islamism or sectarianism. Successive regimes, both martial and civilian, encouraged these impulses, and by 9/11, Pakistani militants were fighting in Afghanistan, India, or against the Shia at home. Overlaps among these areas of activity existed. For example, Pakistani militants from all the major Deobandi groups trained in Taliban-controlled territory in Afghanistan and fought alongside the Taliban against the Northern Alliance. Most of these groups prioritized other theaters, however, with some focused on India and others on sectarian violence in Pakistan.

Since 2002, the number of militant focal points has increased. Afghanistan became a major focal point for almost every militant group based in Pakistan—Afghan, Pakistani, and foreign—and a host of smaller networks and splinter groups. The presence of U.S. forces; the robust Taliban-led insurgency and growing Pakistani support for it; and declining fortunes of the Kashmir jihad helped to make Afghanistan the most popular front for Pakistan-based militants. It is important to keep mind that many of these militants were Afghans fighting to "liberate" their homeland. But numerous Pakistani jihadists also joined the fight. With the exception of Lashkar-e-Tayyiba, India ceased to be the main target for most militant groups in the region as the Kashmiri jihad waned and the insurgency in Afghanistan intensified.[55] Sectarian attacks in Pakistan escalated following a lull during which LeJ members were either on the run or launching attacks against official targets.[56] By the end of the decade after 9/11, targets included Pakistani Barelvis and Ahmadis as well as the Shia.[57] In addition to these three areas of focus—all of which had existed before 9/11—revolutionary jihad against Pakistan became a new locus of activity. By the latter years of the decade, a revolutionary ideology had fully taken hold among many established jihadists and a new generation of militants who had little, if any, affiliation with recognized organizations.[58] Finally, although most Pakistan-based militants remained motivated by local and regional factors, al-Qaida's global jihadist ideology, which entails striking U.S. and allied targets wherever they may be found, influenced a subset of militants in Pakistan.[59] At the same time, al-Qaida became more active in regional areas, providing operational support for the Taliban's insurgency in Afghanistan and the TTP-led revolutionary jihad against the Pakistani state.

The expansion in the number of areas of militant activity was accompanied by a growing integration among the militants. First, India's perceived malevolent involvement in Afghanistan contributed to the integration of these two areas of activity in the minds of some militants who remained allied with the Pakistani state. The 2008–10 time period witnessed an escalation of attacks on Indian targets in Afghanistan by Pakistan-based actors, with the Lashkar-e-Tayyiba and the Haqqani Network primarily responsible.[60] LeJ is also believed to have been responsible for attacks against Shiite Afghans in three cities in December 2011. Second, sectarian ideology infused the revolutionary jihad against the Pakistani state.[61] This integration owed to the overrepresentation of LeJ members in anti-state violence and the historical connections that some TTP commanders had to SSP and LJ.[62] In addition to prior organizational affinity, revolutionary and sectarian militants complemented one another operationally. Those associated with SSP and LeJ exploited the Talibanization in FATA and Khyber Pakhtunkhwa for safehaven, and their sectarian attacks, in turn, became "an extension of the TTP war against cities," to quote one scholar.[63]

Whether or not to participate in violence against the Pakistani state became the single greatest dividing line among militants.[64] Although a bifurcation exists at the organizational level, longstanding ties among militants created opportunities for collaboration on the ground. Personal connections formed through training or fighting together can lead to ad hoc support at the rank-and-file level.[65] The intensifying integration of the militant milieu widened the prospects for collaboration. This has enabled anti-Pakistan groups to leverage the resources and infrastructure belonging to state-allied organizations and sometimes also the religious parties associated with them.[66] For example, mosques and madaris associated with state-allied groups may also function as hideouts, transit points, staging grounds, and storage depots for attacks against Pakistan.[67] Individuals in these state-allied organizations also sometimes provide assistance—knowingly or unknowingly—to anti-state militants, through transportation, money, food, or even reconnaissance.

These dynamics have created operational challenges for the Pakistani authorities intent on thwarting attacks at home. Despite the fact that the TTP claims credit for attacks, a single attack might have one group provide money, a second logistics, a third reconnaissance, a fourth a vehicle, a fifth explosives, and a sixth a bomber. This further confuses and complicates counterterrorism efforts.[68]

Interaction and integration is even more common in FATA, where state-allied and anti-state groups collaborate. For example, the Haqqani Network has acted as an enabler for the TTP, a host of smaller anti-state entities (including many Punjabi splinter groups), and al-Qaida.[69] Although it has worked to limit any public association with the insurgency in Pakistan, the Haqqani Network actively benefits from TTP manpower. In return, it acts as a "platform for operational development and force projection" for segments of the TTP and other anti-state entities.[70] This includes providing access to training, expertise, resources, and the prestige that comes from participating in certain operations in Afghanistan.[71] Moreover, the Haqqani Network has been al-Qaida's main enabler in the region for more than two decades. Al-Qaida's resilience and, until recently, ability to project power transnationally arguably owed more to this assistance than to that proffered by any other local ally. Pakistani military and ISI leaders undoubtedly are aware of these dynamics and seek to control the Haqqani Network the same way they have numerous other assets, providing resources on the one hand and arresting some of their commanders and limiting their capacity to operate on the other.[72] Their ability to do so, however, is limited by the need to maintain it as an asset in Afghanistan and in FATA as well as by the fear of what a real crackdown would entail. Similar dynamics are at play with lesser-known FATA-based outfits that have struck nonaggression pacts with the military.

The State Adapts

Pakistan's approach toward the groups operating on its soil is predicated on the utility they provide externally *and* internally, and the perceived threats they pose to the state (especially Pakistani elites). There are three broad positions that Pakistan takes toward the Islamist militant groups on its territory: collaboration, belligerence, and benign neglect. In some cases, the authorities may adopt disparate positions toward the same group at the same or different times. Borrowing from the literature in the field of economics, this approach could be termed this "co-opetition" to capture the degree to which the state treats the some groups as belligerents and collaborators.[73] In non-academic parlance, we might call groups that fall into this fourth category "frenemies" of the state.[74] This section explores lessons learned in terms of how the state seeks to counter anti-state militants (belligerence) and works with state-allied ones (collaboration).

Upon assuming his position as army chief, Kayani took steps to increase the army's "ownership of and commitment to Pakistan's internal security duties."[75] The security establishment started making more sustained counter-insurgency and counterterrorism efforts against anti-state militants inside and outside FATA. By 2008, Pakistani military forces were fighting in all seven tribal agencies.

Years of experience operating in the FATA combined with training assistance and capacity building provided by the United States meant Pakistan's security forces were better prepared to clear and hold territory. Tactical improvements in areas such as communications and precision-strike capability enabled military operations that were relatively more effective. At the same time, the Pakistani military continued to exploit and exacerbate existing fissures among anti-state militants. For example, the Pakistani military has made efforts to prevail on various FATA-based factions to withhold support from anti-state militants attacking Pakistan and instead focus on fighting in Afghanistan.[76] In exchange, the Pakistani military avoided targeting these entities during military campaigns in FATA.[77] Sometimes, these arrangements went beyond benign neglect. For example, Pakistan's security services provided Hafiz Gul Bahadur and Maulvi Nazir with support to attack Uzbek militants allied with their rival, Baitullah Mehsud, who led the TTP until his death in 2009.[78]

After a drawn-out, civilian-led effort to engage the TTP in negotiations failed, the Pakistani military finally launched a long-awaited offensive (named Zarb-e-Azb) in the North Waziristan Agency in 2014. Attempts to split the TTP and reorient more of its members toward fighting in Afghanistan preceded Zarb-e-Azb.[79] Most notably, the Pakistani military came to a modus vivendi with TTP leader Khan Said (commonly known as Sajna), who was upset about Mullah Fazlullah, a non-Mehsud commander, taking control of the TTP after Hakimullah Mehsud was killed in a U.S. drone strike.[80] Sajna condemned the Fazlullah-led TTP for attacks against the Pakistani government and security forces and indicated he would focus his attacks across the border in Afghanistan. In exchange, the Pakistani security establishment refrained from attacking Sajna's forces during operations in the FATA.[81] Zarb-e-Azb also spared state allied militant groups, most notably the Haqqani Network.[82]

State-associated groups are deemed useful not only for offensive operations against India and Afghanistan, but also to help counter the militants waging a revolutionary jihad against the state. Indeed, since the insurgency developed in Pakistan, the military and ISI have increasingly used state-associated groups for internal as well as external purposes. For example, Lashkar-e-Tayyiba has carried out a propaganda campaign against al-Qaida and the TTP, demonizing them for launching attacks in Pakistan.[83] The Pakistani security services have also used Lashkar-e-Tayyiba to gather intelligence on anti-state militants and, at times, to neutralize them.[84] Although the Taliban and Haqqani Network do not directly fight revolutionary groups like the TTP, with which they both have a relationship, the military has relied on them to temper the TTP and reorient anti-state militants toward Afghanistan.[85] The Haqqani Network and Taliban have also acted as diplomatic interfaces with the TTP.[86] Haqqani leaders reportedly helped mediate a number of the cease-fire agreements and peace deals between the military and TTP commanders in North and South Waziristan.[87] The Haqqanis also may have helped to facilitate the aforementioned alliance that pitted Nazir and Bahadur against Baitullah Mehsud.[88]

Pakistan's support for state-associated groups is critical for maintaining influence over them. In the years that followed 9/11, military officials, civilian politicians, and others close to the security establishment complained that anti-state militant groups emerged as a result of crackdowns undertaken in response to U.S. pressure. Talking about many of the groups supported by the state in Kashmir, one ISI officer asserted, "Pakistan banned these organizations under pressure from the U.S. and this was a mistake. At the time, these people were in the system. Now they are outside the system."[89] This complaint is coterminous with one that the United States pressured Pakistan to launch military incursions into FATA that in turn catalyzed the insurgency currently facing the state. It is true that Pakistan launched early incursions under U.S. pressure. Yet these were in keeping with Islamabad's agreement after 9/11 to pursue al-Qaida members who fled across the border. Moreover, these operations were often poorly resourced and targeted narrowly to avoid state-allied militants. These constraints combined with the army's proclivity for peace deals contributed to the growing insurgency in Pakistan.

Members of the security establishment are concerned that the cessation of active support for state-associated groups could lead to a concomitant rise in anti-state violence.[90] These officials also recognize that inducements provide a way to rein in erstwhile militants when necessary. In some cases, such support is also perceived to be necessary to enable state-associated groups to beat back anti-state challenges or to reengage erstwhile members. For example, for several years al-Qaida has been attempting to poach Lashkar-e-Tayyiba members, compete for its recruits, and co-opt its anti-India platform.[91] Members from Lashkar-e-Tayyiba were also becoming involved in anti-state violence. This was an even bigger problem with JeM. Leaders from both organizations claim the state provided them additional resources to keep current members in line and induce former members who might be assisting anti-state militants to return to the fold.[92] The aim may have been to gather information from these former members, monitor them, and control their activities as much as possible. ISI officers also reportedly goaded Lashkar-e-Tayyiba leaders to re-indoctrinate former and current members against launching attacks in Pakistan, and local clerics were encouraged to deliver the message that jihad in Pakistan was *haram* (forbidden).[93] Similar efforts, according to one of their number, were undertaken with some JeM members.[94]

Conclusion

Pakistan has made sufficient gains against anti-state militants in recent years, retaking control of most territory in FATA and driving many remaining anti-state militants across the border into Afghanistan. Although Zarb-e-Azb assiduously avoided the Haqqani Network in North Waziristan, the military reportedly targeted some of the factions that might qualify as "frenemies" such as the one led by Hafiz Gul Bahadur.[95] The military also launched airstrikes in areas controlled by Sajna, the former TTP leader who forged a temporary reconciliation with the government.[96] He was killed in Afghanistan in November 2015 by a U.S. drone strike.[97] Finally, in 2015, the authorities have carried out a series of extrajudicial killings that eliminated top LeJ leaders, including Malik Ishaq, possibly because the group was drifting toward the Islamic State of Iraq and the Levant (ISIL).[98] These actions should not be perceived as a strategic shift in Pakistan's policy toward militants. Rather, the security establishment appears to be cleaning house when it comes to groups and factions it deems either belligerents or unreliable allies. There are no indications Pakistan plans to end its support for longstanding state-allied groups like Lashkar-e-Tayyiba, the Taliban, or Haqqani Network.

U.S. policymakers should have learned a lot of hard lessons since the invasion of Afghanistan after 9/11. One of them is that no realistic inducements or threats of coercion are likely to change the Pakistani military's strategic calculus regarding support for militant groups. The security establishment's segmented approach is informed by militants' external utility against India and in Afghanistan, internal value managing other security issues, and perceived threats to the state. In addition, numerous domestic barriers to action against the militant infrastructure exist. These include concerns about blowback in the form of attacks in the settled areas and against civilian and military officials; systemic deficiencies in the country's judicial, law enforcement, and intelligence capabilities; civilian-military divides; competition among politicians; and militants' growing influence in the political, media, and social spheres.

Although potentially successful in the near-term, Pakistan's triage approach constrains its policy options over the medium- to long-term, further locking the establishment into a reactive as opposed to forward-leaning posture and making it more difficult for the country to face either its geopolitical or domestic challenges. The cumulative creeping expansion of jihadist influence also contributes to an identity crisis that threatens to corrode Pakistan's cohesion. At this stage, however, Pakistan's approach to militancy is path dependent. The state and the militants on its soil will continue to evolve and adapt. There is not likely to be an inflection point where decisionmakers elect to dismantle the militant infrastructure or cease support for state-allied groups. Any progress in these areas will be incremental, reversible, and often ad hoc. If Pakistan ever moves from its current path onto one where it is more committed than not to dismantling the militant infrastructure, Pakistani decisionmakers probably won't recognize the moment they've crossed the Rubicon. The United States almost certainly will not.

Chapter 6 is an extension of ideas that appeared previously in Stephen Tankel, "Beyond the Double Game: Lessons From Pakistan's Approach to Islamist Militancy," *Journal of Strategic Studies*, June 16, 2016, 1–13. Used by permission.

Chapter 6 also includes extensions of ideas that appeared previously in Stephen Tankel, "Domestic Barriers to Dismantling the Militant Infrastructure in Pakistan," U.S. Institute for Peace, September 2013. Used by permission.

CHAPTER 7
Chinese Views on the U.S. Wars on Afghanistan and Iraq

David Lai

The United States has fought two wars in the last 15 years.[1] One was against al-Qaida terrorists and the Taliban regime in Afghanistan from 2001 to 2014. The other toppled the regime of Saddam Hussein in 2003 and subsequently fought Iraqi anti-U.S. insurgents until 2011. In both wars, the United States won decisive military battles at the initial stages, yet was unable to translate those military victories into desired war outcomes. In the end, as Chinese observers put it, the United States won the battles but lost the wars.[2]

These two wars will have lasting impact on the United States and international affairs. While the United States has much to reflect on from its experience (achievements and mistakes), other nations also draw their own lessons from these major U.S. foreign policy undertakings. The United States will do itself a good service to take both into account. Indeed, the United States has many thorny and unsettling foreign policy issues and will be operating in an increasingly constrained environment, domestic as well as international, in the future; it pays for the United States to learn about the lessons, to know itself better and the others as well.

Chinese Concerns With the Two Wars

Among the nations in the world, China is arguably the one most concerned with U.S. foreign policy conduct in general, and the two wars in particular, for several special reasons. First, China has many conflicts of interest with the United States, some of which carry the danger of getting the two nations into armed conflicts. There is the risk of direct confrontation in the Western Pacific over contested interests, as well as the risks created by U.S. defense commitments to allies or partners (such as Taiwan, Japan, the Philippines, or even Vietnam) that are in contentious and at times explosive territorial disputes with China.

Second, China is in a power transition process with the United States as a result of its phenomenal economic rise. This power transition is complicating China's decades-long, precarious relationship with the United States and bringing changes to the Asia-Pacific region; it presumably also will affect the international system in the future.[3] Use of force by the dominant and rising powers to deal with similar changes has occurred repeatedly throughout history.[4] The Chinese worry that the U.S. use of force in the two wars, especially the invasion of Iraq, set dangerous precedents for international conflict and will also make U.S.-China conflict more prone to escalation and the clash of armed forces.

Finally, China is in the midst of its military modernization. The Chinese People's Liberation Army (PLA) has been learning from its U.S. counterpart to improve its fighting capability. U.S. military operations in the two wars thus are of great interest to the Chinese.

For these reasons (and undoubtedly more), Chinese analysts have paid close attention to the strategic as well as operational aspects of these U.S. wars. This study includes a broad survey of open-source Chinese observations on the two U.S. wars as they unfolded and presents the following key Chinese views, which appear to remain current: 1) The two wars were blatant cases of the U.S. drive for global hegemony. 2) As a result, and due to U.S. failures, the United States lost much soft power in this drive. 3) The U.S. "preemption and prevention" conduct set inappropriate standards in international affairs. (The Chinese hold that the war on Iraq was both preemptive and preventive and that the George W. Bush administration blurred the difference between the two on purpose so that it could launch the war on Iraq.)[5] 4) The U.S. military strategies and tactics in the two wars provide valuable lessons for the Chinese military.

A Note on Methodology

Before detailing these Chinese observations, a few cautious notes are in order. First, although the research is extensive, it is by no mean exhaustive.

Second, there is no known comprehensive Chinese study on the lessons learned from these two wars. This analysis pieces many scattered observations together. Nevertheless, this survey reflects widely shared Chinese views on the two U.S. wars.

Third, most, if not all, Chinese analysts look at the two wars through the prism of Marxism, Leninism, Maoism, and Dengism. From this ideological perspective, Chinese analysts dogmatically cast U.S. conduct in waging those two wars as the pursuit of U.S. world hegemony.

Finally, most of the Chinese analyses of the two wars suffer from a lack of proper theoretical framework, logical consistency, and independent assessment. These methodological problems led to a "collective blindness" ("集体失明") among the Chinese analysts in predicting the course and outcome of the two wars. Most analysts also "followed the crowd" (随大流) to say the same things about the wars. For instance, before the Afghan war, most, if not all, predicted that the United States would not be able to destroy the Taliban regime and al-Qaida, or to make any progress in the War on Terrorism. Many asked variants of, "How could the U.S. win if the enemy was invisible?"[6] However, when the United States decisively destroyed the Taliban regime and al-Qaida strongholds in Afghanistan in late 2001, most Chinese analysts quickly switched their views—the U.S. military seemed almighty and the United States would easily gain a strategic and operational stronghold in Central Asia and the Middle East.[7]

On the War in Afghanistan

The Chinese argue that the Afghan War was initially the right thing for the United States to do. But, they believe, it was not done right.

The 9/11 terrorist attacks on the United States put the whole world in shock. Deep sympathies poured from all corners of the world to the United States. When the United States presented solid evidence that the al-Qaida masterminds in Afghanistan were responsible for orchestrating the attacks, the United Nations quickly passed resolutions to support the U.S.-led efforts to fight against the terrorists in Afghanistan, including the use of force, and against the Afghan Taliban regime that was providing shelter to the terrorists. Russia and China set aside their differences with the United States and offered unprecedented support to the latter on its mission. NATO members also invoked for the first time the alliance's obligation of collective defense and joined hands with the United States to fight against the terrorists and Taliban in Afghanistan.

The U.S. military's decisive victories over the Taliban and al-Qaida made the anti-terrorism mission initially look very promising. Yet the Chinese insist that two major U.S. undertakings came to tarnish this noble cause: the U.S. invasion of Iraq and the questionable nation-building measures in Afghanistan.

The Chinese strongly hold that the U.S. invasion of Iraq was fundamentally wrong and that it brought fatal damage to the U.S. mission in Afghanistan. The biggest damage was the loss of U.S. soft power and moral authority.[8] The Chinese from the outset saw U.S. conduct in the Iraq War as a U.S. drive for world hegemony, leading them then to see the Afghan War, although started with a just cause, as another part of the U.S. hegemonic design. As a result, they believe, international support faded away.

In the meantime, the invasion of Iraq took U.S. leaders' attention and efforts away from Afghanistan. This move prevented the United States from

135

taking full advantage of its initial military victory over the al-Qaida terrorists and the Taliban regime to completely eradicate the terrorist safehavens in Afghanistan. The al-Qaida terrorists and Taliban remnants thus got a chance to regroup and make a comeback, derailing the Afghan War and making the Afghan nation-building program extremely difficult. Yet even with the disturbance from the al-Qaida terrorists and Taliban outlaws aside, the Chinese argue that the U.S. formula for Afghan nation-building was questionable, to say the least, and was doomed to fail eventually.

Chinese analysts generally believe that the United States, for its strategic and ideological interests, wanted to create a pro-U.S. government in Afghanistan and could offer the Afghans the only model the United States knew and was eager to promote: democracy. Chinese argued that the U.S. efforts were doomed to fail for the following reasons. First, Afghanistan was a nation without a functional government for decades and a highly fragmented society with scattered tribes still operating on primitive rules. Second, Afghanistan did not have a modern economy except for the opium business. Third, following the destruction of the Taliban regime, Afghanistan badly needed stability, order, and economic development. In theory, a strong and efficient central government should have been a prerequisite for the rebuilding of this nation. But democracy is not meant to be efficient; it is a form of government for more developed nations rather than for developing countries.[9] According to the Chinese view, the U.S. approach was inappropriate and had only made nation-building in Afghanistan more difficult.[10]

On the Iraq War

Unlike their views on the "good-beginning-bad-ending" war in Afghanistan, Chinese observers unanimously hold that the United States did not do a right thing by launching the Iraq War and did not conduct it effectively either. Chinese observations on the Iraq War thus have been mostly about U.S. hegemonic lust, "preemptive/preventive" bullying, and the negative consequences of the war. With respect to the actual conduct of war, most Chinese initially expected the U.S. to win the military battles but regretted that Saddam did not stage a decent fight against the invaders. They held this view not because they liked Saddam, but because they did not like the United States and its conduct.

The Chinese argued that the Iraq War was doomed to fail from the beginning. It had an unjust strategic nature (非正义的战略属性)—going without a UN mandate and violating international standards. The United States had excessive and unattainable strategic objectives (过高的战略目标): 1) the elimination of weapons of mass destruction (WMD) in Iraq; 2) the destruction of the Saddam regime; 3) control of oil supplies and the world energy market; 4) the recreation of the Middle East's strategic landscape; 5) the transformation of Iraq into a model of democracy in the Middle East and the promotion of Western values in the region; and 6) a step toward U.S. world hegemony.

The United States resorted to a controversial strategic approach (极有争议的战略方针和手段), namely the "preemption/prevention approach," to launch the Iraq War. This conduct violated all the standards of international relations, and it was not appropriate for fighting against terrorists; hence, the Chinese argue that heavy-handed and violent U.S. measures only begot further terrorist acts (以暴除暴, 越反越恐). The Chinese also argue that the United States adopted an inappropriate strategic guidance. Specifically, the United States did not see clearly who the enemy was and wrongly paired up terrorism with Saddam.[11]

With the above-mentioned problems, most Chinese insisted at the outset that the United States could not win the Iraq War and would sink into a quagmire in the Middle East. Indeed, 10 years after the war, the Chinese felt vindicated that the United States must have much to regret. Iran emerged as the biggest winner in the U.S. wars on Afghanistan and Iraq—the United States had destroyed Iran's two enemies. Furthermore, with the toppling of the Saddam regime, the United States opened a can of worms—the ethnic, religious, and many other problems that were tightly controlled by Saddam had all come to the surface. In addition, the democratic government apparently did not work for Iraq.[12]

"U.S. Hegemonic Drives"

Among all the people in the world, the Chinese are unquestionably the ones who talk about "U.S. hegemony" the most. They have been characterizing U.S. foreign policy conduct as hegemonic moves for decades and criticize the "U.S. hegemonic drives" whenever they can. It comes therefore as no surprise that the Chinese took the two U.S. wars as naked acts of U.S. pursuit of hegemony (赤裸裸的霸权行径).

U.S. Imperialism and Hegemony

The Chinese follow Marxism, Leninism, Maoism, and Dengism to view imperialism as the highest stage of capitalism and hegemony as the conduct of imperial states. They argue that the United States has been a capitalist nation since its beginning and long has followed its capitalist impulse to expand. They also assert that the United States has a deep cultural desire for its hegemonic pursuit, the so-called "sense of Americans being God's chosen people to carry out a divine mission," a calling to transform the world "in God's image."[13]

In the Chinese view, the United States rose from the ashes of World War II to become an imperial state. Its hegemonic ambitions, however, were frustrated by the Soviet Union, which, from the Chinese perspective, also became an imperial state during the Cold War. With the collapse of the Soviet empire, the United States became the sole superpower and was eager to pursue a unipolar world under U.S. control, the so-called *Pax Americana*.[14]

U.S. Hegemonic Conduct

The late Chinese statesman Deng Xiaoping asserted that in the post-Cold War era the United States would use "human rights over sovereign rights" as a pretext to intervene in other nations' internal affairs; that it would instigate trouble everywhere; that the U.S. hegemonic drives would become sources of war; and that the United States would pursue its hegemonic world order at the expense of other nations' interests.[15]

Chinese analysts also believe that U.S. hegemonic drives have taken on other new features as well, including: from hegemonic competition to dominance (争霸到独霸); from regional to global hegemony (从区域到全球霸权); from hegemony in certain areas to all-dimension hegemony (全方位霸权); and from interest-based to system order-based hegemony (制度霸权).[16]

Moreover, with its unmatched military power, the United States has dominated the "right to initiate war," exposed its intent to unilaterally rule the world more fervently, attempted to legitimize its intervention in other nations' internal affairs, and emphasized its use of force in international affairs as a decisive factor, Chinese analysts believe.[17]

Chinese analysts maintain that, driven by its urge to pursue world hegemony, the United States quickly turned the 9/11 tragedy into an opportunity to launch a "foreign policy revolution" that aimed to push the U.S. drive for hegemony to a new level.[18]

The Cost of U.S. Hegemony

The Chinese argue that the relentless U.S. drive for world hegemony has backfired. The United States has paid a heavy price for the Iraq War. First, there was a huge bill for blood and treasure (according to the 2012 data, U.S. casualties were 4,487 killed and 32,000 wounded, and the war cost $800 billion.)[19] In the Gulf War of 1991, the United States had many other nations—such as Kuwait, Saudi Arabia, and Japan—to pay the bills. Yet the United States could not get any other nation to do the same for the Iraq War of 2003.

The United States overthrew the Saddam regime, yet it created, and sank into, a quagmire in Iraq. Terrorism has increased, and Iraq has become a new breeding ground for terrorists. The Iraq War had turned the War on Terrorism

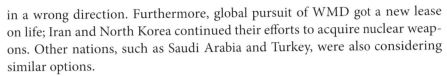

in a wrong direction. Furthermore, global pursuit of WMD got a new lease on life; Iran and North Korea continued their efforts to acquire nuclear weapons. Other nations, such as Saudi Arabia and Turkey, were also considering similar options.

Another unintended consequence, according to the Chinese analysts, is that the reputation of the United States, perceived U.S. trustworthiness, and the attractiveness of U.S. ideals have been tarnished. While the United States spent 10 years in the wars in Afghanistan and Iraq, other major powers, especially China, were able to concentrate on their national development.[20] As a result, multipolarity has gained strength, accelerating the global challenge to U.S. unipolar hegemony.

In waging the Afghan War, the United States received unprecedented support from the other great powers, especially Russia and China, and overwhelming sympathy and support from the world community. The United Nations gave the mandate for the United States to fight against the Taliban regime and al-Qaida terrorists. However, by launching the invasion of Iraq, the United States not only had ruined its gains in Afghanistan, but also made itself a problem for the world.[21]

The Chinese believe that the United States has always wanted to bring the Muslim world under its control. Yet the U.S. invasion of Iraq did not serve the U.S. objective. On the contrary, it hurt U.S. soft power. In waging this war, the United States turned diplomacy into war and its regional objective into regime change—the removal of Saddam Hussein. This was a big mistake in the U.S. pursuit of its grand strategy.[22]

In the meantime, the U.S. adventure in Iraq showed that U.S. military power could not guarantee that the United States could attack other nations at will without suffering casualties of its own (想打死谁就打死谁, 而自己却不受伤); and the United States could not go it alone to control the world single-handedly (独步天下).[23]

The Chinese maintain that the primary reason the United States got itself into a quagmire in Iraq was the Bush administration's efforts to spread democracy with military force and the hope to end terrorism with democracy (以武力推广民主, 以民主终结恐怖主义暴政). The Bush administration mistakenly believed that terrorism was special to Islam and turned the War on Terrorism into an ideological confrontation, according to Chinese analysts. But terrorism is a form of violence; it is the means extremists use to confront stronger opponents. In history, there have been many examples of terrorism. It is not a copyrighted property of any particular nation or religion. Moreover, the Bush administration related the root of terrorism to the political and religious systems of the Middle Eastern nations, rather than to economic underdevelopment and biased U.S. support for Israel in the Israel-Palestine conflict. Most Chinese insist that with this misconception, the Bush administration did not try to resolve the Israel-Palestine conflict, but instead chose to push for the spread of democracy, hoping that Western democracy could transform the political systems in the Middle East and use Western values to reform the Muslim communities. This effort was incorporated in the Bush administration's "Greater Middle East Initiative" put forward in 2004.[24] The result turned out to be a repressive Iraqi government by the few replaced by a repressive government by the majority (只是用多数人的暴政代替了少数人的暴政). Moreover, the Bush administration blindly believed in military power and completely oversimplified an extremely complicated Middle East problem, according to Chinese analysts.[25]

The Chinese argue that terrorism is the direct result of the U.S. hegemony. For a long time, the United States acted as the world's policeman, interfered with other nations' internal affairs at will, emphasized its own interests, imposed its values on others, and made enemies everywhere. This was especially the case in the Middle East. The success in the Afghan War led the United States to believe more in the power of its military force. But, they believe, the U.S. way of using violent force against violent force only breeds more violence. Thus, hegemony and terrorism have formed an insoluble deadlock (解不开的死结). Terrorism and hegemony have become two public enemies of world peace and development.[26]

On the Preemptive/Preventive War

The line between preemptive and preventive wars has been traditionally blurred, and the legality of both is also in question. The Chinese argue that the United States made a seemingly reasonable call for the use of preemptive strike against terrorists following the 9/11 terrorist attacks, yet used it as a cover for a preventive war against Iraq.[27]

Chinese analysts insist that the U.S. turn to the preemptive and preventive approach was not an impulsive act, but rather an intentional game changer in U.S. foreign policy and military tactics.[28] They also contend that the U.S. use of what they call "the preemptive/preventive approach" had made the United States a dangerous hegemonic power in international affairs. The United States wanted to be the one that sets the rules in international politics, serves as a judge determining who broke the rules, and then acts as a policeman to implement the rules (with the preemptive/preventive strikes). This approach is dangerous because there are no international checks and balances on U.S. hegemonic power. Against this backdrop, the 9/11 terrorist attack served as a "blasting fuse;" and antiterrorism war was thus a pretext. The United States believed that it could use force to overthrow those rogue regimes that did not comply with U.S. demands. If the Iraq War went well, the United States would then move on to attack Iran or North Korea.[29]

There are broader and far-reaching consequences of this approach as well. From a political perspective, the United States would go unilateral, putting the United Nations and international order in peril. From a security perspective, this approach had changed the norms of international security. The United States would seek absolute security at the expense of other nations' security. From a military perspective, this approach violates international norms about the use of force. On the technical side, in order to pursue surprise in military action, the United States would develop more advanced high-tech weapons, further widening the gap between its military power and those of other nations. In order to reduce logistics burdens, the United States would explore acquisition of more overseas bases and allies' support. Ultimately, in order to have absolute superiority, the United States would seek space dominance, rendering a peaceful use of space impossible. The United States would pursue new interventionism. The Chinese concluded that when the United States gets used to invading other nations, there is no stopping it anywhere.[30]

Chinese analysts believe the Iraq War was the debut of the U.S. preemptive/preventive war doctrine (伊拉克战争是先发制人军事战略的开山之作). However, with this heavy-handed approach, the United States did not establish a democratic, stable, and secure Iraq; instead, it made the Iraq situation even more turbulent. After the invasion, the United States could not create a new Iraq as an example of U.S.-style democracy and security. The U.S. setback in Iraq spells the failure, if not demise, of the preemptive/preventive war doctrine and the effort to promote democracy.[31]

On the War Strategies and Tactics

Chinese analysts observe that the United States relied on the following to win the battles in the Iraq War: large-scale precision-strike and space-guided weaponry; aircraft carrier battle groups; information control; air superiority; and new-concept weapons tailored for Iraq.[32] Because Iraq had no countermeasures, it was practically an experimental site for the U.S. high-tech weapons, new operational tactics, preemption, democracy promotion, and construction of a world order under U.S. hegemony.[33]

Although Chinese military analysts agree that the U.S. forces and operations were impressive and mostly successful, they nevertheless find some shortcomings. They believe the United States made a mistake in its relations with Turkey and the possibility of using Turkey as a launch pad for the invasion of Iraq in 2003. Because Turkey did not allow U.S. troops to attack Iraq from Turkey, the U.S. military had to make contingency plans that affected the course of the invasion. (They failed to note General Tommy Franks' memoir, which revealed that the United States misled Iraq and got Saddam to prepare for a war from the north that would never come.[34])

The Chinese initially held that the United States did not have good intelligence so that it had to start the war 10 hours before the plan. (They did not realize that this was the result of a quick decision to try to decapitate the Iraqi regime by killing Saddam Hussein.) They also held that the United States underestimated the will of Iraqis to resist the invasion. Thus, in its fast move toward Baghdad, the U.S. military stretched its logistics supply lines, which Iraqi forces attacked. As a result of this setback, President George W. Bush planned to send an additional 100,000 troops to Iraq.[35] In sum, the decapitation and shock-and-awe strategies felt short.

Third, Chinese also noted that following their victory in Mosul on March 21, 2003, U.S. troops prominently displayed U.S. flags everywhere. This act stirred a big uproar in Iraq and the Arab world generally. There was also widespread bragging of victory and bravery. All of these insensitive acts generated resentment among the Iraqi people.[36]

Although the Chinese initially believed that the United States would win the major battles in the Iraq War, they nonetheless expected Saddam Hussein and his followers to stage a decent fight against the U.S. troops.[37] Before the onset of the Iraq War, the Chinese had high hope that Saddam and his troops would learn from Mao's theories about the weak overcoming the strong and the tricks in the protracted people's war. They also strongly held that Saddam was a skillful statesman and a mastermind in dealing with the United States. The Chinese predicted that Saddam had learned his lessons from the Gulf War of 1991 and would avoid a head-on collision with the invading U.S. troops. Moreover, the Chinese expected Saddam to lure the U.S. troops in and then launch guerilla warfare and tactics to confront them. The Chinese argued that since the invasion was unjust, illegal, and influenced by greedy designs, the United States would not be able to win the war and that Saddam would eventually wear the U.S. troops down with a protracted people's war of attritions and street fights in the cities.[38]

The war unfolded initially as the Chinese had expected. There was no serious resistance on the Iraqi side. As the invading forces moved swiftly toward Baghdad without any resistance, the Chinese chose to believe that Saddam knew what he was doing and that letting the U.S. troops move toward Baghdad was part of his plan. Indeed, the attacks by some of the Iraqi forces deployed in the southern provinces on the U.S. logistics supply lines appeared to confirm the Chinese view that Saddam was doing the right thing. The Chinese felt vindicated when the United States had to call in more troops to protect the supply lines and fight against the Iraqi forces in the south.

That exchange of fights slowed the U.S. advance a little bit. But when the U.S. troops re-secured the supply lines and resumed their advance toward Baghdad, Chinese military analysts still believed that Saddam was playing the game of "empty fortress" ("空城计").[39]

With their preconceived views on the war and Iraqi options, Chinese commentators initially hailed the success of Saddam's strategy, arguing that he opened the door to Iraq wide and lured the enemy deep into the country. He resisted the invading forces with multilayered defense, dispersed his troops, and counterattacked the invading forces with selective emphases. Saddam used guerilla tactics and attacked the enemy's weak spots (游击袭扰); conducted Iraqi media resistance effectively; and used "precision-guided misleading" ("精确误导")[40] to confuse the invading troops. According to the Chinese, he countered the high-tech enemy with low-tech capabilities and staged street fights and an all-people and whole-nation resistance (巷战, 全民皆兵, 整体御敌).[41]

Chinese analysts also initially believed that Saddam retained a formidable air force, and they still hoped that it would make a surprise attack on the U.S. forces.[42] The Chinese also noted that the Iraqi troops used the tactics of attacking at night, faking surrender, pretending to be civilians, and fighting at close range (短兵战). They asserted that Iraqi guerilla warfare was taking place even at the beginning of the war.[43] The Chinese also held that the U.S. military underestimated Iraqi military's resistance capacity and Saddam's strategic intelligence, yet overestimated the coalition's coordination capacity. Iraqi troops' resistance appeared to be well organized, planned, and targeted. Saddam had many years of experience with the United States and with keeping Iraq under his tight control.[44] Although the U.S. military had fought many wars in the last two decades, it did not have much recent ground war experience.[45] The Chinese even asserted that the United States had already admitted that it was the people who would ultimately make a difference, not the high-tech weapons (美国已经认账, 战争的最终决定因素还是人).[46]

The Chinese were very delighted to hear that the Iraqis used Chinese terms to characterize their fight against the U.S. invaders. Chinese reports at the time noted that Iraq claimed to "make strategic retreat, lure the enemy deep in, and prepare to strike back after the invaders (战略撤退诱敌深入后发制人)." There was also a report that Iraqi Defense Minister Mahdi said that the Iraqis "let the U.S. troops get to Baghdad early so that we can encircle them and beat them up like dogs (关起门来打狗)." The report also suggested that many Iraqis were still loyal to Saddam.[47] As the war continued, Chinese commentators continued to expect Iraq to make a counterattack.[48]

Chinese believed that U.S. psychological warfare failed.[49] They continued to doubt the U.S. ability to attack Baghdad and engage in street fighting.[50] The Chinese believed that the Iraqi people would stand by Saddam to fight against the U.S. invaders. Even if they did not fight for Saddam, they would fight for Iraq.[51]

With the fall of Baghdad and U.S. troops closing in on Tikrit, Saddam's hometown, Chinese commentators still believed that Saddam "followed the Chinese strategy" to do what the Chinese had mistakenly celebrated initially, before the Iraqi collapse in Baghdad, as described above.[52] Chinese observers could not accept the fact that several hundred thousand Iraqi troops had simply evaporated. They chose to believe that the Iraqi troops disappeared on purpose and that Saddam would stage a final showdown with the U.S. invaders in Tikrit and northern Iraq.[53] Chinese military commentator, PLA National Defense University professor Han Xudong (韩旭东), characterized Saddam's move as "Iraqi troops withdrew from Baghdad with dignity (从容地撤出)" and "orchestrated a well-organized evaporation of troops (蒸发行动)." He also said that this "empty fortress" could have been the best note in Saddam's life (空城计是萨达姆一生最精彩的一笔).[54]

The battles in Iraq were eventually all one-sided. Saddam' regime fell without making any serious countermeasures. Chinese commentators simply could not accept this result. Some started to speculate that Saddam had an under-the-table deal with the United States to save his life.[55] Other reluctantly expressed regret that Saddam had not followed the Chinese "prescription" to fight against the U.S. invaders: Street fights regrettably did not happen. Guerilla warfare had a seemingly formidable start but faded away too fast. A "scorched earth" strategy was never attempted. The burning of oil fields and destruction of infrastructures were not executed. Saddam did not follow through with his threat of a protracted war of attrition. And, finally, a major showdown had never taken shape.[56]

Many Chinese commentators also regretted that: 1) Saddam had a mistaken assessment of the overall situation and incorrectly judged that the war would not break out; 2) Saddam had insufficiently prepared for war; 3) Saddam's strategy and tactics were dated and not flexible (落后呆板); 4) Saddam had lost popular support; and 5) the United Nations did not prevent the United States from waging war.[57]

While most Chinese commentators showed their disappointment, a few reasonable Chinese observers argued that the people's war could not take place in Iraq because Saddam did not have the support of the Iraqi people.[58] Some Chinese commentators started to realize that Saddam never intended to fight a bloody street war in Baghdad. His troops did not have the power or will to do so.[59]

Some also pointed out that simply because the U.S invasion was not justified does not mean Saddam had justice in his hand. Even if the Iraqi people found it justified to resist the U.S. invasion, it does not mean that Saddam could rally the people around him to fight. The Iraqi people's spontaneous resistance could not succeed without effective national leadership. Saddam was in no position to lead the Iraqi people and wage a people's war against the U.S. invasion.[60]

The U.S. War Experience Is Without Universal Significance

Although the U.S. use of force in Iraq and Afghanistan, and in other countries since the end of the Cold War, has been successful and impressive, it has been, as PLA Senior Colonel Fan Gaoyue (樊高月), head of the PLA Academy of Military Science (AMS) Department of Foreign Military Studies, argues, special cases with no universal significance (不具有普遍性意义的特殊战争). Iraq in 2003 was a severely degraded nation after years of U.S.-led sanctions. Its early industrial-age military capability suffered a huge generational gap when compared with the information-age U.S. military, and the war was a highly asymmetric one.[61] Another AMS analyst, Senior Colonel Zhao Xiaozhuo (赵小卓), went a step further to raise the question: If the U.S. military gets in a fight with a well-matched opponent, will the war follow the U.S. rules and wills? The answer, Sr. Col Zhao put it, should be a "no."[62]

The Chinese also argued that because several hundred thousand Iraqi troops disappeared mysteriously, it is difficult to say that the U.S. new military strategy and tactics had succeeded, for they did not have a real test. As such, the U.S. military was lucky that Saddam did not stage a street fight in Baghdad or wage guerilla warfare in Iraq to wear the invaders down.[63]

Lessons of War for China and Its Military Modernization

The U.S. use of force in the Gulf War of 1991 was a wake-up call to the Chinese, who subsequently embarked on a major military modernization program. The U.S. use of force in the wars in Afghanistan and Iraq was also an eye-opening experience for the Chinese. They got to see how much the U.S. military had progressed since 1991, especially the U.S. use of information-age capabilities. All of these motivated the Chinese military to accelerate its modernization drive and, they hope, catch up with the U.S. military.[64]

The Iraq War was a test of the U.S. military transformation. Through the U.S. operations, the Chinese saw precision-guided munition and weapon systems; joint and integrated military forces; real-time command, control, communications, computers, and intelligence (C4I); multidimension operations; and systems of operations. Many Chinese observers believe that China should get a clear understanding the U.S.-led "Revolution in Military Affairs" and develop Chinese military capabilities more quickly.[65]

From their observation of the conduct of U.S. wars, the Chinese reflect on the following propositions: 1) it is important to strengthen weapon development, especially "assassins maize" (a term referring to special weapons designed for dealing with U.S. forces); 2) nuclear deterrence is key to preserving major power standing and protection; 3) improvement of missile survival is imperative; 4) anti-aircraft carrier capabilities are important means in future wars against the United States; 5) anti-access and area denial (A2/AD) and other anti-carrier platforms will make the U.S. military think many times before sending troops into war zones; 6) low-cost but high-performance conventional missiles should be given priority, as should precision-guided missiles and munitions; and 8), air superiority is key to keeping enemies at bay.[66]

Chinese observations of the conduct of U.S. wars and U.S. military developments also led them to see that China's future military modernization needed a new direction. For most of the history of the People's Republic, China's military modernization strategies were concerned with immediate threats, preparations to react to attacks, and maintenance of the status quo. China is now much more powerful. Its homeland is much more secure. China therefore should learn from the U.S. military to have a capability-based strategy. China wants to become first-class military power. It therefore must have a military that has the capability to project power globally.[67]

During the two wars, the Chinese military had an opportunity to get an extensive and close look at, and commented on, a wide variety of U.S. military equipment, doctrine, and operations, such as: the U.S. Marine Corps' role and its weaponry,[68] medical support,[69] battlefield medical treatment,[70] non-combatant medical treatment,[71] logistic support,[72] information warfare and propaganda,[73] the U.S. Army Corps of Engineers' experiences in Iraq and its lessons for the PLA,[74] new battle concepts,[75] military equipment,[76] impact of information technology,[77] air raid operations by the U.S.-British coalition forces in the Iraq War,[78] soldier suicide,[79] psychological warfare,[80] soldier psychological problems,[81] transportation,[82] guided munition,[83] airborne weapons,[84] U.S. Army brigade operations,[85] battlefield water supply,[86] armor vehicle maintenance,[87] GPS jamming and counterjamming techniques,[88] and many others. One should not be surprised to see the Chinese learn from the U.S. experiences and accelerate China's military modernization.

CHAPTER 8
Japan's Lessons in Iraq and Afghanistan

Michael W. David

Japan is the major ally of the United States in northeast Asia, a region that has witnessed tremendous economic, social, and military changes over the past 20 years. Weapons of mass destruction add to the conventional and asymmetric challenges that confront established nations such as Japan. In response to the strategic global changes, on April, 27, 2015, the United States and Japan announced the results of the Security Consultative Committee meeting, also known as the "2-plus-2" meetings. These included the first revision of The Guidelines for U.S.-Japan Defense Cooperation ("the Guidelines") in almost 20 years. The next day the White House issued the "U.S.-Japan Joint Vision Statement," the essence of which was:

> The new Guidelines for U.S.-Japan Defense Cooperation will transform the Alliance, reinforce deterrence, and ensure that we can address security challenges, new and old, for the long term. The new Guidelines will update our respective roles and missions within the Alliance and enable Japan to expand its contributions to regional and global security.[1]

This chapter will look at analyses the Japan Self Defense Force (JSDF) conducted of its activities related to the wars in Iraq and Afghanistan, and the influence of the analyses on shaping the roles of the JSDF under the new Guidelines. It will also address the extent to which these new Guidelines reflect lessons learned by Japan from the Iraq and Afghanistan wars, and the lessons learned implications related to Japan's expectations about potential U.S. involvement in future crises.

Historical Background

Understanding the 2015 Guidelines depends on a review of the evolution of Japan's national security policy and the earlier 1997 Guidelines. Japan's military and defense situation is unique. Article IX of the postwar Japanese Constitution forbids the use of military force as a means of settling international disputes and forbids Japan from maintaining an army, navy, or air force. The government circumvents these restrictions by maintaining that requirements for a minimum level of self-defense do not constitute "war potential." The majority of Japanese citizens approve the spirit of Article IX, but since the 1990s, considerable numbers of Japanese have come to believe that Japan should commit the JSDF to collective defense efforts, like those authorized by the UN Security Council in the Gulf War. But, until September 19, 2015, the JSDF was not permitted to participate in collective defense or coalition activities.

The dispatch of the Overseas Minesweeper Force (OMF) to the Persian Gulf (April to November 1991) was the first overseas mission for the JSDF and the first time since World War II that Japanese military forces had ventured abroad in an operational military capacity.[2] The timing was curious, coming as it did almost 2 months after Iraqi forces had been driven from Kuwait and Iraq had accepted a UN Security Council—mandated ceasefire that ended the first Gulf War. The Japanese government had previously committed $13 billion (USD) to the coalition's military forces, yet when the Kuwaiti government used a *Washington Post* advertisement to express its appreciation to the liberating coalition forces, it conspicuously omitted the Japanese flag.[3] This public relations slight in part triggered the OMF deployment of six JSDF ships to the Persian Gulf on April 26, 1991. Subsequent to the Kuwaiti advertisement, in 1992 the Japanese Diet approved the Law Concerning Cooperation for United Nations Peacekeeping Operations and Other Operations, which permitted JSDF participation in UN peacekeeping operations. The Act on Dispatch of the Japan Disaster Relief Team was also revised to include participation abroad by the JSDF.[4] These laws formed the basis for later JSDF participation in various UN peacekeeping operations missions such as Cambodia (1992–93), Mozambique (1992–95), Golan Heights (1996–2014), Honduras (1998), East Timor (2002–04), and Sudan (2011–?).

The 1997 Guidelines, however, were more specifically the result of the North Korea nuclear crisis that occurred between February 1993 and June 1994. On April 1, 1993, the International Atomic Energy Agency declared North Korea to be in noncompliance with the Treaty on the Non-proliferation of Nuclear Weapons. The United States and North Korea initiated negotiations to discuss inspections on June 2, 1993, but by April 1994 diplomatic efforts reached an impasse.[5] That same month U.S. military units conducted a Reception, Staging, Onward Movement, and Integration (RSOI) exercise in South Korea. The primary purpose of the exercise was to train Combined Forces Command, United States Forces Korea staff, and related logistics organizations on the deployment and integration of units from the mainland United States into South Korea. On May 24, 1994, Senator John McCain urged the deployment of additional U.S. land, air, and naval forces to South Korea and the region. During this period of heightened tension, former President

Jimmy Carter unofficially visited North Korea in June 1994, and as a result of President Carter's discussions with senior North Korean leaders, the United States and North Korea opened talks that resulted in the signing of an Agreed Framework in Geneva on October 21, 1994.[6]

The staging and movement components of the RSOI exercise involved the use of U.S. bases and other facilities in Japan. The exercise included contingency planning for the potential use of Japanese airport and harbor facilities; storage and movement of food, fuel, ammunition and other supplies; medical support; and numerous other service support activities. The existing defense guidelines were far from clear on possible implementation of these types of measures, much less their legality under the Japanese constitution, and American and Japanese planners identified many shortcoming, gaps, and problem areas.[7] Due to the Korean nuclear crisis and the RSOI shortcomings, the U.S. Joint Chiefs of Staff revised Operations Plan 5027, a plan for wartime operations in Korea. Also, U.S. Defense and State Department officials formalized a new agreement with Tokyo to ensure that Japanese bases would be available if the United States went to war with North Korea.[8] The 1997 Guidelines were the official terms of the agreement and defined its revised details.[9] Operating under these guidelines, after the 9/11 terrorist attacks against the United States, the JSDF deployed to the Indian Ocean and Kuwait and, based on the Anti-Terrorism Special Measures Act, participated in peace-building activities in Iraq and Afghanistan.[10]

Selected Overview of Japanese Assessments

What did the Japanese learn from the Iraq and Afghanistan experiences that influenced the Guidelines agreed to in April 2015? A review and analysis of selected Japanese assessments of experiences and events related to the wars in Iraq and Afghanistan suggest ways to better understand Japan's perspective and enhance their contribution to the U.S.-Japan alliance.

Maritime Operations

Many publications in Japan related to the Iraq and Afghanistan wars start with comments on the minesweeping activities in the Persian Gulf from April to November 1991 after the first Gulf War. Observers of all political persuasions saw this as the initial or inaugural year of JSDF participation in overseas deployments. Based on lessons learned from this experience, the Japan Maritime Self Defense Force (JMSDF) was better prepared to participate in replenishment activities in the Indian Ocean 10 years later.[11] However, the JMSDF had also built on its Cold War experience of cooperation with the U.S. Navy in antisubmarine warfare and protection of sea lines of communication (SLOCs).

This cooperation produced tactics, know-how, and communications procedures that facilitated the JMSDF's ability to provide prolonged replenishment activities in the Indian Ocean. This experience, in turn, supported and facilitated subsequent deployments in antipiracy operations in the Indian Ocean.[12]

The initial dispatch of the 1991 OMF was not as smooth as it appeared. In early February 1991, the JMSDF began preparatory planning for the mission but faced a serious lack of information and intelligence. It needed tactical specifics on the operational areas of the multinational force, as well as details on the types of floating and tethered mines in the area. It also lacked details on the weather, water temperatures, water salinity and transparency, sea life, and related information. Upon receiving the deployment order on April 16, 1991, the JMSDF asked the U.S. Navy for this information. They received little detailed data because, according to Japanese opinion makers, the U.S. Navy did not really expect the JMSDF to deploy and operate.[13] The OMF did deploy, and it arrived in the Straits of Hormuz on May 26, 1991. In the interim, sufficient intelligence and information had been collected, and the OMF was able to successfully complete its mission.[14] In the process, the OMF and JMSDF coordinated and cooperated with the UN Multinational Interception Force and participated in Maritime Commander Meeting sessions. One might say the main lessons learned were that policy credibility and physical presence are key elements of cooperation in international coalitions.[15] Acceptance and understanding come in strange ways. The OMF did what billions of dollars could not—it got the Japanese flag on the multinational force T-shirt. Humorous perhaps, but Tokyo understood that it could no longer buy its way out of responsibility to help resolve international crises.[16]

The story was different following the 9/11 attacks in New York and Washington, DC. Within a week, Prime Minister Koizumi Koichi's government pledged military support to the United States and U.S. forces. The Japanese Diet passed the Anti-Terrorism Special Measures Law on October 29, 2001, that allowed the JSDF to provide rear-area support and security for U.S. and UN forces.[17] NATO partners had already activated Article 5 of the Washington Treaty—an attack against one NATO member is an attack against all—and a week later European AWACS aircraft deployed to U.S. airspace.[18] The Japanese decision reflected the result of lessons learned 10 years earlier. More specifically, it provided for visible support delivered in a timely manner, with a focus on material support and presence.[19] This was implemented to the extent that the JMSDF deployed ships and personnel in the Indian Ocean over a period from December 2001 to January 2010. During this period over 13,300 personnel and 73 ships of the JMSDF supported the U.S., UK, French, German, and Pakistani navies in the region.[20]

Japan's deployments related to the wars in Afghanistan and Iraq, along with antipiracy operations, provided close cooperation and coordination with not only the U.S. Navy's 7th Fleet and United States Pacific Command, but also with the U.S. Navy's 5th Fleet, United States Central Command, and navies of the multinational forces in the Persian Gulf and Horn of Africa regions.

One of the first lessons learned was reconfirmation of the fact that in the realm of international diplomacy and public relations, contributions to peace and security missions that feature troop presence and visibility are more important than financial contributions. The JMSDF deployments to the Indian Ocean over roughly 8 years cost about $700 million (USD). These operations drew laudatory comments from the UN, as well as from Afghanistan, Pakistan, the United States, and other nations. This was in sharp contrast to the situation of the 1991 Gulf War described above in which Japan's financial contributions did not draw public appreciation.[21]

At the operational level, the JSDF learned a great deal about what a "coalition" is, and the difference between an alliance and a coalition. An alliance is based on (1) a treaty and provides long-term structure; (2) shared national values and interests; and (3) an obligation to participate in military operations to defend a partner. A coalition is based on: (1) specific defined duties; (2) narrow scope of national interests; and (3) limited, self-defined operational activities. For example, some nations may provide large conventional forces for a full spectrum of operations, but others may limit their participation to only aerial reconnaissance, medical assistance, or other specified areas. The level of commitment is up to each participating coalition member, and although no treaties are involved, all participants must strictly meet their level of commitment.

A coalition structure was ideal for Japan because it permitted the JMSDF units to act within limitations imposed by Japanese laws. It also limited the JMSDF role because the Japanese could not participate in the fullest scope of intelligence sharing. Since Japan was not a part of the Five Eyes group (United States, United Kingdom, Canada, Australia, and New Zealand) or a NATO or International Security Assistance Force (ISAF) member nation, its only access was to general Operation ENDURING FREEDOM–related intelligence. Conversely, Japan learned that by permitting the use of its facilities, and providing support based on the U.S.-Japan Alliance, the importance of the Alliance was strongly reinforced. That is, Japan's support of coalition operations increased the mutual trust and respect between U.S. and Japanese forces and laid the basis for participation in future coalitions.[22] This represented the first time the JMSDF deployed as part of a multinational force, and was central to gaining a high degree of expertise in naval operations supporting international stability and security. Japan honed its expertise about international counterterrorism and counterpiracy operations, as well as the security of SLOCs from Japan to the Middle East. With respect to SLOC activities, the lesson learned was the need for advanced and ongoing coordination with nations bordering the entire length of the SLOC, without regard to a specific geographic radius or region. That concept mandated revision of Cold War limitations of JMSDF operations within a 1,000 nautical mile radius of Japan.[23]

High-quality Japanese maritime equipment and institutional experience have important roles in coalition operations. For example, JMSDF AEGIS escort cruisers have search, warning, and information collection capabilities that could be useful at any time. Japan is one of the few nations, including the United States and Spain, with AEGIS ships, which could be called important public property of the international community. Japan's P-3 patrol aircraft fleet is one of the largest in the world. Previously focused on antisubmarine warfare, the expanding, multipurpose capabilities of P-3s have been demonstrated in ongoing antipiracy operations off the coast of Somalia.[24]

Another notable SLOC-related lesson learned may be reflected in Japan's plans to give planes to the Philippines to use for patrols in the South China Sea. This move would deepen Tokyo's security ties with the Southeast Asian nation most at odds with Beijing over the disputed waterway. Four sources with knowledge of the matter told Reuters that Japan was looking to offer three Beechcraft TC-90 King Air planes that could be fitted with basic surface and air surveillance radar.[25] They said talks within the Japanese government were preliminary and would need to overcome legal hurdles. Japan has yet to formally propose the planes as an alternative to the more sophisticated Lockheed Martin P3-C aircraft that Manila wants to track Chinese submarine activity. Equipping Manila with maritime-capable patrol planes would dovetail with Prime Minister Shinzo Abe's more muscular security agenda but likely would anger China, which has repeatedly accused Japan of interfering in the South China Sea dispute.[26]

Ground Operations in Iraq

On December 9, 2003, the Japanese Diet passed the Humanitarian Relief and Iraqi Reconstruction Special Measures Law. This allowed the government to send the JSDF to Iraq. The government justified the operation based on UN Security Council Resolutions 1483 and 1511, which permitted the contribution of humanitarian and reconstructive assistance to Iraq. Troops from the Japan Ground Self Defense Force (JGSDF) 2nd Division selected personnel for deployment, and the first troops arrived at the Dutch military base in Samawah, Iraq, on January 19, 2004.[27]

This was, however, not a UN peacekeeping mission, but a "coalition of the willing" operation, organized by the United States, and without the detailed UN guidelines under which Japanese peacekeeping forces had previously operated. Much of the planning had to be conducted on a day-to-day basis through liaison with the Iraqi public and coalition forces. Although this ad hoc arrangement posed many challenges, Japan gained valuable experience participating in an actual multilateral operation for the first time by working closely with the Dutch, Australian, and British forces in Iraq. A principal outcome was that Japan learned to integrate its diplomatic and military resources into a process that differed significantly from its previous UN-organized deployments. Integration created a uniting principle among the various Japanese government agencies and JSDF services involved, and was essential to the safe completion of the mission.[28]

Comments by the first commander of the JGSDF troops in Iraq set the stage for understanding the overall Japanese experience. "We are here [in Iraq] to invest in the future and stabilize hearts. Our mission is to deepen ties not only with the Iraqi people, but with the region's nations as well. The mission of the JGSDF, who arrived in February 2004, is based on three pillars: medical support, water supply, and engineering support."[29]

The Iraq mission differed from previous JGSDF reconstruction efforts because the existing infrastructure in Samawah was already more highly developed than places such as Cambodia, where the basic construction skills of the JGSDF engineers had been sufficient. Rehabilitating Samawah required more sophisticated skills, which forced the JGSDF to contract out work to local civilian firms. This need for advanced construction techniques motivated the then-Japan Defense Agency, renamed the Ministry of Defense in January 2007, to dispatch civilian specialists in the engineering and construction fields from the Japan Defense Facilities Administration Agency in late 2004.[30] Linguists and other specialists from the Ministry of Foreign Affairs (MoFA) were also needed, and two were provided on a rotational basis out of Kuwait. The MoFA officials hired their own security guards and initially stayed inside the Dutch camp while the JGSDF was building its own base camp.

This duality eventually evolved into what came to be known as the "two wheels of the cart" approach. The JGSDF represented the humanitarian face of Japan's support through reconstruction activities, and MoFA represented the financial aspect through its dispersion of Official Development Assistance (ODA) funds. The ODA programs for Iraq were likewise divided into two types—local and national. In one, MoFA provided grassroots grants for the local government in Samawah area that authorities synchronized with JGSDF reconstruction efforts there. The other, the national program, was larger as

ODA grants for major humanitarian and reconstruction assistance were channeled through the central government in Baghdad.[31]

LTC Yoshiyuki Sakaemura, a later member of the JGSDF contingent in Samawah, provided more specific details on how matters developed.[32] Using ODA funds, the JGSDF contingent employed local people in mainly two areas: the management of the JGSDF contingent's camp and the reconstruction of public facilities. Inside the camp, locals worked as interpreters and mechanics to maintain and repair the facilities and equipment. Outside the camp, the JGSDF hired locals as technical engineers, interpreters, and coordinators between the JGSDF contingent and local authorities or contractors to reconstruct public facilities. Through their work with the JGSDF contingent, these local companies improved their capabilities, selection methods, and materials, and as of 2011 the companies were succeeding in reconstructing public facilities.

An example of collaboration between the operations of the JGSDF and the MoFA's ODA programs was the donation of medical equipment in Al Muthanna Province. The JGSDF contingent restored and rehabilitated the medical facilities and provided training on medical procedures. It was beyond the JGSDF's mandate to grant the appropriate supplies, such as medical equipment and ambulances. Instead, the Japanese MoFA, using ODA funds, provided grants to the locals to enable them to purchase such items. The JGSDF contingent restored or rehabilitated 30 primary healthcare centers while MoFA grants secured the medical equipment, medicine, ambulances, radios, and generators for the centers, that is, the actual equipment to bring the restored facilities online. The JGSDF contingent in turn offered the hands-on training for the ODA-granted medical equipment for Iraqi medical staffs. By combining advantages of the JSDF contingent's operations and the ODA's donation of medical equipment, the Japanese created synergy to improve overall health care environment in Al Muthanna Province.[33]

Several lessons learned related to local coordination and negotiation. Although the provincial government was supposed to be the focal point for determining local needs, it became evident there was also a very critical need to gain the understanding and meet the expectations of local leaders and people at the city, town, and village levels. Furthermore, the JGSDF was not working in isolation, and had to adjust to differences in the "local view" held by U.S., UK, and Dutch forces.[34]

Finally, the JGSDF and MoFA faced different local expectations than other coalition partners. The Iraqis viewed Japan as a major economic powerhouse, not a military one, and had unusually high levels of expectation for financial aid. The disillusioned Iraqis had anticipated full scale investment and expansion of facilities, businesses, and employment in the province. In reality, the laws governing the Japanese deployment only permitted "reconstruction" and "humanitarian assistance," not financial assistance.[35]

Resolving this perception gap proved to be a major challenge and was the source of constant local disagreements related to the scope and functionality of the reconstruction and assistance efforts. Defining needs started at the Provincial Development Coordination Committee (PRDC). However, as noted, it required constant interface with each provincial bureau, city and town council, and tribal chief.[36] The PRDC became the final point of decision for matters up and down the chain of command, but any decisions still required continual contact, coordination, and confirmation down to the local village and tribal leaders.[37] For instance, once a project was approved, evaluating the submissions and related cost proposals became a highly contentious issue at the budgetary and engineering levels. The potential for bribery and leaks of proprietary information was an ongoing concern. The PRDC had to fairly subdivide projects into city and local shares to ensure overall acceptance and support. Eventually, the PRDC established a model for an open bidding and review process that required explanations of costs and scope of work. The general populace accepted this solution.[38]

Support from the MoFA was critical in helping to ensure the smooth operation of this process. When working on a major project and defining critical items like cost, schedule, terms and conditions, it was necessary to check the various Arabic translations of proposals as paperwork moved from the provincial to local levels. The MoFA provided local interpreters and Arabic qualified MoFA officers to review and vet the final documentation.[39]

Conversely, in the early stages of implementing humanitarian and reconstruction assistance for Iraq, MoFA officials had difficulty identifying on-site development projects. Staff of the Japan International Cooperation Agency (JICA) were not initially permitted to enter Iraq. The JSDF contingent in Iraq, as a coalition member, shared the military information with the multinational force that the MoFA could not otherwise access, but that was very important for proper implementation of its projects. The JSDF contingent did mediate the relationship between the MoFA and the other coalition armed forces by serving as a "development facilitator" in support of the MoFA's ODA activities. The cooperation between the ODA and the JSDF enabled the personnel to work in a more secure environment. In addition, although the JSDF contingent was one of the coalition armed forces, it left a positive impression on the local people due to its close association with ODA, which provided financial assistance that the Iraqis expected from Japan. By supporting the ODA, the JSDF contingent contributed indirectly to improving security, in spite of not having an official direct security and stabilization mission.[40]

When the order for the redeployment of the JGSDF out of Iraq came in June 2006, all major Japanese news organizations carried editorials highlighting the operation's achievements: the JGSDF had not suffered any casualties, had not used force themselves, and had contributed to the reconstruction and stabilization of public life in the Samawah area.

The Iraq experience demonstrated that participation in further peacekeeping operations would require Japan to develop new systems for dispatching and maintaining troops in the field, new training programs, and more flexible personnel recruitment policies. To this end, the JGSDF established a training unit for international missions in March 2007 at the JGSDF's Camp Komakado in Gotenba, Shizuoka Prefecture. The new peacekeeping operations training unit educates JGSDF members on international law and on regulations governing the use of weapons. The same year, the JGSDF also created a 700-member rapid response regiment in anticipation of future overseas missions.[41] This should not be interpreted, however, to mean that Japan will become involved in every future international peacekeeping opportunity.[42]

The new Guidelines announced in April 2015, and passage of new laws on September 19, 2015, relating to the security of Japan, are a reflection of "lessons learned" from the experiences in Iraq and Afghanistan, and represent efforts to develop policy designed to implement those lessons. The opening statement of the Guidelines outlines the key focus of the U.S.–Japan agreement:

> In order to ensure Japan's peace and security under any circumstances, from peacetime to contingencies, and to promote a stable, peaceful, and prosperous Asia-Pacific region and beyond, bilateral security and defense cooperation will emphasize: seamless, robust, flexible, and effective bilateral responses; synergy across the two governments' national security policies; a whole-of-government Alliance approach; cooperation with regional and other partners, as well as international organizations; and the global nature of the U.S.-Japan Alliance.[43]

The perceived success of the Iraq deployment created a favorable political environment within Japan's Liberal Democratic Party and may have helped foster the passage of new laws on September 19, 2015, that have raised peacekeeping operations to a central priority of the JSDF on par with the defense of Japan.[44]

Perceptions of American Lessons Learned

A commentary by Professor Tomonori Yoshizaki of Japan's National Institute of Defense Studies (NIDS) on U.S. Army Field Manual 3-24, *Counterinsurgency*, (published in December 2006) provides some insights into Japan's potential role in future counterinsurgency operations. Professor Yoshizaki focused sharply on a section related to "Paradoxes of Counterinsurgency Operations."[45]

The first and most shocking paradox is that "Some of the best weapons for counterinsurgents [the U.S.] are not to shoot." This indicates a 180-degree about-face in the traditional U.S. approach to counterinsurgency, since the United States sought decisive battles to overthrow the Taliban in Afghanistan and the regime in Iraq. The second paradox is that "money is ammunition." Once security is restored, "dollars and ballots will have more important effects than bombs and bullets." In other words, coordination between reconstruction and restoration of security determines the success and failure of an operation. The third is that "Sometimes, the more you protect your force, the less secure you may be." Support from the people is indispensable for the suppression of insurgents. "If military forces remain in their compounds, they lose touch with the people," reinforcing fears on the part of the people with the end result of insurgents snatching the initiative away from stabilization forces. The fourth is that "Sometimes, the more force is used, the less effective it is." The use of force in a major way could provide insurgents with a good opportunity for their propaganda. Lastly, the fifth paradox is that "Sometimes doing nothing is the best reaction." Terrorist acts and guerrilla operations by insurgents are often aimed at provoking excessive responses from counterinsurgents. If the counterinsurgents respond to a provocation by opening fire on a crowd or executing a clearing operation, they may create more enemies among the otherwise apolitical indigenous population.[46]

The author then comments that the paradoxes presented in the *Counterinsurgency* Field Manual exactly describe the very restrictive stance of the JSDF in its international peace cooperation activities. It is possible to construe the JSDF's stance of not firing a shot and causing not a single casualty as performing a certain "function" in the form of humanitarian assistance and reconstruction support operations. According to Colonel Masahisa Sato, the commander of Japan's first contingent in Iraq, the JGSDF provided troops escalation control training to, insofar as possible, not create a situation where gunshots are fired. This suggests that the JGSDF troops operated under self-discipline, so that the existence of the JGSDF in Iraq would not provide a pretext that would lead to any deterioration in the country's security situation. As Professor Yuji Uesugi points out, the process of working out "techniques not to shoot and not to be shot" and creating a "sea of confidence and safety" present useful lessons for other countries as well.[47]

Yoshizaki goes on to acknowledge that the JGSDF in Iraq was not participating at the same level of responsibility and rules of engagement as those of other coalition forces. Current Japanese law, for example, did not allow the JSDF to engage in security, stability, and restoration (SSR) operations.

Thus, Japan's contribution was geared toward civilian assistance within the SSR context. At a meeting of the SSR Working Group for Afghanistan, Japan became a leading nation, together with the UN, in planning "disarmament, demobilization and reintegration (DDR) of ex-combatants," but the actual work was coordinated by civilians in the DDR unit of the Japanese embassy in Kabul. In the case of Iraq, when the JGSDF withdrew from Samawah, its commander delivered a note on the handover of its Samawah camp to the 10th Division of the Iraqi Army, but this hardly represents SSR. The contingent from the 10th Division, JGSDF left behind only tents, housing units, bullet-proof containers, television sets, refrigerators, beds, blankets and other fixtures as well as cafeteria facilities, air conditioners, generators and commercial off-the-shelf water supply systems. The JGSDF could not leave behind "anything that could pose security issues such as weapons, communication equipment and vehicles, according to under Japan's long-standing three principles for arms exports."[48]

The Afghan Experience

It has been widely publicized that the Japanese government has contributed greatly to Afghanistan's reconstruction and peace-building since the fall of the Taliban regime in 2001. It is not widely known, however, that many Japanese personnel have been engaged in-country supporting the Afghan people in returning to peaceful daily lives and reconstructing their country. Even less is known about what the Japanese did, how they struggled, and what they have accomplished in Afghanistan.[49]

In 1968 the Japanese government concluded a yen loan agreement with the government of Afghanistan for water supply projects. Thus, Japan's experience in Afghanistan pre-dates the 1991 JMSDF operations in the Persian Gulf by 23 years, and the JSDF deployments to Iraq by at least 36 years. It also means that the MoFA, not the Japan Defense Agency or its successor the Ministry of Defense, has been the primary overseer and director of Japanese activities and operations in Afghanistan.

In this capacity, two members of Peace Winds Japan, an NGO associated with MoFA, visited the province of Sar-e Pul in northern Afghanistan in July 2001, where nearly 60,000 people had evacuated from remote regions to the suburban plain in search of fresh water. Peace Winds Japan and other NGOs were taking part in the Japan Platform (JPF), and conducted a field survey from August 25 to September 7, 2001.[50] The Japan Platform is a system established by the MoFA in August 2000 in cooperation with the Japanese business community and NGOs. Its purpose is to enhance cooperation for the use of ODA funds with the private sector, and it is specifically designed to facilitate emergency humanitarian assistance activities implemented by Japanese NGOs effectively and quickly on the occasion of disasters and conflict, to avoid any delay in initiating the provisions of emergency humanitarian assistance, and to extend the effect of the activities.[51] (See note for further background on JPF.[52]) Just as the Peace Winds Japan staff moved to neighboring Pakistan, the 9/11 attacks occurred. Due to the 9/11 attacks, the JPF suspended its preparatory survey of relief activities inside Afghanistan and shifted its focus to supporting the refugees in neighboring countries, including Pakistan, Tajikistan, Uzbekistan, and Iran. Although these neighbors had closed their borders, they still received an influx of Afghan refugees. Conditions in existing refugee camps quickly deteriorated, and the JPF began relief activities for refugees in Pakistan.[53]

Following the U.S. military intervention and the rapid defeat of the Taliban, Japanese aid personnel returned to Kabul, Mazar-e Sharif, and other cities. From December 2001 to February 2002, emergency aid activities were underway in earnest. Japanese aid workers distributed relief supplies, conducted medical activities, supported domestic refugee camps, and provided mine risk education. The JPF's operations were Japan's first large-scale emergency aid activity and served a cumulative total of at least 100,000 people.[54] JICA set up its own office in Kabul and appointed Takanori Jibiki as its first Resident Representative in July 2002.[55]

Subsequently, based on the Bonn Accords of late 2001, the Group of Eight (G8) member states identified five key security issues for Afghanistan, with different countries assigned to each. The United States was responsible for creating a national army; Germany for reorganizing the police force; the United Kingdom for counternarcotics; and Italy for judicial reforms. Japan, meanwhile, worked together with the UN on disarmament, demobilization, and reintegration (DDR). The challenge of DDR—creating an environment that encouraged the soldiers of the tribal military cliques to turn in their weapons and leave their units to return to civil society—was regarded as one of the most difficult and important of the five key problems.[56] Although the military cliques (warlords) had created a military alliance to resist the Taliban, they had not agreed to disarm after the collapse of the Taliban regime. DDR is normally carried out after conflicts when there is an agreement between the military forces to disarm and a neutral organization (such as a UN peacekeeping mission) to oversee the implementation of the agreement. This was not the case for the DDR in Afghanistan, and the process had to proceed on a voluntary basis, based on the presidential decree that the national army would be the only legitimate army. To make disarmament a success, the Afghan government had to establish trust in the new national army, namely that it would be a politically neutral army and would provide for the defense of the entire country not just individual warlords. The DDR then became very closely linked to the reform of the national army.[57] The Afghan government declared the completion of the DDR program in December 2006.[58] The Japanese tried to promote disarmament, but deep-rooted vestiges of tribalism and warlord influence persisted within the country, regardless of the formation of an Afghan National Army. Further complicating matters, the Afghan government has even asked the warlords for assistance.[59]

In 2012, the JICA Research Institute summarized its experiences in Afghanistan. It described the situation there over the preceding 10 years as extremely unusual, even for a developing nation. The country faced a range of simultaneous challenges: the problems unique to countries that have experienced many years of war; difficulties resulting from the diversity of ethnic groups, languages, and religions; and an extremely unstable security situation. The Afghan people had been deprived of educational and employment opportunities after experiencing a long period of war, so development of human resources was necessary to provide aid effectively. The state framework, including the constitution, had to be rebuilt from scratch, and government administrative organizations had no semblance of organization.[60] In such circumstances, the Japanese turned to the Afghans they had trained earlier. The waterworks, hospitals, and television stations provided by Japanese aid in the 1970s prior to the Soviet invasion, as well as the Japanese-trained technical experts, became the foundation for post-2001 nation-building more than 20 years later. Tokyo's assistance programs for the reconstruction of Afghanistan from 2002–12, supplemented by the indigenous Japanese-trained skilled workers, enabled Japan to far surpass anything that they provided in the 1970s and to feel confident their efforts will surely continue to support nation-building for Afghanistan for many decades yet to come.[61]

An April 2015 MoFA report described relations with Afghanistan. At the July 2012 Tokyo Conference on Afghanistan, Japan announced that it would "provide up to around $3 billion (USD) of assistance to Afghanistan over about five years from 2012, in the fields of socioeconomic development and enhancement of security capacity."[62] As of February 2015, a total of $2.451 billion (USD) of assistance had been disbursed. Japan has also committed to assistance in three key areas: (1) Japan will pave the way for the Afghans to take their own security responsibilities by supporting the National Police (with salaries, training, and literacy education); (2) for reintegration and long-term reconciliation with insurgents, Japan will provide assistance for vocational training of former combatants as well as small-scale programs for job creation; and (3) based on Afghanistan's development strategy, Japan will provide assistance for Afghanistan's sustainable development focusing on the agricultural sector, infrastructure development, and human resource development, as well as education and health/medical care. The MoFA report

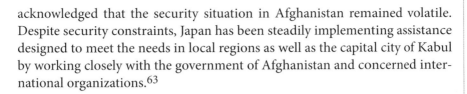

acknowledged that the security situation in Afghanistan remained volatile. Despite security constraints, Japan has been steadily implementing assistance designed to meet the needs in local regions as well as the capital city of Kabul by working closely with the government of Afghanistan and concerned international organizations.[63]

Observations and Conclusions

To what extent do the new (U.S.-Japan) Guidelines reflect lessons learned by Japan from the Iraq and Afghan wars and what are their implications for potential U.S. involvement in a confrontation between China and Japan?

The JMSDF and JGSDF activities in Iraq and Afghanistan created an awareness of the need for a "whole of government approach," and the importance of coalition coordination, intelligence sharing, and participation in international security and stabilization activities. The cooperation between the JGSDF and the MoFA in Iraq, and their "two wheels of the cart" approach, certainly reflects the former, and Japan's new legislation passed on September 19, 2015, to permit "collective defense" reflects cognizance of the importance of participation of civilian and military organizations as equal partners in coalition operations. The new laws allow the JSDF to defend the country's close allies in combat for the first time under its constitution, which renounces "war as a sovereign right of the nation and the threat or use of force as means of settling international disputes."[64] Another important lesson is that in the realm of international contributions to peace and security missions, *presence* and *visibility* are more important than financial contributions. Hence, it is reasonable to expect Japan will be a more active participant in UN and international coalition activities in the future. This may be reflected in the near term in South Sudan, where Japan is participating in the United Nations Mission in the Republic of South Sudan.

Japan's ongoing efforts in Afghanistan reflect efforts to cooperate with regional and other partners, as well as international organizations. They also demonstrate the global nature of the U.S.-Japan alliance. Japan's September 2015 legislation related to collective defense has drawn domestic and international protests based on concerns over being drawn into overseas conflicts and potential JSDF casualties.[65] However, it also reflects recognition of the importance of not only the U.S.-Japan alliance, but coalition cooperation and partnership.

JMSDF Admiral Tomohisa Takei's remarks in Washington, DC, on July 29, 2015, provide another indication of Japan's new security awareness.[66] Takei made no mention of North Korea, which has test-fired missiles over Japan, or the Senkaku Islands, claimed by China, or a resurgent Russia,

Japan's neighbor to the north. In his remarks at the Carnegie Endowment for International Peace, the admiral did not even talk much about "the Pacific," preferring the more expansive "Indo-Pacific." Instead of discussing northeast Asia, Takei warned that continued chaos in Somalia and new instability in Yemen keep piracy alive in the Gulf of Aden, where the Japan Maritime Self Defense Force provides escort ships and patrol aircraft. And, after some thinly veiled remarks about "a certain country" causing "anxiety and distrust" by its actions in the South China Sea, Takei came right out and named China, with an un-Japanese directness.

Another example of Japan's security perceptions can be found in the following overview of the *Defense of Japan 2015*, published by the *Japan Times*.[67]

> Japan's defense white paper for 2015 examines a range of global threats and pays particular attention to China's growing military assertiveness in the East China Sea and South China Sea, accusing it of "highhanded" actions to change the status quo by force. "Coupled with a lack of transparency in terms of military and security affairs, China's military development is of concern to the regional and international community, including our country," Defense Minister Gen Nakatani told a news conference following Cabinet approval of the annual paper. "Our country needs to observe it closely," he added. The white paper says in its assessment that China "has been continuing activities seen as high-handed to alter the status quo by force and has attempted to materialize its unilateral claim without making compromises." It adds that some of these activities "could trigger contingencies." China has been building an offshore gas platform in the East China Sea since June 2013, the paper says. Japan and China agreed in 2008 to jointly develop natural gas fields in the East China Sea, where the two countries have not agreed on a boundary between their exclusive economic zones. Under a demarcation Japan has proposed, China's new gas platform would lie on the Chinese side. The paper states Japan has raised its concerns over the project, and quotes "Our country has repeatedly lodged protests with China's unilateral development and urged it to stop the construction work." The reference to China's action in this matter was added after the LDP [Liberal Democratic Party] rejected the first draft. The party reportedly said it lacked details about China's building of a platform that it fears could be used for military purposes. The paper notes that China "routinely" sends ships to waters around the disputed Senkaku Islands in the East China Sea. On the situation in the South China Sea, the paper cites international concerns about China, including some expressed by the United States, saying it has

conducted reclamation work "rapidly" and "on a large scale" at seven reefs in the Spratly Islands. "China . . . is believed to be promoting the construction of infrastructures including a runway and port on parts of the reefs," the paper says. Beijing claims sovereignty over almost all of the South China Sea, but parts are also claimed by Brunei, Malaysia, the Philippines, Taiwan, and Vietnam. The paper notes that a Chinese fighter jet intercepted a U.S. Navy aircraft at close range in August last year.[68]

The *Defense of Japan 2015* focus on the East and South China Seas, and reference to events there that "could trigger contingencies," is noteworthy and indicative of a need for close cooperation and coordination by all concerned parties. However, there are other important evolutionary factors driving change in Japan's defense posture. These include the lessons learned from two decades of the JSDF gradually expanding regional and global missions, and a desire to maximize efficiencies in response to the changing nature and rising costs of military technology, fiscal constraints, a shrinking and aging population, and the Japanese public's persistent, deep-seated skepticism about military power. In response to these challenges, Prime Minister Abe and his predecessors have pursued incremental changes to bolster deterrence, to deepen cooperation and interoperability with the United States as well as other partners, and to facilitate a more rapid, flexible, and effective response to a range of perceived traditional and non-traditional security threats.[69]

Probably the greatest challenge in managing the U.S.-Japan Alliance in the coming years will be how to maintain synergy and formulate active, effective coordination across the two governments' national security policies to deal with the challenges of the international political, economic, and security environment both governments are facing.

CHAPTER 9
Perspectives of International Nongovernmental Organizations

Pauline H. Baker

A 2014 survey of global nongovernmental organizations (NGOs) conducted by European Universities on Professionalization on Humanitarian Action (EUPRHA) estimated roughly 4,400 NGOs then worked on humanitarian action on a daily basis worldwide. In 2010, the combined estimated total expenditure for international NGOs was U.S. $7.433 billion. Thirty-eight percent of this amount went to only five organizations: Doctors Without Borders (*Médecines sans Frontières* or MSF), Catholic Relief Services, Oxfam International, Save the Children Alliance, and World Vision International.[1] This paper explores the lessons learned by humanitarian NGOs such as these in the Iraq and Afghanistan wars.

There are three major types of NGOs concerned with issues of war and peace: 1) humanitarian and relief organizations that provide basic services directly to civilian populations, including refugees and war casualties; 2) democracy, rule of law, and human rights organizations that conduct investigations and advocate programs to promote their cause; and 3) mediation, conflict resolution, and peace-building organizations that run projects to reduce violence, advance peacebuilding, and promote state-building. There are also a number of smaller international NGOs, some of which partner with the larger entities, and several for-profit and non-profit development organizations, which concentrate on improving civilian livelihoods. Western think tanks are involved as well, and a growing number of local or national NGOs, often referred to as Southern International NGOs (SINGOs), receive direct funding from Western donors. Private-sector engagement is also increasing, although it still represents a comparatively small part of overall humanitarian and development resources and usually is limited to specific regions or contexts relevant to business interests.

This paper looks at the first cluster—humanitarian NGOs—many of which operate in the field throughout the conflict cycle: before the military arrives, during the conflict, and in the post-conflict stage. Humanitarian organizations are the ones that are most exposed to violence in war zones, and they are often closest to the people.

Including NGOs in a book on potential hostile forces is unusual. NGOs are not combatants. Although they have different perspectives, including occasionally being critical of military activities that encroach on their traditional field of operations, they are not "hostile" in the military sense of the term. Indeed, their role is critical in conflict zones, and the military often depends on them to help address social needs. There are also day-to-day interactions between the military and NGOs in the field that are often overlooked, and NGOs look to the military to provide them with a safe enabling environment. But new challenges are complicating civil-military relationships. Rising casualties among humanitarian workers and the tendency of aid donors to incorporate humanitarian strategies into their security campaigns pose enormous practical, ethical, and financial strains on humanitarian organizations that are yet to be resolved.

This paper examines three major NGO issues that have arisen in the Afghan and Iraq wars—security, shrinking humanitarian space, and funding. It concludes that, although each humanitarian organization has carved out its own doctrine and procedures, NGOs as a whole continue to uphold the classic Red Cross principles of neutrality, non-partisanship, and independence in some way. In the future, they are likely to adhere even more to these traditional principles, or devise innovative ways to apply them, in order to preserve their moral legitimacy, enhance physical security, sustain revenue, and fulfill their mission to protect civilians threatened by natural or manmade disasters.

Security

Security has become the most urgent issue of concern for NGOs operating in war zones. If ever there was an epochal event—a precise moment in time that serves as a reference point—demonstrating this point, it is the October 3, 2015, air attack by an American AC-130 gunship on a crowded hospital in Kunduz, Afghanistan. Run by MSF, a highly-respected international humanitarian organization, the hospital had been providing trauma medical services to war wounded, and its presence in the area was well-known. The attack occurred for over an hour, despite desperate calls by the staff to military authorities begging them to halt the mission, which killed 30 people, including patients still on operating tables and wounded in wheelchairs and beds. The incident triggered a firestorm of accusations and counter-accusations that shattered trust, ignited outrage, and complicated civil-military relations. It raised fundamental questions, not only about how to ensure civilian protection, but about the risks humanitarian workers were facing in the field, the wisdom of using airpower in counterinsurgency operations, and how the United States should proceed in the longest war in American history.

The incident reignited grievances that had been brewing for years. Stated simply, many NGOs feel that the U.S. government and its coalition partners lack a sense of urgency about NGO security and fail to appreciate the profound impact that changing trends in military engagement are having on their operations. The Kunduz attack keyed into these concerns. For one thing, NGO risk assessments presumed that the greatest physical threats would come from irregular forces and insurgents, not members of the Western coalition. The Kunduz attack showed that NGOs are threatened from all sides. The lethality of the attack also illustrated the increased violence directed against aid workers, a trend that had not been given much official government attention. And it highlighted the debate raging within the community about how to deal with military strategies that are encroaching on humanitarian imperatives.

The controversy goes beyond assigning blame. The U.S. military quickly took responsibility for the "mistake" and ordered an investigation, as did the Afghan government. In a highly unusual gesture, President Barack Obama personally apologized to MSF. But those actions did not address the fundamental issue: the military's tendency to dismiss such tragedies as "collateral damage" in the "fog of war" (which seems to belittle humanitarian lives), and to disregard the steady expansion of military actors into the humanitarian domain (which seems to distort the humanitarian mission).

Rising violence against humanitarians has not been given much media coverage or official attention. Yet, casualties among aid workers in the 21st century have increased substantially, chiefly from conflicts in Sudan (Darfur), Afghanistan, and Somalia.[2] Data collected by the Aid Worker Security Database showed a steady increase in the number of violent incidents affecting aid workers from 1997 to 2008. The average annual number of major incidents (127) from 2006 to 2008 represents an 89 percent increase from the previous three year period (2003 to 2005) and a 177 percent increase from the annual average going back to 1997.[3] According to the Humanitarian Policy Group, "all manner of NGOs have suffered increasing attacks irrespective of their funding and partnerships...and every major international humanitarian agency has paid for armed security in at least one operational context."[4]

This trend is partly a result of changing perceptions. Insurgents have grown increasingly suspicious of NGOs, viewing them as government collaborators, foreign agents, or integral parts of a wider Western agenda (an assumption that is underscored by the undeniable Western nature and orientation of the international aid community). Fewer NGOs are perceived as neutral by the beneficiary populations. Counterterrorism policies and Western efforts to "win the hearts and minds" of local populations have reinforced such suspicions. For example, when provincial reconstruction teams (PRTs) were first set up in Afghanistan, distinctions had been made between NGOs that were willing to work with the coalition forces and those that were not. That distinction began to dissolve when the military sent out its own humanitarian teams, with civilian clothes and vehicles similar to those used by NGOs, making it difficult for local populations and insurgents to see the difference.

The Kunduz tragedy also showed the failure of existing security measures. Before the attack, both MSF and the United States had taken standard precautions to ensure that there would be no accidental encounters of this kind. Strongly criticized in the past for causing excessive civilian casualties, the United States was cutting back on its air campaign. In fact, it had been in the process of drawing down its forces to comply with the 2016 deadline previously set by President Obama to reduce combat American forces in Afghanistan, except those needed for embassy protection.

For its part, MSF had also taken precautions. It had informed both the United States and Taliban forces of its identity and location. MSF had given its GPS coordinates to all combatants, put flags on the roof identifying the site as a hospital, and phoned U.S. authorities to call off the attack as soon as the hospital was fired upon. According to reports from those on the ground, the U.S. gunship continued the attack, aiming at the main hospital building for over a half hour after frantic calls for a cease fire.

Curiously, the Kunduz incident triggered a larger outcry than usual. Civilians had much higher casualties in other incidents that had occurred in the Afghan and Iraqi wars. Bombs and airstrikes destroyed hospitals in Yemen, Syria, and Afghanistan around that period, including an alleged Saudi-coalition airstrike on a hospital in Saada Province in Yemen just a few weeks after the one in Kunduz.[5] Except for protests from the Afghan government, they did not result in as much public criticism as the one in Kunduz.[6] Underscoring the seriousness with which it viewed the attack, MSF asked the International Humanitarian Fact-Finding Commission (IHFFC) to carry out an independent investigation. The IHFFC is not a UN body, but a mechanism created in 1991 from an additional protocol to the Geneva Conventions that governs the rules of war.[7] It had never been used before. The mechanism requires the consent of both the United States and Afghanistan, an unlikely occurrence.

A number of conditions were present that created, in effect, a "perfect storm" for a major controversy to erupt. First, there were operational errors, particularly the failure of the U.S. special operations forces to confirm the target visually before calling in the strike. The "eyes on the target" requirement was needed because the AC-130 gunship, which flies at a low altitude, relies on visual targeting, not GPS coordinates, to strike accurately on the ground.[8]

Second, the attack hit a hospital run by one of the best-known and highly respected NGOs in the world, which works in 80 countries, helps tens of millions of people, and won a Nobel Peace Prize in 1999. Kunduz represented the biggest loss of life in the history of the organization, and it closed down its operations in response. MSF had withdrawn from Afghanistan once before, following the killing of five of its aid workers by insurgents in 2004 after 24 years of working in the country. At that time, MSF said the U.S. coalition's attempt to use humanitarian aid to "win hearts and minds" had compromised the agency's neutrality and undermined Afghan trust in the organization, a frequent accusation that was shared by many humanitarian workers. The 2015 attack—this time from a U.S. strike—was particularly difficult for MSF to bear as it opened an old wound of suffering from attacks based on misperceptions. Stephen Cornish, the Executive Director of MSF in Canada, cited being seen as too close to the U.S. government as the reason why MSF was targeted by insurgents in 2004. Feeling vulnerable to attacks from both sides is why the organization relies on funding from private donors. "We don't take institutional or government funds for our work in contexts where it may appear to compromise our principles. It's not just a matter of pride—it's a matter of life and death, both for our patients and our workers," said Cornish.[9]

Third, U.S. trustworthiness suffered from the Kunduz attack, not only because of the high casualty rate and the fact that it occurred at a designated "protected site," one of several schools, hospitals, mosques, and other buildings that were supposed to be exempt from targeting. It also was because of multiple U.S. accounts of what had happened. Initially, the attack was described as a justified response to protect endangered American troops, implying that the Taliban was in the area. Then, the United States said it was a strike called in by Afghan forces when they came under fire, though MSF denied that there were any insurgents in the hospital. Finally, the U.S. commanding officer, General John F. Campbell, admitted that the strike was "a U.S. decision made within the U.S. chain of command" due to a "chain of mistakes" made by troops who "did not follow their own rules."[10] Three weeks after the attack, American investigators further revealed that Afghan and U.S. troops had been rushed from other areas to defend Kunduz from the Taliban assault on the town. The AC-130 pilots had not previously worked with either the Afghan or the U.S. special operations forces in that area. The operation was described by the Defense Department as "hasty" with "insufficient time for deliberate planning."[11]

Fourth, battlefield conditions were chaotic. Control of Kunduz was in flux. It had been overrun by the Taliban days earlier, the first time that the insurgency had taken control of a major urban center. The defeat was a severe blow to Afghan security forces and American strategy; it was seen as the biggest military victory for the Taliban since the U.S.-led invasion in 2001.

Indeed, according to the *New York Times*, the fall of Kunduz showed that the "expanding insurgency.... has spread through more of Afghanistan than at any point since the Taliban government was deposed."[12] Fifteen days after Kunduz fell to the Taliban, the city was retaken by Afghan forces, helped by U.S. air-strikes, but not before a terrible tragedy detracted from the battlefield victory.

Finally, there was the political context. President Obama was considering whether to delay the withdrawal of the remaining 9,800 American troops in the country by the end of 2016, as he had originally planned. The 2016 presidential campaign was also in full swing, politicizing issues of national security. On October 15, 2015—12 days after the attack on the hospital—Obama reluctantly announced that U.S. forces would extend their mission in Afghanistan until 2017, beyond his term of office. He said that Afghan forces were not ready to stand alone. No doubt, the defeat and recapture of Kunduz shaped the decision, and perhaps the hospital attack did too, but no mention of it was made in the President's statement.

The hospital attack was also pivotal because it raised questions about the morality of American military operations in the region as a whole. In the eyes of some NGOs, this incident was not only an unfortunate tragedy, it was an atrocity. MSF called it a war crime, accusing the United States of intentionally targeting civilians. As horrific as it was, however, unless intent is proven, historians are not likely to see this tragedy as morally equivalent to other post-9/11 human rights abuses committed in war zones, such as the Abu Ghraib prison in Iraq or the U.S. base in Guantánamo Bay, Cuba, where the most dangerous captured terrorists were held. Prisoners at the U.S. Army-run prison at Abu Ghraib were subjected to torture, sexual abuse, and murder, resulting in a major scandal and military court-martials. The prison was eventually closed, and a U.S. contractor that had helped run the detention center agreed to pay modest compensation to the victims' families. President Obama also pledged to close down the Guantánamo Bay prison (nicknamed Gitmo). During his tenure, hundreds of detainees were released or transferred to other countries, but by November 2015, the prison remained open, largely due to a congressional ban on the transfer of prisoners to U.S. soil; 114 men were still held, many without charge, including dozens who had reportedly been cleared for transfer out of the facility.[13]

The Kunduz attack probably will not be seen in the same vein as these scandals. The U.S. military accepted responsibility. According to Neta Crawford, NATO allies had earlier "changed their procedures for airstrikes in mid-2009—reducing their number and making the criteria for a strike more restrictive and the number of civilian deaths due to airstrikes had gradually decreased. By 2014, 2 percent of all casualties in Afghanistan were caused by pro-government airstrikes."[14]

Nonetheless, in the eyes of the NGO community the incident raises questions about the U.S. government's war strategy. Was this incident a sign that, in its frustration over the duration of the war, the United States would accept civilian deaths if suspected insurgents or terrorists were in the crosshairs? Media reports asserted that some U.S. analysts thought the hospital attack was justified because there had been reports that some patients affiliated with high-ranking Taliban insurgents were taking shelter in the hospital. But hospitalized wounded warriors are protected under international law.[15] "Even if there had been 'enemy' activity within the compound," wrote Jason Cone, the U.S. executive director of MSF, "the warring parties would still have been obligated by the laws of war to respect the protected status of hospitals, understand the nature of targeted structures, and factor in the potential civilian toll."[16]

The biggest military loss in this incident was U.S. credibility. As one commentator put it, "There is only so much distance we can claim."[17] Christopher Stokes, MSF's general director, stated that "the reality is the U.S. dropped those bombs."[18] "If a violation of international humanitarian law on this scale can be dismissed as a 'mistake,' 'the fog of war,' or even 'a terrible tragedy,'" said Jason Cone of MSF, "then all of our medical staff, projects, and patients in conflict zones could be jeopardized. What is at stake is the ability of humanitarian organizations to continue their life-saving work at the front lines of conflict."[19]

It did not take long for the headlines on Kunduz to fade from public view as other horrific incidents, such as the downing of a Russian civilian airliner in Egypt and a massive terrorist attack in Paris, both of which occurred a few weeks after the Kunduz attack, grabbed media attention. Nonetheless, the Kunduz hospital attack has been seared in the memory of the humanitarian community as a continuing reminder of the vulnerability of humanitarian workers.

Humanitarian Space

After security, a closely related concern of NGOs that emerged in the Afghan and Iraq wars is "shrinking humanitarian space," a term that refers to conditions that are reducing the ability of humanitarians to safely provide material goods and services to populations in need.

Humanitarian organizations began to find themselves confronted with environments that were far different than traditional battlefield configurations that were typical two decades before when most wars were between states, not within them. Previously, humanitarian workers operated in areas where fighting was minimal and their presence was not controversial. But the nature of war is changing. With rare exceptions, most post-Cold War wars are irregular or asymmetrical conflicts in which the frontlines are in constant flux and combatants include a diffuse array of nonstate militias and terrorist groups.

No longer can aid organizations assume that combatants will respect the right of credible humanitarian organizations to freely evaluate, deliver, and monitor assistance in an impartial and independent way, without fear of attack. NGOs also face growing disdain from host countries who suspect that they are aiding their enemies. In addition, they are being pushed by the UN to integrate humanitarian relief under the umbrella of its own agencies. The terrain of humanitarian action has thus been transformed, with fewer protections, heightened threat levels, more pressure to conform to national security interests, and growing skepticism by local populations.

The term "humanitarian space" is itself somewhat controversial. It was first coined during the Cold War era to describe the limitations placed on humanitarian agencies in Central America.[20] Its usage broadened in the 1990s when the then-President of MSF, Rony Brauman, invoked the term to describe the need for humanitarian organizations to be free from any political agenda. The International Committee of the Red Cross (ICRC) and other well-known organizations also adopted the phrase in the late 1990s. However, there have been some differences in how the term has been applied. Some NGOs, such as MSF, equate humanitarian space with respect for International Humanitarian Law. Some, like Mercy Corps and Save the Children, use the term to refer to specific conditions for operating locally, such as their objection to U.S. Agency for International Development's (USAID's) contract language that required prior agency approval for their contacts with the news media in Iraq.[21] Some, such as the International Rescue Committee, CARE, and World Vision, use the term to defend the primacy of their mission, declining to apply for USAID grants because they feel that providing basic services in the country took priority over promoting democracy and that other countries with pressing humanitarian crises, such as those in Africa, needed more help.[22] Some NGOs use it in reference to practical measures they want the military to provide to protect civilians, such as humanitarian corridors, refugee camps, demilitarized zones, and safe areas. Others, like the ICRC, equate humanitarian space with the principles of neutrality, non-partisanship, and independence. Still others employ the term to mean everyday challenges that limit action, such as administrative delays, transportation bottlenecks, criminality, local disputes, competition over resources, and other frustrations. Some interpret the term to refer simply to the deterioration of security.[23]

A report by the Overseas Development Institute (ODI) in London challenged the very idea of "shrinking humanitarian space" for lacking historical perspective. It claimed that there was never a humanitarian golden age when neutrality was respected and NGOs could work in conflict zones free of political considerations.[24] While admitting that humanitarian workers are in more danger from direct attacks than they have been in the past, the report argues that the number of workers in the field and the scope of their operations have also expanded massively. At least 200,000 aid workers are estimated to have been employed in 2010 by the UN and international NGOs, the report asserts, not including local NGOs. Proportionally, they are no more at risk than those who worked in the field earlier, ODI alleged.

This criticism is somewhat misleading. It lumps independent NGOs with UN workers, ignoring the fact that UN personnel have far more financial support and physical protection in the field, and that they perform a variety of functions, including armed peacekeeping, election monitoring, and diplomatic initiatives. The UN often coordinates operations of humanitarian organizations, especially in conflict zones, but the organizations are independent and do not necessarily answer to the UN or enjoy the same level of support. The ODI also lumps development personnel with humanitarians, obscuring the lines between development and relief. Development personnel work directly for national governments, with all the burdens and privileges that affords, whereas humanitarian organizations, though often funded by governments, are on their own. Sometimes NGOs hire local bodyguards, who may be linked to insurgents. That, of course, creates ethical and security issues that have not been fully resolved by the NGO community, including the fact that it makes the humanitarian organizations look like they are taking sides. The practice is frowned upon by donors as well. But NGOs who do this explain it as a temporary arrangement that allows them access to needy populations.

Whatever the definition used or the precise accuracy of the term, humanitarian organizations feel that their humanitarian space has narrowed. "If the military enjoyed increased hegemonic control of civil-military relations in Somalia and Kosovo," wrote Michael Pugh, an independent analyst, "then the evolution of this trend can be seen as complete in Afghanistan and Iraq."[25] NGO fears of encroachment were confirmed when Colin Powell, a retired four star general officer and then-U.S. Secretary of State, in 2001 explicitly described NGOs as "force multipliers," saying they were "an important part of our combat team."[26] While he meant it as a compliment to underscore the central importance of humanitarian assistance and he urged government officials to work toward having good relationships with NGOs, his language piqued NGO sensibilities about neutrality and were alarming. Indeed, an MFS spokesperson asserted that Powell's view exposed NGOs to more dangers. He cited a Taliban official who accused MSF of "spying for the Americans"—the alleged reason for the brutal killing of five of their workers in 2004—and warned that further attacks were to be expected.[27]

A concrete illustration of the militarization of humanitarian assistance is the decision by the United States and its allies to set up joint civil-military teams in Afghanistan that would combine security with development and humanitarian assistance. The military first established coordinating mechanisms through Coalition Humanitarian Liaison Cells (CHLCs—called "chicklets"). Soldiers performed a variety of functions in civilian clothes and supported USAID logistics and security in key urban areas. But a second mechanism went further. PRTs were a multinational initiative begun in 2002 that folded civilian tasks into the military stabilization strategy.

The PRTs were intended to link the central government with the poorest populations, bringing it closer to the people in rural areas. They were supposed to "win hearts and minds," showing how the Western presence was not a hostile foreign occupation, but a positive force. Twenty-six PRTs were set up, of which 12 were led and paid for by the U.S. Department of Defense and manned mostly by defense employees. Other members of the Western alliance set up their own PRTs, but there was no overall plan, methodology, exit strategy, or metrics of performance agreed upon. Though some officials claimed success, in the end, the PRTs were found to have suffered from poor planning, inadequate oversight, a lack of international coordination, corruption, and negative public perceptions due in part to the fact that PRTs were run by foreigners with little local input.

Most international NGOs were critical of the PRTs for their mission, structure, lack of effectiveness, and invasion of humanitarian space. They complained that soldiers worked in plain clothes, drove the same unmarked cars that NGOs used, and undertook many of the same reconstruction and relief projects that NGOs were doing. Some PRTs distributed leaflets that conditioned continued delivery of relief and aid on the willingness of the local population to provide information on the Taliban and al-Qaida, expanding the goals of the PRTs to intelligence collection as well. Local partners of CARE reported that the Taliban had warned them that if they accepted funding from the PRTs, their security would be threatened.[28]

After 10 years, the U.S. alliance decided to end the experiment. The Afghan government saw PRTs as a parallel government and refused to take them over. The UN declined to run them. In 2012, they were shut down completely. Although there were some accomplishments, such as new schools, there was little to show for the billions of dollars spent.

The NGO experience in Iraq was somewhat different than in Afghanistan. NGOs had operated in Afghanistan since the 1950s and there were large numbers of local relief and reconstruction organizations there with experience. By contrast, there was virtually no civil society in Saddam Hussein's Iraq, and international NGOs had little presence in the country when the 2003 invasion occurred. In addition, Afghanistan's battleground consisted of irregular warfare after the Taliban was overthrown. The United States aimed at stabilization of a poor, largely underdeveloped tribal society. Iraq's battle-ground consisted of conventional war plans at the outset and, after the over-throw of Saddam Hussein, the stabilization effort focused on de-Baathification, a process that essentially destabilized the country by dismantling all the state institutions, causing widespread unemployment and the demobilization of an army whose troops had nowhere to go. Some of the discharged soldiers became insurgents as the situation deteriorated. Iraq was also a more developed coun-try than Afghanistan, with an educated population, a natural resource base, and better infrastructure. Many thought, prematurely, that this would negate the need for substantial international humanitarian relief.

The heightened level of sectarian violence that followed the overthrow of Saddam Hussein soon disabused people of the notion of an easy ride to sta-bility. The intense bloodletting discouraged humanitarian organizations from engaging at first. As time passed, humanitarian organizations moved in where they could. The military coordinated with NGOs, but the relationship was tense since many of the humanitarian organizations questioned the justness of the war and took a strong stand against it. The military also confronted an unanticipated insurgency that endangered security, obstructed access routes, and undermined safe environments for the humanitarians.[29]

In addition, the United States initially decided to unify the entire stabi-lization effort in Iraq, placing security, governance, humanitarian response, and reconstruction under the control of the Department of Defense. Dep-uty Assistant Secretary of Defense for Stability Operations Joseph Collins, the main Defense Department interlocutor with the NGO community, said that the decision to place the management of humanitarian and recon-struction work within the Pentagon was made on the basis of an assess-ment of lessons learned from recent post-conflict efforts. The Pentagon felt that a single command of all aspects of the post-conflict response was essential to avoid the confusion and difficulties of coordinating so many diverse actors—government leaders, peacekeeping forces, UN agencies, and NGOs—that had plagued efforts in Kosovo and Afghanistan.[30] The United States required NGOs to emphasize their links to the government if they wanted to be funded. Although the State Department and USAID got heavily involved in Iraq by mid-2004, the pressure was still on for NGOs to conform to government requirements. USAID Director Andrew Natsios echoed Sec-retary Powell's view, cited earlier, that NGO work was inextricably linked to America's strategic goals in Iraq.

This centralized approach by the U.S. government put international NGOs in a bind. Many depended upon U.S. government funds to provide a humani-tarian response, but accepting these terms meant that they were surrendering to a forced association that would put their staff in danger. The International Rescue Committee withdrew, but other NGOs, such as CARE and Save the Children, took a different tact. They required a clause be included in their agreements that enabled them to report only to civilian agencies. Technically, this allowed them to appear to be working with civilians, but it is not clear that it had any measurable effect on local perceptions or resolved the larger security problem. InterAction, the U.S.-based membership organization for relief and development NGOs, called for the UN to be the coordinator of humanitarian and reconstruction efforts instead of the U.S. government. The UN did get involved in Iraq but pulled out temporarily after a truck bomb killed 23 people in August 2003 at the UN headquarters in Baghdad, including Sergio Viera de Mello, who headed the mission. That attack underscored the risks that all non-military actors were facing. Oxfam, an international confederation of NGOs, left the country, citing its belief that international organizations were becoming increasingly targeted. Others closed down for a short time, moved their staff to satellite offices in neighboring countries, or downsized and called for more security.[31] But the United States continued to tie its NGO funding to counterinsurgency and counterterrorism efforts, a practice that it extended elsewhere, such as Pakistan.

To many NGOs, this meant that humanitarian space was becoming part of the battlespace. In an article in the *New Republic*, David Rieff, a foreign policy analyst, chastised the United States for using NGOs as "pawns in the war on terrorism."[32] NGOs that agreed to work with the U.S. government, albeit at arm's length, found that they could not sufficiently maintain distance and a working relationship with the U.S. government. Staff complained that the distinction between those with guns and those who had come to provide humanitarian relief was often compromised or little understood by civilian populations.[33] Most of the humanitarian organizations had to be based in the "Green Zone," which they felt skewed their perception of the situation on the ground, inhibited their access to the public, and made them appear as spies affiliated with occupation forces. A 2007 report by the NGO Coordination Committee in Iraq (NCCI), an independent network of NGOs formed in 2003, concluded that, with the notable exception of the ICRC, the requirements imposed by linking humanitarian aid to counterinsurgency strategy undermined their ability to do their work. Their report concluded that the NGO community had "failed to respond to the needs in Iraq," because they had 1) not "adapted and adjusted their responses to the evolving and complex context," 2) "focused on Government capacity and reconstruction—which has been a slow process producing few milestones," and 3) "lacked acceptance among the Iraqi population due to 12 years of sanctions against Iraq and the need to use military escorts for their logistics and security."[34]

The ICRC exception points to an interesting split within the humanitarian community. In balancing adherence to the principles of neutrality and impartiality with managing everyday realities, the ICRC carved out a unique rationale to explain its acceptance of the approach advocated by the government. It argued that there is a hierarchy within the set of humanitarian principles, with the most important obligation being adherence to the belief that "the humanitarian imperative comes first."[35] In other words, regardless of the perceived association with counterterrorism strategy or the risks that this implies for its workers, the humanitarian obligation is to "stand and deliver." This contrasts with the position of MSF, which is equally emphatic about the importance of maintaining neutrality and impartiality to fulfill its mission. Although these positions represent two ends of a continuum, the gap was not as wide as it appears. Other NGOs adopted the "stand and deliver" position, bending toward the ICRC stance. But even the ICRC recognized the need to take account of the dangers. It backed off the "stand and deliver" imperative and reduced its staff by half after the devastating Taliban attack on the UN headquarters in Kabul in 2003.

In a study by World Vision, NGOs were categorized into three schools of thought:[36]

1. *The Refuseniks*, who advocate no military contact, particularly at the field level, and strictly uphold NGO principles (e.g., MSF).

2. *Principled Pragmatists*, who attempt to uphold humanitarian principles while also accepting certain trade-offs to find the best means of operating in terms of security and logistical support, (e.g., World Vision).

3. *Ambivalents*, who are neither for, nor against, military engagement. These may be multi-mandated agencies who are pursuing development, emergency humanitarian, and advocacy needs simultaneously, or agencies that decide to apply the intended principles to each specific country context where they work in the same operating space as military forces (e.g., CARE).

The World Vision study also made an important observation regarding how the military understands the notion of humanitarian space. It reported that in interviews it had conducted, "military actors…tended to view [humanitarian space] as physical operating space, and thus were unable to comprehend why NGOs would argue for their own bubble of operations, given that in reality the 'humanitarian' and 'military' or 'security' spheres of action necessarily overlap and are barely distinguishable in some cases."[37] World Vision's remedy was to propose a different term—"humanitarian operating environment"—and to advise NGOs to "emphasize to military and government actors that within such an environment, NGOs expect to be able to operate independently and impartially, without fear of attack."[38] The true meaning of "humanitarian space," the report argued, is for NGOs "to maintain their ability to assist populations in need, not constrained by political or physical barriers to their work."[39] Although it is doubtful that a new term will resolve this complex issue, World Vision accurately explained the gap between military and NGO interpretations of humanitarian space.

The ICRC, a preeminent global organization that provides humanitarian assistance to civilians in natural disasters and wars, is in a league of its own. Although often grouped with NGOs, it is actually a private association formed under the Swiss Civil Code in 1863 that adheres to the principles of the Geneva Conventions.[40] It has "delegations" in over 50 countries and an annual budget over $550 million, most of which comes from governments—the United States, the European Union, Scandinavian countries, and Switzerland. Staff members are known as "delegates" who work with national Red Cross and Red Crescent societies in the field, mostly through local workers. It has wrestled for years with the ethical issues posed by neutrality and impartiality. Sometimes it has chosen to speak out against governments that commit human rights abuses (as in Serbian detention camps in Bosnia) and sometimes it has chosen to remain silent (as in its failure to reveal what it knew about Nazi concentration camps and extermination of the Jews in World War II). It insists it is independent, distancing itself not only from governments but also from other NGOs and UN agencies. Its operating mantra is "first in and last out." The commitment to retaining access to all sides in war zones has resulted in the ICRC taking courageous stances in the face of danger. For example, it remained in Bosnian Serb territory in 1995 during NATO airstrikes, though NGOs from NATO countries were evacuated. It stayed in Kabul to keep hospitals running when Tomahawk missiles attacked an Afghan facility in 1998 that the United States said was a terrorist training camp, though the UN and NGOs left. And it stayed in Chechnya, where six of its workers were murdered in 1996. Its "stand and deliver" motto allows it to work within government guidelines, but the ICRC retains its neutrality by refusing to accept military escorts for its convoys or to post armed guards inside its hospitals.

As time passed and violence mounted in Iraq, NGOs that stayed in the country ran into skepticism, mistrust, and distain from the local population. Iraqi expectations of NGOs had been high and when they were not fulfilled, public opinion turned on them. They were accused of ulterior motives, such as working for money, intelligence agencies, or missionary purposes.[41] Even local NGOs began to be viewed with increasing skepticism by the public, as they were seen as vehicles of local politicians and strongmen. The Iraqi Red Crescent, for example, was said to be linked to Iraqi Prime Minister Nouri al Maliki's Da'wa Party, though it denied the accusation.

Funding

As the U.S. military presence in Iraq waned, Western funding of humanitarian aid declined. The number of NGOs operating in Iraq was never authoritatively established, but NCCI calculated that there were about 80 international humanitarian NGOs, and 200 newly formed Iraqi humanitarian NGOs in the country in 2003, when the United States removed Saddam Hussein. In all, according to a local charity, this number grew to roughly 12,000 NGOs by 2006—including democracy advocates, human rights activists, employment counselors, reconciliation organizations, humanitarian organizations, and so-called "briefcase NGOs."[42] By 2013, only about 2,000 NGOs were said to remain due to funding cuts and security threats. Between 2003 and 2007, 94 aid workers were killed in Iraq.[43]

Iraq's lucrative oil resources and its status as a middle-income country also played a role in the reduction of humanitarian workers, as donors felt that a larger proportion of funding should be borne by the Iraqi government. At the same time, security worsened. NGOs coped by maintaining lower profiles to avoid becoming targets. They did not reveal where their funding came from or with whom they were partnering. They minimized communications and information sharing with coalition forces. They adopted remote programming strategies, relocating to safehavens, such as the more stable Kurdish region, and they partnered more with local NGOs. The situation led to a "bunkerization" mentality in which NGOs retreated into fortified compounds, residences, and offices; adopted restrictive travel policies; and outsourced activities to subcontractors. This distanced humanitarian aid organizations from the societies in which they worked.[44] Effectiveness declined as access became more restricted, the quality of the aid delivered was questioned, and aid organizations had less information about actual conditions on the ground.

The enactment of counterterrorism laws and other security measures had an impact on financial flows as well. It criminalized the transfer of resources to individuals or groups suspected of being affiliated with terrorists. Even if the humanitarian nature of transactions was well established and there was no evidence of any intent to support terrorist groups, international NGOs that accepted donor funding were required to comply with new security regulations that raised operating costs, slowed down administrative functions, undermined humanitarian partnerships, reduced access, and made humanitarian workers personally responsible for any infractions.

In 2002, USAID required NGOs to sign grant agreements that included a clause that: 1) reminded them of the ban on transactions with organizations on the list of Specially Designated Nationals,[45] 2) required them to certify that grant funds would not assist any terrorist activity, and 3) required that they have a Partner Vetting System to ensure that there would be no inadvertent transfer of funds to terrorists. This was a serious burden for NGOs. Most did not have the capacity to screen foreign nationals, and they did not want to be put in a position in which they would appear to be working with military and intelligence organizations.

These laws and regulations significantly narrowed the operational freedom of NGOs. For example, sometimes local strongmen require humanitarian organizations in dangerous areas to pay registration fees or "taxes" and to tolerate a diversion of resources. Military, diplomatic, and intelligence agencies face similar demands in conflicted territories. They, too, have been known to tolerate some aid diversion and have "paid off" local leaders as "the cost of doing business." The NGO view, by and large, was that such practices should be avoided, but if they enabled access, they could be tolerated so long as they did not significantly benefit the military situation to the advantage of one side over the other. But the new counterterrorism regulations had no such provision. Unintentional "material support" to armed opposition groups or listed individuals constituted potential violations of the law, resulting in criminal liability. Understandably, this new operating environment generated considerable concern within the NGO community. Tensions rose as the U.S. government provided different definitions of what constituted "material support" and "terrorism." Some agencies side-stepped the requirements by adopting a "don't ask, don't tell" policy or by applying different standards to different conflicts. A representative of a donor country who was interviewed on this issue revealed that the United States was not applying the new regulations with any degree of uniformity or consistency: "I am not being asked to apply to same level of scrutiny in Afghanistan as in Somalia."[46] The ambiguity did not help clarify the situation for NGOs in any meaningful way; there was always the threat of prosecution if they crossed the line.

Counterterrorism laws also posed a fundamental ethical dilemma for NGOs. On the one hand, they had to conform to international humanitarian law, which does not draw a distinction between victims and perpetrators of war. On the other hand, they were being forced to comply with counterterrorism laws that say helping a victim who aids, or is affiliated with, terrorism and other offenses is a criminal offense. Some NGOs chose not to engage with proscribed groups or avoided them out of fear of prosecution. Others abstained from accepting government donations to avoid the conflict altogether. MSF included a generic exemption clause in its contracts that said that nothing in its donor agreements "shall be interpreted in a way that prevents MSF from fulfilling its mission as an impartial humanitarian actor bound by medical ethics."[47]

A study by the Humanitarian Study Group documented the impact of counterterrorism requirements on donations and operating efficiency.[48] Some donors withheld funds, or threatened to do so, when NGO compliance was judged inadequate. Administrative burdens mounted, delaying the timeliness and efficiency of humanitarian aid. Humanitarian workers were reluctant to go to high risk areas. Humanitarian bureaucracy grew as NGOs had to devote substantial staff time and financial resources to comply with the rules, such as applying for exemptions, scrutinizing lists, vetting recipients, and collecting personal information. Charitable giving became less transparent and accountable. Private donors redirected their contributions to less regulated organizations, using cash, which is more difficult to track. Concern about banking restrictions also affected transfers to and from Islamic organizations and may have encouraged diaspora communities in extreme emergencies, like the 2010 Pakistan floods that put one-fifth of the country's landmass under water and affected 20 million people, to give cash donations to individuals. This, in turn, opened up opportunities for money laundering. In the long term, the threat of criminal sanctions added another barrier blocking open discussions and information sharing between humanitarian organizations and donor officials.

Although the vast majority of NGOs evidently complied with the demands, it made the NGO community more cautious about publicly discussing their activities. Some may be reluctant to admit that they have complied with certain conditions or restrictions, and others may not want to suggest that they could be operating in violation of them, cultivating an atmosphere of self-censorship. The net outcome was that the political strategy, which had been designed to fight terrorism, had the unintended effect of constraining NGOs, narrowing the humanitarian space in which they had traditionally operated, and undermining their ability to lessen tensions on the ground.

NGOs are not as dependent upon official funding as is commonly thought. In 2012, official funding from U.S. government agencies and other official donors represented about 25 percent of the total revenue of all NGOs registered with USAID that provide relief and development services.[49] (This omits many international NGOs that do not receive grants or contracts from the United States and are involved in missions other than relief and development.) Private donations, including cash and in-kind contributions, represented 57 percent of the total revenue of international NGOs, and other revenue (i.e., sales, user fees, and investment income) represented the remaining 18 percent.[50] By contrast, private funding accounted for only 5 percent of UN income and 28 percent of income for the Red Cross Movement.

Among government donors, the United States is the biggest contributor to humanitarian aid, but the picture is somewhat skewed. American aid soared in Afghanistan and Iraq after the military interventions, greatly enlarging the reservoir of funding that NGOs could access. The NGOs that were funded by the United States were limited to those that had the ability to provide relief in war conditions, meaning that the organizations that were considered qualified were those that had worked in Afghanistan and Iraq before the military interventions. However, other NGOs with significant private resources also flocked to these countries. MSF and Care International in Afghanistan both refused government money for these engagements because they objected to the militarization and conditionality of official assistance. Of all the major international humanitarian organizations, MSF receives the largest proportion of its income from private sources. Generally, only 10 percent of its budget is based on institutional or government donations. In 2010, it received a staggering $1 billion in private funding. "If it were a country," commented one report, "MSF would have been the second largest humanitarian donor after the United States and ahead of the United Kingdom."[51] Faith-based NGOs, such as Catholic Relief Services, also have access to independent funding and, like MSF, can afford to reject official donations.

Private funding is a vital component of financing and the single most important factor that allows NGOs to be independent, both in name and in practice. Unlike official donations, private contributions are not a zero-sum game in which the fundraising success of one NGO is a loss for others. All NGOs with operations in Afghanistan and Iraq seem to have benefited from the fundraising efforts of their peers (or competitors) because the publicity raised awareness of need, expanding the collective pool of contributions. Media coverage also helped expand private contributions, especially when civilian suffering was widely depicted in both traditional and social media. For example, in the Syrian war, donations to NGOs increased in 2015 when pictures were aired of the body of a three-year Syrian refugee boy who drowned while escaping the conflict, along with his mother and brother, after his boat capsized.[52]

But long wars tend to bring "compassion fatigue." Controversy over the rationale and effectiveness of military interventions, media reports on pervasive corruption and waste, and lack of success in stabilizing the situations generate an impression that recipients either do not deserve support or misuse it. Under these conditions, the closer the NGO community gets to the official community, the harder it is for them to sustain their identity as independent and non-partisan providers of humanitarian relief.

Another common misperception is that NGOs compete fiercely for government resources, despite the risks, as a way to prevail in the humanitarian marketplace. Country choice, it has been alleged, is not based so much on need, as on proximity to acquiring government funds. NGOs go where the wars are for monetary reasons. This does not seem to be true in Afghanistan and Iraq. In a study of NGO activity in these two countries, Youngwan Kim and Peter Nunnecamp, two researchers from South Korea and Germany, found that there "is no compelling evidence that it pays for NGOs to engage where the United States intervenes."[53] In other words, NGOs do not necessarily obtain easier access to government funding by engaging in high-risk endeavors where the U.S. military is active, as compared to NGOs that chose not to engage.[54] Official donations do not always make up for the loss of private contributions, especially if there are mounting doubts about the rationale of the wars, the effectiveness of the U.S. presence, and the integrity and performance of the host governments.

Because private funding is the most important source of support for NGOs, it is in the financial as well as the security interest of the organizations to retain their distinct identity and reputation for independence to appeal to prospective donors. Those NGOs that do not have the luxury of significant private funding, however, are much more likely to work in dangerous zones and are less likely to be able to stand their ground. The larger and better-known NGOs have more freedom of action whereas the smaller and lesser-known NGOs are more vulnerable to government influence. When the host government also becomes unfriendly, many NGOs then may confront existential problems. In 2012, when it was clear the United States was downsizing its military presence in Afghanistan, Kabul ordered 175 local NGOs to shut down, ostensibly because they failed to submit annual reports due to inefficiency, corruption, and lack of oversight. As a result, the operating environment for NGOs, both international and local, became highly unfavorable and donations began to dry up. This raised further doubts about the ability of Afghanistan to care for the welfare of its own citizens after NATO combat troops depart.[55]

Conclusions

Three major trends in the Afghanistan and Iraqi wars impacted the ability of international humanitarian NGOs to fulfill their missions. The first was worsening security that resulted in direct attacks against aid workers, despite precautions designed to avoid such tragedies. The second was a "shrinking humanitarian space" that incorporated humanitarian operations into wider U.S. national security objectives, such as counterterrorism and counterinsurgency. The third trend concerned funding. Large NGOs receive a greater share of their revenue from private sources than from official government donors, enabling them to assert their independence, but their operational freedom was still affected by concerns over security, shrinking humanitarian space, and the resulting impact these trends had on private donations.

NGOs are thus torn between two contradictory poles. On the one hand, they can maintain their independence and shape their terms of engagement with the military as long as private funding is available. On the other hand, they have a smaller space in which to exercise that independence due to increased physical threats to their staff and tighter counterterrorism laws that require them to conform to U.S. government policies. Whether they are *refuseniks, principled pragmatists,* or *ambivalents,* NGOs are likely to invoke humanitarian principles of neutrality, non-partisanship, and independence in some form in order to enhance their security and legitimacy. If NGOs are to play a meaningful role in the stabilization of fragile states, then donors and governments need to devise approaches that will protect them physically and respect them operationally as they navigate increasingly dangerous and complex environments.

CHAPTER 10
Learning by Insurgents

Lawrence E. Cline

It long has been a truism that insurgents win by simply not losing. This precept certainly has been reinforced following U.S. interventions in Iraq and Afghanistan. In many ways, the survival—and in some cases, the relative thriving—of insurgent groups may be considered as somewhat Darwinian, in which only the most capable groups and individuals survive.[1] In large measure, this of course is physical survival. Beyond this, however—and equally important—is that the message of these groups also survives. Battlefield success may in fact be less crucial than the war of the idea. In many ways, the most successful lesson incorporated by modern insurgent movements has been that of the absolute criticality of effective information operations.

One key point needs to be stressed about learning and changes in organization and operations: both insurgents and counterinsurgents are (or at least should be) learning groups and individuals. Both are simultaneously learning from each other. As General John Abizaid, then commanding general of the United States Central Command, noted early in the U.S. war in Iraq, the insurgent campaign "is getting more organized, and it is learning. It is adapting, it is adapting to our tactics, techniques and procedures, and we've got to adapt to their tactics, techniques and procedures."[2] Ultimately, whichever side is better at learning and more skilled at adaptations based on this learning probably will prevail.

One other important point regarding insurgent group learning is that for those organizations expecting survival, such learning is cumulative. That is, successful groups not only learn from their own experience, but also incorporate lessons learned from other groups, both contemporaneous and historical. A good example of how this has worked in practice was the so-called Manchester Manual, an operational training document published by al-Qaida and seized by British police in a raid in Manchester, United Kingdom, in 2000. This manual provided basic instruction for al-Qaida members. Particularly in the section on intelligence collection and counterintelligence, many of the tactics, techniques, and procedures would look familiar to any Western intelligence officer.[3] Such willingness to learn from not only one's own experiences but also those of opponents suggests an active learning organization. This of course is a critical advantage for such groups.[4] In Iraq during the U.S. occupation, insurgents obtained many training manuals from the Iraqi army. As Ahmed S. Hashim noted, "They have apparently sought to learn from more established and successful groups elsewhere, and have studied the tactics of Hezbollah and Palestinian groups such as Al-Aqsa Martyrs' Brigades and HAMAS."[5] Likewise, another al-Qaida publication, *al Baqaa fi al-Zuruf al-Sa'ba* (Survival in Difficult Circumstances) is a translation of a U.S. field manual.[6]

The focus of this chapter is on three movements. The first two are those the United States faced in Iraq and Afghanistan. In some ways, these two cases must be viewed in terms of general movements rather than "pure" organizations. In both cases, multiple groups have been involved, with varying degrees of success. Generally, however, the main focus will be on al-Qaida in Iraq (AQI) and the Taliban in Afghanistan. The third group might be viewed as the lineal descendent of AQI: the self-proclaimed Islamic State of Iraq and the Levant (ISIL).[7] ISIL will receive the most attention because it thus far has proven to be the most successful of these groups.

Organizational Structure

Newer groups, particularly ISIL, appear recently to have learned a number of organizational lessons. In the early 2000s, it was a truism among most analysts that the basic rule for success as a terrorist group was to shift from "old" hierarchical structures to a network structure.[8] Certainly, groups such as al-Qaida seemed to embrace networking, with concomitant success. Groups that were very hierarchical were subject to decapitation strategies; most such groups seemed to be fading away. Purely (or overwhelmingly) networked groups have had a number of advantages. They are more adaptable, the individual components are harder to counter, and the "centers of gravity" are more difficult to identify and target. In addition, they can provide an overall ideological base for the continuance of a widespread and long-term movement. Although the concept of "fourth generation warfare" may in some ways be viewed as somewhat ahistorical, Thomas X. Hammes offers some useful insights into this approach:

> The United States must understand that fourth-generation organizations are different. Since Mao, they have focused on the long-term political viability of the movement rather than on its short-term tactical effectiveness. They do not see themselves as military organizations but rather as webs that generate the political power central to this type of warfare. Thus, these organizations are unified by ideas. The leadership and the organizations are networked to provide for survivability and continuity when attacked. And the leadership recognizes that their most important function is to sustain the idea and the organizations, not simply to win on the battlefield.[9]

At the same time, however, groups based on a purely network structure faced one critical problem. This was to translate short-term successes—some of which, such as the 9/11 attacks, Bali bombings, the London subway, and Spanish railroad attacks, represented major individual victories—into larger and longer-term strategic outcomes. Likewise, networks inherently feed on successes; potential recruits and other forms of support tend to gravitate to networks that show prospects for achieving their goals. Retaining the initiative may be the most critical lesson that such groups have learned.

Personalities and leadership also continue to play a role in networked ideological movements. According to two major ideologues—Abu Muhammad al-Maqdisi and Abu Qatada—who have a long history of supporting al-Qaida and who are known to have had close ties with the current leadership, much of the network system of al-Qaida has in fact collapsed after the death of Usama bin Ladin.[10]

Groups that have shown the better chances of long-term success generally have formed a combination of hierarchy and network.[11] The admixture has varied with the environment and with each group's particular objectives, but both elements seem to have been critical, particularly for insurgent organizations. One lesson that ISIL apparently has taken to heart is the need to strengthen alliances with groups that might prove useful. In particular, ISIL seems to have been willing to work with former Baathists who never reconciled with the Iraqi government.[12] Many of these groups (and individuals) never accepted direct alliances with AQI, but remained inalterably opposed to U.S. occupation.[13] As such, the native Iraqis probably are viewed as more "authentic" by much of the Iraqi Sunni populace than was AQI with its preponderance of foreign fighters; ISIL seems to have learned to take better advantage of Iraqis, even if they came out of exile. Two caveats should be noted, however. The first is that such alliances have been rare to nonexistent with most other jihadist groups; ISIL in fact has been more likely to fight them than to ally with them. Fellow jihadists are more likely to be viewed as direct competitors for recruiting potential supporters; therefore, opposing like-minded (in theory) groups likely is in the long-term interests of ISIL. The second note is that ISIL certainly is using a large number (and probably a preponderance) of foreign fighters both in Iraq and Syria. The point for ISIL is that using local elements who possess critical skills and local knowledge and connections can provide critical enablers for their operations even if the bulk of their fighters are not local.

Spiegel Online has published what it states are organizational documents for ISIL found in Syria, which reportedly originally belonged to Samir Abd Muhammad al-Khlifawi, also known as Haji Bakr, a senior leader in ISIL.[14] Although a sole source, the documents fit with other reporting. They indicate a group whose organization and structure were carefully planned from the start, rather than an organically developing loose network. Almost certainly as a result of learning lessons from American successes in rolling up AQI networks earlier, based in large measure on security weaknesses within and between AQI cells, the ISIL organizational structure was built around a multi-layered security and counterintelligence system.

Also, from the beginning, ISIL stressed the need to collect local intelligence. According to some documents, elements of information included:

- List the powerful families.
- Name the powerful individuals in these families.
- Find out their sources of income.
- Identify names and the sizes of (rebel) brigades in the village.
- Find out the names of their leaders, and find out who controls the brigades and their political orientation.
- Find out their illegal activities (according to Sharia law), which could be used to blackmail them if necessary.[15]

Parenthetically, the first elements of this list are similar to the arguments advanced in Major General Michael Flynn's influential 2010 report on "white" intelligence.[16] The necessity for understanding local dynamics, whether by insurgents or counterinsurgents, clearly is widely seen as a key ingredient of success in this struggle.

Based on these elements of essential information, ISIL was able to quickly identify and neutralize opposing centers of power. AQI also eliminated competitors for power, but it seemed to be much less systematic and not as understanding as ISIL of social, traditional, or emergent leaders in the areas it temporarily controlled. ISIL appears to have learned the criticality of creating an early power vacuum that it could fill.

The pattern that the Taliban and other groups in Afghanistan have used to learn and to adapt in order to survive has been somewhat different than that of ISIL. In the case of Afghanistan, relatively loose alliances have become the longer-term pattern. The hierarchy versus network system for the groups varies widely, but in general Seth G. Jones's conclusion that the "typical pattern has been loose strategic guidance at senior levels, with considerable autonomy at tactical level" remains accurate.[17] At the same time, however, such an alliance pattern can result in problems achieving strategic goals. Harald Håvoll correctly notes:

The lowest common denominator is that the presence of foreign support to the Karzai government, especially security forces, is against the interests of all the above [Taliban, militias, and criminal groups]. This shared goal is, however, an operational goal, a means to an end—and not necessarily their strategic goals. The strategic goals, more often than not, differ among the various insurgent groups, and to a significant degree.[18]

In some cases, such loose alliances might provide advantages to an overall movement. At the very least, they make responses by counterinsurgency forces more difficult, particularly in trying to develop strategies tailored to the differing end goals of the myriad of groups. This might also represent an accurate assessment of the strategic environment and the result of learning the appropriate lessons from the course of the insurgency. Given the historical pattern of local power centers in Afghanistan, smaller groups with their bases in these power centers probably will have more local success than a geographically broad unified movement. Importantly, this reinforces the truism that "one size does not fit all" in insurgencies.

Tactical and Operational Learning

Due to space limitations, only limited discussion of examples of insurgent improvements in tactics, techniques, and procedures can be provided. In many ways, these are significantly less important than learning leading to improved organization and strategy. Nevertheless, a clear pattern of learning at this level has been displayed by multiple insurgent groups, particularly ISIL. Some innovations such as the use of up-armored vehicles to serve as the shock force for attacks almost certainly were derived from the observation of their use by U.S. forces.[19] Likewise, studies have noted significant steady improvements in Taliban tactics over the course of the war, including a higher success rate of explosive devices; a greater capability of coordinating complex attacks; and long-range rifle fire.[20]

Some "sub-contracting" has developed among insurgent groups. In several locations, autonomous cells with expertise at particular skills seem to be "for rent" to the highest bidders. This was the case earlier in Iraq with some improvised explosive device (IED) cells.[21] Likewise, some criminal groups in Iraq kidnapped Westerners and "sold" them to insurgent groups, which then used them for political purposes.[22] Reports have surfaced of similar relationships being established in South Asia with criminal and/or independent specialist cells. These types of what essentially are business relationships can result in some potential issues for insurgent organizations in regard to security and lack of control of these cells, but insurgents seem to have learned that using what might be termed "private insurgent corporations" can provide economy of scale for them.

Insurgents have learned to use technology to their advantage both in tactical operations and in tactical training. In particular, this was reflected in the virtually continual measures/countermeasures/counter-countermeasures surrounding the use of IEDs in Iraq. Most information about this campaign remains very justifiably classified, but the various methods of emplacing and detonating the IEDs ranged up and down the technology scale; essentially, the insurgents proved very adaptable in determining what would work best in a particular situation. Clearly, the coalition forces (after some time lag) generally "won the IED battle," but the various detonation techniques certainly have entered the insurgent playbook.[23]

Several other creative uses of various technological tools have been noted. For example, in Afghanistan in 2007, a US Army press release noted:

> When a new fleet of helicopters arrived with an aviation unit at a base in Iraq, some Soldiers took pictures on the flightline.... From the photos that were uploaded to the Internet, the enemy was able to determine the exact location of the helicopters inside the compound and conduct a mortar attack, destroying four of the AH-64 Apaches.[24]

More recently [2015] (and more worryingly), ISIL released videos of its use of unmanned aerial vehicles in its attacks in Baiji, Iraq, and Raqqa, Syria.[25]

Insurgents and terrorists have learned to use the Internet to expand their operational training system. For example, a seven-part series was posted on the web on how to use a GPS receiver.[26] Also, as noted by Michael Kenney, "the fifth and sixth installments of *In the Shadow of the Lances*, another al Qaeda publication, details lessons learned in the Afghanistan campaign .... a senior operative wrote the installments as a sort of after action review to be shared with Islamic insurgents then preparing to fight American forces in Iraq."[27] Conversely, insurgent groups also may have learned the limitations of relying almost exclusively on online training. For example, according to figures compiled by *The Long War Journal*, ISIL has operated 57 training camps (30 in Iraq, 27 in Syria).[28] In part this reflects simply the opportunity for the group to establish such camps with relative security. More importantly, though, it also suggests that successful groups have re-learned the advantages of actual hands-on training.

Strategy

One important note should be raised at the beginning of a discussion of insurgent strategy. This is that insurgent successes achieved through a carefully thought-out strategy cannot always be distinguished from successes that might be viewed as almost accidental. In other words, successes achieved on the battlefield may occur despite the leadership's strategy rather than through some grand plan. Insurgent performance also, of course, is affected by the relative skills of the counterinsurgents. Awareness of this truth could be reflected by a Rhodesian officer's comment in 1979: "If we had been fighting the Viet Cong, we would have lost the war a long time ago."[29] Similarly, if a particular insurgent group faces unskilled governmental security forces or governments with losing (or nonexistent) strategies, its success may be more due to ineptitude by the other side than by any particular skills it possesses.

The recruiting strategy of ISIL appears to be intimately connected with its larger strategy. For many years, there was a debate within jihadist circles as to whether to focus on "near enemies" (local regimes) or "far enemies" (Western powers).[30] This issue became particularly germane with the rise of AQI during the U.S. occupation of Iraq. With the differing priorities between AQI and AQ "Central" in Afghanistan, the split between the two quickly was publicly very apparent.[31]

Viewed from the outside, ISIL has learned how to square this particular ideological circle. First, it abandoned the al-Qaida tag to emphasize its independence. More importantly, its various propaganda outlets provide relatively equal emphasis on near and far enemies. For near enemies, it is very easy for ISIL to find examples of abuses against Sunnis in Syria, in particular, but also in Iraq. Without stretching the historical analogy too far, some of the propaganda themes of "fighting the good fight against injustice" and their appeals are similar to those that attracted young people from other countries to fight in the Spanish Civil War. This theme can provide a significant number of recruits for operations within the region. According to U.S. official statements, ISIL had an estimated 22,000 fighters from 100 countries in mid-2015.[32] Thus far, this recruiting appeal does not appear to have waned.

At the same time, ISIL has paid at least rhetorical attention to the "far enemy." Open sources provide few indications that ISIL actually has devoted many practical resources to out-of-area operations, however. The continued internationalization of the movement (at least via information operations) could represent both a carefully calculated strategy and learning from previous mistakes made by al-Qaida and AQI. Pushing the global jihad theme can provide further legitimacy for the group in some circles, increasing the flow of recruits and other forms of support, without incurring major costs. More broadly, it also can complicate the responses of countries to ISIL. At best for the group, such international threats can deter some countries from engaging in operations against ISIL. Even if these results are not achieved, however, the potential for an internal threat from ISIL can create a more complicated strategic calculus and resourcing decisions for governments in balancing homeland security requirements against the level of resources devoted to offensive operations against ISIL. At best (from the standpoint of ISIL), it can create a virtuous cycle: individuals and groups that have declared allegiance to ISIL (no matter how tenuous the actual practical links) and that attempt even low-level operations can increase the international perception of ISIL as having global reach even while it devotes its principal efforts to more localized insurgencies. This ultimately can create self-fulfilling prophecies by its opponents as to the power of ISIL.

A second key aspect of ISIL strategy is emphasizing its desire for, and capability to build, an actual state. In part, this has been rhetorical, but there also have been practical steps taken. Following the elimination of real or potential rivals—in many cases, fellow jihadists—ISIL has established local governance under its auspices. For example, Christoph Reuter noted that "when Raqqa fell to the rebels in March 2013, a city council was rapidly elected. Lawyers, doctors, and journalists organized themselves. Women's groups were established. The Free Youth Assembly was founded, as was the movement 'For Our Rights' and dozens of other initiatives."[33] In some areas, the local governance may in fact have become more regularized and effective than it previously was under putative central government control.[34] To boost its claims for improved governance, according to a BBC report, ISIL has released a promotional video publicizing the health care provided to the population under its control. And, according to the video filmed at Raqqa General Hospital in Syria, which featured an ISIL Health Service logo and an Australian doctor, ISIL offers a wide range of health services to both fighters and civilians.[35]

Clearly, such governance has been marked by increasing brutality and probably increased disgruntlement of the population under ISIL control.[36] The main point, however, is that virtually any level of practical governance provides ISIL with a number of advantages, particularly by boosting the credibility of its claims for its legitimacy and for garnering at least a measure of local support. It almost certainly learned these lessons from the earlier failures of AQI. Although now largely forgotten, during the U.S. occupation of Iraq AQI in fact declared an "Islamic State of Iraq" that was at least ostensibly somewhat independent of, and higher than, AQI.[37] Given the paucity of structures and practical governance, however, virtually no one appeared to take this claim seriously. ISIL's more practical provision of at least some services suggests that it has learned that establishing actual mechanisms for at least pockets of support may be crucial for long-term survivability.

Afghanistan presents a rather different strategic picture for the insurgents. As noted, with multiple loosely coordinated violent groups in Afghanistan, identifying a single overarching strategy based on lessons learned likely is futile. Some trends as a result of lessons learned do seem apparent, however. Perhaps the key lesson—and one decidedly not difficult to learn—is that major Western military involvement in Afghanistan is almost certainly coming to an end very soon. As such, based both on the Taliban's propaganda and its actual operations, the key takeaway by the group's leaders seems to be the need to focus operations to increase their perceived strength vis-a-vis the Afghan government. In some ways, the Western militaries still in the country may be increasingly less salient in Taliban strategy. The pattern for 2014–15 (after a significant drawdown of Western forces) was more focused on high-visibility attacks against government targets and larger assaults against Afghan security forces.[38]

The Taliban in the last five or so years has taken a strategy for its operations involving intelligence services that differs from that of ISIL. According to the Jamestown Foundation *Terrorism Monitor*, "Along with these major and well-coordinated battles in the field, insurgents are now being used as assets in a clearly drawn intelligence war targeting the Afghan security establishment, with a particular focus on the Afghan domestic intelligence agency."[39] These efforts to "blind" the Afghan government suggest that the Taliban has learned the criticality of winning the intelligence war. Also, there has been a marked incidence of attacks against critical security figures in the Afghan government.[40] Rajiv Chandrasekaran of the *Washington Post* summarized the current strategy as "The Taliban are fighting a political war while the United States and its allies are still fighting a tactical military war…We remain focused on terrain. They are focused on attacking the transition process and seizing the narrative of victory."[41]

This "narrative of victory" is critical for the Taliban and its allied groups. Even if they do not actually win back control of the country, seizing the initiative could be crucial in any future peace agreements with the Afghan government. Again using a historical analogy, the so-called "Final Offensive" by the insurgent Farabundo Marti National Liberation Front (FMLN) group in El Salvador in 1989–90 (despite being an operational failure) was critical because it enhanced the group's political stature in the subsequent peace talks and ensured the FMLN's inclusion in the Salvadoran political process.

One operational-level issue may be associated with these efforts. This is the spike in so-called "green on blue attacks"—attacks by members of the Afghan security forces against ISAF members—beginning in late 2011 shortly after the United States announced its plans for shifting security responsibilities to Afghan forces. According to data collected by *The Long War Journal*, "in 2012, attacks by Afghan forces on coalition forces surged; in 2012, they accounted for 15 percent of coalition deaths. In 2011, green-on-blue attacks accounted for 6 percent; in 2010, 2 percent; in 2009, 2 percent; and in 2008, less than 1 percent."[42] The official U.S. stance on these attacks has been that virtually all of them have been by disgruntled Afghan troops or police with individual grievances, with one unnamed U.S. spokesperson claiming that fewer than 10 percent of the attackers had any connection to the Taliban.[43] Unsurprisingly, Taliban spokesmen and propaganda broadcasts have claimed credit for all these attacks, together with announcements that the group has increased efforts to infiltrate Afghan security forces.[44]

Following the major increase in insider attacks in 2012, ISAF was able to sharply decrease their incidence, both through instituting a series of self-protection measures (many of which understandably remained classified) and by at least attempting to improve vetting procedures for members of the Afghan security services.[45] Although some of these measures apparently have been eased, the key point was that the green-on-blue attacks and the subsequent measures to reduce them created some major gaps both in trust and in operational cooperation between ISAF and Afghan allies. These results almost certainly will continue to create problems in supporting ISAF efforts to transition security control to government of Afghanistan. It might also be noted that if ISIL is an effective learning organization, it will note the issues created in Afghanistan by insider attacks. Given the 2015 U.S. initiatives in training Iraqi forces, the value of infiltration of these recruits by ISIL (or potentially by Shia militias for that matter) certainly would seem to be an obvious lesson.

Information Operations

In many ways, the most important lesson learned by insurgent groups has been the criticality of information operations. Indeed, numerous insurgent and terrorist organizations have absorbed this lesson more effectively than have most governments. The goals of the information operations campaigns necessarily include strategic communications, operations, recruiting, and building a support structure. The actual information operations systems developed by insurgent groups deserve further examination to uncover the processes developed as a result of learning best practices.

One important information operations factor surrounding ISIL is branding, to use a Madison Avenue term. The tag line might be, "these are not your father's jihadists." The Madison Avenue analogy is apt because ISIL propaganda and information operations are relatively sophisticated, which is consistent with a fairly long-standing effort by virtually all terrorist groups. Any such group now must compete for attention. As Neville Bolt notes, terrorist organizations must use "subversive principles of commercial and political marketing to chart ways through an overcrowded media-world of information and symbols."[46] Much of ISIL's propaganda focus is on its success in actually taking

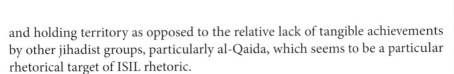

and holding territory as opposed to the relative lack of tangible achievements by other jihadist groups, particularly al-Qaida, which seems to be a particular rhetorical target of ISIL rhetoric.

The ISIL successes actually are a continuation of earlier lessons learned by insurgents in Iraq (and elsewhere). All the insurgent groups in Iraq became much more skilled at information operations over the course of the U.S. occupation. In reality, they likely were quicker learners on information operations than were U.S. forces, and they seemed to start from a higher skill level. The one lesson decidedly learned by the Iraqi insurgents was the advantage of making the war visual. Virtually every attack was recorded on electronic media and was quickly posted to electronic media. One reflection of how essential AQI viewed this tool and how extensively they used it was provided by the fact that between June and about November 2007 (roughly the period corresponding to the "surge"), American forces captured eight media labs belonging to AQI, in which they found a total of 23 *terabytes* of material that had not yet been uploaded to the web.[47]

The Taliban presents a similar pattern in having developed a sophisticated information operations strategy. According to an International Crisis Group study, this includes targeting multiple audiences:

> [1] English language, for international audiences. Disseminated primarily through a regularly updated website and almost daily contact with international media outlets, it aims at gaining global coverage and an international audience through reputable outlets; [2] local languages, particularly Pashtu (with some Dari and Urdu), aimed at regional groups, including on both sides of the Afghan-Pakistan border. This has several objectives: to obtain wider public support through folk imagery and culture (songs/poems) which appeal to national and religious sentiments; fear and intimidation through night letters (*shabnamah*, pamphlets or leaflets usually containing threats) and violent DVDs; and recruitment through morale-boosting martial songs, orations and statements about operations on the website, magazines, DVDs and audio cassettes; and [3] Arabic, for wider transnational networks. More closely linked with global issues and movements online as well as through a few publications, aimed at building wider support and presumably gaining recruits and financing. Global groups also seek to link the conflict in Afghanistan to their wider narrative of a battle between the West and Islam.[48]

When in power before the U.S. invasion, the Taliban regime displayed little skill in media management; at best, it might be viewed as exhibiting efforts at control rather than persuasion.[49] The successors to the earlier Taliban (the so-called neo-Taliban), however, clearly learned the skills required for information operations. As a U.S. military officer put it, "unfortunately, we tend to view information operations as supplementing kinetic [fighting] operations. For the Taliban, however, information objectives tend to drive kinetic operations....virtually every kinetic operation they undertake is specifically designed to influence attitudes or perceptions."[50]

Insurgent groups have demonstrated their commitment to their information operations experts in practical ways. One source has reported that Al Hayat Media Center, the ISIL media organization, offered a young Syrian an $18,000 salary and a house and car to work for it.[51] An indicator of the importance that the Taliban places on media operations is cited by Cori E. Dauber:

> According to Lara Logan, CBS News' Senior Foreign Correspondent and one of the very few reporters to have continued reporting regularly from Afghanistan during the time she was stationed in Baghdad, the Taliban always give the person with responsibility for media and information in an operational cell the number two position in the cell overall.[52]

There continues to be debate among analysts as to the relationship between terrorist (or insurgent) groups and "mainstream" media, which largely is beyond the scope of this chapter. In terms of insurgent learning, however, one related issue should be noted. This is how well various insurgent groups have learned to feed their propaganda into various news feeds as "straight" news. As one analyst has noted, "The area where the neo-Taliban have made great strides is in using outside media to portray themselves as a legitimate opposition group in Afghanistan, not as a terrorist group set on destroying the government."[53] Likewise, in looking at insurgents during the U.S. occupation, Cori E. Dauber in a Strategic Studies Institute paper argues that:

> Key issue in all this is internet connectivity. They no longer have to try to create "buzz" to move a clip into the mainstream press: they are now the press's primary source of news footage when it comes to the vital issue of attacks on American military personnel in Iraq. All they have to do is make the material available.[54]

Insurgents similarly have learned to use the Internet in very creative ways for their propaganda themes. For example, Andrew Exum noted that Iraqi insurgents operated a website called BaghdadSniper on which viewers could watch sniper attacks against coalition forces, with narration in six languages.[55]

Insurgent and terrorist groups clearly have learned that information operations and strategic communications represent a U.S. weakness that is the equivalent of a "center of gravity" they can exploit. A number of American officials and senior officers have noted this weakness. For example, U.S. Army

Brigadier General Kurt Crytzer said, "Our adversaries are constantly one step ahead of U.S. in the IO [information operations] realm."[56] Other U.S. officials also have argued that the United States—after perhaps a slow start—rapidly caught up with insurgents in Afghanistan and Iraq. Two notes might be made on these arguments. The first is that information operations that did in fact succeed in Iraq appeared to be more focused on tactical-level actions rather than sustained strategic communications and information operations.[57] The second issue might be noticed from a generally positive official assessment on U.S. information operations: "The importance of strategic communication has only recently been fully recognized within [the Department of Defense], and therefore relevant policy and doctrine are still evolving."[58] This statement was published in 2009, after eight years of combating insurgents, which suggests a continued lag in U.S. learning and adaptation.

The following excerpt from an official ISAF press release reflects the difference between the U.S. approach to information operations and those of the insurgent groups it has faced:

> [The Taliban] are not bound by a responsibility to tell the truth. In fact, they routinely exaggerate casualty numbers and damage figures to elevate their stature and generate a larger impact...There are numerous instances where the spokesman's first notification of an event is a request for comment from the media. Rather than admit lack of knowledge of the event, the spokesmen provide fabricated data and adjust their numbers incrementally as they gain better fidelity from their networks.[59]

However laudable the intent to provide nothing but completely accurate information, this comment misses one of the key aspects of information operations campaigns. Controlling the message remains critical, which in large measure involves being the first to present particular issues and themes. Waiting for "certainty" can put the information operator constantly in a reactive mode and quite possibly lead to irrelevance.

In many ways, the United States has self-created barriers in the information operations realm. In large measure, this is due to legal restrictions. The U.S. Information and Educational Exchange Act of 1948 (commonly known as the Smith-Mundt Act) has been legally construed as prohibiting U.S. information operations efforts against American citizens.[60] Some relief was provided in what became known as the Smith-Mundt Modernization Act, which was introduced in 2010 and made part of a larger piece of legislation in 2012.[61] This offers the major U.S. international information systems (such as Radio Free Europe) somewhat more flexibility in the content they are able to provide online, but does not address military information operations efforts.

AQI found a number of propaganda themes of considerable use with, at least, the Sunni population of Iraq. All of these resonated well during the U.S. occupation of Iraq, and they likely will continue to be of use in any further potential U.S. counterinsurgency efforts in the region. One interesting source providing the most useful themes is a U.S. Marine Corps study of the formation of the *Sahwa* (Awakening) Movement; this movement became a principal counterinsurgency tool during the U.S. surge. In a series of oral history interviews, key members of *Sahwa* described both why they joined the movement and the conditions precipitating their decision to join.

These *Sahwa* leaders and members provided details of local perceptions of the U.S. operations in Iraq that provided grist for AQI propaganda efforts. Certainly, the very presence of U.S. forces underlay everything, but the way U.S. operations initially were conducted seemed to be almost as important. As a senior U.S. officer observed:

> [T]hey would state that after Baghdad fell and throughout the summer of 2003, the Americans overreacted to small acts of resistance or violence and fought in a way that was cowardly and without honor. Here they would talk about the senseless use of firepower and midnight raids on innocent men. They said that by our escalation, we proved true the rhetoric of the nationalist firebrands about why we had invaded, and our actions played directly into the hands of organizations like Zarqawi's al-Qaeda in Iraq and Sadr's militia.[62]

Clearly, such perceptions were overcome—and in fact, several *Sahwa* leaders noted that they received more support from the U.S. than from the Iraqi government—but AQI's themes probably continue to be usable in the future by groups facing the United States.[63] In the particular case of Iraq, this might be even more complicated. As noted, the Iraqi government never provided much support to the Sunni anti-AQI elements while the United States was still in the country, and Baghdad was even less helpful (with some arguing that it became actively hostile) after the American withdrawal.

The "war of perceptions" may be even more complex currently. With the United States attempting in 2015 two rather distinct simultaneous goals— supporting largely Sunni anti-Assad forces in Syria while trying to at least contain the Sunni ISIL in Iraq—local populations may be understandably confused as to how to understand the situation. In fact, U.S. Army Brigadier General Kurt Crytzer, Deputy Commander of Special Operations Command Central, has been cited as claiming that many Iraqis believe that the United States is secretly arming ISIL.[64] There is no evidence that ISIL has directly taken advantage of such perceptions in its propaganda themes, but they offer possible topics and issues for insurgent messaging.

Insurgent Learning and the Future

In many ways, counterinsurgents also have had to re-learn past lessons from history, at times painfully. Certainly, earlier writers on counterinsurgency such as David Galula, Frank Kitson, and Robert Thompson would agree with most of the doctrine provided in Field Manual 3-24, *Counterinsurgency*, particularly since much of it was derived from their observations and experience. Likewise, insurgent groups seem to have also re-learned some of the key lessons both from other groups and their individual experiences operating against the United States and its allies.

Both the Taliban and ISIL appear to have learned the most critical lessons surrounding insurgency and, perhaps more importantly, have adapted these lessons to their particular environments. Both the Taliban and ISIL clearly have benefited from the learning from their earlier experiences against the United States, but the forms of their responses seem to have differed. In the case of the Taliban, the overwhelming bulk of attention appears to have been directed to what might best be described as the local insurgency environment. In other words, despite continuing to try to maintain and enhance regional alliances of various stripes, the Taliban and associated groups remain focused on improving their effectiveness within Afghanistan itself. As such, the most critical learning processes—and implementing these lessons learned—have been associated with operational-level actions. As previously argued, the basic Taliban strategic goal of either regaining control of Afghanistan, or at least strengthening its hand in future political negotiations, seems to have remained rather consistent. The learning and subsequent changes have seemed to be more a matter of emphasis of new tools and focuses rather than a major re-shifting of priorities.

This can be contrasted with ISIL. Viewing ISIL as the lineal descendant of AQI, the lessons learned from the overall failure of AQI during the U.S. occupation seem to have created a somewhat subtle but significant change in strategy. During the heyday of al-Qaida "Central," there was much discussion and debate among Western analysts as to whether the world was viewing a global insurgency.[65] In terms of actual operations, this never quite appeared to be the case. More significantly, AQI—much more of an insurgent group than the larger al-Qaida—did not succeed particularly well as insurgents (as opposed to terrorists). ISIL clearly has learned lessons from these earlier cases, and it seems to have managed to bridge many of the gaps between local and international.

One of the major lessons incorporated by ISIL and the Taliban is that of the criticality of information operations. This certainly is not a new feature of insurgent movements, whether under the rubric of propaganda, indoctrination, or psychological operations. The key improvement these two groups has made, however, is fully utilizing all the available tools to spread their message. As noted earlier, many would view their information operations as having been superior to those of the counterinsurgents fighting them. Clearly, as recent battlefield setbacks by ISIL have shown, even the best-crafted information operations campaigns cannot win an insurgency. Nevertheless, even groups (perhaps including ISIL) that are relatively weak can maximize their longevity by using effective information campaigns.

Perhaps the most important lesson the Taliban and ISIL have learned is the importance of strategic patience. Their apparently improved operations, strategies, and information operations in many ways simply provide them with additional breathing space to continue to survive as coherent movements. Both groups have incorporated lessons learned earlier through their own experience and through those of other groups to establish "facts on the ground." Neither group may ultimately succeed, but their existence as learning organizations will make them much more difficult to counter. The fresh lessons they have provided almost certainly will be studied by other groups in the future, whether or not they are of similar ideological stripes.

CHAPTER 11
U.S. Intelligence Credibility in the Crosshairs: On the Post-War Defensive

Bowman H. Miller

Intelligence services have an inherent disinclination to share what they know and how they know it, but any notion that a single country's services can operate effectively without partners, including foreign ones, is no longer sensible. However, when it comes to sharing from the world of secrets, trust is the coin of the realm. Moreover, trust and risk management in the world of intelligence partnering confront a complication when the credo, drawn from the negotiation history of superpower arms control, is deemed to be "trust but verify." There is a major rub in trying to verify that the trust one places in a partner is deserved, since that very act of verifying of necessity tends to involve "spying on one's partner."

The purpose of this brief assessment is to analyze how that trust factor has been affected by recent U.S. and other actions, especially in the two war zones of Iraq and Afghanistan and in confronting terrorism on a global basis. The examination weighs the importance for intelligence partnerships of foreign reception of various U.S. intelligence practices, many of them new in light of the post-2001 terrorism challenge and often controversial. The analysis also treats overarching concerns as well as reactions and responses in three key, allied partner states—the United Kingdom, Germany, and Japan. The former two were directly involved in either or both Iraq and Afghanistan. Japan, on the other hand, is deemed to have been affected, in part, by U.S. moves and behaviors as Tokyo, albeit also for other reasons, extends its development and embrace of more unilateral intelligence and defense capabilities. However, despite the diminution of trust between the United States and some of its partners among scores of countries with which the United States cooperates in intelligence, the fact remains that they are so dependent upon U.S. cooperation and capabilities that there is little, if any, inclination to cast aside that U.S. source of cooperation and assistance.

The Intelligence Community (IC) of the United States is the world's largest, most versatile, most technologically advanced, and most expensive. It is now also as complex and challenged as is any on earth, given America's global interests, presence, and engagement. Tens of thousands of people toil in the U.S. IC, and tens of billions of dollars go into its budget each year. However, Americans by themselves, even given the advanced technology and sophisticated methods at their disposal, cannot monitor, let alone master, all of the world's festering challenges to U.S. and allies' national security. As globalizing interdependence demands more networking and cooperation among governments, the U.S. IC has realized increasingly that it needs willing and able foreign partners to achieve the intelligence success and insights the United States requires.

As if the IC required further impetus, the terrifying events of 9/11, mounds of Congressional legislation, the recommendations from various hearings and commissions, President Barack Obama's 2010 and 2015 National Security Strategies, the Director of National Intelligence's strategy, and public and media commentary all insist that the U.S. IC do a better job of sharing information domestically across agency lines among the IC's 17 different services and agencies. In addition, the community is explicitly enjoined by all of the aforementioned authorities to be more assertive and effective in partnering with counterpart services abroad.[1] Despite inherent misgivings over sharing secrets, U.S. intelligence, under the aegis of the Director of National Intelligence, has endeavored to do more of just that.

Quid Pro Quo?

Partnering with foreign intelligence services takes many forms, but in virtually all cases what the United States offers or provides its counterparts outweighs, at least in quantity, what it receives in return. The array of these partnerships, with a mix of foreign agencies, varies from virtual integration with very close partners to ad hoc sharing.[2] The intention or motivation, on the U.S. side, is to better inform allies and partners so that they are more effective in carrying out operations of benefit both to the United States and to them, to train them to be more adroit in their operations and analysis, to relieve the U.S. of some operational and collection tasks, and to equip coalition partners with vital intelligence in a common endeavor. The United States primarily partners with individual agencies bilaterally—with one country or service at a time. But such partnering also occurs in some areas multilaterally, e.g., in NATO, and in larger groupings when conducting coalition operations, with the U.S. either in the lead or performing cooperatively as the "best supporting actor" when it comes to intelligence and military operations. Regardless of the arrangement, the pivotal issue of trust in one's partner is ever-present when it comes to sharing secrets or in operating jointly and clandestinely.[3]

Partnerships with counterpart intelligence and security services also seek, in many instances, to influence foreign attitudes and decisions as much as to simply inform them. Herein lies the crux of concern when and if U.S. intelligence's truthfulness, accuracy, credibility, and objectivity are called into question. As noted, every country's intelligence enterprise inherently distrusts foreign intelligence services. Recruited new hires are subjected to the admonition that they should never assume that information or an approach from a foreign intelligence and security counterpart is honest, well-intentioned, or without an ulterior motive. Information security, counterintelligence awareness, and constant wariness typify the world of intelligence services. Indeed, one of the barriers to better use of intelligence within the United Nations system is this very suspicion, i.e., that countries cull out only the intelligence they want people in the UN to see, in order to further their own aims and priorities.[4]

No more telling case in point regarding such suspicion came in the February 2003 presentation to the UN Security Council by Secretary of State Colin Powell concerning Iraq's reported possession of weapons of mass destruction (WMD). That effort—to market the need to intervene against Saddam Hussein in Iraq—proved hollow in some key aspects. Thus, foreigners (both partners and adversaries) remain wary of U.S. motives, making it incumbent upon the United States not to be caught cooking the books when it comes to intelligence partnering and sharing.[5] The U.S. community of intelligence, security, and law enforcement agencies is not where it should be, or wants to be, concerning its global reputation. The United States clearly has been and wants to remain being considered the foremost professional, credible, capable, and secure intelligence enterprise in the world. The fact that it is the largest, best funded, and most technologically adept intelligence apparatus, certainly in the democratic world, does not automatically bestow any elevated stature on the U.S. intelligence establishment, however.

Numerous episodes in the last decade and a half have cost the U.S. IC some of its precious credibility. Today, the U.S. IC finds itself devoting too much time and effort defending and justifying itself, all while seeming to lose the offensive against a burgeoning array of vexing foreign-origin threats and challenges. The wars in Iraq and Afghanistan, their rationale, conduct, and aftermath, have taken a toll on the stature of U.S. intelligence and, concomitantly, on personnel morale within it. The community no longer enjoys the same reputation for excellence in the eyes of many of its foreign partners or adversaries. In addition, many outside the U.S. remember all too well President George W. Bush's bipolar dissection of the post-9/11 world into friends and enemies, those either with the United States or against it. At the time, France and Germany, having spearheaded the UN effort to head off the U.S.-led intervention, were counted among the latter.[6] That said, the U.S. IC still remains of fundamental importance to virtually all of its foreign partners, who enjoy, for the most part, asymmetrical benefits from this kind of relationship. Those advantages tend to come in exchange for special geographic, linguistic, and at times operational and analytical access and contributions.

Coalition Denouement: Time for a New Intelligence Cost-Benefit Analysis?

As the coalition deployments in Iraq and Afghanistan approach their presumed endpoints, traditional U.S. allies worry that the level of intelligence partnering, imperfect though it has been, will be reduced as various countries' will and capacity to intervene abroad wanes. U.S. and allied defense budgets are under extreme pressures. Defense system procurements are either being canceled, stretched out, or displaced by extending the life span of key elements, i.e., the UH-1 Huey helicopters of the U.S. Air Force, the UK's Nimrod maritime intelligence, surveillance, and reconnaissance aircraft, etc. The 1990s Balkans interventions, Iraq, Afghanistan, and most recently Libya all have shown that European NATO allies' claims to field a major, deployable, and sustainable expeditionary force of their own are hollow. If they were ever realistic goals, those goalposts of spending and defense modernization have clearly been moved back. If the allies are less willing and able to engage and deploy abroad in coalition with U.S. forces, many in the U.S. intelligence enterprise wonder if the rationale for sharing intelligence with them is as valid as it has been. Do the inherent risks of sharing (and they do persist) warrant the outlays and exposure of sensitive U.S. intelligence collection and analysis? Is that perennial mantra of intelligence partnering—based on quid pro quo—being realized or likely to come about in future years?

European defense spending continues to remain flat or trend downward. In a sign of the times, even the United Kingdom recently inquired of NATO whether London could now count its intelligence spending as part of its NATO outlays in an effort to come closer to agreed spending objectives. Despite their laggard status, allies worry that the U.S. will draw back from existing commitments in long-established, operational sharing relationships, as the U.S. intelligence and defense budgets shrink along with most of their own. This impending retrenchment comes despite the fact that more, not less, partnering would be advantageous to all parties. While individual nations devote less to defense, global threats both miniaturize and multiply, and globalization's growing interdependence and the intrinsic common vulnerabilities it creates for states persist.

Some representatives of Five Eyes partners (Australia, Canada, New Zealand, and the United Kingdom) utter an almost plaintive plea that the United States not cut back the level and intensity of sharing that those same partners have grown accustomed to—in places ranging from Kosovo to Kandahar, from Baghdad to Benghazi. The United States long has been deemed to be overly protective, if not niggardly, in providing operationally significant intelligence to even its closest strategic partners, including the United Kingdom. There is now a palpable worry that the U.S. will further dilute and delimit intelligence partnering, even as the number and complexity of likely contingencies grows. Thus, even though key partners have wounds from their relationship with U.S. intelligence over aspects of the Iraq and Afghanistan contingencies, none of them wants to forego those relationships, upon which so much of their own analytic insights and security preparedness depend. They continue to press the case that the United States partnering with them still yields a net benefit to Washington. Their position remains that, for the most part, those prized relationships, even when troubles arise, have proved to be cost effective, even as they recognize that any intelligence sharing poses a greater risk of exposure, compromise, or other hostile exploitation.

Chinks in America's IC Armor

In the last decade and a half, the United States IC has confronted no less than a half dozen major challenges to its reputation for credibility, ethical methods, and professional behavior. It has been the focus of allegations of malfeasance, illicit methods, illegal collection and confinement, violation of foreign nations' sovereignty and laws, and an inability to control and protect its own intelligence information, sources, and collection methods. Although not all of these instances reflect direct U.S. intelligence involvement or direction, all of them have harmed the standing of U.S. intelligence both at home and abroad. What belongs in that inventory of negative episodes? Pride of place certainly goes to the late-2002, woefully mistaken U.S. National Intelligence Estimate (NIE) that posited "with high confidence" continuing WMD programs in Iraq.[7] It also goes to the ill-fated UN Security Council briefing of similar purported findings in February 2003.

Many close partners, often beholden to the U.S. IC for both raw and finished intelligence, parroted the U.S. proposition that Saddam Hussein had acquired at least WMD know-how, if not an actual capability and available stocks. They were misled by U.S. judgments rooted in a kind of global IC groupthink, a pro-war policy orientation of President George W. Bush's administration, and unsubstantiated analytical presumptions not based on recent intelligence or convincing evidence. At the UN Security Council, Secretary of State Powell drew upon selected elements of that NIE and other data, significant parts of which were flawed or false.[8] Flawed, cherrypicked intelligence was used to justify the war and, later, to sell the need for intervention in Iraq to the world at the UN. (Much of what transpired in the United States concerning Iraqi WMD "intelligence" was evident in the United Kingdom as well, as will be discussed below.) The somewhat lurid role of an Iraqi source, ironically code named Curveball, contributed to the mistakes and misjudgments in the lead-up to the intervention.

In 2004, images of U.S. mistreatment of Iraqi prisoners at Abu Graib, made all too public with streaming videos, were conjoined with allegations of U.S. "extraordinary renditions," waterboarding and other "enhanced" interrogation techniques in "elicitation" of information, and alleged secret CIA prisons abroad.[9] As noted below, an Italian court tried some 20 Americans in absentia for the reported seizure and transfer to Egypt of a radical Islamic imam from Milan. All the while U.S. leaders have dealt with the issue of housing/incarcerating "unlawful combatants" at Bagram Air Base in Afghanistan and on Guantanamo Bay Naval Base in Cuba, the latter intermittently threatened with closure but still operating today. A whole new vocabulary of intelligence euphemisms arose as the United States and its partners faced a new kind of terrorist and insurgent enemy operating outside the scope of previous international norms and legalisms.

Leaks in the U.S. Intelligence Vessel

Equally, if not more, damaging to the reputation of both U.S. intelligence and American diplomacy have been the mammoth, unlawful disclosures of diplomatic reporting by U.S. Army Specialist Bradley (now Chelsea) Manning via Wikileaks and the hemorrhaging of even more costly leaks by Edward Snowden exposing a variety of sensitive U.S. intelligence efforts and capabilities. These two millennials, claiming high-minded motivations for their criminal behavior and violation of public trust, have caused untold harm to U.S. national security with their actions. Regardless of their reasoning, the fact remains that some in the United States and many abroad, particularly in political, parliamentary, and media ranks, were all too pleased to have access to such supposed "hard evidence" of alleged U.S. intelligence malfeasance and illicit activity. Tales of espionage, snooping, and such make for lively press, if not media sensationalism, but there is ample fire behind the smoke to make many of these recent accounts and accusations of U.S. misdeeds and violations of trust appear accurate.

The Snowden case and its revelations continue. The fact that reporters for the *Guardian* in Britain write about them and draw from them not while on British soil but writing from Brazil—beyond the normal reach of UK intelligence and security agencies MI5 and MI6—is testimony to the supposition that their publication is most likely in violation of the UK Official Secrets Act's provisions. The "temporary" Russian exile of Snowden likewise attests to similar fugitive status in his own case but also perhaps, for a while at least, to Snowden being a welcome and apparently informative houseguest of the Federal Security Service (FSB), a KGB successor agency. All of this has generated considerable political mayhem in some partner countries—as well as added demands at home for more IC transparency and accountability.

Though some of the foreign reactions to Snowden's troubling claims are clearly disingenuous, the fact remains that perennial American references to being the "indispensable nation" are now also greeted with a growing concern that some of the U.S. intelligence enterprise's actions appear untruthful, unlawful, and impeachable. Rather than being exceptional and indispensable, the United States is also seen by too many as untrustworthy for having obtained some of its intelligence using measures outside accepted democratic and legal norms. Although the feigned alarm in countries like France—renowned for its own highly intrusive intelligence collection activities—is widespread, partner intelligence services have been hard pressed to explain what they know of U.S. practices and to what extent they are party to them or are themselves employing similar methods. Suffice it to say that foreign counterpart intelligence services are being whipsawed between wanting to maintain their still highly valued relationships with U.S. agencies and serving and being valued as protectors of their own sovereign national security, intelligence equities, and political processes.

Analysis Under the Gun

Much has been written, alleged, and reported about the rushed, ill-considered, and politicized U.S. NIE concerning claims that Saddam Hussein's Iraq had WMD in at least two of the three categories, i.e., chemical and biological. Paul Pillar, an acknowledged critic of Bush administration Middle East policy, is one of those whose perspectives on this sordid episode have been expressed in first-person detail. Pillar's recollections point to the Bush administration's "pressing the community for juicier tidbits that would make more of an impression on the public when talking about Iraqi weapons programs."[10] Pillar writes knowingly of the sad saga of the WMD in Iraq NIE. He notes that the White House spokesman's claim (much later in 2007) that the President's main reasons for intervention came from the NIE on Iraq and Saddam's own actions was, in Pillar's words, a "lie." "[I]t was impossible for the intelligence estimate in question…to have been a basis for the decision" since the NIE came after President Bush had decided on the path to war and a campaign to sell it to the public.[11]

Pillar's study of the nexus between intelligence and policy highlights one essential fact: "as a shaper of policy, ideology decisively trumps intelligence."[12] Equally significant, however, and galling among analysts, is that British counterparts suffered constraints, biases, and pressures of their own. Pillar has a direct counterpart in the UK's Brian Jones. In his extremely detailed, blow-by-blow account of the experiences of British intelligence in dealing with Iraq and anti-Saddam intervention issues, Jones recounts all of the political efforts to steamroll the analysis of the existence of Iraqi WMD in order to echo the Blair government's policy and war preparations. Like his late colleague Sir Percy Craddock, former chief of the UK Joint Intelligence Committee (JIC) under Prime Minister Margaret Thatcher, Jones stresses the necessary distinction and separation between intelligence and policy, one all too often ignored or overridden in the Iraq case:

> I suspected he [Deputy Chief of UK Defence Intelligence] was keen to provide uncritical support to the policy community. There is an important line between intelligence and policy and I was worried that it was becoming blurred under his influence.... At the heart of it was our duty to strive to ensure [the intelligence assessment dossier on WMD in Iraq] represented our assessment of the intelligence.[13]

Jones's entire account is rather painful to read for any intelligence analyst. It documents the kind of pressures inflicted by a rush to a pre-ordained policy judgment, as well as the politicization of the analytic product, i.e., decision-makers pressing for the analysis to assert what policymakers want it to say.

Such was also the case, whether implicit or explicit, in Washington concerning WMD in Iraq, of course.

Compound Interest Can Prove Harmful

Many different but related events and issues have contributed to a lessening of outsiders' faith and confidence, both in the ways the U.S. intelligence enterprise conducts itself as well as in the product of its analysis. World opinion witnessed in graphic videos U.S. mistreatment of some prisoners in Iraq at the hands of some U.S. military guards. What happened at Abu Graib, despite the behavior being confined to several individuals, only served to cause much of world opinion to conflate those disgusting images with other allegations of secret (and presumably equally humiliating and brutal) CIA foreign prisons. In those alleged confinement facilities, waterboarding and other questionable, if not unacceptable, interrogation techniques were reportedly in use. Various American euphemisms, carefully crafted for U.S. consumption, did little to blunt negative perceptions in the United States and abroad of such excessive American intelligence actions and methods.

Adding to the negative perceptions being fed outside the United States were a number of reported "extra-territorial renditions," acts which most people would label kidnapping. One such major case, referred to earlier, involved the reported seizure of an outspoken, radical imam from the streets of Milan, Italy, and his rapid transfer to Egyptian custody, reportedly without the knowledge or consent of any Italian authority. The reported seizure and transfer deeply offended Italian government and public sensitivities. Italian courts subsequently indicted and tried, in absentia, 22 alleged CIA operatives and one U.S. Army officer involved in the case. The ability of such personnel to again work abroad was harmed.[14] On the Italian side, two very senior officials, eventually identified publicly as having been forewarned of the reported operation, were convicted for their role in this case, only to see their sentences quashed on appeal. The imam in question is now pressing a case against Italy in the European Court of Human Rights in Strasbourg.[15]

It is this guilt by association issue which comes up repeatedly when foreign counterparts of U.S. intelligence are caught in the web of allegations of U.S. abuses. Thus, if an Italian, German, Pakistani, or other official is deemed to have been party to or aware of some questionable U.S. intelligence collection or other operation, he or she often pays the price of "name and shame" public exposure, lost stature, and frequently a forfeited position. If a foreign political leader has reportedly been the target of U.S. intelligence collection, his or her own services are put in a bind: either they were cognizant of the U.S. activity and did nothing about it; or they were ignorant of the alleged U.S. intrusion and thus seemingly incompetent. For U.S. partners, these events thus can be the ultimate lose-lose situation for them—and for the relationship's level of trust and confidence.

The Saga Turns Cyber

This trail of sometimes lurid miscues or poorly veiled actions became even more troublesome after the Wikileaks episode. This so-called whistle-blower website received and made available to international news outlets and others hundreds of thousands of SECRET-level, internal State Department diplomatic reporting telegrams. Thanks to the leak perpetrated by Manning, since convicted on a variety of counts and sentenced to some 30 years confinement, masses of sensitive U.S. diplomatic and intelligence reports and confidential foreign contacts' names were compromised. His leaks, like other such massive hemorrhages of classified, sensitive information, have proved even more damaging than much classical espionage.[16] The difference, of course, is that a leak into the public domain has a potentially unlimited global audience, whereas a clandestine, state-run espionage operation is carried out in secret and the intruder endeavors to keep the harvest of intelligence secret for as long as the operation is lucrative and beyond.

The Wikileaks fiasco, occurring in the midst of the Iraq war and borne of Manning's computer access in that theater of conflict, brought with it a range of complications and disclosures. Several of its manifestations included the foreign ouster of two U.S. ambassadors, those to Ecuador and Mexico, from their positions. In addition, the number of U.S. inside contacts in foreign governments, who saw their identities as sources revealed or threatened with publication, yielded a much larger span of Wikileaks vulnerability to being named as a confidential source and promises to curtail some of the access and insight the United States had enjoyed while it maintained those sources' trust and confidentiality.

The fact is that great doubts and misgivings were introduced worldwide into the business of U.S. confidential diplomacy and international candor by the Wikileaks affair, and it has yet to run its full course.[17] All of that said, key partners of the U.S. IC—even with their previously shielded ties to the U.S. now publicized—have generally remained wedded to that relationship, despite suffering catcalls and worse. They try to reassure their U.S. partners and themselves that whatever low points have afflicted the relationship would prove a short-lived episode. They focus on the fact that many of these intelligence partnerships are longstanding, of necessity quite resilient in the face of criticism, and usefully enduring, even durable enough to withstand harsh exchanges and chilled political relations between capitals. It is not uncommon for intelligence professionals in foreign services to seek American reassurance that, though the political leaders of the partnering nations may be at odds over a policy, the intelligence partnership should continue unabated. The investment is too great to write off, in their view.

Enter Snowden — Better Said, Snowden Departs

On top of the amalgam of a misguided NIE concerning the presumed existence of Iraqi WMD, graphic pictures or accounts of U.S. torture at Abu Graib and elsewhere, allegations of the United States scooping up radical Islamists as suspected terrorists in various foreign countries, and the Wikileaks mega-leak to the world public, another American intelligence insider has wreaked huge havoc on sources, methods, and secrecy. Edward Snowden, a contract employee at the U.S. National Security Agency (NSA), walked away from his sworn duties at its Hawaiian location and headed for exile, or at least a way station, in Hong Kong. After some peregrinations, he eventually reached Russia where he enjoys continuing "asylum," his respite and protection from the long arm of U.S. justice. In the interim, he has leaked hordes of sensitive data and operations, been widely interviewed, seen himself become the subject of an Academy Award-winning documentary, and emerged as an unlikely folk hero and media darling within anti-establishment circles across the globe. His revelations have proved very costly to a range of partnerships the U.S. IC has carefully fostered and maintained.

Perhaps taking a cue from Manning but with much greater, more devastating access to highly classified programs, capabilities, and operations, the more savvy Snowden has paired up with several journalists, primarily the *Guardian's* Glenn Greenwald and the *Washington Post's* Barton Gellman.[18] The latter have published one expose after another, claiming to shed light into NSA's operations, techniques, and practices; they have published information of great interest and value to America's adversaries and hostile intelligence services, and to anti-Western, malevolent forces globally. Moreover, the United States has seen the pivotal trust it has worked so long and hard to build up with allies and partners be diminished as a result of his disclosures, compounding Manning's damage. Snowden's allegations and leaked documents have bred huge doubts of the veracity of U.S. assertions that America does not "spy" on friends and allies. In addition, his disclosures have prompted a firestorm of protest over, and investigation of, alleged wholesale NSA domestic surveillance of Americans' Internet and email activities. Those revelations resulted eventually in calls for U.S. legislation restricting NSA's work in this regard and major domestic judicial decisions castigating such collection as excessive and violating the bounds of the U.S. Patriot Act.

Most troubling, in some respects, is that Snowden's claims and releases continue to trickle out from his safehaven (and from co-conspirators) abroad. Moreover, the fact that Russia's Vladimir Putin saw fit to free Snowden from his no-man's-land in Moscow airport all but confirms that the FSB is part of this cabal. The FSB seems to be making Snowden comfortable as a uniquely placed source: presumably he is talking to FSB officers in greater depth and detail than what has been made public to date, notwithstanding Snowden's denials. One can only wonder and await what more will be exposed—whether it be true or false. For many observers, however, it matters little how true any of Snowden's revelations are or may be; much of the semi-informed world public has become convinced that his claims are true, given his access and the masses of stolen data. Many of the uninitiated, especially among America's detractors, clearly believe that the NSA has exceeded the bounds of its mission and violated both democratic norms and U.S. Constitutional protections.

Making Intelligence Fit the Policy

The United Kingdom, led by Prime Minister Tony Blair during the Iraq and Afghanistan wars, has been the most involved, most directly affected, and the most structured in its response to both contingencies, but primarily involving the entry, alongside the United States, into Iraq in 2003. British and American intelligence, joined at the hip since World War II, were equally and simultaneously confronted by the Iraq contingency and questions about how intelligence was to be involved in its planning, rationalizing, and execution.[19]

Both nations' responses have been dissected at length. The British post-mortem has included several major commission and parliamentary inquiries, various hearings, and private, first-person accounts. Two seminal examinations of what led up to the Iraq intervention and the convoluted role British intelligence played in it (or was played, as some have indicated) are Brian Jones' account (referenced earlier) entitled *Failing Intelligence: The True Story of How We Were Fooled into Going to War in Iraq* and a quite different portrait in William Shawcross' *Allies: The U.S., Britain, Europe and the War in Iraq.* Jones' version dates from 2010, while Shawcross wrote his much earlier, first published in 2003.

Shawcross finds little to fault in the shared Anglo-U.S. decision to invade Iraq, seeing it as inevitable at some point and in some fashion, given Saddam Hussein's track record of abuse, flaunting of the UN, and intimidating moves at home and in the region. Brian Jones, on the other hand, makes what one reviewer termed a "compelling case" against misguided policy and misuse of intelligence. Jones was, to borrow a phrase from U.S. history, a "witness at the creation," this time of the intelligence and analysis designed to inform British policy vis-a-vis Iraq, war, WMD, and more. His book provides insight into the political machinations of the British government under Blair as it undertook to rationalize and publicly sell the need to intervene in Iraq. Like the U.S. presentation to the UN Security Council in February 2003, intelligence in the UK was to be the handmaiden of that effort, had Blair and his aides had their way. The likes of Jones, however, withstood as best they could mounting pressures to sing from Blair's song sheet, regardless of the paucity of intelligence to support the Prime Minister's preferred course of action.

Jones recounts the protests of some of his key weapons analysts that they lacked any credible intelligence since 1991 on aspects of WMD suspicions and that some of the purported more recent intelligence claims were such that "anyone with a passing knowledge of published information on Iraq's WMD could have made them up."[20] In addition, despite their protests, analysts were also told that there existed new, more credible intelligence (a "Report X") and that its sensitivity precluded access, an untenable claim in the world of sensitive, all-source intelligence analysis.[21] Jones, a senior Defence Intelligence Service (DIS) analyst, goes on to critique the source verification work and UK intelligence community pre-eminence of MI6, Britain's civilian secret foreign intelligence service, airing more British dirty laundry.[22]

The British response to how intelligence was acquired and handled before the Iraq intervention, along with the sometimes spotty cooperation with the U.S. in military theater operations in Iraq, has not led to any wholesale remake of British intelligence or to rethinking the partnership with the United States.

However, concern was again heightened that, even with its closest partner, Britain needs to have a fully informed, highly competent all-source intelligence capability of its own. Moreover, insiders in British intelligence remain wary of being steamrolled or having their products cherrypicked to suit their political masters' wishes or preferred policies.[23] Intelligence consumers remain free to act as they choose, but it is not their privilege to blame their intelligence providers when misguided or ill-considered policies go awry. Such a credo sounds eminently reasonable to intelligence professionals, but its continuing abuse is what intelligence professionals should expect.

Germany: But I Thought We Were Friends

Looking at how all of this Iraq and WMD intelligence has played out in Germany thus far can be equally instructive. Germany, a very important if not the closest U.S. intelligence partner, chose not only to opt out of the Iraq episode politically but to actively seek to derail it. While the Schröder government was doing its best, in concert with France, to stop the intervention, German intelligence representatives in Washington pleaded with counterparts to preserve that relationship among intelligence agencies, notwithstanding the acute irritation in the wider bilateral German-American relationship.[24] However, intelligence ties directly related to Iraq and the intervention there with non-player Germany were not seriously affected. On the other hand, later publication of allegations of National Security Agency (NSA) snooping on high-level German targets caused a political firestorm for Berlin.

Claims in 2013 that NSA had intercepted the cell phone of German Chancellor Angela Merkel caused an outcry of angry protest, hurt feelings, and anti-American hand-wringing. (It even took on the name "Handygate;" *handy* is the German slang for a cell phone.) German intelligence leaders were put in the unenviable position of either admitting they were witting of such an adversarial collection intrusion (by their key NATO ally) or claiming ignorance—and thus appearing either incompetent or attempting to resort to "implausible denial." Worse was yet to come, however. A second chapter opened in early 2015 when German media and the German parliament's left-ist factions accused Berlin's *Bundesnachrichtendienst* (BND, or Federal Intelligence Service) of knowingly cooperating with America's NSA in collecting against European communications targets—foremost among them France, the European Union, and Airbus.

Piling on, the media's accusations then re-focused on the German Chancellery because the BND comes directly under its supervision and oversight. Was the Chancellery also ignorant of both NSA and BND "cooperation" or have staff members of Merkel's Chancellery been at least disingenuous, if not blatantly untruthful, as to what they knew and when? Adding to the complications was a parliamentary demand, from Merkel's political opposition, for access to a purported roster of NSA-provided email and IP addresses, reportedly provided for the BND itself to track and intercept—in effect, the alleged "joint NSA-BND target list."[25] As of mid-2015, the NSA-focused saga continues to roil politics in Germany, with weekly magazine and online commentary and accusations from the likes of *Der Spiegel*, Germany's most widely read (left-leaning) weekly, but also from most mainline print media—keeping the pot boiling. Time will tell whether the German Federal Prosecutor's June 2015 decision not to pursue the alleged NSA intercepts of Merkel for lack of evidence will dampen the furor.

Japan: Maybe We Should Become More Self-Reliant?

Japan presents a quite different story with respect to post-Iraq intervention intelligence and larger security questions. The government of Prime Minister Shinzo Abe appears committed to a more forward-leaning, less constricted attitude toward the constitutionally mandated Self-Defense Forces and their employment. Those initiatives have unleashed a storm of protests, both in public and parliament, reacting to the concern that Tokyo under Abe would be departing from its post-World War II restraint concerning a limited territorial defense force. Abe has suggested that Japan's military needs to be prepared to intervene in external conflicts and/or on behalf of threatened foreign partners. Related to such a reorientation is the perceived need to have more and better, also independently acquired, intelligence.

In Japan, intelligence is heavily compartmented. Very few agencies of government or personnel ever have access to it. That said, it does not prevent intelligence (both indigenous and U.S.-provided) from frequently being leaked in the media, often for political purposes. Now, in light of the Abe government's proposed defense enhancements, expected increasing demands involving future offshore interventions have brought renewed interest and commitment to enhancing Japan's unilateral intelligence collection capacity. With parliamentary backing, moves are afoot to expand its satellite-based signals collection capabilities, to strengthen foreign intelligence based on recruiting and controlling human assets, and to flesh out more analysis drawing on those products. Whether those moves have anything directly to do with Japanese perceptions of U.S. intelligence fidelity and credibility is hard to discern, but their timing hardly seems coincidental.

The fact that the conservative Abe government is pursuing these kinds of enhancements would seem to owe less to hedging Japan's bets in counting on the United States for meeting many of its intelligence and security needs than to the heightened regional tensions with Beijing over unrelenting historical and maritime issues. Thus, perhaps more important than a U.S. factor, rising Japanese concerns over Chinese muscle-flexing and the continuing worry about a North Korea with nuclear weapons, missiles, and a barely penetrable ideology have prompted efforts by Japan to acquire more intelligence relying upon its own resources. It goes without saying that, thanks in large part to 20th century history, Japan has no basis to seek direct intelligence partnering within its own region.

Conclusion

Much of what has transpired around the world concerning the reputation of U.S. intelligence collection, analysis, and operations during and after the wars in Iraq and Afghanistan appears to outsiders to contradict American values and their showcasing as models for the world to see and imitate. What heretofore have been heralded as the acceptable methods, values, and avowed ideals of intelligence and law enforcement in keeping with U.S. rule of law, relative transparency, and defense of democracy seem out of sync with recent American intelligence practices and pronouncements. U.S. policy and actions are often deemed hypocritical, more reminiscent of might makes right and the ends justify the means. Thus, when a sitting U.S. Attorney General (Alberto Gonzales) issued a legal finding that waterboarding and other "enhanced" interrogation techniques did not constitute torture, many questioned his motives, legal interpretations, and moral and ethical judgment. The political cartoonists had a field day with this interpretation, as they have with a veritable avalanche of intrusive U.S. intelligence and law enforcement measures in the last decade and a half.

In light of the foregoing—and the less than ideal outcomes of conflicts in and over Iraq and Afghanistan—the U.S. intelligence reputation has taken many hits in foreign perceptions and portrayals. Much of this also has to do, however, with the mistrust of U.S. motives behind the Iraq intervention per se. Although many U.S. allies understand the conundrum that the 9/11 terrorist attacks brought about, they do not share the U.S. choice of methods to confront terrorism and Islamist extremism globally.[26] One must add, of course, that virtually no other country on earth has the capacity or will to deploy major forces, including special operations troops, to the far corners of the earth in extremely threatening conditions to take the fight to terrorists where they live, train, and operate.

Although some of the trust in the United States has lessened, relations with and dependence on the United States show few signs of marked diminution. U.S. credibility is questioned more often and demands for greater transparency have grown, but in intelligence the United States is, indeed, still the indispensable nation. Thus, all is not lost by any means, since the United States remains the dominant global actor in intelligence and counterterrorism/counterinsurgency. However, recouping some lost trust and stature will take a series of positive developments, marked U.S. image improvement, and greater willingness to partner even-handedly with others abroad in order to redress any misgivings and doubts that have arisen. In the interest of U.S. national security and global stability, those trust-enhancing measures toward foreign intelligence partners need to be ushered in soon.

CHAPTER 12
Conclusion: Lessons of the Lessons

John A. Gentry

The preceding 11 chapters illustrate a wide range of views about recent American wars held by important non-U.S. government actors. The perceptions and "lessons" of this volume should be considered tentative, however. The war in Iraq, once thought moderately successfully concluded in 2011, has morphed into a different and, in some respects, more dangerous conflict. The war in Afghanistan continues as of this writing, with its outcome uncertain. Both conflicts presumably will continue to evolve and undoubtedly will generate more perceived lessons, and lessons revised, as time passes. Still, some learning already is evident in the actions of insurgent groups still fighting in both countries and in the policies of states globally. This chapter summarizes contributors' findings, examines their judgments for broader patterns, and suggests some similarly tentative lessons of the lessons and implications for government officials and for scholars.

The lessons countries and nonstate actors encountered, and sometimes learned and operationalized, span a variety of topics. The word *encountered*, following Richard Hooker and Joseph Collins's use of the term, emphasizes a few critical observations: not all learnable lessons are in fact learned accurately, quickly, or well by national leaders; only some are converted into useful military equipment and doctrine or national policies; and often even fewer are internalized with some permanence into government organizational cultures.[1] Hooker and Collins's study, commissioned by Chairman of the Joint Chiefs of Staff General Martin Dempsey and published in 2015, makes the point clear by its title—*Lessons **Encountered**: Learning from the Long Wars* [bold added]—suggesting a lack of confidence that the U.S. government will effectively learn this time or, perhaps more diplomatically and positively, posing a challenge to do it well this time.

The lessons non-American actors identified and turned into policies and actions vary dramatically. Domestic political, diplomatic, alliance, and military/security situations seem to have been among the major causes of such differences in both perceptions and lessons. Countries with which the United States has troubled relationships unsurprisingly focus more on strategic political and military lessons applicable to a potential future conflict with the United States. U.S. allies' perceptions concentrate on the implications of their involvement in the wars in the context of continuing, valued alliance ties to the United States as well as a variety of domestic political and defense policy issues.

These and other significant differences suggest that effective learning about the wars even from narrowly U.S.-centric perspectives, while reasonably addressing lessons immediately useful for U.S. military commanders, planners, and policymakers, should also account for the lessons of friends involved in the conflicts whom Washington may want to engage again in coalition military operations. In addition, actors that did not participate but were watching intently surely will use their lessons when dealing with American leaders in the future. Disconcertingly from the U.S. perspective, most of the lessons of friends (Japan and France are partial exceptions) spring from, and focus on, negative experiences, while most of the lessons of potential or actual adversaries give them hope for better domestic and international situations. Iran, most especially, sees the wars as directly beneficial to the Islamic Republic and its agenda.

This chapter summarizes and assesses the lessons of the preceding chapters, generally in two overlapping ways: by country groups and by functional topic. It focuses primarily on perceptions and judgments that recur in chapters that were written independently to answer the questions posed in the Introduction of this book. More speculatively, it also suggests additional lessons for the U.S. government, other governments, and researchers.

U.S. Allies

Four chapters discuss lessons of seven countries with which the United States has treaties of alliance. In the cases of the United Kingdom, France, Germany, Italy, and Japan, lessons related to the maintenance and strengthening of their alliance ties played major roles in decisions to participate in operations in Afghanistan, mainly. Peter Viggo Jakobsen notes that the European allies entered the wars (or did not) for different reasons, had very different experiences in the conflicts in which they did participate, and unsurprisingly derived different lessons, which he tests by assessing their attitudes toward, and roles in, subsequent operations in Libya and Mali and against the Islamic State. Jakobsen's four-part model of determinants of West Europeans' judgments about the efficacy of the use of force in the two wars (and more broadly) (Table 4 in Chapter 1) includes assessment of whether a contemplated mission is good for long-term alliance ties with the United States. He concludes that most of the major European NATO states he assesses, and thence also the smaller member states that generally follow their lead, may not be willing to follow the United States into another major deployment unless the operation is in defense of core national interests, meets rigorous humanitarian standards, or is important to maintain alliance ties. Jakobsen's construct also helps explain why France, which did not participate in Iraq but had a generally positive experience in Afghanistan, has been the most aggressive European user of force in recent years. Jakobsen's assessment closely tracks Patrick Keller's more detailed look at Germany's lessons from its experience in Afghanistan.

Jakobsen's model seems generally applicable to Japan and Turkey as well. Maintenance and expansion of U.S. ties were major, and generally positive, factors for Japan. But less-than-ideal economic, domestic political, and internal security situations contributed markedly to Turkey's negative views of the consequences of the war in Iraq and its later spillover consequences in Syria, and to Turkey's view that internal stability is more important than the still-significant alliance relationship with the United States. Indeed, K.A. Beyoghlow argues that Turkey sees the Iraq war as spawning existential threats to Turkey, suggesting that Turkey may be reluctant to accommodate future U.S. interests not clearly linked to those of Turkey.

Strikingly, the American goal in planning the invasion of Iraq in 2002–03 largely excluded planning for a European role.[2] Aiming to win quickly and efficiently, largely with American power and that of close allies such as the United Kingdom and Australia, U.S. military planners wanted to avoid the coordination problems they experienced in past alliance and coalition operations, including NATO's war against Yugoslavia in 1999, then hand off post-conflict repairs, humanitarian assistance, and "nation-building" chores to others, including allies and the United Nations. France, Germany, and Belgium very publicly opposed the Iraq war, however, blocking NATO planning for a role in Iraq and making the "coalition of the willing" much smaller for the 2003 war against Iraq than it was in 1990–91.[3]

In contrast, NATO countries invoked Article 5 of the Washington Treaty immediately after the 9/11 attacks. NATO member states and other coalition partners nevertheless saw the mission in Afghanistan very differently, generating tasks and rules of engagement that Jakobsen, Keller, and Michael David discuss at length. These different views frustrated some American military personnel who did not understand or appreciate reasons for the divergent national political directives that complicated the International Security Assistance Force mission considerably. Presumably Germany, Japan, and some other allies will help again under similar circumstances, but recent experience suggests that they want clearer, more consistent, and more effective U.S. leadership than they experienced in both Iraq and Afghanistan.

Jakobsen argues that conventional wisdom that European NATO's military postures are weakening is incorrect. His case rests mainly on the robust actions of France since 2011 and the reasonable assertion that NATO countries will fight to defend core national interests. While the prospect of needing to defend themselves seems more imaginable as Russia flexes its muscle in Ukraine and against the Baltic states, Germany, Italy, and even the United Kingdom showed high and evidently growing sensitivity to casualties in Iraq and Afghanistan—among local civilian populations and their own troops. Japan displayed similar casualty aversion. These evidently strongly held convictions help explain why, in the absence of an existential threat to them, Washington may find enlistment of its allies in risky ventures challenging unless their core national interests are at stake or a humanitarian emergency seems particularly compelling. Policymakers, diplomats, intelligence officers, and soldiers should continue to be alert for signs of the evolving criteria by which states assess the worth of military missions and the consequences of such decisions. This is essential for identifying changes in the political, military, and normative appeals necessary to recruit members of coalitions in the future.

Pakistan was nominally cooperative with the U.S.-led coalition in Afghanistan but operated in ways it viewed as nationally advantageous. In Stephen Tankel's view, Pakistan saw the United States as an important actor in Afghanistan that it needed to accommodate rhetorically, while keeping its primary focus on its rivalry with India and domestic concerns. Pakistan therefore supported groups it thought useful at home even if they also fought the U.S.-led coalition in Afghanistan, angering U.S. officials. Tankel observes that the groups now seem to pose considerable dangers to the Pakistani military and political leadership, suggesting that they may have misjudged situations. But Pakistani actions may not have been mistakes—just the best way to handle difficult situations as they arose.

Potential U.S. Adversaries

Perhaps the dominant perception of countries with which the United States has challenged relationships is U.S. strategic ineptitude. Both the George W. Bush and Barack Obama administrations get poor marks for strategic coherence and consistent, effective political/military operations over time. Potential adversaries of the United States see the wars and their outcomes as negative for U.S. interests while having a range of implications for their own concerns. Although there is some admiration for U.S. technological and tactical military prowess, the perceptions of U.S. strategic incompetence should worry American officials because they reflect a lack of respect for the United States as a responsible international actor. Officials should also be concerned about the implications of what Russia, China, and Iran see as U.S. strategic- and operational-level political/military bumbling. Such views seem to lead them to see opportunities to operate more freely and in ways differently than Washington would like and, in some cases, to see American weaknesses as vulnerabilities they have opportunities to exploit.[4] Presumably, other actors have seen the wars similarly and drawn similar conclusions.

Russia and China see geostrategic lessons of the wars similarly: the United States was dangerously aggressive in Iraq, especially, but was strategically confused and ultimately ineffective in achieving its goals for the wars despite being tactically and technically proficient in winning battles. Wars the United States initiated spun out of U.S. control because they were poorly conceived, leading to numerous unintended consequences, including the rise of terrorist groups in many countries. Chinese analysts cite the phenomenon generally while Russians blame the United States for the spillover of Islamist terrorism into their country, which they consider to be a big and growing problem. These concerns are mirrored elsewhere, including by American analysts and even senior officials such as former Secretary of Defense Robert Gates.[5] Stephen Blank argues the Russians go further, concluding that Russia, too, as a great power can act as independently of international norms as the United States has—and get away with it.[6] And, both Russia and China used the years of U.S. distraction in south and southwest Asia to strengthen their national militaries in ways directly applicable to a potential fight with American forces.

Analysts in both countries see the U.S. wars through national historical and ideological lenses, in some cases predisposing them to see lessons more objective observers, or at least analysts with other paradigmatic perspectives, may interpret differently. But those perceptions are nevertheless real, meaning it behooves observers of all varieties, including intelligence analysts, to make sure they do not commit the cardinal error of mirror-imaging when assessing others' lessons.[7]

Iran actively, if indirectly, fought U.S.-led coalitions in both Iraq and Afghanistan and emerged more confident in its political/military strategy and political/theological prospects regionally, in the Muslim world generally, and vis-a-vis the United States. Convinced that the United States is a determined enemy, Iran practiced forms of low-level, asymmetric conflict that it thinks were effective and will be useful in the future to advance its interests and goals at U.S. expense. Thomas Dowling's analysis suggests that Iran, perhaps more than Russia and China, identifies the sources of U.S. failings in both wars as exploitable vulnerabilities.

U.S. Strategic Confusion

Most countries, including U.S. allies, see American strategies as ineffective and often unclear. The most common critique is that the United States entered both wars without knowing the regions in which it would be operating. Committed to furthering American values, the United States failed to advance them because it did not understand how to accomplish them in the very different political cultures of Iraq and Afghanistan. Many Americans have made similar observations, including the severe critique of then-Major General Michael Flynn cited in the Introduction.[8] Lawrence Cline makes a key point: once again the United States, and especially the U.S. military, focused on tactical fighting—usually doing it well—while ignoring the political and other strategic aspects of whole wars. The point was made succinctly in a conversation U.S. Army Colonel Harry Summers reports that he had with a North Vietnamese Army colonel in 1975, soon after the American war in Vietnam was over, and published in 1982 in a book once read widely by U.S. military officers:

> "You know you never defeated us on the battlefield," said the American colonel [Summers]. The North Vietnamese colonel pondered this remark a moment. "That may be so," he replied, "but it is also irrelevant."[9]

U.S. enemies again did not make America's mistake.

Patrick Keller notes that Germany, keen to support the United States in keeping with its goal of keeping NATO strong, saw shifts in publicly stated U.S. strategic goals damaging the credibility and effectiveness of operations in Afghanistan, thereby also diminishing German popular support for the effort. Berlin also was confused about American policy regarding Libya in 2011. Turks and Iranians think the Americans showed little understanding of the Middle East, making major mistakes derived from cultural ignorance and insensitivity—a problem for Turkey but a good thing from Iran's perspective.

Chinese analysts argue that American ideological commitment to spreading democracy in south and southwest Asia was severely misplaced, leading to ineffective strategies and operations in both Iraq and Afghanistan. David Lai notes that Chinese analysts, seeing the world through Marxist-Leninist-Maoist-Dengist-colored glasses, also see the U.S. wars as part of an American quest for global "hegemony." While the terminology may seem inflammatory at first, it is not far from that of Western scholars of the realist perspective on international relations, who talk about the unipolarity of a post-Cold War world led by the United States as hegemon. And U.S. government rhetoric during the early days of the Iraq War, at least, featured the goal of reshaping the Middle East into a version of America's image by establishing democracy in Iraq.

Stephen Tankel argues that Pakistan understood that U.S. interests were not its own and opted to act in ways superficially supportive of U.S. goals while focused on its own. Islamabad took some actions that helped the Taliban, and correspondingly opposed U.S. interests, in part because Pakistan doubted U.S. staying power. Temporal commitment is a key element in strategy, and many observers have noted the short-term focus of U.S. policies and commitments—especially President Obama's once-firm calendar date, now predictably extended, for ending the U.S. military mission in Afghanistan.

This common view is disturbing from an American perspective because it suggests both diminishing international respect for the United States and evidently growing concerns about perceived U.S. strategic incompetence. It also gives several countries, especially actual (Iran) and potential rivals (Russia and China) hope that they, too, can enhance their power at U.S. expense, with positive results for themselves.

Ideas and Information Operations

The importance of effective use of information operations (IO), including political messaging, appears in different ways in several chapters. Three authors discuss the power of ideas to change strategic cultures of countries. Patrick Keller and Michael David note that the constitutions the United States imposed on Germany and Japan after World War II significantly limited those countries' roles in the wars. Stephen Blank observes that Russia wants to use IO to create similar effects in other countries—to its advantage. Yet unlike in the 1940s, U.S. efforts to impose democracy in Iraq and Western efforts to promote democracy in Afghanistan both failed and met considerable derision as ideologies inappropriate for the political cultures they were thrust upon. Left unasked, and unanswered, is whether U.S. efforts were less competent than those of the immediate post-World War II period or whether situations were dramatically different. Certainly Japan in 1945, like Iraq and Afghanistan in 2001, had no strong national tradition of democracy.

Russia seems to have made major changes in its doctrine and operations in this arena. Unlike the U.S. emphasis on technical aspects of cyber warfare—usually defined as attacks on computer networks—the Russians also focus upon control of the content of electronically communicated messages useful for shaping whole societies. In contrast, the United States does "public diplomacy" notoriously poorly and bans IO aimed at Americans and even messages Americans may receive indirectly via "blowback" from abroad. Stephen Blank argues that the Putin regime sees this kind of IO as applicable in both domestic and international contexts. Other analysts point to sophisticated Russian irregular warfare operations in Ukraine in 2014–15, especially, that employed IO to legitimize Russian intervention to protect ethnic Russians allegedly oppressed by Ukraine.[10] Many actors in recent years in a wide variety of conflicts have sought to defeat or manipulate enemies or third parties by appealing to sensitivities to casualties, or what some call the instrumental use of casualty aversion norms.[11] Russia has added a new twist on such norm entrepreneurship by appending nationalism to the list of rights that allegedly merit external intervention to defend. The liberal West, including the United States, appears to be most vulnerable to such instrumental use of norms.[12]

Iran, too, is using both aspects of IO—cyberattacks and the shaping of content. It seems to have built its "Cyber Army" in partial reaction to the Stuxnet attacks it experienced in 2010. And, U.S. failures in Iraq and Afghanistan, and its ongoing struggle against the Islamic State, give Tehran opportunities to portray itself as a legitimate regional power and the only effective force protecting all Muslims from the Islamic State and oppressed people globally from alleged American predations.

Insurgent groups have learned the importance of IO to control the initiative in political discourse, regardless of the accuracy of the information they purvey, and its importance for many other purposes. As Lawrence Cline notes, the Taliban and Islamic State devote significant resources to using IO to recruit, train, and raise funds. They gather, create, and disseminate information that trumpets their operational successes and their enemies' failures, and otherwise supports their strategic agendas. Recognizing the importance of IO, they have built IO units into their force structures. Even the Islamic State is now using a more established variant of the instrumental use of norms—using Iraqi civilians as human shields to both protect their fighters and generate favorable publicity if Iraqi security forces and their allies accidentally kill civilians.[13]

For NATO states and Japan, Jakobsen, Keller, and David argue that future deployments will depend in part on the domestic political discourse, driven by information-shaped perceptions, about the justice of future operations. This makes contestation over perceptions of evolving situations critical for partisans of all persuasions. It makes still more important the development of effective American "public diplomacy" capabilities, at minimum. But while this effort requires technical skills that have been very weak for years, it also must be based on facts, and the wars have cost the United States credibility in important respects.

U.S. Learning and Adaptation Critiqued

Our authors and the actors they assess repeatedly comment that the lessons that Americans took from the conflicts differ from other actors' perceptions, sometimes markedly, and that Americans should have learned faster and better—perhaps thereby avoiding their strategic errors. The chapters note the dearth, and/or slowness, of U.S. government learning in absolute terms and relative to actual or potential adversaries. The slow learning is followed by ineffective adaptation. These assessments should concern U.S. government officials but not surprise them. A large body of literature on U.S. foreign policy decisionmaking, intelligence, and military lessons-learned processes notes chronic deficiencies in these areas.[14]

Stephen Blank makes the point most explicitly and strongly about Russian learning compared to U.S. learning, but Iran, China, and U.S. allies also note slow and ineffective U.S. learning and adaptation. Blank observes that American officials have not well monitored Russian developments generated partly in response to the wars in Iraq and Afghanistan—and partly also from ongoing Russian learning and adaptation processes stemming from operations in Chechnya and elsewhere. And, Thomas Dowling and David Lai note that Iranian and Chinese commentators, respectively, almost universally argue that the United States did not learn about the Middle East. Indeed, analysts in both countries maintain that the United States still does understand the region.

Stephen Tankel reminds us of the central importance of irregular forces in Pakistan's strategic competition with India, and remarks that U.S. government officials should have known that Islamabad would protect perceived core strategic assets despite what Washington wanted. Yet they clearly did not. Senior U.S. officials repeatedly blasted the Pakistani government for accommodating groups that fight the United States in Afghanistan but are of major domestic importance to Islamabad, including the Haqqani Network.

Lawrence Cline notes a troubling pattern for the U.S. and other Western governments: insurgent groups continue to learn and adapt faster than they do. This phenomenon is not new; it also is not surprising. Weak nonstate actors fighting materially strong states must be agile or they will be crushed. Nonstate enemies have indeed learned to adapt quickly and well to U.S. and coalition strategies. For example, the xenophobic Taliban, isolationist in the late 1990s, displayed considerable ineptitude in 2001, leading to its quick defeat. But it staged a considerable comeback, in significant part by learning from its past mistakes and from American practices. The Islamic State, largely a descendant of al-Qaida in Iraq, has managed, as of this writing in early 2016, to create a proto-state and a huge challenge for its many enemies. The Islamic State also is turning its attention to the "far enemy," leading to terrorist attacks in Western Europe and perhaps the United States in late 2015. Stephen Tankel notes the substantial evolution in the thinking of jihadist groups in Pakistan, which in some cases led to increased opposition to the Pakistani state, in part due to questionable government actions taken at U.S. behest.

States learn at different speeds, and Cline's assessment that U.S. learning and adaptation are relatively slow and ineffective is consistent with other comparisons.[15] A true superpower can get away with slow learning in situations that do not involve existential threats. But it is much more damaging to lesser powers and states that rely on organizing and leading disparate coalitions to achieve their foreign policy objectives and need finesse to do so—as Washington has increasingly tried to do in recent years.

Domestic Political Ramifications

The wars prompted appreciable political debate and some national soul-searching in several countries. Failure was not the only cause. Japanese military experiences and successes, while modest by American standards, controversially suggested variously to Japanese that their country should—or should not—be somewhat more muscular in its international political/military doings. Japan's experiences also raised again the issue of the wisdom of Japan's post-1945 constitutional prohibition on use of armed force to resolve international disputes and thence to its unusually conservative national strategic outlook. In contrast, many Germans seem to have decided that a primary German lesson of 1939–45 was a good one; the use of military force for optional purposes really is a bad idea. The war in Iraq, in particular, contributed to intense policy debates in Turkey and growing anti-American sentiment. Stephen Blank describes a dramatic change in Russian domestic policy, triggered also by lessons of internal conflicts in Chechnya and elsewhere, that IO should be used to control domestic thought processes; this goal surely is not without precedent in authoritarian Russian/Soviet history, but the techniques and the counterterrorism focus of recent efforts are new. And, Thomas Dowling observes that Iran's ruling elites are pleased with their successes in both wars, presumably strengthening their domestic positions.

Foreign Aid

The role of foreign aid agencies and the nongovernmental organizations (NGOs) they employ and otherwise support, and of military units operating in humanitarian assistance-type roles, appears in three chapters. Pauline Baker focuses on international humanitarian NGOs and the problems they encountered in dealing with belligerents in the conflicts, including the U.S. government. As Baker notes, the U.S. Agency for International Development relies extensively on NGOs under contract to perform its functions, and other countries' aid agencies do the same. Baker's discussion of how U.S. policies endanger aid workers physically, threaten the operational environments they treasure, and endanger their funding suggests another variant of U.S. strategic confusion. The U.S. and other governments have decided that they will rely on NGOs to perform much of their foreign assistance, but make it hard for NGOs to perform in ways those NGOs consider essential to their principles and organizational well-being. At the same time, military doctrine for counterinsurgency operations per Field Manual 3-24, the latest edition of which is called *Insurgencies and Countering Insurgencies*, makes clear that military engagement with local people is essential for strategic political/military success—precisely what NGOs do not want.[16] NGOs long have been in war zones before foreign troops arrive, stayed during the fighting, and remained after the troops go home. That pattern seems likely to continue. This fairly obvious policy contradiction remains unresolved.

A major civil-military effort to contribute to "nation building"—the Provincial Reconstruction Teams—did not perform particularly well and eventually was discontinued in Afghanistan. This suggests that core elements of U.S. and NATO doctrine and force structure—civil affairs or what NATO terms Civil-Military Cooperation, or CIMIC, units and functions—also need re-consideration.

Michael David emphasizes the importance of Japan's Ministry of Foreign Affairs and its use of Official Development Assistance funds to support many Japanese military and NGO operations in Afghanistan, especially. Japanese armed forces in both countries and German troops in Afghanistan understood that core parts of their missions as assigned by their national governments were to help local people, not to kill enemies. Because such attitudes are likely in future conflicts, U.S. planners and decisionmakers, and their coalition partners, have much to do. They must ensure that military and civilian government personnel, and NGO staff, understand their often very different missions and appreciate the underlying, strongly held principles that lead NGOs and governments to specify sometimes very different operational tasks and rules of engagement than U.S. troops have and like.

Lessons for Intelligence

The strategic muddle of the wars and global reactions to it suggest significant challenges for U.S. intelligence. Starting with the 9/11 surprise that prompted the war in Afghanistan and the weak intelligence behind the flawed National Intelligence Estimate of 2002 on Iraqi weapons of mass destruction that was part of the Bush administration's rationale for the invasion of Iraq, U.S. intelligence on the wars has been widely criticized.[17] As Bowman Miller notes, publicity about politically validated but unsavory interrogation techniques and renditions did not help.

The chapters of this book, which amount to a form of open-source intelligence analysis, suggest other kinds of failings and challenges that are more closely associated with traditional intelligence collection and analytic practices. Perhaps most significantly, American and foreign observers widely if implicitly believe the Intelligence Community in 2001 did not adequately help (and has not since helped) senior U.S. leaders to develop long-range, effective strategic vision. Intelligence cannot, of course, prevent decisionmakers from making mistakes, and ineffective and/or inconsistent strategies have been common features of both the Bush and Obama administrations.

Intelligence does as senior leaders ask it to do, but senior leaders cannot ask for information or intelligence about what former Secretary of Defense Donald Rumsfeld famously called "unknown unknowns." Intelligence arguably has a responsibility to anticipate and study situations senior leaders do not yet know will one day concern them greatly, to look "over the horizon," in former Director of Central Intelligence Robert Gates's vernacular—a practice some now call anticipatory intelligence. The Intelligence Community also can better assess whether U.S. policies, threats, requests, or inducements are likely to be effective abroad, under what circumstances, and whether they may generate unintended negative consequences.

The National Intelligence Priorities Framework gives intelligence leaders some flexibility to look at issues and areas not currently of policy concern.[18] These chapters suggest they may need to do so more aggressively. U.S. intelligence traditionally has better identified and assessed tactical-level capabilities rather than strategic intentions. But General Flynn's critique indicates that even tactical intelligence was flawed by design—its priorities were skewed. Tactical intelligence personnel traditionally work closely with and for operators, who to some degree understandably focus mainly on the here and now, suggesting that decisions to look more broadly and deeply, and at different issues including strategically important political factors, should mainly be a national-level responsibility.[19] Sometimes it is best *not* to focus primarily on immediate, tactical support to combat troops in the field.

At strategic levels, these chapters and history suggest another reason for American concern. Only years later did American intelligence personnel become aware that Soviet leaders saw the U.S. military buildup of the early 1980s and a major exercise in 1983 as indicating an intent by President Ronald Reagan to initiate a nuclear attack on the USSR.[20] Focused on other issues, and aware that the Reagan administration had no such plan, U.S. intelligence officers were slow to appreciate that the Soviets had a drastically different view. Have U.S. actions (or inactions) during the wars in Iraq and Afghanistan, or strategic muddling including a lack of U.S. "staying power," generated reactions U.S. intelligence has not yet identified whose negative consequences have yet to appear? Russia, China, and Iran fairly clearly are pondering their lessons carefully.

Consequences and Concluding Comments

The wars and their lessons have consequences that promise to be significant for years to come, complicating U.S. foreign policymaking in new ways. The war in Afghanistan, and Pakistani government policies, may have exacerbated instability in Pakistan. The war in Iraq and its aftermath have deepened

Turkish unhappiness with many U.S. policies, damaging the NATO solidarity. For Japan, effective operations in both Iraq and Afghanistan have strengthened self-confidence, while perhaps making Japan a more willing partner in future U.S. operations. In Germany, the bitter aftertaste of operations in Afghanistan may make Berlin even less willing to use force except in immediate national defense, while French confidence in military options has grown. Both Russia and China seem to have learned many lessons. And, a more confident and emboldened Iran may be an even bigger challenge for many countries.

While these assessments of the wars' implications are partial and preliminary, some things are clear. The war efforts thus far have not only been costly non-successes from the U.S. perspective, they appreciably affected many other aspects of international life, with generally negative implications for U.S. interests that surely are not yet fully apparent. Potential and actual adversaries have learned and adapted, and perhaps become more adventuresome, while U.S. allies question the quality of American leadership. The U.S. government continues to struggle with its national security decisionmaking and implementing processes.[21] The consequences of the wars seem likely to make reforms both more important to make and tougher to accomplish. They also have expanded the types and complexity of issues U.S. intelligence, policymakers globally, and the scholarly community should address.

ENDNOTES

INTRODUCTION

1 For example, Richard D. Hooker, Jr., and Joseph J. Collins, *Lessons Encountered: Learning from the Long Wars* (Washington: National Defense University Press, 2015); Christopher Chivvis, Olga Oliker, Andrew Liepman, Ben Connable, George Wilcoxon, William Young, *Initial Thoughts on the Impact of the Iraq War on U.S. National Security Structures* (Santa Monica, CA: RAND, 2014), www.rand.org.

2 Anthony H. Cordesman, *Irregular Warfare: Learning the Lessons of "Worst Case" Wars* (Washington: Center for Strategic and International Studies, 2014); Stephen Biddle, "Afghanistan's Legacy: Emerging Lessons of an Ongoing War," *Washington Quarterly* 37, no. 2 (2014): 73–86.

3 Michael T. Flynn, Matt Pottinger, and Paul Batchelor, *Fixing Intel: A Blueprint for Making Intelligence Relevant in Afghanistan* (Washington: Center for a New American Security, 2010), 7.

CHAPTER 1
Less Capable and Less Willing? European Involvement in Combat Operations After Iraq and Afghanistan

1 U.S. Department of Defense, "The Security and Defense Agenda (Future of NATO)" (speech by Secretary of Defense Robert Gates, Brussels, June 10, 2011).

2 See for instance Ellen Hallams and Benjamin Schreer, "Towards a 'Post-American' Alliance? NATO Burden-sharing After Libya," *International Affairs* 88: 2 (2012): 322–24; International Institute of Strategic Studies, "War in Libya: Europe's Confused Response," *Strategic Comments* 17:4 (2011): 1–3.

3 Steven Erlanger, "Shrinking Europe Military Spending Stirs Concern," *New York Times*, April 23, 2013. For similar assessments, see Jeffrey. H. Michaels, "Able but Not Willing: A Critical Assessment of NATO's Libya Intervention," in *The NATO Intervention in Libya: Lessons Learned from the Campaign*, ed. Kjell Engelbrekt, Marcus Mohlin and Charlotte Wagnsson (New York: Routledge, 2014), 17–37; Richard Norton-Taylor, "First Afghanistan, Now Libya. Can Nato Actually Win Any of Its Wars?" *Guardian*, July 26, 2011.

Chapter 1 Endnotes

4   Michael Shurkin, "Allied Fronts. European Armies Approach Austerity in Instructive Ways," *RAND Review* (Fall 2013), http://www.rand.org/pubs/periodicals/rand-review/issues/2013/fall/alliedfronts.html.

5   Pew Research Center, *NATO Publics Blame Russia for Ukrainian Crisis, but Reluctant to Provide Military Aid*, June 10, 2015, 17, http://www.pewglobal.org/files/2015/06/Pew-Research-Center-Russia-Ukraine-Report-FINAL-June-10-2015.pdf.

6   European Union, *Special Eurobarometer* 432, *Europeans' Attitudes Towards Security*, April 2015, 20, http://ec.europa.eu/public_opinion/archives/ebs/ebs_432_en.pdf.

7   European Union, *Special Eurobarometer* 432, *Europeans' Attitudes Towards Security*, 36.

8   Pew Research Center, *NATO Publics Blame Russia for Ukrainian Crisis*, 6, 10.

9   Peter Viggo Jakobsen and Jens Ringsmose, "Size and Reputation—Why the United States Has Valued Its 'Special Relationships' with Denmark and the United Kingdom Differently Since 9/11," *Journal of Transatlantic Studies* 13:2 (2015).

10   Peter Viggo Jakobsen, "The Indispensable Enabler: NATO's Strategic Value in High-Intensity Operations Is Far Greater Than You Think," in *Strategy in NATO: Preparing for an Imperfect World*, ed. Liselotte Odgaard (New York, NY: Palgrave Macmillan, 2014), 59–74.

11   NATO, *Operation UNIFIED PROTECTOR, Final Mission Stats*, November 2, 2011.

12   Ivo H. Daalder and James G. Stavridis, "NATO's Victory in Libya: The Right Way to Run an Intervention," *Foreign Affairs* 91, no. 2 (2012): 6; Michael J. Williams, "Implications for British Defense Dependency on Foreign and Security Policy," in House of Commons Defence Committee, *Operations in Libya*, Vol. II (London: The Stationery Office Limited, 2012), 7.

13   Michael Hastings, "Inside Obama's War Room," *Rolling Stone*, October 27, 2011; Scott Wilson and Joby Warrick, "Obama's Shift Toward Military Action in Libya," *Washington Post*, March 19, 2011.

14   Scott Bade, "The British Aren't COMING—Why the French Intervene in their Former African Colonies and the British Do Not," Stanford Center for International Security and Cooperation 2013, 5.

Chapter 1 Endnotes

15 See Steven Erlanger, "The French Way of War," *New York Times*, January 20, 2013; Bastien Irondelle and Olivier Schmitt, "France," in *Strategic Cultures in Europe: Security and Defence Policies Across the Continent*, ed. Heiko Biehl, Bastian Giegerich, and Alexandra Jonas (Potsdam: Springer VS, 2013), 125–37.

16 Michael Shurkin, *France's War in Mali: Lessons for an Expeditionary Army* (Santa Monica, CA: RAND), 22–23.

17 Madelene Lindström and Kristina Zetterlund, *Setting the Stage for the Military Intervention in Libya: Decisions Made and Their Implications for the EU and NATO* (Stockholm, FOI, 2012), 20–22.

18 Camille Grand, "The French Experience: Sarkozy's War?," in *Precision and Purpose: Airpower in the Libyan Civil War*, ed. Karl P. Mueller (Santa Monica: RAND, 2015), 189.

19 Paul Cornish, "United Kingdom," in *Strategic Cultures in Europe*, in ed. Biehl, Giegerich, and Jonas, 370–86.

20 Michael Clarke, "The Making of Britain's Libya Strategy," in *Short War, Long Shadow—The Political and Military Legacies of the 2011 Libya Campaign*, ed. Adrian Johnson and Saqeb Mueen (London: Royal United Services Institute, 2012), 8; Bagehot, "The War Drums Boom in Britain," *Economist*, March 18, 2011.

21 Jakobsen and Ringsmose, "Size and Reputation."

22 Ben Clements, "Public Opinion and Military Interventions: Afghanistan, Iraq and Libya," *The Political Quarterly* 84, no. 1 (January 2013): 119.

23 Clarke, "The Making of Britain's Libya Strategy," 7–9.

24 David Cameron, "Foreign Policy in the National Interest," (speech to the Lord Mayor's Banquet, November 14, 2011), http://www.number10.gov.uk/news/lord-mayors-banquet/.

25 Alice Pannier, "A Crisis Within the Crisis: Franco-British Negotiations in the War in Libya (2011)," (paper presented at the 13ème Congrès National de l'Association Française de Science Politique Aix en Provence, June 21–23, 2015), 8.

26 See Alessandro Marrone and Federica Di Camillo, "Italy," in *Strategic Cultures in Europe*, ed. Biehl, Giegerich, and Jonas, 192–206.

27 Linda Basile, Pierangelo Isernia, and Francesco Olmastroni, *Italians and Foreign Policy* (research report by CIRCaP/LAPS (University of Siena) and IAI, 2013), 20–21.

Chapter 1 Endnotes

28 Jason W. Davidson, "Italy-US Relations since the End of the Cold War: Prestige, Peace, and the Transatlantic Balance," *Bulletin of Italian Politics*, 1, no. 2 (2009), 290; Alessandro Marrone, Paola Tessari and Carolina De Simone, *Italian Interests and NATO: From Missions to Trenches?* (Rome: Istituto Affari Internazionali, 2014), 20–22; Alessandro Marrone and Alessandro R. Ungaro, "Relations Between the United States of America and Italy in the Post-Cold War Period: a Defense-Industrial perspective," *Cahiers de la Méditerranée*, 88, 2014, 157–181, https://cdlm.revues.org/7542.

29 Marrone and Ungaro, "Relations between the United States of America and Italy in the Post-Cold War Period," para 46.

30 Marrone, Tessari and De Simone, *Italian Interests and NATO*, 28.

31 Gregory Alegi, "The Italian Experience: Pivotal and Underestimated," in *Precision and Purpose*, ed. Mueller, 216; David P. Auerswald and Stephen M. Saideman, *NATO in Afghanistan, Fighting Together, Fighting Alone* (Princeton: Princeton University Press, 2014), 172–73.

32 Ben Lombardi, "The Berlusconi Government and Intervention in Libya," *International Spectator* 46, no. 4 (2011): 42.

33 Clements, "Public Opinion and Military Interventions," 122.

34 David Cenciotti, "Cleared Hot: The Italian AMX Light Combat Planes To Be Cleared To Carry (and Use) Bombs in Afghanistan," January 28, 2012, http://theaviationist.com/2012/01/28/cleared-hot/.

35 Alegi, "The Italian Experience: Pivotal and Underestimated," 220–21.

36 Osvaldo Croci and Marco Valigi, "Continuity and Change in Italian Foreign Policy: The Case of the International Intervention in Libya," *Contemporary Italian Politics* 5 no. 1 (2013): 47–49; Valentina Pop, "Italy Presses for NATO Command of Libya War," *EU Observer*, March 22, 2011.

37 Alegi, "The Italian Experience: Pivotal and Underestimated," 226; Tom Kington, "Italy Gives Bombing Stats for Libya Campaign," *Defense News*, December 14, 2011.

38 See Julian Junk and Christopher Daase, "Germany," in *Strategic Cultures in Europe*, ed. Biehl, Giegerich, and Jonas, 138–52.

39 *Rede Joschka Fischers auf dem Außerordentlichen Parteitag in Bielefeld*, May 13, 1999, http://staff-www.uni-marburg.de/~naeser/kos-fisc.htm.

40 Jakobsen, "The Indispensable Enabler."

Chapter 1 Endnotes

41 Christopher Alessi, "Learning to Fight: How Afghanistan Changed the German Military," *Spiegel Online International*, October 15, 2013.

42 James D. Bindenagel, "Afghanistan: The German Factor," *Prism* 1, no. 4 (2010): 106; Michael F. Harsch, "A Reluctant Warrior. The German Engagement in Afghanistan," *PRIO Paper* 2011, 5.

43 Sarah Brockmeier, "Germany and the Intervention in Libya," *Survival* 55, no. 6 (2013): 63–90.

44 Ibid., 79.

45 Lindström and Zetterlund, *Setting the Stage for the Military Intervention in Libya*, 26.

46 Ralf Beste and Dirk Kurbjuweit, "SPIEGEL Interview with Defense Minister De Maizière: 'We Will Not Get Involved' in Syria,'" *Spiegel Online International*, June 20, 2011.

47 Ekkehard Brose, "Recalibrating German Security Policy Three Years After Libya," March 17, 2014, http://www.swp-berlin.org/en/publications/point-of-view/recalibrating-german-security-policy-three-years-after-libya.html; Alison Smale, "Spurred by Global Crises, Germany Weighs a More Muscular Foreign Policy," *New York Times*, February 2, 2014.

48 Daryl Lindsey, "Atoning for Libya: Germany Seeks Low Profile in Syria," *Spiegel Online International*, August 30, 2013.

49 Sergei Boeke and Bart Schuurman, "Operation 'Serval': A Strategic Analysis of the French Intervention in Mali, 2013–2014," *Journal of Strategic Studies*, 2015, doi: 10.1080/01402390.2015.10454946-7, 2.

50 Bruno Tertrais, "Leading on the Cheap? French Security Policy in Austerity," *The Washington Quarterly* 36, no. 3 (Summer 2013): 51.

51 Shurkin, *France's War in Mali*, 2–3.

52 Grand, "The French Experience;" Phillipe Gros, *Libya And Mali Operations: Transatlantic Lessons Learned* (Washington: The German Marshall Fund of the United States), 14.

53 Tertrais, "Leading on the Cheap?," 53.

54 BVA, Les Français et l'intervention militaire au Mali, January 15, 2013, http://www.bva.fr/data/sondage/sondage_fiche/1220/fichier_les_francais_et_lintervention_militaire_au_mali0144e.pdf.

Chapter 1 Endnotes

55 Olga Khazan, "In France, the Mali Intervention Is More Popular Than Gay Marriage," *Washington Post*, January 16, 2013; Gabriele Parussini, "Mali Campaign Lifts Hollande in France," *Wall Street Journal*, January 15, 2013.

56 Tertrais, "Leading on the Cheap?," 53; Boeke and Schuurman, "Operation 'Serval,'" 6–7.

57 Roland Marchal, "Briefing: Military (mis)adventures in Mali," *African Affairs* 112: 448, 2013, 489.

58 David Gauthier-Villars and Adam Entous, "After French Criticism, Washington Drops Payment Demand," *Wall Street Journal*, January 20, 2013.

59 Boeke and Schuurman, "Operation 'Serval,'" 17; Gros, *Libya and Mali Operations*, 12.

60 Agence France-Presse, "France Displaces Britain as Key US Military Ally," *DefenseNews*, March 19, 2015; François Heisbourg, "Hollande's Martial Prowess," *New York Times*, February 10, 2014; Barack Obama and François Hollande, "France and the U.S. Enjoy a Renewed Alliance," *Washington Post*, February 10, 2014; Michael Shurkin and Peter A. Wilson, "France Is Replacing the UK as America's Top Ally in Europe," *Newsweek*, March 30, 2015.

61 Nicholas Cecil and Peter Allen, "U.K. Troops 'Must Not Get Bogged Down' on Mali Training Mission," *London Evening Standard*, January 15, 2013; Michael Codner, "The British Military Contribution to Operations in Mali: Is This Mission Creep?," *RUSI Analysis*, January 30, 2013; Philip Hammond, "UK Intervention in Mali Is Strategy for Future, Says Defence Secretary," *Guardian*, January 29, 2013; Nicholas Watt and Luke Harding, "Mali: Britain Prepared to Send 'Sizeable Amount' of Troops To Support French," *Guardian*, January 28, 2013.

62 Nick Squires, "Mali: Italy to Offer France Logistical Support," *Telegraph*, January 16, 2013.

63 *Speech by Federal Foreign Minister Westerwelle in the German Bundestag on the Bundeswehr mission in Mali*, February 20, 2013, http://www.auswaertiges-amt.de/sid_A39A760BAB1CF45AC55C5D60BB55081E/EN/Infoservice/Presse/Reden/2013/130220-BM-BT-Mali-Rede.html?nn=354316.

64 "Militäreinsatz in Mali Frankreich bittet Bundeswehr um Tankflugzeuge," *Süddeutsche Zeitung*, January 25, 2013.

Chapter 1 Endnotes

65 The 12 countries that have conducted strike missions are Australia, Bahrain, Belgium, Canada, Denmark, France, Jordan, Netherlands, Saudi Arabia, Turkey, the United Arab Emirates, and the United Kingdom.

66 Embassy of France in London, "Prime Minister Explains French Action in Iraq to Parliament," September 24, 2014, http://www.ambafrance-uk.org/Prime-Minister-explains-French-23725.

67 Eleanor Beardsley, "Why French Troops Are Intervening in Africa—Again," NPR, December 15, 2013, http://www.npr.org/2013/12/15/251171604/once-again-french-troops-intervene-in-africa; David Smith and Kim Wilsher, "Clashes in Central African Republic as UN Authorises French Intervention," *Guardian*, December 5, 2013.

68 Myriam Benraad, "France Joins Fight Against Islamic State Group to Revive Ties to Iraq," *World Politics Review*, September 30, 2014.

69 Embassy of France in London, "Prime Minister Explains French Action in Iraq to Parliament."

70 Anna Mulrine, "US Strategy Against Islamic State: Iraq First, But Not Iraq Only, Dempsey Says," *Christian Science Monitor*, November 19, 2014, http://www.csmonitor.com/USA/Military/2014/1119/US-strategy-against-Islamic-State-Iraq-first-but-not-Iraq-only-Dempsey-says-video.

71 Peter Dominiczak, "Syria: 'National Soul-Searching' Needed After Commons Defeat," *Telegraph*, August 30, 2013.

72 Tim Ross, "Poll: Majority Back Military Action Against Islamic State," *Telegraph*, September 6, 2014; Steven Swinford and Georgia Graham, "Britain Goes To War Against ISIL," *Telegraph*, September 26, 2014.

73 Jakobsen and Ringsmose, "Size and Reputation."

74 Michael Clarke, "Cameron Failed To Take the Lead Against ISIS," *Daily Telegraph*, September 26, 2014; Louisa Brooke-Holland and Claire Mills, "ISIS: The Military Response in Iraq and Syria," *House of Commons Standard Note*, SN/IA/6995, December 2014, 5.

75 Con Coughlin, "Army Chief: Don't Rush Into War Against Isil," *Telegraph*, September 7, 2014; Ben Farmer, "'Bare Bones' RAF Will Struggle To Mount Iraq Operation," *Telegraph*, September 25, 2014.

76 Brooke-Holland and Mills, "ISIS," 7.

77 House of Commons Defence Committee, *The situation in Iraq and Syria and the response to al-Dawla al-Islamiya fi al-Iraq al-Sham (DAESH)* (London: The Stationery Office Limited, 2015).

Chapter 1 Endnotes

78 Will Dahlgreen, "British Public Call for Increased UK Involvement in ISIS Strikes," *YouGov*, February 8, 2015, https://yougov.co.uk/news/2015/02/08/increase-isis-air-strikes-public/.

79 Iain Watson, "Consider Syria IS Strikes, Defence Secretary Urges MPs," *BBC News*, July 3 2015.

80 Andrew Grice, "British Airstrikes on Syria," *Independent*, July 30, 2015.

81 Patrick Wintour. "Britain Carries out First Syria Airstrikes After MPs Approve Action Against Isis," *Guardian*, December 3, 2015.

82 The continuing influence of the "special relationship" on British thinking and practice is evident from House of Commons Foreign Affairs Committee, *Government foreign policy towards the United States* (London: The Stationery Office Limited, 2014).

83 Kathleen J. McInnis, "Coalition Contributions to Countering the Islamic State," *CRS Report*, R44135, August 4, 2015, 1.

84 Sean MacCormac "Islamic State Threatens Italy," *Washington Times*, February 19, 2015; Steve Scherer and Massimiliano Di Giorgio, "Italy To End Sea Rescue Mission That Saved 100,000 Migrants," Reuters, October 31, 2014.

85 Agence France-Presse, "Germany Rules Out Air Strikes, Troops in Iraq," September 22, 2014.

86 Alison Smale, "Germany Puts Curbing Russia Ahead of Commerce," *New York Times*, August 14, 2014.

87 Gero Schliess, "Larger Role for Germany in Expanded 'IS' Campaign?," *Deutsche Welle*, September 20, 2014; Frank-Walter Steinmeier, "Why Germany Is Sending Weapons to Iraq," *Wall Street Journal*, September 2, 2014.

88 "Germany to Supply Arms to Kurds Fighting 'IS' Militants," *Deutsche Welle*, September 1, 2014, http://dw.com/p/1D4W8 (accessed October 5, 2015); Justin Huggler, "Merkel Plan to Send German Troops to Iraq 'May Require Law Change,'" *Telegraph*, December 11, 2014.

89 Auswärtiges Amt, *Rede von Außenminister Steinmeier anlässlich der Bundestagsdebatte zur Ausbildungsmission der Bundeswehr in Nordirak*, January 15, 2015.

90 Jakobsen, "The Indispensable Enabler."

Chapter 2 Endnotes

CHAPTER 2
The Country of Unrequited Dreams: Lessons From Germany's Mission in Afghanistan

1 The author thanks his research assistants Judith Weiß and Daniela Braun for their hard work and dedication.

2 Timo Noetzel and Thomas Rid, "Germany's Options in Afghanistan," *Survival* 51, 5 (2001): 71–90; and Timo Noetzel, "Germany's Small War in Afghanistan: Military Learning Amid Politico-Strategic Inertia," *Contemporary Security Policy* 31, no. 3 (2010): 486–508.

3 Christian Thiels, "Die Kosten des Krieges" [On military costs], *Tagesschau*, March 20, 2015, http://www.tagesschau.de/ausland/kosten-des-krieges-in-afghanistan-101.html.

4 Sebastian Enskat and Carlo Masala, "Einsatzarmee Bundeswehr? Fortsetzung der Deutschen Außenpolitik mit anderen Mitteln?" [Deployment Force Bundeswehr: Continuation of Germany foreign policy with other means?], in *Früher, entschiedener und substantieller? Die neue Debatte über Deutschlands Außenpolitik* [Earlier, more decisively and more substantial? A new debate about Germany's foreign policy], ed. Gunther Hellmann, Daniel Jacobi, and Ursula Stark Urrestarazu, *Zeitschrift für Außen- und Sicherheitspolitik*, (Special Edition No. 6, Springer, 2015): 365–378, 371.

5 German Foreign Office, "Fortschrittsberichte Afghanistan" [Progress Reports Afghanistan], accessed August 2, 2015, http://www.auswaertiges-amt.de/DE/Aussenpolitik/RegionaleSchwerpunkte/AfghanistanZentralasien/Fortschrittsbericht-node.html.

6 German Ministry of International Development and Cooperation, accessed July 2015, http://www.bmz.de/de/was_wir_machen/laender_regionen/asien/afghanistan/zusammenarbeit/index.html.

7 "Bevölkerung: Afghanistan-Einsatz war Aufwand nicht Wert" [German public opinion: The mission in Afghanistan was not worth the effort], *Spiegel* online, December 20, 2014, http://www.spiegel.de/spiegel/vorab/umfrage-afghanistan-einsatz-war-aufwand-nicht-wert-a-1009343.html.

8 Christian-Democratic Union, Christian-Social Union, Social Democratic Party, Free Democratic Party ("Liberals"), Alliance 90/The Greens.

Chapter 2 Endnotes

9 From the parties in the German Bundestag, only the socialist Die Linke has consistently opposed the German mission in Afghanistan.

10 As such, they reflect both the thinking of the government and the author; I will note the distinction where appropriate.

11 For a fine overview, see also NATO's RESOLUTE SUPPORT website: http://www.rs.nato.int/article/nic/nic-focus-on-germany.html.

12 John Vinocur, "Terror Strikes America/Political Strategies: Schroeder Urges Europe To Stand Against Foes," *International New York Times*, September 20, 2011, http://www.nytimes.com/2001/09/20/news/20iht-chirac_ed3_1.html.

13 Deutscher Bundestag, "Stenografischer Bericht," [Stenographic report, session 210], December 22, 2001, accessed August 2, 2015, http://dip21.bundestag.de/dip21/btp/14/14210.pdf; Deutscher Bundestag: "request of the Federal Government," December 21, 2011 accessed August 2, 2015, http://dipbt.bundestag.de/dip21/btd/14/079/1407930.pdf.

14 "Violence on the Rise: German Troops Kill First Person in Afghanistan," *Spiegel* online, August 28, 2008; and German Ministry of Defense, "Taschenkarte für die Soldaten des deutschen Anteils International Security Assistance Force in Afghanistan. Regeln für die Anwendung militärischer Gewalt" [Rules of Engagement for the German Soldiers in the International Security Assistance Force in Afghanistan], 2002. Soldiers of the German Bundeswehr operated under very strict rules of engagement in Afghanistan until mid-2009. They were not allowed to use firearms except in self-defense while under an attack or if an attack was imminent.

15 Struck first used that phrase in an undocumented Radio interview in 2002. He reiterated it many times since, most notably in this speech in the Bundestag: Declaration of the Government of the Federal Republic of Germany by Defense Minister Dr. Peter Struck, March 11, 2004, accessed July 9, 2016, http://www.bmvg.de/portal/a/bmvg/!ut/p/c4/NYoxDoMwEATfkg_4REGRdPkFpLGMOZ1XxA7ync33QUjRdDNDH7oooUOC4VfClyaaI17L4ZbcxWUUqHFFy05YY0JMxv5unasxVkgrov_RK8P88BxHt9adL6NWW9xo396PE6UZows!/.

16 Stephan Bierling, *Vormacht wider Willen. Deutsche Außenpolitik von der Wiedervereinigung bis zur Gegenwart* [Reluctant hegemon. German foreign policy from reunification till present], (München: C.H. Beck 2014), 80–106.

Chapter 2 Endnotes

17 Deutscher Bundestag, "Beschlussempfehlung und Bericht" [Report of the Investigation Committee of the Bundestag], October 25, 2011, http://dip21.bundestag.de/dip21/btd/17/074/1707400.pdf.

18 Speech of Angela Merkel, "Regierungserklärung zu den aktuellen Ereignissen in Afghanistan" [On current events in Afghanistan], September 8, 2009, accessed August 2, 2015, http://www.bundesregierung.de/Content/DE/Bulletin/2009/09/93-1-bk-bt-regerkl.html.

19 Jennifer Abrahamson, "Guttenberg Refers to War in Afghanistan Breaking Berlin Taboo," *Deutsche Welle*, November 3, 2009, http://www.dw.com/en/guttenberg-refers-to-war-in-afghanistan-breaking-berlin-taboo/a-4852436. In a typical—yet effective—publicity stunt, zu Guttenberg made that point in an hour-long TV interview broadcast from the Bundeswehr camp in Mazar-e Sharif, with the minister and the journalist Johannes B. Kerner sitting among soldiers. Such images were completely unknown to German TV audiences at the time.

20 See NATO website on Mission RESOLUTE SUPPORT: http://www.rs.nato.int/images/media/PDFs/150601placemat.pdf, accessed September 29, 2015.

21 For a more fully developed presentation of the two narratives, see Patrick Keller, "German Hard Power: Is There a There There?," American Enterprise Institute, October 8, 2013, accessed August 2, 2015, https://www.aei.org/publication/german-hard-power-is-there-a-there-there/.

22 For more information about the debate on Germany's role in international affairs, see the speech of President Joachim Gauck at the 2014 Munich Security Conference, "Germany's Role in the World," January 31, 2014, accessed August 2, 2015, http://www.bundespraesident.de/SharedDocs/Reden/DE/Joachim-Gauck/Reden/2014/01/140131-Muenchner-Sicherheitskonferenz.html; as well as the report of the German Marshall Fund and the German Institute for International and Security Affairs, "New Power. New Responsibility," 2013, accessed August 2, 2015, http://www.swp-berlin.org/fileadmin/contents/products/projekt_papiere/GermanForcignSecurityPolicy_SWP_GMF_2013.pdf.

23 Nicholas Kulish, "German Limits on War Face Afghan Reality," *New York Times*, October 26, 2009, http://www.nytimes.com/2009/10/27/world/27germany.html?_r=0.

Chapter 2 Endnotes

24 Klaus Naumann, *Der Blinde Spiegel. Deutschland im afghanischen Transformationskrieg* [The blind mirror: Germany and the war of transformation in Afghanistan] (Hamburg: Hamburg Edition 2013), 96.

25 Kateri Jochum, "New rules of engagement for German troops in Afghanistan," *Deutsche Welle*, July 26, 2009, accessed August 2, 2015, http://www.dw.com/en/new-rules-of-engagement-for-german-troops-in-afghanistan/a-4519627; German Ministry of Defense, Taschenkarte für die Soldaten des deutschen Anteils International Security Assistance Force in Afghanistan. Regeln für die Anwendung militärischer Gewalt [Rules of engagement for the German soldiers in the International Security Assistance Force in Afghanistan], 2009.

26 Patrick Keller, "Strategic Posture Review: Germany," *World Politics Review*, March 18, 2004, http://www.worldpoliticsreview.com/articles/13631/strategic-posture-review-germany.

27 Kate Connolly, "The German Case," *Telegraph*, September 14, 2006, http://www.telegraph.co.uk/news/worldnews/1528855/The-German-case.html.

28 Annual Studies/Polls of the Social Sciences Institute of the Bundeswehr, e.g. http://www.dmfk.de/fileadmin/downloads/Sicherheits-_und_verteidigungspolit_Meinungsklima.pdf, accessed August 3, 2015.

29 Bernd Ulrich, "*Wofür Deutschland Krieg führen darf. Und muss.*" [For what Germany goes to war], (Reinbek: Rowohlt 2011). This attitude could also explain why the Afghanistan mission received its highest approval ratings when most Germans still believed it a primarily humanitarian mission.

30 Speech of Horst Köhler, *Einsatz für Freiheit und Sicherheit* [Effort for Freedom and Security], October 10, 2005, accessed August 2, 2015, http://www.bundespraesident.de/SharedDocs/Reden/DE/Horst-Koehler/Reden/2005/10/20051010_Rede_Anlage.pdf?__blob=publicationFile.

31 Strong commitments by NATO and EU nations will remain a prerequisite for support while a UN mandate, as evidenced by the case of Kosovo, might provide a critical advantage but is not a sine qua non.

32 Rainer Glatz, "ISAF Lessons Learned: A German Perspective," *PRISM* (2:2), March 2011, 169–176.

33 Naumann, *Der Blinde Spiegel*, 100.

Chapter 2 Endnotes

34 Timo Noetzel and Thomas Rid, *Mehr Köche als Diplomaten* [More cooks than diplomats], February 5, 2010, http://www.stiftung-nv.de/publikation/mehr-k%C3%B6che-als-diplomaten. (Simultaneously published in Financial Times Deutschland, page unknown)

35 "Polizeiausbildung in Afghanistan: Bundeswehrverband Deutschland wirft der EU Versagen vor" [Training the police in Afghanistan: The German association of the Bundeswehr accused the EU of failing the mission], *Spiegel* online, July 18, 2007, http://www.spiegel.de/politik/ausland/polizeiausbildung-in-afghanistan-bundeswehrverband-wirft-deutschland-und-eu-versagen-vor-a-512132.html.

36 Reflected in the Afghanistan Concept of the German Federal Government 2003 and 2006, accessed August 2, 2015, https://www.boell.de/sites/default/files/assets/boell.de/images/download_de/weltweit/afghanistankonzept_bundesregierung2006.pdf.

37 German Ministry of Defense, "Ressortbericht zum Stand der Neuausrichtung der Bundeswehr" [Interagency report on the state of the reorientation of the Bundeswehr], May 8, 2013, www.bmvg.de/portal/a/bmvg/!ut/p/c4/NYvBCsIwEET_aDcBRerNEhSvvdh4S9sQVpqkrJt68eNNDs7AO8xj8Im1ye0UnFBObsUR7Uzn6QNT3AO8cuG6QqREb_FMJeKjfRYPc05eGsUnocrATjLDllnWZgpzNUALWqqVNr7T6R3-70-1qzUEfzb0fcIvx8gOBJaR2/, 13–16; Bundeswehr, "Die Starke der Streitkräfte" [Strength of forces], August 9, 2013, accessed August 3, 2015, www.bundeswehr.de/portal/a/bwde/streitkraefte/grundlagen/staerke/.

38 For a detailed discussion of the re-orientation, see Keller, "German hard power: Is there a there there?"

39 Airborne Warning and Control System; an integrated NATO surveillance capability under German leadership.

40 Deutscher Bundestag, *Unterrichtung durch die Kommission zur Überprüfung und Sicherung der Parlamentsrechte bei der Mandatierung von Auslandseinsätzen der Bundeswehr* [Final report about the review of the parliamentary rights to deploy the Bundeswehr], June 16, 2015, accessed August 2, 2015, https://www.bundestag.de/blob/379046/ec2f468a9323c99f9bff783edb611c9b/bericht-data.pdf.

41 Barry Buzan, Ole Waever, and Jaap de Wilde, *Security: A New Framework for Analysis* (Boulder, CO: Lynne Rienner, 1998).

Chapter 3 Endnotes

42 "Considerable progress has been made in recent years in the civilian reconstruction of the country. Afghan gross domestic product (GDP) per capita increased more than six-fold between 2001 and 2013, totaling an estimated USD 670 per capita in 2013. Today, more people than ever before have access to water, electricity, medical care and education. Infrastructure has been created and reconstructed on a major scale, and significant progress has been made in developing administrative and rule-of-law structures," German Federal Government: "Fortschrittsbericht Afghanistan 2014" [Progress Report Afghanistan], November 2014, accessed August 2, 2015, http://www.auswaertiges-amt.de/cae/servlet/contentblob/694822/publicationFile/200835/Fortschrittsbericht2014.pdf.

43 Nils Wörmer, "Changing Times in the Hindu Kush? Afghanistan Facing the Transformation Decade," KAS International Reports, January 2015, accessed August 2, 2015, http://www.kas.de/wf/doc/kas_40191-544-2-30.pdf?150126095403.

CHAPTER 3
What Did Russia Learn From the U.S. Wars in Iraq and Afghanistan?

1 Aleksandr' Golts, "Military Reform Going Nowhere Again," *Moscow Times*, May 7, 2003, http://www.themoscowtimes.com/opinion/article/military-reform-going-nowhere-again/238667.html.

2 In 1999, when the author was a professor at the U.S. Army War College during the Kosovo crisis of that year, the Russian military made it clear to the Russian students who had been and were then studying at the War College that they had no interest in what the students had learned in America.

3 Roger McDermott, *The Reform of Russia's Conventional Armed Forces: Problems, Challenges, & Policy Implications* (Washington, DC: Jamestown Foundation, 2012).

4 Stephen Blank and Younkyoo Kim, "Insurgency and Counterinsurgency in Russia: Contending Paradigms and Current Perspectives," *Studies in Conflict and Terrorism* 36, no. 11 (November 2013): 917–32.

5 Reuben F. Johnson, "Hybrid War Is Working," *Jane's Defence Weekly*, February 26, 2015.

6 Aleksandr V. Rogovoy and Keir Giles, *A Russian View on Landpower* (Carlisle Barracks, PA: Strategic Studies Institute, U.S. Army War College, 2015).

Chapter 3 Endnotes

7 *ITAR-TASS News Agency*, in Russian, October 2, 2003, LexisNexis.

8 Moscow, *Krasnaya Zvezda*, in Russian, February 7, 2003.

9 Moscow, *Moskovskiy Komsomolets*, in Russian, January 9, 2003.

10 "Putin, Ivanov Point to Bigger Policy Role for Military," *Current Digest of the Post-Soviet Press* (Henceforth CDPP) LVII, no. 46 (December 14, 2005), LexisNexis; "Chief of General Staff on Changes in Russia's Military Policy," *RIA Novosti*, January 27, 2006.

11 For an example of the new defense doctrine, *Voyennaya Doktrina Rossi-iskoi Federatsii*, December 26, 2014, www.kremlin.ru.

12 Moscow, *Interfax-AVN Online*, in English, May 26, 2011; Albert Avramov, "Fiasco-NATO's New Musical," Sofia, *Duma*, in Bulgarian, February 1, 2012.

13 Kabul, *TOL News Online*, in English, September 13, 2013.

14 "Interview with Russian Ambassador to Afghanistan, Andrey Avetisyan," Paris, *LeMonde*, in French, July 3, 2012.

15 Viktor Sergeyev, "The USA in Afghanistan," *International Affairs* (Moscow) no. 3 (2012): 58–66.

16 Fedor Lukyanov, "Russia-2011: Regional Conflicts in Focus," *Moscow Defense Brief*, no. 3 (2011): 3; "CSTO Warns of Afghan Fallout Post-2014," *Jane's Defence Weekly*, February 28, 2013, https://janes.ihs.com; "NATO Pullout From Afghanistan to Change Central Asian Strategic Configuration, CIS ATC," *Interfax*, February 12, 2013, cited in *Johnson's Russia List*, February 12, 2013; Zamir Kabulov, "Leaving Afghanistan, the United States Wants to Strengthen Their Presence in [the] Asia Pacific," *Security Index* 19, no. 1 (2013): 5–9.

17 Dexter Filkins, "After America," *New Yorker*, July 9 and 16, 2002, 54–67; Lewis G. Irwin, *Disjointed Ways, Disunified Means: Learning From America's Struggle to Build an Afghan Nation* (Carlisle Barracks, PA: Strategic Studies Institute, U.S. Army War College, 2012).

18 Moscow, *Tass*, in Russian, December 10, 2014; "Russian Ambassador Warns of Afghan Problems Spilling Across Border," *Radio Free Europe Radio Liberty*, December 29, 2014, Moscow, *Interfax*, in English, December 29, 2014.

19 Kabul, *TOL News Online*, in English, January 3, 2015.

20 Kabul, *1NewsTV*, in Dari, December 15, 2014.

Chapter 3 Endnotes

21 Moscow, *Ministry of Defense of the Russian Federation*, in Russian, December 10, 2014.

22 Joshua Kucera, "Kremlin Talks UP ISIS Threat to Central Asia, Russia," *Eurasia Insight*, January 6, 2015, www.eurasianet.org.

23 Moscow, *Interfax*, in English, December 29, 2014; Moscow, *Interfax*, in English, December 8, 2014.

24 Istanbul, *Yeni Safak Online*, in Turkish, November 20, 2014.

25 Moscow, *Interfax*, November 18, 2014.

26 Recknagel; "IS Militants Asked Baghdadi for Permission to Fight 'Infidels' in Tajikistan," *Radio Free Europe Radio Liberty*, January 5, 2015; Joanna Paraszcuk, "IS Militants Asked Baghdadi for Permission to Fight 'Infidels' in Tajikistan," *Eurasia Insight*, January 5, 2015, www.eurasianet.org.

27 Ibid.

28 Moscow, *Interfax*, in English, December 23, 2014.

29 Kucera, "Kremlin Talks UP ISIS Threat to Central Asia, Russia."

30 Moscow, *Interfax*, December 29, 2014.

31 Moscow, *Interfax*, in English, December 29, 2014.

32 "Border Alert: Nuke War Risk Is Rising, Russia Warns," www.rt.com, November 17, 2011.

33 Ibid.; Roger N. McDermott, "General Makarov Highlights the 'Risk' of Nuclear Conflict," *Valdai Discussion Club*, December 8, 2011, www.valdaiclub.com.

34 Andrei Lebedev, "Yuri Baluevsky: The Russian Military Has a Chance to Straighten Its Spine," *Izvestiya*, March 2, 2005, LexisNexis.

35 Moscow, *Interfax*, in English, September 21, 2011.

36 Russian foreign Minister Sergei Lavrov's Interview with Rossiyskaya Gazeta, *Ministry of Foreign Affairs of the Russian Federation*, September 21, 2011, www.mid.ru.

37 "Genshtab Gotovitsia k 'liviskomu Stsenariiu' v Rossii," www.66.ru, October 4, 2011, www.66.ru/news/society/102896/print.

38 Ibid, Alexander Mikhailov, 2.

39 "Russia on the Brink of Civil War," Moscow, *Vlasti*, in Russian, April 19, 2009.

Chapter 3 Endnotes

40 Ibid.

41 Ibid.

42 Stephen Blank, "Russian Information Warfare as Domestic Counter-insurgency," *American Foreign Policy Interests* 35, no. 1 (2013): 31–44.

43 Iriana Borogan, "In Shoulder-Boards: The Kremlin's Anti-Crisis Project: When OMON Rushes to Help," Moscow, *Yezhenedevnyi Zhurnal*, in Russian, December 15, 2009.

44 Moscow, *Agentstvo Voyennykh Novostey Internet Version*, in Russian, July 4, 2008.

45 McDermott, *The Reform of Russia's Conventional Armed Forces.*

46 Ibid.; Rod Thornton, *Organizational Change in the Russian Airborne Forces: The Lessons of the Georgian Conflict* (Carlisle Barracks, PA: Strategic Studies Institute, U.S. Army War College, 2011); Keir Giles and Andrew Monaghan, *Russian Military Transformation—Goal In Sight?* (Carlisle Barracks, PA: Strategic Studies Institute, U.S. Army War College, 2014).

47 Ibid.

48 Ibid.

49 Rogovoy and Giles, *A Russian View on Landpower.*

50 Moscow, *Interfax-AVN Online*, in Russian, September 19, 2013.

51 Stephen J. Cimbala, *The New Nuclear Disorder: Challenges to Deterrence and Stability* (Farnham, Surrey, UK: Ashgate, 2015), 45–46.

52 Konstantin Sivkov, "The Russian Navy's Drones: What Kind of Unmanned Aerial Vehicles Does the Domestic Navy Primarily Need?" Moscow, *VPK Voyenno-Promyshlennyi Kuryer Online*, in Russian, October 30, 2013.

53 Ibid.

54 Stephen Blank, "Russian Information Warfare as Domestic Counter-insurgency," *American Foreign Policy Interests* 35, no. 1 (2013): 31–44.

55 Oleg A. Stepanov, "The Role of Internal Affairs Agencies in Efforts to Fight Terrorism Under High-Technology Conditions," in, *Russian Views on Countering Terrorism During Eight Years of Dialogues: Extracts From Proceedings of Four U.S.-Russian Workshops* ed. Glenn Schweitzer and Marc Fox (Washington, DC, National Research Council of the National Academies, 2009): 75.

Chapter 3 Endnotes

56 Henry Shue, "Target-Selection Norms, Torture Norms, and Growing US Permissiveness," in *The Changing Character of War*, ed. Hew Strachan and Sybille Schieperes (Oxford: Oxford University Press, 2011): 466–73.

57 Moscow, *NTV,* in Russian, August 15, 2007.

58 Colonel-General Boris Cheltsov, "Approaches to the Creation of the National Aerospace Defense System and the Future Network-Centric Wars," *Military Thought* no. 4 (2008): 1–11.

59 Roger McDermott, "Russia's Conventional Armed Forces, Reform and Nuclear Posture to 2020," Paper presented to the Conference Strategy and Doctrine in Russian Security Policy, Washington, DC, National Defense University, Fort Lesley J. McNair, June 28, 2010; Timothy L. Thomas, *Recasting the Red Star: Russia Forges Tradition and Technology Through Toughness* (Ft. Leavenworth, KS: Foreign Military Studies Office, 2011).

60 Lt. General Nikolai A. Molchanov, "Information Resources of Foreign States as a Threat to Russia's Military Security," *Military Thought* no. 4 (2008): 22–31.

61 Moscow, *Voyenno-Promyshlennyi Kuryer Online*, in Russian, September 15, 2010.

62 Ibid.

63 Moscow, *RIA Novosti Online*, in Russian, October 19, 2013.

64 Moscow, *Interfax-AVN Online,* in English, January 30, 2012.

65 Vladimir Vasilyevich Karyakin, "The Era of a New Generation of Warriors—Information and Strategic Warriors—Has Arrived," Moscow, *Nezavisimaya Gazeta Online*, in Russian, April 22, 2011.

66 John E. Bolen, Jr., *Operational Art Goes Digital: Information Warfare and the Future of Russian Operational Theory*, Summer Student Paper, U.S. Army War College, August, 2012, 16.

67 Ibid.

68 William M. Darley, "Clausewitz's Theory of War and Information Operations," *Joint Forces Quarterly* 40 (2006): 73–79.

69 Franklin Kramer, Stuart H. Starr, and Larry Wentz, Editors, *Cyberpower and National Security* (Washington, DC: Potomac Books, 2009).

70 Col. Richard G. Zoller, "Russian Cyberspace Strategy and a Proposed United States Response," in *Information as Power: An Anthology of Selected*

Chapter 3 Endnotes

United States Army War College Papers Volume 5, ed. Jeffrey L. Caton, John H. Greemyer, Jeffrey L. Groh, and William O. Waddell (Carlisle Barracks, PA: Strategic Studies Institute, U.S. Army War College, 2011), 118.

71 Vladimir Vasilyevich Karyakin, "The Era of a New Generation of Warriors—Information and Strategic Warriors—Has Arrived," Moscow, *Nezavisimaya Gazeta Online*, in Russian, April 22, 2011.

72 Ibid.

73 Stephen Blank, "Class War on the Global Scale: The Culture of Leninist Political Conflict" in *Conflict, Culture, and History: Regional Dimensions*, ed. Stephen J. Blank et al. (Maxwell AFB, Alabama: Air University Press, 1993), 1–55.

74 Blank, "Russian Information Warfare as Domestic Counterinsurgency," 31–44.

75 "Russian President Threatens to Target U.S. Missile Shield," *Radio Free Europe Radio Liberty*, November 23, 2011, https://www.rferl.org/a/medvedev_outlines_response_to_us_missile_shield/24399845. html.

76 Ibid.

77 Ibid.

78 Ibid.

79 Ibid.

80 Blank, "Russian Information Warfare as Domestic Counterinsurgency," 31–44.

81 Col. (ret) Timothy L. Thomas, USA, *Recasting the Red Star: Russia Forges Tradition and Technology Through Toughness* (Ft. Leavenworth, KS: Foreign Military Studies Office, 2011), 247.

82 Aleksandr' Gorbenko, "Second General Staff: Why Make Sergey Shoigu First Vice Premier," Moscow, *Odnako Online*, in Russian, November 1, 2013.

83 Ibid.

84 Ibid.

85 Stephen Blank, "No Need to Threaten Us, We Are Frightened of Ourselves: Russia's Blueprint for a Police State" in *The Russian Military Today and Tomorrow: Essays in Memory of Mary Fitzgerald*, ed. Stephen J. Blank and Richard Weitz (Carlisle Barracks, PA: Strategic Studies Institute, U.S. Army War College, 2010), 19–150.

Chapter 3 Endnotes

86 Russian Security Doctrine To Be Adjusted After Arab Spring, Ukraine Turmoil—Official, *Russia Today*, May 6, 2015, https://www.rt.com/politics/256025-russia-security-doctrine-patrushev/.

87 General M.A. Gareyev, "Applying Zhukov's Command Heritage To Military Training and Reform in Today's World," *Journal of Slavic Military Studies* 12, no. 4 (December, 1999): 83; Alexander M. Kirov, "Soviet Military Intervention in Hungary" in *1956: Soviet Military Intervention in Hungary*, ed. Jeno Gyorkei and Mikolos Horvath (Budapest: Central European University Press, 1999), 188.

88 Ilan Berman, "The Caliphate Comes Home," *Journal of International Security Affairs*, no. 20 (Spring-Summer, 2011), http://www.securityaffairs.org/issues/2011/20/berman.php.

89 Moscow, *Interfax*, in English, December 20, 2011.

90 Berman, "The Caliphate Comes Home."

91 Ibid.

92 Ibid.

93 Ibid.

94 Olof Staaf, "Moscow Unable to Afford New Development Program for North Caucasus," *Central Asia Caucasus Analyst*, August 17, 2011, www.cacianalyst.org.

95 Eugene Miakinov, "The Agency of Force in Asymmetrical Warfare and Counterinsurgency: The Case of Chechnya," *Journal of Strategic Studies* 34, no. 5 (2011): 648.

96 Ibid., 648–649.

97 Dean Cheng, "Chinese Lesson From the Gulf Wars" in *Chinese Lessons From Other People's Wars*, ed. Andrew Scobell, David Lai, Roy Kamphausen (Carlisle Barracks, PA: Strategic Studies Institute, U.S. Army War College, 2011), 176.

98 Max G. Manwaring, *The Strategic Logic of the Contemporary Security Dilemma* (Carlisle Barracks, PA: Strategic Studies Institute, U.S. Army War College, 2011), 18.

99 Stephen Blank, "Russian Information Warfare as Domestic Counterinsurgency," *American Foreign Policy Interests*, 35, no. 1 (2013): 31–44.

100 Manwaring, *The Strategic Logic of the Contemporary Security Dilemma*, 666–67.

Chapter 4 Endnotes

101 Ibid.

102 V.V. Panchenkov, "Lessons From the Information War in the North Caucasus," Moscow, *Vooruzhenie, Politika, Konversiia*, no. 4, 2002, February 5, 2004.

103 Robert W. Schaefer, *The Insurgency in Chechnya and the North Caucasus: From Gazavat to Jihad* (Santa Barbara, CA: Praeger Security International, 2011), 199–200, 221–232.

104 Ibid., 215.

105 D.J. Peterson, *Russia and the Information Revolution* (Santa Monica, CA: RAND Corporation, 2005), 89–94.

106 Moscow, *Agenstvo Voyennykh Novostei*, July 25, 2000, in Russian.

107 Miakinov, "The Agency of Force in Asymmetrical Warfare and Counterinsurgency," 666–67.

108 Conversations with Russian Journalists, "Russian Army Cracks Down on Media in Chechnya," Reuters, July 26, 2001.

109 Edwin Bacon and Bettina Renz with Julian Cooper, *Securitizing Russia: The Domestic Politics of Russia* (Manchester: Manchester University Press, 2006), 16.

110 Blank, "Russian Information Warfare as Domestic Counterinsurgency," 31–44.

111 *Voyennaya Doktrina Rossiiskoi Federatsii*, December 26, 2014, www.kremlin.ru; Rogovoy and Giles, *A Russian View on Landpower*.

CHAPTER 4
Iran: Goals and Strategy "Steadfast," but Open to Tactical Innovation

1 Laura Smith-Spark and Yousuf Basil, "Iran's Supreme Leader Vows No Change in Relations with 'Arrogant' United States," CNN, July 19, 2015, http://www.cnn.com/2015/07/18/middleeast/iran-us-relations-khamenei/index.html.

2 Saeid Golkar, "Iran's Revolutionary Guard: Its Views of the United States," *Middle East Policy* 21, no. 2 (Summer 2014): 1, http://www.mepc.org/journal/middle-east-policy-archives/irans-revolutionary-guard-its-views-united-states.

3 Ibid., 1.

Chapter 4 Endnotes

4 In the IRGC view, the United States employs four methods to achieve this: "(1) hard war, (2) semi-hard war, (3) soft war and (4) intelligence war." Arguing that hard war efforts to defeat Iran have failed, the IRGC is especially concerned with soft war which involves "...nonmilitary measures and includes both cultural and political elements, such as promoting Western culture and the American lifestyle." See Golkar, "Iran's Revolutionary Guard," 1.

5 Kayhan Barzegar, "Balance of Power in the Persian Gulf: An Iranian View," *Middle East Policy* 17, no. 3 (Fall 2010): 74–87, http://www.mepc.org/journal/middle-east-policy-archives/balance-power-persian-gulf-iranian-view.

6 Some Iraqi officials echo this judgment. Minister of Planning Ali al-Shukri described the withdrawal of U.S. forces as a failure for which "Washington feels ashamed. The Americans sustained 5,000 deaths during the occupation of Iraq and finally left the country shamefully." See "Minister Views Military Pullout from Iraq as US Failure," Fars News Agency, January 9, 2012, 1, https://www.highbeam.com/doc/1G1-276646031.html. Much less attention was given to U.S. actions in Afghanistan.

7 Nasser Saghafi Ameri, "The Middle East after U.S. Troops' Withdrawal from Iraq," *Iran Review*, December 28, 2011, 1, http://en.merc.ir/Home.aspx.

8 Naser Asadi, "Coercive Diplomacy: A Study of U.S. Policies Towards Iraq (1990–2003)," *Foreign Relations* 1, no. 3 (Fall 2009): 169–99, Iranian Scientific Information Database, http://en.journals.sid.ir/ViewPaper.aspx?ID=183702.

9 See, for example, Ahsan ur Rahman Khan, "Realities Relating to US Withdrawal from Afghanistan," *Iran Review*, July 14, 2013, http://www.iranreview.org/content/Documents/Realities-Relating to US' Withdrawal from Afghanistan.

10 Kourosh Ziabari, "US Troops Surge in Afghanistan, Repetition of Mistake Committed in Iraq—Iran Review's Exclusive Interview with Najibullah Lafraie," *Iran Review*, October 20, 2014, http://www.iranreview.org/content/Documents/US-Troops-Surge-in-Afghanistan-Repetition-of-Mistake-Committed-in-Iraq. See also "US-Afghan Security Agreement Brings Negative Consequences for Region," *Iran Review*, December 3, 2013, http://www.iranreview.org/content/Documents/EU-Decision-to-Maintain-Iran-Sanctions-Lacks-Legal-Basis.htm; Nasser Saghafi Ameri, "America

Chapter 4 Endnotes

Needs Iran in Afghanistan," March 12, 2009, http://isrjournals.ir/en/america-a-europe/795-america-needs-iran-in-Afghanistan.

11 Mohammad Javad Zarif, "Occupying Armies Bring No Democracy," *Iran Review*. August 11, 2015, 3. Accessed November 23, 2015 at http://www.iranreview.org/content/Documents/Occupying-Armies-Bring-No-Democracy.

12 Ibid., 3.

13 Ardeshir Ommani, "U.S. Colonialism in Iraq," *Tehran Times*, June 21, 2008, 1, http://www.tehrantimes.com/Index_view.asp?code=171204.

14 Kayhan Barzegar, "Balance of Power in the Persian Gulf: An Iranian View."

15 Mohammad Javad Zarif, Minister of Foreign Affairs, "What Iran Really Wants: Iranian Foreign Policy in the Rouhani Era," *Foreign Affairs*, May/June 2014, https://www.foreignaffairs.com/articles/iran/2014-04-17/what-iran-really-wants.

16 Ibid.

17 Hossein Amir-Abdollahian, "Two Views to Regional Developments," *Iran Review,* October 26, 2014, http://www.iranreview.org/content/Documents/Two-Views-to-Regional-Developments.

18 "Iraqi popular force questions US anti-terror fight in Iraq," Mehr News Agency, October 7, 2015, http://en.mehrnews.com/news/110808/Iraqi-popular-force-questions-US-anti-terror-fight-in-Iraq.

19 Naser Hadian and Shani Hormozi, "Iran's New Security Environment Imperatives: Counter Containment or Engagement with the US," *Iranian Review of Foreign Affairs* 1, no. 4 (Winter 2011): 17.

20 Ibid., Hadian and Hormozi offer a more elaborate typology of Iranian motives, which they identify as Ideological Sources, Threat Perceptions, Past Experiences, National Pride, Economic Imperatives, and Geopolitical Considerations, 25–28.

21 Saideh Lotfian, "Prevent and Defend: Threat Perceptions and Iran's Defence Policy," *Iranian Review of Foreign Affairs* 2, no. 3 (Fall 2011): 27.

22 Ibid., 9 10.

23 One Iranian analyst argues that the regime should be viewed from two perspectives. First, as any other power, Iran is concerned with interests and threats. However, "at the same time, this system, given its theological nature,

Chapter 4 Endnotes

has certain unique characteristics, which would demand attention from an angle different from other countries." Seyed Mahdi Hosseini Matin, "Iran's Desired Power Status," *Iranian Review of Foreign Affairs* 3, no. 1 (Spring 2012): 183–206.

24 "Leader Underlines Washington's Failure in Suppressing Islamic Awakening," Fars News Agency, June 4, 2014, http://en.farsnews.com/newstext. aspx?nn=13930314000504.

25 Ibid., 190.

26 Annie Tracy Samuel, *Perceptions and Narratives of Security: The Iranian Revolutionary Guards Corps and the Iran-Iraq War*, International Security Program Discussion Paper Series, Belfer Center for Science and International Affairs, 8, http://belfercenter.hks.harvard.edu/publication/22042/ perceptions_and_narratives_of_security.html.

27 "Supreme Leader: Attacking the Islamic Republic is Costly," Website of the Office of the Supreme Leader, Seyed Ali Khamenei, October 13, 2011, http://www.leader.ir/langs/en/index.php?p=contentShow&id=8696.

28 "Civil Defense Chief: US Convinced of Inability to Attack Iran," Fars News Agency, October 28, 2015, http://english.farsnews.com/print. aspx?nn=13940806001248.

29 *The Daily Star*, Beirut, Lebanon, April 15, 2014, http://www.highbeam. com/doc/1G1-364872209.html/print.

30 As an example of Iranian perceptions of success, see Abdelhak Mamoun, "We dominate Iraq and Syria, says Iranian Revolutionary Guard Commander." *Iraqi News.Com*, December 5, 2014, http://www.iraqinews.com/ arab-world-news/dominate-iraq-syria.

31 This participation assumes that conditions at home permit the absence of such forces for prolonged periods and that the Lebanese and/or Iraqi Shia populations remain willing to tolerate the resulting casualties.

32 Ali Alfoneh, *Generational Change in the Iranian Revolutionary Guards Corps Quds Force: Brigadier General Iraj Masjedi*, Washington, DC: American Enterprise Institute for Policy Research, no. 2, March, 2012, 4, https://www.aei.org/publication/generational-change-in-the-iranian-revolutionary-guards-corps-quds-force-brigadier-general-iraj-masjedi/.

33 These senior level costs are growing steadily. For the latest analysis, see Robin Wright, "Iran's Generals Are Dying in Syria," *The New Yorker*,

Chapter 4 Endnotes

October 26, 2015, http://www.newyorker.com/news/news-desk/irans-generals-are-dying-in-syria.

34 The public's disinterest in foreign adventures was reflected in a popular chant during the 2009 elections "No to Gaza, No to Lebanon, My life is for Iran," YouTube video, https://www.youtube.com/watch?v=dLOldK79sAg.

35 Unconfirmed press reports claim that the IRGC has established special courts martial to review the resignations of several senior and a number of lower ranking IRGC officers unwilling to serve in Syria. "IRGC Members Avoiding Service in Syria." Originally reported in *Sharq al Awsat*, April 11, 2015. Repeated at *NOW*, April 11, 2015, https://now.mmedia.me/lb/en/NewsReports/566169-irgc-members-avoiding-service-in-syria-report.

36 Martin Rudner, "Hizballah: An Organizational and Operational Profile," *International Journal of Intelligence and CounterIntelligence* 23, no. 2 (February 2010): 226–46.

37 Joseph Felter and Brian Fishman, *Iranian Strategy in Iraq Politics and "Other Means,"* Combating Terrorism Center at West Point Occasional Paper Series, October 13, 2008, 62–63, https://www.ctc.usma.edu/posts/iranian-strategy-in-iraq-politics-and-"other-means".

38 Ibid., 65.

39 Michael McBride, "Evolution of the Immortals: The Future of Iranian Military Power," *Small Wars Journal*, June 29, 2014, 2, smallwarsjournal.com/printpdf/15885.

40 Ned Parker, Babak Dehighanpisheh, and Isabel Coles, "Special Report: How Iran's Military Chiefs Operate in Iraq," Reuters, February 24, 2015, 6:00am EST. http://www.reuters.com/article/us-mideast-crisis-committee-specialrepor-idUSKBN0LS0VD20150224

41 "Iran Sends Tanks Into Iraq to Fight Islamists," August 22, 2014, Accessed October 30, 2015 at https://warisboring.com/iran-sends-tanks-into-iraq-to-fight-islamists-d130c9fa58bb#.x6aeybu3b

42 McBride, "Evolution of the Immortals," 1.

43 "The ministries of defense, interior, oil, as well as the Law Enforcement Forces (LEF) are staffed by commanders linked to this same network". Will Fulton. *The IRGC Command Network—Formal Structures and Informal Influence*, Washington, DC, American Enterprise Institute Critical Threats project, 2013, 7–8.

Chapter 4 Endnotes

44 Ibid., 6.

45 Ibid., 4.

46 Alfoneh, *Generational Change in the Iranian Revolutionary Guards Corps Quds Force*, 4.

47 For a thorough discussion of the topic, see Monroe Prince, "Iran and Soft War," *International Journal of Communications* 6 (2012): 2397–2415. The Basij shares the responsibility for combating soft war. See Greg Bruno, Jayshree Bajoria, and Jonathan Masters, *Iran's Revolutionary Guards*, Washington, DC: Council on Foreign Relations, updated: June 14, 2013, http://www.cfr.org/iran/irans-revolutionary-guards/p14324.

48 First Corps, also known as the "Ramazan/Ramedan Headquarters," covers Iraq; Second Corps handles Pakistan; Third Corps, aka Al-Hamzah Command Center, deals with Turkey and the Kurds; and Fourth Corps, aka al-Ansar Command Center in Mashhad, is responsible for projecting Iranian influence in Afghanistan and Central Asia. Felter and Brian Fishman, *Iranian Strategy in Iraq Politics and "Other Means,"* 18–19. The term "Corps" in these instances seems to be a generic term for a large subordinate organization not the designation of formal, standardized military units.

49 Paul Quinn-Judge, "Iranians Staffed Terrorist Base in Bosnia, US Says," *Boston Globe*, February 17, 1996.

50 Jonathan Schanzer, "The Islamic Republic of Sudan?" Defend Democracy.Org, June 10, 2010. Accessed November 10, 2015, at http://www.defenddemocracy.org/media-hit/the-islamic-republic-of-sudan/#sthash.FzCeg61M.dpuf.

51 For example, in 2010, Quds Force terrorist plots were reportedly disrupted in Azerbaijan, Turkey, and Kuwait. See Matthew Levitt, *Hizballah and the Quds Force In Iran's Shadow War With the West*, Washington Institute for Near East Policy, Policy Paper 123, January 10, 2013, 4.

52 Briefing by Major General Kevin Bergner in Baghdad October 3, 2007, cited in Bill Roggio, "Iran's Ramazan Corps and the Ratlines into Iraq," December 5, 2007, http://www.longwarjournal.org/archives/2007/12/irans_ramazan_corps.php.

53 Vincent J. Schodolski, "U.S. Officials Claim That Iran Is Hampering Efforts in Iraq," *Chicago Tribune*, July 11, 2003.

Chapter 4 Endnotes

54 "Shia Strength—Iraqi Militants Adapt to the US Drawdown," *Jane's Intelligence Review*, September 30, 2011, https://www.washingtoninstitute.org/uploads/Documents/opeds/4e8b0eba7c0a2.pdf.

55 Lolilta Baldor, "Pentagon Chief Says Iranian Support for Militias in Iraq on the Increase," AP Worldstream, April 11, 2008, https://news.google.com/newspapers?nid=1774&dat=20080412&id=nhIfAAAAIBAJ&sjid=aYYEAAAAIBAJ&pg=6227,1376074&hl=en.

56 "Iran Denounced Recent US Allegations of Iranian Support for Iraqi Militants," *Iran Review*, April 29, 2008, http://www.iranreview.org/content/Documents/Iran_Denounced_Recent_US_Allegations_of_Iranian_Support_for_Iraqi_Militants.htm.

57 "Iraq's Territorial Integrity Maintained Due to Iran's Help," Fars News Agency, January 23, 2016, http://en.farsnews.com/newstext.aspx?nn=13941103000856.

58 There is even evidence that some in the force have transferred explosives to certain members of the Taliban—a longtime enemy of Iran—for use against NATO troops. No byline, *The Islamic Revolutionary Guard Corps: Military and Political Influence in Today's Iran*, Washington, DC: Brookings, Institution, November 18, 2008, http://www.brookings.edu/events/2008/11/13-iran.

59 "U.S. Cites New Evidence of Iranian Support for Taliban," *US Fed News Service*, April 30, 2008.

60 Ibid. The Iranians deny such support, arguing that "U.S. charges of likely Iranian help to the Taliban are part of the stereotyped U.S. and British claims and their feverish psychological war." Iranians also argue that the U.S. and Britain's aim in indulging in such allegations is to insinuate that Iran is a threat to peace and stability; whereas in the Iranian view, the main threats are the American and British forces. See, for example, Ali Omidi, "Iran and the Security of Afghanistan After NATO's Pullout," *Iranian Review of Foreign Affairs* 3, no. 2 (Summer 2012): 46.

61 The captured rockets were identical to Iran-provided rockets seized from Iraqi Shia militants. Matt Schroeder, *Rogue Rocketeers: Artillery Rockets and Armed Groups*, A Working Paper of the Small Arms Survey, Graduate Institute of International and Development Studies, Geneva, 2014, 31, http://www.smallarmssurvey.org/fileadmin/docs/F-Working-papers/SAS-WP19-Rogue-Rocketeers.pdf.

Chapter 4 Endnotes

62 Dexter Filkins, "The Shadow Commander," *New Yorker*, September 30, 2013, http://www.newyorker.com/magazine/2013/09/30/the-shadow-commander.

63 See Carl Anthony Wege, "Hezbollah's Communication System: A Most Important Weapon," *International Journal of Intelligence and CounterIntelligence* 27, no. 2 (February 2014): 240–52. For a bit more dated account, see "Lebanon: Hezbollah's Communication Network," *Stratfor*, May 9, 2008, https://www.stratfor.com/analysis/lebanon-hezbollahs-communication-network.

64 Stephen E. Hughes, *Armed Forces of the Islamic Republic of Iran*, 44, http://www.academia.edu/8069971/ARMED_FORCES_OF_THE_ISLAMIC_REPUBLIC_OF_IRAN.

65 "Over 30 Brave Iranian Soldiers Martyred in Northern Syria This Month Fighting ISIS and Al Qaeda Affiliated Terrorists," October 30, 2015, http://www.liveleak.com/view?i=f89_1446205447&selected_view.

66 Saeid Golkar, *Captive Society: The Basij Militia and Social Control* (New York: Cambridge University Press, 2015).

67 Will Fulton, "The IRGC Command Network—Formal Structures and Informal Influence," Washington, DC, American Enterprise Institute Critical Threats project, 2013, 40.

68 Michael Connell, *The Iran Primer—Iran's Military Doctrine*, Washington, DC: United States Institute of Peace, http://iranprimer.usip.org/resource/irans-military-doctrine?print.

69 U.S. Treasury Department, "Treasury Designates Iranian Ministry of Intelligence and Security for Human Rights Abuses and Support for Terrorism," February 16, 2012, https://www.treasury.gov/press-center/press-releases/Pages/tg1424.aspx.

70 *Iran's Ministry of Intelligence and Security: A Profile*. Washington: Federal Research Division, Library of Congress, 2012, 37 and 44.

71 Ibid., 33.

72 Ibid.

73 Ibid., 29–30.

74 Ibid., 45.

Chapter 4 Endnotes

75 Ali Alfoneh, "IRGC Intelligence: The Driving Force Behind Iran's New Crackdown," Foundation for the Defense of Democracy Policy Brief, November 10, 2015, http://www.defenddemocracy.org/media-hit/ali-alfoneh-irgc-intelligence-the-driving-force-behind-irans-new-crackdown/#sthash.S1Wo06m.pdf.

76 "Shia Strength—Iraqi Militants Adapt to the US Drawdown," *Janes Intelligence Review*, November 1, 2011, 2, https://www.washingtoninstitute.org/uploads/Documents/opeds/4e8b0eba7c0a2.pdf.

77 Nicholas Blanford, "Hezbollah Cuts Back on Troops Fighting for Assad," *Times of London*, October 4, 2013, http://www.thetimes.co.uk/tto/news/world/middleeast/article3885951.ece.

78 "Nasrallah: Hezbollah in Syria for Long Haul," Al Jazeera, November 15, 2013, http://www.aljazeera.com/news/middleeast/2013/11/nasrallah-hezbollah-syria-long-haul-2013111414617430132.html.

79 Christoph Reuter, "Syria's Mercenaries: The Afghans Fighting Assad's War," *Spiegel Online International*, May 11, 2015, http://www.spiegel.de/international/world/afghan-mercenaries-fighting-for-assad-and-stuck-in-syria-a-1032869.html.

80 "The Hashid consist of pre-existing Shia militias, increased in size as a result of Sistani's fatwa, alongside formed militias and a small number of Sunni tribal fighters." Jonathan Spyer, "Rise of Shia Militias Shapes the Future of Iraq," *Jane's Intelligence Review* 27, no. 8, August 1, 2015, http://www.grouph3.com/index.php/intelligence/entry/analysis-the-rise-of-shia-militias-shape-future-of-iraq. For a detailed discussion of the Iraqi Shia forces, see Phillip Smyth, "Iranian Proxies Step Up Their Role in Iraq," Washington Institute for Near East Policy, *Policy Watch 2268*, June 23, 2015.

81 Leith Fadel, "More Iraqi Paramilitary Arrive in Aleppo Under Orders from the Iranian Revolutionary Guard," Al Masdar News, October 26, 2015, http://www.almasdarnews.com/article/more-iraqi-paramilitary-arrive-in-aleppo-under-orders-from-the-iranian-revolutionary-guard/.

82 Spyer, "Rise of Shia Militias Shapes the Future of Iraq," *Jane's Intelligence Review*.

83 Hossein Bastani, "Iran Quietly Deepens Involvement in Syria's War," *BBC Persian Service*, October 20, 2015, http://www.bbc.com/news/world-middle-east-34572756.

Chapter 4 Endnotes

84 Ibid.

85 Ibid.

86 A variety of press reports indicate the Iranians have been recruiting Afghan mercenaries since 2014. These fighters receive rudimentary tactical training and monthly pay of $500–$1000 a month. See, for example, Nick Paton Walsh, "'Afghan' in Syria: Iranians Pay Us To Fight for Assad," CNN, October 31, 2014, http://www.cnn.com/2014/10/31/world/meast/syria-afghan-fighter/. See also "Is Iran Paying Afghan Mercenaries To Fight in Syria?" BBC, June 19, 2015, http://www.bbc.com/news/world-middle-east-33195694.

87 Ari Heistein and James West, "Syria's Other Foreign Fighters: Iran's Afghan and Pakistani Mercenaries," *The National Interest*, November 20, 2015, http://nationalinterest.org/feature/syrias-other-foreign-fighters-irans-afghan-pakistani-14400.

88 Ibid. See also Saeed Kamali Dehghan, "Afghan Refugees in Iran Being Sent to Fight and Die for Assad in Syria," *Guardian*, November 5, 2015, http://www.theguardian.com/world/2015/nov/05/iran-recruits-afghan-refugees-fight-save-syrias-bashar-al-assad.

89 Bassam Khabieh and Adam Rawnsley, "Inside Iran's Secret War in Syria," *Daily Beast*, November 13, 2015, http://www.thedailybeast.com/articles/2015/11/13/inside-iran-s-secret-war-in-syria.html.

90 Heistein and West, "Syria's Other Foreign Fighters." Pakistanis also are reportedly fighting with rebel forces. A 2013 Russian TV report quoted claims by unidentified leaders of the Tehrik-i-Taliban Pakistan that they had sent fighters and established their own camps in Syria. See "Pakistani Taliban Sent Hundreds to Syria to Fight Shoulder-to-Shoulder With Rebels," July 14, 2013, 19:42 https://www.rt.com/news/pakistan-taliban-rebel-syria-086/.

91 However, Armed Forces General Staff HQ Deputy IRGC Maj. Gen. Gholam Ali Rashid reportedly "claimed that Iran had modeled the NDF (militia forces allied with the Syrian government) on Iran's Basij." "Iran has built a second Hezbollah in Syria—IRGC" Accessed November 23, 2015 at http://www.liveleak.com/view?i=4a2_1399455701#mpLvToMr47ysk9tJ.99 or http://www.uskowioniran.com/2014/05/iran-has-built-second-hezbollah-in.html May 7, 2014.

Chapter 4 Endnotes

92 The reports generally either precede or follow the actual event; reporting of ongoing exercises is relatively rare. For reports of recent exercises, see "Muharram' War Game Staged in Western Iran," Mehr News Agency, October 19, 2015, http://en.mehrnews.com/print/111181/Muharram-war-game-staged-in-western-Iran; "Air Defense Stages Maneuver at Khondab Nuclear Site," Mehr News Agency, October 20, 2015, http://en.mehrnews.com/print/111223/Air-defense-stages-maneuver-at-Khondab-nuclear-site; "Army Launches Final Phase of Drill," Mehr News Agency, November 19, 2015, http://en.mehrnews.com/print/112100/Army-launches-final-phase-of-drill.

93 For an examination of what the Iranians term "Mosaic defense," see the discussion of "Land Warfare Doctrine" in Michael Connell, *Iran's Military Doctrine*, U.S. Institute of Peace, http://iranprimer.usip.org/resource/irans-military-doctrine.

94 "Great Prophet 9 Exercise, phase two." February 27, 2015. Accessed November 23, 2015 at http://www.uskowioniran.com/2015/02/great-prophet-9-exercise, phase two.

95 Carl Anthony Wege, "The Hizballah-North Korean Nexus," *Small Wars Journal,* January 23, 2011, http://smallwarsjournal.com/jrnl/art/the-hizballah-north-korean-nexus.

96 Bill Roggio, "Iran, Quds Force and the Karbala Attack," *Long War Journal*, April 27, 2007, www.longwarjournal.org/archives/author/Bill-Rogio.

97 Gabi Siboni and Sami Kronenfeld, *INSS Insight No. 598: The Iranian Cyber Offensive During Operation Protective Edge*, Israel Institute of National Security Studies, August 26, 2014, http://www.inss.org.il/index.aspx?id=4538&articleid=7583.

98 Amy Kellogg, "Iran Is Recruiting Hacker Warriors for Its Cyber Army to Fight 'Enemies,'" Fox News, March 14, 2011, http://www.foxnews.com/world/2011/03/14/iran-recruiting-hacker-warriors-cyber-army.html.

99 LTC Eric K. Shafa, *Iran's Emergence as a Cyber Power*, U.S. Army Strategic Studies Institute, August 20, 2014, www.strategicstudiesinstitute.army.mil/index.cfm/articles/Irans-emergence-as-cyber-power/2014/08/20.

100 Frederick W. Kagan and Tommy Stiansen, *Cyber Threat From Iran, The Initial Report of Project Pistachio Harvest*, American Enterprise Institute Critical Threats Project and Norse Corporation, April 2015, 21.

Chapter 4 Endnotes

101 For an overview of the Stuxnet issue, see Ellen Nakashima and Joby Warrick, "Stuxnet Was the Work of U.S. and Israeli Experts, Officials Say," *The Washington Post*, June 2, 2012, https://www.washingtonpost.com/world/national-security/stuxnet-was-work-of-us-and-israeli-experts-officials-say/2012/06/01/gJQAlnEy6U_story.html. For an Iranian view of Stuxnet and claimed subsequent cyberattacks on Iran, see "Commander: Iranian Armed Forces Ready for Cyber War," Fars News Agency, February 18, 2014, http://en.farsnews.com/newstext.aspx?nn=13921129001186.

102 Andretta Towner, Senior Intelligence Analyst at CrowdStrike, quoted in Ashish Kumar Sen, *Iran's Growing Cyber Capabilities in a Post-Stuxnet Era*, Washington, DC, The Atlantic Council, April 10, 2015, http://www.atlanticcouncil.org/blogs/new-atlanticist/iran-s-growing-cyber-capabilities-in-a-post-stuxnet-era.

103 Shane Harris, "Forget China: Iran's Hackers Are America's Newest Cyber Threat," *Foreign Policy*, February 18, 2014, http://foreignpolicy.com/2014/02/18/forget-china-irans-hackers-are-americas-newest-cyber-threat/.

104 Shafa, *Iran's Emergence as a Cyber Power*.

105 "Iran Unleashes Cyber Army to Attack 'Enemy Websites,'" Live Leak. Com, March 16, 2011, http://www.liveleak.com/view?i=374_1300289092.

106 James P. Farwell, and Darby Arakelian, "What Does Iran's Cyber Capability Mean For Future Conflict?" *The Whitehead Journal of Diplomacy and International Relations* 14, no.1 (Winter 2013): 7, 49–65.

107 Kagan and Stiansen, *Cyber Threat From Iran*, 42.

108 Ashish Kumar Sen, "Iran's Growing Cyber Capabilities in a Post-Stuxnet Era."

109 Farwell and Arakelian, "What Does Iran's Cyber Capability Mean For Future Conflict?" 4.

110 Kagan and Stiansen, *Cyber Threat From Iran*, 21.

111 Siboni and Kronenfeld, *The Iranian Cyber Offensive During Operation Protective Edge*.

112 Farwell and Arakelian, "What Does Iran's Cyber Capability Mean For Future Conflict?" 1.

113 Jeremy Kirk, "Iranian Cyber Army Running Botnets, Researchers Say," *IDG News Service*, October 25, 2010, http://www.computerworld.com/article/2513597/network-security/iranian-cyber-army-running-botnets-researchers-say.html.

Chapter 4 Endnotes

114 Dana Schwarz, *Iran on the Cyber Offensive*, Israel Institute of National Security Studies, January 7, 2013, http://i-hls.com/2013/01/iran-on-the-cyber-offensive/.

115 "Commander Reiterates Iran's Preparedness to Confront Enemies in Cyber Warfare," Tasnim News Agency, February, 18, 2014, http://www.tasnimnews.com/en/news/2014/02/18/287797/commander-reiterates-iran-s-preparedness-to-confront-enemies-in-cyber-warfare.

116 On page 21 of their report, Kagan and Stiansen state their "study has traced significant volumes of malicious activity to systems controlled by the IRGC and organizations close to the Iranian government." Kagan and Stiansen, *Cyber Threat From Iran*, 21.

117 Siboni and Kronenfeld, *The Iranian Cyber Offensive during Operation Protective Edge*, 1.

118 Ibid.

119 Ashish Kumar Sen, "Iran's Growing Cyber Capabilities in a Post-Stuxnet Era."

120 Ben Elgin and Michael Riley, "Now at the Sands Casino: An Iranian Hacker in Every Server," *Bloomberg Business*, December 11, 2014, http://www.bloomberg.com/bw/articles/2014-12-11/iranian-hackers-hit-sheldon-adelsons-sands-casino-in-las-vegas.

121 Cylance, *Operation Cleaver Report*, 2014, https://www.cylance.com/operation-cleaver-cylance.

122 Ibid., 10.

123 Ibid., 7.

124 "Larijani Urges Unity Among Muslims," Fars News Agency, January 10, 2015, at http://en.farsnews.com/newstext.aspx?nn=13931020001359.

125 "Leader: Western Spy Agencies Behind Anti-Islam Plots in Region," Fars News Agency. January 9, 2015. What exactly is meant by "(so-called) Shiism linked to the UK's MI6" remains unexplained. http://en.farsnews.com/newstext.aspx?nn=13931019000690.

126 "Senior Iranian Cleric Urges Muslims to Grow United Against Extremism, Enemies' Plots." Fars News Agency, December 14, 2014, http://en.farsnews.com/newstext.aspx?nn=13930923000919.

127 "Enemies Plotting to Create Rift among Muslims," Fars News Agency, June 26, 2013, http://en.farsnews.com/newstext.aspx?nn=13920405000608.

Chapter 4 Endnotes

128 "Islamic Unity Conf. Releases Final Statement 30 December 2015," Mehr News Agency, http://en.mehrnews.com/news/113226/Islamic-Unity-Conf-releases-final-statement.

129 "Senior MP Warns Against US, Israel's Plots for Middle East," Fars News Agency, July 21, 2013, http://en.farsnews.com/newstext.aspx?nn= 13920430000443.

130 "Iran, Mexico in Agreement over US Role in Creation of Takfiri Groups," Fars News Agency, December 7, 2014. Despite the article's title, it does not identify any Mexican individual or organization that supposedly agrees with this assertion. http://en.farsnews.com/newstext.aspx?nn= 13930916001101.

131 "Leader's Aide: ISIL Product of US-Israeli Plots," Fars News Agency, September 9, 2014, http://en.farsnews.com/newstext.aspx?nn= 13930618001306.

132 "Senior Iranian Cleric Urges Muslims to Grow United Against Extremism, Enemies' Plots."

133 "Senior Cleric: ISIL to Backfire on West Soon," Fars News Agency, January 9, 2015, http://en.farsnews.com/newstext.aspx?nn=13931019000780.

134 "Tehran Rejects Possibility for Cooperation with West against ISIL," Fars News Agency, December 10, 2014, http://en.farsnews.com/newstext. aspx?nn=13930919001236.

135 "No But, If or Else: Muslim Nations Must Unite to Combat Terrorism," Fars News Agency, December 27, 2015, http://en.farsnews.com/newstext. aspx?nn=13941006001179.

136 "MPs Approve Bill to Fight International Terrorism," Mehr News Agency, January 12, 2016, http://en.mehrnews.com/news/113541/MPs-approve-bill-to-fight-intl-terrorism. The report did not identify who "generally believes" this claim.

137 "Iraq's will, not countries' positions, to eradicate ISIL," Mehr News Agency, December 28, 2015, http://en.mehrnews.com/news/113190/Iraq-s-will-not-countries-positions-to-eradicate-ISIL.

138 "Iran Rejects US Sincerity in Fight against ISIL," Fars News Agency, February 4, 2015, http://en.farsnews.com/newstext.aspx?nn= 13931115000223.

Chapter 5 Endnotes

139 "Iranian Speaker Describes US-Led Anti-ISIL Coalition as Useless." Fars News Agency, December 24, 2014, at http://en.farsnews.com/newstext. aspx?nn=13931003001270.

140 "Iran, Mexico in Agreement over US Role in Creation of Takfiri Groups."

141 "Islamic Unity Conf. Releases Final Statement 30 December 2015," Mehr News Agency.

142 "Some Regional States Seeking Restoration of Former Empires," Mehr News Agency, December 24, 2015, http://en.mehrnews.com/news/113105/ Some-regional-states-seeking-restoration-of-former-empires.

143 "Salehi: Muslims Awakened by Enemies' Antagonistic Moves," Fars News Agency, June 3, 2013, http://en.farsnews.com/newstext.aspx?nn= 13920313000591.

144 "Senior MP Blasts US for Dividing Terrorists to Good and Bad," Fars News Agency, January 7, 2015.

145 Deputy Foreign Minister for Europe and America Majid Takht Ravanchi Iran has been seeking to broaden ties and cooperation with Latin American states, including Venezuela, Bolivia, Brazil, Ecuador, Nicaragua, Cuba, Mexico, and Colombia. See "Iran Wants Faster Growing Ties with Latin America," Fars News Agency, November 9, 2015, http://en.farsnews.com/ newstext.aspx?nn=13940818001237.

CHAPTER 5
America's Wars and Turkish Attitudes: A Slippery Slope

1 Stephen Kinzer, *Crescent and Star: Turkey between Two Worlds* (New York: Farrar, Straus and Giroux, 2008), 243.

2 Andrew Finkel, *Turkey: What Everyone Needs to Know* (New York: Oxford University Press, 2012), 130–34.

3 Former U.S. Ambassador to Turkey, Eric Edelman, referred to these bumps as a "turbulent period." See The Washington Institute, Eighth Turgut Ozal Memorial Lecture, June 22, 2006, Policy Paper # 1115.

4 Ibid., 4.

5 Ibid., 5.

6 Interview with General Norman Schwarzkopf, Cox News Service, March 27, 1991. Also see Norman Schwarzkopf, *It Doesn't Take a Hero: The Autobiography of General H. Norman Schwarzkopf* (New York: Bantam, 2010), 475 94.

Chapter 5 Endnotes

7 Graham E. Fuller, *The New Turkish Republic* (Washington, DC, The U.S. Institute of Peace, 2008), 155. More recent reports say that the cost of the war in neighboring states to Turkey is in the billions of U.S. dollars. For example, "Turkey Opposition Puts $16 Billion Price Tag on Neighborhood Wars," Voice of America, May 4, 2015.

8 Nicole Pope and Hugh Pope, *Turkey Unveiled* (New York: Overlook Press, 2004), 159–79, 169–70, and 345.

9 Finkel, *Turkey*, 51. Dervis's reform ideas echoed to some extent the work of John Williamson who in 1989 outlined a set of economic policies known as the Washington Consensus to help ailing economies such as Turkey's address structural problems of development including microeconomic stabilization, economic opening in the direction of trade, foreign direct investments (FDI), and the expansion of market forces domestically through privatization. See John Williamson, ed., *Latin American Readjustment: How Much Has Happened* (Washington, DC: Institute for International Economics, 1989). For an update of Williamson's ideas, see his lecture, "The Washington Consensus as Policy Prescription for Development," (Washington: Institute for International Economics, January 13, 2004).

10 Finkel, *Turkey*, 75–77. Davutoğlu's vision centers on two key concepts: strategic depth and "zero problems with neighbors"—a refinement on Ataturk's original idea. The underpinnings of the former are based on the notion that Turkey inherited from its Ottoman past a rich endowment of historical links and cultural ties with its neighbors. Turkey therefore should embrace, not discard, that legacy, as it not only links Turkey to its neighbors but also binds Turkey's citizens to one another. On the other hand, Davutoğlu's regional pursuit of "zero problems with neighbors"—a doctrine that stresses close diplomatic and economic with Turkey's neighbors—stresses an effort to dilute national boundaries. Zero problem with neighbors and the policies emanating from it did not sit well with Turkey's traditional allies including the United States who felt that Turkey was moving eastward, away from its traditional Kemalist Western alliances and commitments. See Harvey Morris, "Turkey Hints at a Breakup With Europe," *International Herald Tribune*, February 6, 2013. Also see Patrick Cockburn, "Whose Side Is Turkey ON?" *London Review of Books* 36, no. 21 (November 6, 2014): 8–10.

11 Doug Penhallegon, "The Story Behind Turkey's 'No' Vote on Iraq in 2003" in *The Washington Review of Turkish and Eurasian Affairs,* June 2012, www.thewashingtonreview.org/. Penhallegon argues that whereas the United

Chapter 5 Endnotes

States had hoped that the Turkish military would fully support the U.S. political and military domestic and regional agendas, the Turkish military stood silent and ambivalent during the debate that led to the parliamentary vote in 2003. The same point was echoed by Kilic Bugra Kanat, a noted Turkish analyst, who pointed out that "the democratization of Turkish society and the accompanying enrichment of its civil society has transformed foreign policymaking into a more public affair involving other entities such as interest groups, think tanks, and civilian (non-governmental) experts."

12 Kilic Kanat, "AKP Party's Foreign Policy: Is Turkey Turning Away From the West?" *Insight Turkey* 12, no. 1 (2010): 221–23.

13 Editorial, "Valley of the Wolves Movie," *USA Today*, February 16, 2006.

14 Ceylan Yeginsu, "Turkey Agrees to Use of Bases For Airstrikes," *New York Times*, July 25, 2015. Also see Gonul Tol, "Washington-Ankara Tensions Will Shape Obama's Legacy in Turkey," Middle East Institute, Washington, DC, December 5, 2014. Tol argues that Turkey and the United States had deep differences over Iraq and other regional issues ranging from unfair disbursement of revenues of Iraqi oil; to Sunni underrepresentation in the new Iraqi government under Haider Al-Abadi; refusal of the United States to call the toppling of President Mohamed Morsi, in July 2013, a coup; and Turkey's call for more "forceful action" against Asad. For its part, the United States believed that Turkey was not doing enough to rein in ISIL in Syria and elsewhere.

15 TUSKON is today on the defensive in Turkey as President Erdogan sets out to eliminate Gulen's influence from the private and public sector. "Ankara Police Raid Gulenist Business Confederation TUSKON," *Daily Sabah*, November 6, 2015, 1. See also Ishaan Tharoor, "Turkey's Purge Marks the Endgame in Islamist Civil War," *Washington Post*, August 7, 2016.

16 "Ahmet Davutoğlu Discusses Need for End of Cold War Order" in *GWU Today*, February 13, 2012. Davutoğlu emphasized "his nation's role as an advocate for peace in the region, especially in light of Syrian President Bashar al-Asad's violent crackdown against his people. In answer to a question from the audience, Davutoğlu stated that he had repeatedly advised Asad to open up the Syrian political system saying that "Syria can have both democracy *and* internal security and stability" but that Asad had refused to heed his advice.

Chapter 5 Endnotes

17 Jeffrey Mankoff, "Why Moscow Fears Arab Unrest," *Current History*, October 2012: 258–63. Also see Samuel Charap, "Russia, Syria, And The Doctrine Of Intervention," *Survival 55*, no. 1 (February–March 2013): 35–41; Dan Triesman, "Why Russia Supports Syria's Assad," *UCLA TODAY*, (Los Angeles, January 14, 2014); "Russia Seeks Influence, Not Invasion, Analysts Say," *New York Times*, April 10, 2014; A. Barnard and Rick Gladstone, "Russia Seeks to Exert More Influence Over Syria Conflict," *New York Times*, April 4, 2012; Robert Rabil, "Russia Seeks Syrian Foothold in Mideast," *The National Interest*, October 21, 2011.

18 Robert Olson, "Denied a State, Winning a Region: Comparing Kurdish Nationalism after 1918 and 2003," in *The Kurdish Policy Imperative*, ed. Robert Lowe and Gareth Stanfield (London: Chatham House, 2010), 27–57.

19 Ibid., Kemal Kirici, "Turkey's Kurdish Challenge," in Lowe and Stanfield, *The Kurdish Policy Imperative*, 58–78.

20 "The Reluctance To Strike IS May Redound On Turkey's President," *Economist*, October 11, 2014, www.economist.com/node/21623795/comments.

21 Omer Taspinar, Turkey and the Arab Gulf States: A Dance with Uncertain Expectations (Washington, DC: Arab Gulf States Institute in Washington website, March 2015), 45, http://www.agsiw.org/turkey-and-the-arab-gulf-states-a-dance-with-uncertain-expectations/.

22 See interview by Samar Al Moqrin, *Al-Jazira* (Riyadh), November 2, 2015, www.al-jazirah.com/2015/20150211/ar6.htm. Also see *Al-Hayat* (London), May 20, 2015, http://www.alhayat.com/Articles/9354986/; and Saudi columnist Khalaf Al Harbi, "Why Lose Erdogan and His Party?" *Ukaz* (Jeddah), November 3, 2015, http://www.okaz.com.sa/new/Issues/20151103/Con20151103806071.htm. Also see "Under New King, Saudi Arabia May Diverge from Egypt on Muslim Brotherhood," Fox News, March 9, 2015. Also see "Is Saudi Arabia Warming Up to Muslim Brotherhood," Al Jazeera, July 29, 2015.

23 Ceylan Yeginsu, "ISIS Draws a Steady Stream of Recruits From Turkey," *New York Times*, September 15, 2014. The recent bombing of a Kurdish gathering in a Turkish town close to the Syrian border may have played a role in Turkey's change of heart on the need to confront both IS and Kurdish militias in Turkey. See "Bombing Shows Turkey a Vulnerable Target for Islamic State Extremists," Fox News, Associated Press Report, July 21, 2015.

Chapter 5 Endnotes

24 Liz Sly, "Turkey Attacks Kurdish Group in Iraq, Complicating ISIS Fight" *Washington Post*, July 26, 2015. See also Josh Lederman, "White House Says Turkey Has Right To Defend Against Kurds," Associated Press, July 25, 2015.

25 Karen DeYoung, and Liz Sly, "Turkey, U.S. Plan Safe Zone in Syria," *Washington Post*, July 27, 2015. Also see Hugh Naylor, "Syrian Leader Acknowledges Battlefield Losses Top Rebels," *Washington Post*, July 27, 2015.

26 "Turkey Says Russia Violated Its Airspace Near Syrian Border," BBC, January 30, 2016.

27 Keith Bradsher, "Range of Frustrations Reached Boil as Turkey Shot Down Russian Jet," *New York Times*, November 25, 2015.

28 Phil Stewart and Warren Strobel, "Exclusive: U.S. Put Request For Bigger Turkish Air Role on Hold," Reuters, December 4, 2015, http://www.reuters.com/article/us-syria-crisis-usa-turkey-idUSKBN0TO01T20151205.

29 Pew Research Center, *Global Attitudes and Trends: Attitudes Towards the United States Survey*, (Washington, DC 2013; 2008).

30 "Go Home, Yankee," *Economist*, August 13, 2016, 21.

31 Pew, *Global Attitudes and Trends*, 1.

32 Ibid., 3.

33 Ibid., 4–5.

34 Jacob Poushter, *The Turkish People Don't Look Favorably Upon the U.S., or Any Other Country, Really* (Washington, DC, Pew Research Center, 2014). Also see Omer Taspinar, "Turkey's Never Ending Anti-Americanism," *Today's Zaman*, May 4, 2014. Ben Katcher, "The Roots of Anti-Americanism in Turkey," *Middle East Journal* 64, no. 1 (Winter 2010), 51–66; Giray Sadik, *American Image in Turkey: U.S. Foreign Policy Dimensions*, (New York: Lexington Books, 2009).

35 Poushter, Op cit., 1.

36 There is no shortage of insightful prescriptions for improving United States-Turkey relations. See for example, see Steven Cook, et al., *U.S.-Turkey Relations: A New Partnership* (New York: Council on Foreign Relations, 2012); Philip Gordon and Omer Taspinar, *Winning Turkey* (Washington, DC: The Brooking Institution, 2008); Graham Fuller, *The New Turkish Republic* (Washington, DC, The U.S. Institute of Peace, 2008).

37 Stephen Kinzer, "How to Play Nice With Erdogan," *International New York Times*, August 4, 2016, 8.

Chapter 6 Endnotes

CHAPTER 6
How Pakistan Plays Its Double Game: Lessons Learned Since 9/11

1 Akbar Khan, *Raiders in Kashmir* (Karachi: National Book Foundation, 1970); Shuja Nawaz, *Crossed Swords: Pakistan, Its Army, and the Wars Within* (Oxford: Oxford University Press, 2008), Ch. 3.

2 Islamists in Pakistan and Afghanistan forged ties with one another during the 1960s. See Olivier Roy, "The Origins of the Islamist Movement in Afghanistan," *Central Asian Survey* 3, no. 2 (1984): 117–27.

3 Pervez Musharraf, *In the Line of Fire: A Memoir* (New York: Free Press, 2006), 201–202. See also "Wrong Step Can Spell Disaster: Musharraf," *Dawn*, September 19, 2001.

4 Dan Balz, Bob Woodward, and Jeff Himmelman, "Afghan Campaign's Blueprint Emerges," *Washington Post*, January 29, 2002.

5 Ahmed Rashid, *Descent into Chaos: The United States and the Failure of Nation Building in Pakistan, Afghanistan, and Central Asia* (New York: Viking Penguin, 2008), 29–30.

6 Abdul Sattar, *Pakistan's Foreign Policy, 1947–2005: A Concise History* (Karachi: Oxford University Press, 2007), 243.

7 Rashid, *Descent into Chaos*. See also Weinbaum and Harder, "Pakistan's Afghan Policies and Their Consequences," *Contemporary South Asia* 16, no. 1 (March 2008): 25–38.

8 Abdul Salam Zaeef, *My Life with the Taliban*, eds. Alex Strick van Linschoten and Felix Kuehn (New York: Columbia University Press, 2010), 152.

9 Vahid Brown and Don Rassler, *Fountainhead of Jihad: The Haqqani Nexus, 1973–2012* (London: Hurst and Company, 2013), Chs. 1 and 5.

10 Since the Soviet withdrawal, vanquished Afghan parties had either retired from the battlefield or defected to the victors. The Taliban was prepared to follow this tradition. Anand Gopal, *No Good Men Among the Living: America, the Taliban, and the War through Afghan Eyes* (New York, NY: Henry Holt and Co., 2014), Kindle edition, loc 779–81, 1728, 3216.

11 This assessment is a major theme of Anand Gopal's work, *No Good Men Among the Living.*

Chapter 6 Endnotes

12 Vanda Felbab-Brown, *Aspiration and Ambivalence: Strategies and Realities of Counterinsurgency and State Building in Afghanistan* (Washington, DC: Brookings Institution Press, 2013), 265.

13 Gopal, loc. 4523.

14 Many of the men leading the insurgency had attempted to reconcile and been rebuffed. Gopal. See also, Giustozzi, *Koran, Kalishnikov, and Laptop*.

15 Peter L. Bergen, *Manhunt: The Ten-Year Search for Bin Laden—from 9/11 to Abbottabad* (New York: Random House, 2012), Kindle edition, loc 1040–45. These efforts tapered off after roughly 2005; *The Future of al-Qa'ida, Testimony presented before the House Foreign Affairs Committee, Subcommittee on Terrorism, Nonproliferation and Trade*, 112th Cong. (May 24, 2011) (testimony of Seth Jones).

16 Other Taliban factions did not have a major presence in North Waziristan.

17 Antonio Giustozzi, *Koran, Kalashnikov and Laptop: The Neo-Taliban Insurgency in Afghanistan* (London: Hurst and Company, 2009), 1; Alex Strick van Linschoten and Felix Kuehn, *An Enemy We Created: The Myth of the Taliban-Al Qaeda Merger in Afghanistan* (New York: Oxford University Press, 2012), 252–53.

18 van Linschoten and Kuehn, *An Enemy We Created*, 253.

19 Giustozzi, *Koran, Kalashnikov and Laptop*, 34–35.

20 Afghanistan on the Brink: *Where Do We Go from Here?, Testimony presented before the House Foreign Affairs Committee*, 110th Cong. (February 15, 2007) (testimony of Lt. General David Barno (Ret)); no byline, "An Interview with Richard L. Armitage," *Prism: A Journal of the Center for Complex Operations* 1, no. 1 (December 2009): 103–12. Mark Mazzetti, Jane Perlez, Eric Schmitt, and Andrew Lehren, "Pakistan Aids Insurgency in Afghanistan, Reports Assert," *New York Times*, July 25, 2010.

21 On India's presence in Afghanistan, see C. Christine Fair, "Under the Shrinking U.S. Security Umbrella: India's End Game in Afghanistan?" *The Washington Quarterly* 34, no. 2 (2011): 179–92.

22 David Wood, "Commanders Seek More Forces in Afghanistan: Taliban Prepare Offensive against US, NATO Troops," *Baltimore Sun*, January 8, 2007.

23 Khalid Homayun Nadiri, "Old Habits, New Consequences: Pakistan's Posture Toward Afghanistan since 2001," *International Security* 39, no. 2 (Fall 2014): 132–68.

Chapter 6 Endnotes

24 See, for example, Dean Nelson and Ben Farmer, "Hamid Karzai Held Secret Talks with Mullah Baradar in Afghanistan," *Telegraph*, March 16, 2010.

25 Willi Germund, "Rentable Verhaftungen" [Cost-effective arrests], *St. Galler Tagblatt*, March 2, 2010, as cited in Nadiri, "Old Habits, New Consequences," 132–68.

26 Jane Perlez, "Pakistan Is Said to Pursue Role in U.S.-Afghan Talks," *New York Times*, February 9, 2010.

27 On Pakistan's efforts to spoil the peace process, including arresting Taliban members, see "What 2012 Has Meant for Afghanistan," *BBC News*, December 29, 2012. On Washington's evolving approach see Nadiri, "Old Habits, New Consequences," 132–68.

28 Kamran Yousaf, "Islamabad to Ask Kabul To End Anti-Pakistan Propaganda," *Express Tribune*, September 3, 2015.

29 National Commission on Terrorist Attacks upon the United States, *The 9/11 Commission Report: Final Report of the National Commission on Terrorist Attacks Upon the United States* (Washington: Government Printing Office, 2004), 331.

30 Rashid, *Descent into Chaos*, 32.

31 "Pakistani President Bans Islamic Militant Groups," CNN, January 12, 2002. On U.S. pressure and Pakistan's desire to avoid war with India, see Polly Nayak and Michael Krepon, *US Crisis Management in South Asia's Twin Peaks Crisis* (Washington, DC: Henry L. Stimson Center, September 2006).

32 Rashid, *Descent into Chaos*, 147; Stephen Tankel, *Storming the World Stage: The Story of Lashkar-e-Taiba* (New York: Oxford University Press), Kindle edition, loc. 2099–2105.

33 Tankel, *Storming the World Stage*, loc. 3071–76.

34 Improved Indian counterinsurgency efforts, fencing along the Line of Control, and a reduced appetite for conflict in Indian-administered Kashmir contributed as well. On Pakistan's efforts, see Tankel, *Storming the World Stage*, loc. 3071–96, 3123–45.

35 Cyril Almeida, "Kayani Spells Out Threat Posed by India Doctrine," *Dawn*, February 4, 2010.

36 Mumbai Police, *Final Report: Mumbai Terror Attack Cases*, February 25, 2009.

Chapter 6 Endnotes

37 Tankel, *Storming the World Stage*, loc. 3847–75; Sebastian Rotella, "David Headley, Witness in Terror Trial, Ties Pakistani Spy Agency to Militant Group," *Washington Post*, May 23, 2011.

38 Stephen Tankel, "Indian Jihadism: The Evolving Threat," *Studies in Conflict & Terrorism* 37, no. 7 (2014): 567–85.

39 Annie Gowen, "Pakistan, India Spar in Kashmir in Worst Border Violence in Years," *Washington Post*, September 12, 2013. See also, Stephen Tankel, "Beyond the Double Game: Lessons from Pakistan's Approach to Islamist Militancy," *Journal of Strategic Studies*, June 16, 2016.

40 "Lashkar-e-Taiba Behind Gurdaspur Terror Attack, Confirms MHA," *Business Standard*, July 27, 2015.

41 Shafiq Awan, "The Cost of Jhang By-Poll," *Daily Times*, March 10, 2010; Mariam Abou Zahab, "Pashtun and Punjabi Taliban: The Jihadi Sectarian Nexus," in *Contextualising Jihadi Thought*, ed. Jeevan Deol and Zaheer Kazmi (London: Hurst and Company, 2012), 382.

42 Hassan Abbas, "Defining the Punjabi Taliban Network," *CTC Sentinel 2*, no. 4 (April 2009); Zahab, "Pashtun and Punjabi Taliban," 382; Amir Mir, "Punjab Govt May Not Act Against LeJ Due to PML-N's Seat Adjustments with Defunct SSP," *The News*, February 22, 2013; Declan Walsh, "Extremists Pursue Mainstream in Pakistan Election," *New York Times,* May 5, 2013.

43 Zahab, "Pashtun and Punjabi Taliban," 372–73.

44 Ibid.; Ashley J. Tellis, "Pakistan and the War on Terror: Conflicted Goals, Compromised Performance" (Washington, DC: Carnegie Endowment for International Peace, 2008); Mohammad Amir Rana, "Structural Violence," *Dawn*, January 15, 2012; Huma Yusuf, "Sectarian Scourge," *Dawn*, January 31, 2012.

45 Tankel, *Storming the World Stage*, loc. 2099–2105.

46 Other militants sought sanctuary in Pakistan-administered Kashmir and the Northwest Frontier Province Areas (NWFP), known since 2009 as Khyber Pakhtunkhwa (KP). See Amir Mir, *Talibanization of Pakistan: From 9/11 to 26/11* (New Delhi: Pentagon Press, 2009), 108–10; Abbas, "Defining the Punjabi Taliban Network."

47 Stephen Tankel, "Beyond FATA: Exploring the Punjabi Militant Threat to Pakistan," *Terrorism and Political Violence* 28, no. 1 (January 2016): 49–71.

Chapter 6 Endnotes

48 Seth G. Jones and C. Christine Fair, *Counterinsurgency in Pakistan* (Santa Monica, CA: RAND Corporation, 2010); Zahid Ali Khan, *Military Operations in FATA and PATA: Implications for Pakistan* (Islamabad: Institute of Strategic Studies, 2012).

49 Nicholas Schmidle, *To Live or to Perish Forever: Two Tumultuous Years in Pakistan* (New York: Henry Holt and Company, 2009), 143.

50 Fair, "Pakistan's Own War on Terror;" Nasreen Ghufran, "Pushtun Ethnonationalism and the Taliban Insurgency in the North West Frontier Province of Pakistan," *Asian Survey* 49, no. 6 (2009): 1092–1114.

51 Rahimullah Yusufzai, "A Who's Who of the Insurgency in Pakistan's Northwest Frontier Province: Part One—North and South Waziristan," in Hassan Abbas, ed., *Pakistan's Troubled Frontier* (Washington, DC: The Jamestown Foundation, 2009), 32–33.

52 Shehzad H. Qazi, "Rebels of the Frontier: Origins, Organization, and Recruitment of the Pakistani Taliban," *Small Wars & Insurgencies* 22, no. 4 (2011): 574–602.

53 A copy of the Nizam e Adl Regulation, 2009, can be found at "Text of Pakistan's Shari'ah Law 2009," *BBC Monitoring South Asia*, April 14, 2009.

54 Zahab, "Pashtun and Punjabi Taliban," 376; Abbas, "Defining the Punjabi Taliban Network."

55 Lashkar-e-Tayyiba still prioritized jihad against India, but within a half decade after 9/11, Lashkar-e-Tayyiba forces were also fighting in Afghanistan. See Tankel, *Storming the World Stage*, loc. 3109.

56 Rana, "Structural Violence;" Yusuf, "Sectarian Scourge."

57 Mujahid Hussain, *Punjabi Taliban: Driving Extremism in Pakistan* (New Delhi: Pentagon Press, 2011), Ch. 10.

58 Qandeel Siddique, *Tehrik-e-Taliban Pakistan: An Attempt to Deconstruct the Umbrella Organization and the Reasons for its Growth in Pakistan's North-West* (Copenhagen, Denmark: Danish Institute for International Studies, 2010).

59 For example, Faizal Shahzad, who was trained and financed by the TTP, attempted to bomb Times Square in New York in 2010.

60 See for example, Praveen Swami, "Kabul Attack: U.S. Warning Was Accurate," *The Hindu*, August 3, 2008; Mark Mazzetti and Eric Schmitt,

Chapter 6 Endnotes

"C.I.A. Outlines Pakistan Links with Militants," *New York Times*, July 30, 2008; Lynne O'Donnell, "Eight Killed in Suicide Attack Near Kabul Hotel," Agence France-Presse, December 14, 2009; Karin Brulliard, "Afghan Intelligence Ties Pakistani Group Lashkar-i-Taiba to Recent Kabul Attack," *Washington Post*, March 3, 2010; Alissa Rubin, "Militant Group Expands Attacks in Afghanistan," *New York Times*, June 15, 2010.

61 Tankel, "Beyond FATA."

62 Hakimullah Mehsud, the present TTP emir, was previously its leader in Orakzai, where a tribal leader affiliated with SSP first raised a Taliban force using the name Tehrik-e-Taliban in 1999. His relative Qari Hussain Mehsud (known as Ustad-e-Fedayin, or trainer of the suicide-bombers) was a member of the SSP and LeJ before joining the TTP. The local TTP commander in Darra Adam Khel, Tariq Afridi, was another former SSP member. His affiliation with LeJ helped it to become one of the most active groups in Darra Adam Khel, a strategic location on the highway connecting Peshawar with Karachi, on which NATO supply convoys headed into Afghanistan via Torkham. It also provided a jumping off point for SSP/LeJ and JeM militants to participate in operations in Upper Orakzai, where some militants fled following the advent of incursions into South Waziristan in 2004. For a rich discussion of the sectarian influence on the insurgency in Pakistan, see Zahab, "Pashtun and Punjabi Taliban."

63 Zahab, "Pashtun and Punjabi Taliban," 376.

64 Most militants remained preoccupied with local and regional factors, but al-Qaida's global jihadist ideology, which entails striking U.S. and allied targets wherever they may be found, also influenced the militant environment. Pakistani groups, most notably LeT and the TTP, have engaged in or attempted out-of-area attacks against United States and its Western allies.

65 JeM official, interview by author, Multan, 2011; Jamaat-ud-Dawa official, interview by author, Lahore, 2011.

66 Tankel, "Beyond FATA."

67 For example, militants connected to the TTP used the Madrasa Usmania Shadan Lund in Multan as a place to store weapons and ammunition in advance of a failed attack on a government office building. At least two militants involved in this plot also were involved in the attack on the Sri Lankan cricket team bus, for which the Madrasa Usmania Shadan Lund was again used as a storage depot for weapons later transported to Lahore;

Chapter 6 Endnotes

"Attack on Sri Lankan Cricket Team at Lahore," Police Report, Case FIR No. 252, March 3, 2009, author in possession of hard copy; "Interrogation of Amanullah (aka Asadullah, aka Kashif)," Police Report, undated, author in possession of hard copy.

68 Adding to the confusion, groups, networks, and cells also use random names for attacks, often conjured up specifically to divert attention or sow confusion. This practice has local historical roots in Kashmir, where most of the jihadist organizations employed a plethora of aliases at the group or sub-group level to confuse the Indian security forces in Kashmir as well as to avoid retribution from the population. In some instances, they also did it to shield certain activities from their ISI handlers, a rationale that remains today.

69 For more on this dichotomy, see Vahid Rassler and Dan Brown, *The Haqqani Nexus and the Evolution of al-Qa'ida* (West Point: Combating Terrorism Center, 2011).

70 Rassler and Brown, *The Haqqani Nexus*, 46.

71 Ibid., 47; "Attack on Sri Lankan Cricket Team at Lahore."

72 For example, see "Pakistan Releases 3 Relatives of Fugitive Taliban Commander Under Swap Deal," *Frontier Post*, November 14, 2007.

73 Traditionally, co-opetition refers to cooperative competition that occurs between companies with partially congruent interests. See, for example, Adam M. Brandenburger and Barry Nalebuff, *Co-opetition* (New York: Doubleday, 1996).

74 Scholars have identified instances of rebels or insurgents simultaneously clashing and collaborating with one another and a ruling power in civil wars for the purpose of mutual benefit. This concept has yet to be explored in great depth in relation to either Pakistan or the political violence and terrorism literature. On the civil war literature see, for example, David Keen, *Useful Enemies: When Waging Wars Is More Important Than Winning Them* (New Haven: Yale University Press, 2012).

75 Christine Fair, "Why the Pakistan Army is Here to Stay: Prospects for Civilian Governance?" *International Affairs* 87, no. 3 (2011): 571–88.

76 Rana, "Structural Violence;" Christopher Anzalone, "The TTP's Hybrid Insurgency," *Foreign Policy*, November 23, 2011; Jeffrey Dressler, "The TTP Tango," *Foreign Policy*, December 12, 2011; "Peace Negotiations: Ousted TTP

Chapter 6 Endnotes

Deputy Chief Favors Talks with Goverment," Reuters, March 7, 2012. "Pakistan Welcomes Ouster of Taliban Deputy," Associated Press, March 6, 2012.

77 Jones and Fair, *Counterinsurgency in Pakistan*, 73.

78 Ibid., 57.

79 Ismail Khan and Declan Walsh, "After Months of Infighting, a Major Faction Splits From the Pakistani Taliban," *New York Times*, May 28, 2014; Saeed Shah, "Pakistani Taliban Faction Condemns Violence, Breaks Away," *Wall Street Journal*, May 28, 2014.

80 Nader Buneri, "Taliban Infighting Picks Up," *The Nation*, April 11, 2014.

81 Daud Khattak, "Contrasting the Leadership of Mullah Fazlullah and Khan Said Sajna in Pakistan," *CTC Sentinel* 7, no. 7 (July 2014).

82 Salman Masood, "Susan Rice, Obama's Security Adviser, Urges Pakistan to Do More Against Militants," *New York Times*, August 30, 2015.

83 C. Christine Fair, "Lashkar-e-Tayiba and the Pakistani State," *Survival* 53, no. 4 (2011): 29–52.

84 Stephen Tankel, *Domestic Barriers to Dismantling the Militant Infrastructure in Pakistan* (Washington, DC: United States Institute of Peace, 2013); Arif Jamal, presentation at NDU-sponsored conference, "Extremism in South Asia: The Case of Lashkar-e-Taiba," October 12, 2011.

85 Brown and Rassler, *Fountainhead of Jihad*, 159–61.

86 Rassler and Brown, *The Haqqani Nexus*, 2, 10.

87 Brown and Rassler, *Fountainhead of Jihad*, 160.

88 Imtiaz Gul, *The Most Dangerous Place* (Viking, New York 2010).

89 ISI officer, interview by author.

90 Tankel, *Domestic Barriers to Dismantling the Militant Infrastructure in Pakistan*.

91 In 2010, al-Qaida took credit for a joint LeT-Indian Mujahideen attack against the German Bakery in Pune, India, and its threats against India have increased since then. On al-Qaida's claims and threats against India, see Praveen Swami, "Why Pakistan Is Desperate for Lashkar-e-Taiba's Friendship," *Firstpost*, June 21, 2013. On LeT-Indian Mujahideen responsibility for the 2010 Pune blast, see Santosh Sonawane, "Bilal Trained in Pak to Make

Chapter 7 Endnotes

Explosives: Cop," *Times of India*, October 18, 2012; Asseem Shaikh, "Was Mirza Himayat Baig in Aurangabad When Blast Happened?" *Times of India*, October 21, 2012.

92 Hassan Abbas, presentation at NDU-sponsored conference, "Extremism in South Asia: The case of Lashkar-e-Taiba," October 12, 2011; Tankel, *Domestic Barriers to Dismantling the Militant Infrastructure in Pakistan.*

93 Tankel, *Domestic Barriers to Dismantling the Militant Infrastructure in Pakistan.*

94 Ibid.

95 Ismail Khan, "North Waziristan Operation—Daunting Challenge Ahead," *Dawn*, September 15, 2014; Zulfiqar Ali, "Change of Command: Maulvi Halim Replaces Gul Bahadur as Waziristan Taliban Chief," *Express Tribune*, August 15, 2014.

96 Haji Mujtaba, "Air Strikes in Northwest Pakistan Kill 24 Militants: Officials," Reuters, August 17, 2015.

97 Hameedullah Khan, "Pakistan Taliban Commander Allegedly Killed by Drones," Al Jazeera, November 26, 2015.

98 Sameer Lalwani, "Actually, Pakistan is Winning its War on Terror," *Foreign Policy*, December 15, 2015; "Malik Ishaq's Killing a Big Blow to Daesh," *The News*, August 1, 2015.

CHAPTER 7
Chinese Views on the U.S. Wars on Afghanistan and Iraq

1 The United States calls these two wars Operation ENDURING FREEDOM-AFGHANISTAN and Operation IRAQI FREEDOM. However, these two military operations were in every sense wars. This study uses terms the Afghan War and Iraq War throughout.

2 The Chinese overwhelmingly hold this view toward the two U.S. wars. See 樊高月 (Fan Gaoyue), "浅析伊拉克战争的特点" ("An Analysis of the Special Aspects of the Iraq War"), 现代军事 (*Contemporary Military*), No. 7, 2003 and 周桂银 (Zhou Guiyin), "伊拉克战争与美国的大战略失误" ("The Iraq War and Mistake of U.S. Grand Strategy"), 国际观察 (*International Studies*), No. 5, 2003 for a discussion of this view. 孙必干 (Sun Bigan), "重读伊拉克战争" ("Revisiting the Iraq War"), 阿拉伯世界研究 (*Arab World Studies*), No. 2, 2006.

Chapter 7 Endnotes

3 See David Lai, *The United States and China in Power Transition* (Carlisle, PA: Strategic Studies Institute, 2011) for an extensive discussion of the U.S.-China power transition and the assertion that this power transition is now in its second stage made in his recent article "China's Strategic Moves and Countermoves in the Asia-Pacific," *Parameters* 44, No. 4 (Winter 2014–15): 11–26.

4 John J. Mearsheimer, *The Tragedy of Great Power Politics* (New York: Norton, 2001).

5 刘阿明(Liu Aming) and 王联合(Wang Lianhe), "先发制人与预防性战争辨析—以布什政府国家安全战略为例" ("An Analysis of the Difference between Preemptive and Preventive Wars"), 学术探索 (*Theoretical Inquiry*), No. 11, 2004.

6 世界知识封面话题 (*World Affairs Magazine* Cover Story), "大敌无形, 美国怎么打?" ("How Would the United States Fight When the Enemy Is Invisible?"), No. 20, 2001.

7 牛新春 (Niu Xinchun), "集体性失明: 反思中国学界对伊战, 阿战的预测" ("Collective Blindness: Reflection on the Predictions about Iraq and Afghan Wars by the Chinese Analysts"), 现代国际关系 (*Contemporary International Relations*), No. 4, 2014.

8 The Chinese are very receptive to the idea of soft power as articulated by Joseph S. Nye, Jr. in *Soft Power: The Means to Success in World Politics* (New York, Public Affairs, 2004), and his other related works.

9 See the late Harvard University Professor Samuel P. Huntington's classic work, *Political Order in Changing Societies* (New Haven: Yale University Press, 1968) for arguments on this issue.

10 赵华胜 (Zhao Huasheng), "阿富汗: 失去的机会和前景" ("Afghanistan: Lost Opportunity and Future Prospects"), 国际观察 (*International Observer*), No. 6, 2010. 刘青建 (Liu Qingjian), "试析美国在阿富汗的困局" ("An Analysis of the U.S. Dilemmas in Afghanistan"), 现代国际关系 (*Contemporary International Relations*), No. 2, 2009. See also 李建波 (Li Jianbo) and 崔建树 (Cui Jianshu), "美国在阿富汗的困境研究" ("An Analysis of the U.S. Dilemmas in Afghanistan"), 国际展望 (*International Outlook*), No. 6, 2012.

11 随琳 (Sui Lin) and 王成龙 (Wang Chenglong), "伊拉克战争美军战略失误解析" ("An Analysis of the Mistakes by the U.S. Military in the Iraq War"), 国防科技 (*National Defense and Technology*), No. 3, 2007.

Chapter 7 Endnotes

12 雷希颖 (Lei Xiying), "伊拉克战争十年的影响与启示—雷希颖对话华黎明大使和田文林研究员" ("The Impact and Lessons of the 10-Year Iraq War—Interviews with Ambassador Hua Liming and Analyst Tian Wenlin"), 新浪微博: ANU CAIS LXY, March 20, 2013.

13 高祖贵 (Goa Zugui), "美国霸权的根源分析" ("An Analysis on the Origins of U.S. Hegemony"), 和平与发展季刊 (*Peace and Development Quarterly*), No. 4, 2004.

14 戴德铮 (Dai Dezheng) and 邓春晖 (Deng Chunhui), "同性相克, 异曲同工" ("Same Magnets Reject Each Other"), 学习月刊 (*The Studies Monthly*), No. 8, 2004. 周静 (Zhou Jing), "冷战后美国霸权主义的新特点" ("The New Characteristics of U.S. Hegemony in the Post-Cold War Era"), 当代世界经济与政治 (*Contemporary International Economics and Politics*), No. 11, 2003.

15 张树德 (Zhang Shude), 裴佳法 (Pei Jiafa), and 王玉坤 (Wang Yukun), "当代战争主要根源于新帝国主义" ("New Imperialism Is the Main Source of Contemporary Wars"), 中国军事科学 (*China Military Science*), No. 3, 2009.

16 杨玲玲 (Yang Lingling), "美国霸权主义的演变及其实质" ("The Core Meaning and Transformation of U.S. Hegemonism"), 中共中央党校学报 (*Chinese Communist Party Central Cadre School Journal*), Vol. 6, No. 3, August 2002. 唐连风 (Tang Lianfeng), "冷战后霸权主义产生的原因, 特点及反霸举措" ("The Causes and Characteristics of Post-Cold War Hegemonism and Anti-Hegemonism Measures"), 通化师范学院学报 (*Tonghua Normal University Journal*), Vol. 23, No. 3, May 2003.

17 夏小权 (Xia Xiaoquan), "小布什时期美国霸权主义产生根源探析" ("An Analysis on the Root Causes of U.S. Hegemony in the George W. Bush Era"), 当代世界 (*Contemporary World*), No. 7, 2010. 张辰卉 (Zhang Chenhui) and 徐智城 (Xu Zhicheng), "浅析超级大国的新霸权主义是当代战争的主要根源" ("An Analysis of Superpower's Neo-Hegemonism as the Main Source of Contemporary War"), 科技信息 (*Science and Technology Information*), No. 25, 2013. See also 易善武 (Yi Shanwu), "论邓小平的反霸权主义思想" ("On Deng Xiaoping's Anti-Hegemonism Thoughts"), 赤峰学院学报汉文哲学社会科学版 (*Chifeng College Journal of Chinese, Philosophy, and Social Sciences*), Vol. 32, No. 4, April 2011.

18 高祖贵 (Goa Zugui), "美国霸权的根源分析" ("An Analysis on the Origins of U.S. Hegemony"), 和平与发展季刊 (*Peace and Development Quarterly*), No. 4, 2004. 王淑梅 (Wang Shumei), "透视冷战后美国发动的

Chapter 7 Endnotes

四场战争" ("An Analysis of the Four Wars the United States Waged after the Cold War"), 环球经纬 (*Huanqiu Jingwei*), No. 6, 2005. 朱琨 (Zhu Kun), "从霸权主义到新帝国主义" ("From Hegemonism to Neo-Imperialism"), 太平洋学报 (*The Pacific Journal*), No. 1, 2004.

19 社会观察(Social Outlook), "美国结束伊拉克战争" ("The United States Ended the Iraq War"), Issue 1, 2012.

20 雷希颖 (Lei Xiying), "伊拉克战争十年的影响与启示—雷希颖对话华黎明大使和田文林研究员" ("The Impact and Lessons of the 10-Year Iraq War—Interviews with Ambassador Hua Liming and Analyst Tian Wenlin"), 新浪微博: ANU CAIS LXY, March 20, 2013. 陈向阳 (Chen Xiangyang), "应吸取伊拉克战争的教训" ("Must Learned Lessons from the Iraq War"), 国际网 (*International Net*), March 20, 2013.

21 甘苏庆 (Gan Suqing), "美国在阿富汗战争中的收获与教训" ("The Gains and Lessons the United States Had from the Afghan War"), 和平与发展季刊 (*Peace and Development Quarterly*), No. 2, 2002.

22 周桂银 (Zhou Guiyin), "伊拉克战争与美国的大战略失误" ("The Iraq War and Mistake of U.S. Grand Strategy"), 国际观察 (*International Studies*), No. 5, 2003. 李捷 (Li Jie) and 杨恕 (Yang Shu), "阿富汗与美国 '大中亚计划' 评析" ("An Analysis of Afghanistan and the U.S. 'Greater Central Asia' Plan"), 西亚非洲 (*West Asia and Africa*), No. 4, 2008.

23 黄仁国 (Huang Renguo), "美国霸权的困惑" ("The Problems with U.S. Hegemony"), 江南社会学院学报 (*Jiangnan Social Science University Journal*), Vol. 6, No. 3, 2004. 高志虎 (Gao Zhihu), "美国 '反恐' 战争化的思考" ("Thoughts on the U.S. Militarizing the 'Fight against Terrorism'"), 当代世界 (*Contemporary World*), No. 11, 2008.

24 Chinese analysts took note of the initiative. For U.S. analyses, see Marina Ottaway and Thomas Carothers, "The Greater Middle East Initiative: Off to a False Start." Carnegie Endowment for International Peace, Policy Brief, No. 29, March 2004, and Tamara Cofman, "The New U.S. Proposal for a Greater Middle East Initiative: An Evaluation." Brookings Paper, May 10, 2004.

25 刘宗义 (Liu Zongyi), "美国的伊拉克困局及伊拉克战争的遗产" ("The U.S. Iraq Quagmire and Legacy of the Iraq War"), 外交评论 (*Foreign Policy Analysis*), No. 8, 2007. 赵葆珉 (Zhao Baomin), "从伊拉克到阿富汗美国反恐战略评估" ("An Assessment of the U.S. Anti-Terrorism Strategy from Iraq to Afghanistan"), 阿拉伯世界研究 (*Arab World Studies*), No. 2, 2011.

Chapter 7 Endnotes

童毛弟 (Tong Maodi), "美国霸权主义对当前国际反恐合作的负面影响" ("The Negative Impact of U.S. Hegemonism on the Current International Cooperation in Anti-Terrorism"), 和平与 发展季刊 (*Peace and Development Quarterly*), No. 2, 2006. 韩景云 (Han Jingyun), "论美国对伊拉克战争的代价" ("An Analysis on the Price the United States Paid in Waging the Iraq War"), 湖南师范大学社会科学学报 (*Hunan Normal University Social Sciences Journal*), No. 2, 2004. 刘治国 (Liu Zhiguo) and 凡海军 (Fan Haijun), "伊拉克 战争后遗症的文化解读" ("The Iraq War Sequel from Cultural Perspective"), 南京政治学院学报 (*Nanjing College of Politics Journal*), No. 6, 2009. 李翠亭 (Li Cuiting), "伊拉克战争对美国软实力的影响及其反思" ("The Impact of Iraq War on U.S. Soft Power and Reflections"), 武汉理工大学学报社会科学版 (*Wuhan Science and Technology University Social Sciences Journal*), No. 1, 2014.

26 邓春晖 (Deng Chunhui), "恐怖主义与霸权主义关系探微" ("An Analysis of the Relations between Terrorism and Hegemonism"), 太原师范学院学报社会科学版 (*Taiyuan Normal University Journal Social Sciences Edition*), Vol. 4, No. 1, March 2005. 董漫远 (Dong Manyuan), "纵论伊拉克战争" ("An Analysis of the Iraq War"), 国际问题研究 (*International Studies*), No. 2, 2003. 宋丽群 (Song Liqun) and 孟欧 (Meng Ou), "阿富汗战争所体现的局部战争新特点" ("The New Characteristics of Limited War As Reflected in the Afghan War"), 军事历史 (*Military History*), No. 1, 2003.

27 罗峰 (Luo Feng), "美国预防性战争的逻辑" ("The Logic of the U.S. Preventive War"), 世界政治 (*World Politics*), No. 9, 2010. 孙德刚 (Sun Degang), "先发制人战略的实施动因分析" ("An Analysis on the Drive for the Implementation of the Preemptive Strategy"), 外交评论 (*Foreign Policy Analysis*), No. 5, 2009. 周桂银 (Zhou Guiyin), "先发制人战争的道义限度" ("The Moral Limit of Preemptive War"), 世界经济与政治 (*World Economy and Politics*), No. 8, 2010. 蒋晓燕 (Jiang Xiaoyan), "浅析布什政府的 '先发制人' 战略" ("An Analysis of the Bush Administration's 'Preemption' Strategy"), 现代国际关系 (*Contemporary International Relations*), No. 9, 2002. 邵峰 (Shao Feng), "美国先发制人战略及其最新发展" ("The Latest Development in the U.S. Preemptive Strategy"), 前线 (*Frontier*), No. 12, 2004. 史泽华 (Shi Zehua) and 杨云涛 (Yang Yuntao), "重析美国先发制人战略" ("Review of the U.S. Preemption Strategy"), 太平洋学报 (*Pacific Review*), No. 7, 2004. 刘津 (Liu Jin) and 王婧 (Wang Jing), "从伊拉克战争看美国 '先发制人' 战略及其影响" ("U.S. 'Preemption' Strategy and Its Implications from the Case of Iraq War"), 产业与科技论坛 (*Industrial & Science Tribune*), Vol. 12, No. 10, 2013. 罗峰 (Luo Feng), "美国预防性战争

Chapter 7 Endnotes

的逻辑" ("The Logic of the U.S. Preventive War"), 世界政治 (*World Politics*), No. 9, 2010. 刘阿明 (Liu Aming) and 王联合 (Wang Lianhe), "先发制人与预防性战争辨析" ("An Analysis of Preemption and Preventive War"), 学术探索 (*Academic Inquiry*), No. 11, 2004.

28 苏开华 (Su Kaihua), "从 '先发制人' 战略看美国未来霸权主义和强权政治的新动向" ("An Analysis of the 'Preemption Strategy' and Its Impact on the New Directions of the U.S. Hegemony and Major Power Politics") 世界经济与政治论坛 (*World Economic and Political Forum*), No. 2, 2003. 胡欣 (Hu Xin), "从 '遏制威慑' 走向 '先发制人'—后冷战时代的美国新战略" ("From 'Deterrence and Containment' to 'Preemption'—U.S. New Strategy in the Post-Cold War Era"), 世界经济与政治 (*World Economy and Politics*), No. 10, 2002. 刘阿明 (Liu Aming) and 王联合 (Wang Lianhe), "先发制人与预防性战争辨析" ("An Analysis of Preemption and Preventive War"), 学术探索 (*Academic Inquiry*), No. 11, 2004. 邵峰 (Shao Feng), "美国 '先发制人' 战略及其最新发展" ("The Latest Development in U.S. Strategy of 'Preemption'"), 前线 (*Frontier*), No. 12, 2004.

29 雷希颖 (Lei Xiying), "伊拉克战争十年的影响与启示—雷希颖对话华黎明大使和田文林研究员" ("The Impact and Lessons of the 10-Year Iraq War—Interviews with Ambassador Hua Liming and Analyst Tian Wenlin"), 新浪微博@ANU CAIS LXY, March 20, 2013. 萨本望 (Sa Benwang) and 李春宏 (Li Chunhong), "布什政府国家安全战略报告评析" ("An Analysis of Bush Administration's National Security Strategy"), 和平与发展季刊 (*Peace and Development Quarterly*), No. 4, 2002. 何英 (He Ying), "论美国战略思想的转变对中美关系的影响" ("On the Change of U.S. Strategic Thought and Its Impact on U.S.-China Relations"), 国际观察 (*International Observer*), No. 1, 2003. 樊高月 (Fan Gaoyue), "浅析伊拉克战争的特点" ("An Analysis of the Special Aspects of the Iraq War"), 现代军事 (*Contemporary Military*), No. 7, 2003.

30 苏开华 (Su Kaihua), "从 '先发制人' 战略看美国未来霸权主义和强权政治的新动向" ("U.S. Hegemony and Power Politics from the Perspective of Preemption Strategy"), 世界经济与政治 (*World Economy and Politics*), No. 2, 2003. 苏开华 (Su Kaihua), "从 '先发制人' 战略看美国未来霸权主义和强权政治的新动向" ("An Analysis of the 'Preemption Strategy' and Its Impact on the New Directions of the U.S. Hegemony and Major Power Politics") 世界经济与政治论坛 (*World Economic and Political Forum*), No. 2, 2003. 刘阿明 (Liu Aming), "先发制人与国际法" ("Preemption and International Law"), 社会科学 (*Social Sciences*), No. 6, 2004. 郭真 (Guo Zhen), "美国 '先发制人' 战略评析" ("An Analysis of the U.S. 'Preemptive'

Chapter 7 Endnotes

Strategy"), 武汉大学学报哲学社会科学版 (*Journal of Wuhan University Philosophy and Social Science Edition*), No. 2, 2005. 颜剑英 (Yan Jianying), "从 2006 '美国国家安全战略报告' 解读美国霸权主义发展趋势" ("An Analysis of the Development Trend of U.S. Hegemony As Reflected in the 2006 'U.S. National Security Strategy'"), 国际关系学院学报 (*Journal of the College of International Relations*), No. 5, 2007. 张家栋 (Zhang Jiadong), "从强制性外交到 '先发制人' 战略" ("From Coercive Diplomacy to 'Preemptive Strategy'"), 国际观察 (*International Observer*), No. 6, 2003. See also 朴美兰 (Pu Meilan), "论美国 '先发制人' 的对外战略思想" ("An Analysis of the U.S. 'Preemptive War' and Its Foreign Policy Strategy"), 延边大学学报社会科学版 (*Journal of Yanbian University Social Science Edition*), No. 12, 2005. 罗峰 (Luo Feng), "美国预防性战争的逻辑" ("The Logic of the U.S. Preventive War"), 世界政治 (*World Politics*), No. 9, 2010. 孙德刚 (Sun Degang), "'9.11' 后的美国先发制人战略" ("Post-'9.11' U.S. Preemption Strategy"), 国际问题 (*International Issues*).

31 陈良武 (Chen Liangwu), "美国 '先发制人' 军事战略五年评述" ("U.S. 'Preemptive' Military Strategy in Its Fifth Year"), 国防科技 (*National Defense Science and Technology*), No. 4, 2007. 刘津 (Liu Jin) and 王婧 (Wang Jing), "从伊拉克战争看美国 '先发制人' 战略及其影响" ("U.S. 'Preemption" Strategy and Its Implications from the Case of Iraq War"), 产业与科技论坛 (*Industrial & Science Tribune*), Vol. 12, No. 10, 2013. See also 吴先翔 (Wu Xianxiang) and 高义群 (Gao Yiqun), "先发制人与美国霸权" ("Preemption and U.S. Hegemony"), 中国军事科学 (*China Military Science*), No. 1, 2005. 郭真 (Guo Zhen), "美国先发制人战略评析" ("An Analysis of the U.S. Preemptive Strategy"), 武汉大学学报哲学社会科学版 (*Journal of Wuhan University Philosophy and Social Sciences Edition*), April 2003.

32 吕级三 (Lü Jisan), 谷立祥 (Gu Lixiang) and 孟京 (Meng Jing), "伊拉克战争的分析及启示" ("An Analysis and Lessons Learned on the Iraq War"), 导弹与航天运载技术 (*Missiles and Space Vehicles*), No. 5, 2003.

33 彭光谦 (Peng Guangqian), "中国专家论伊战" ("Experts on the Iraq War"), 解放军报 (*PLA Daily*), March 24, 2003.

34 Tommy Franks, *American Soldier* (New York: HarperCollins Publishers Inc., 2004), 406–407, 429, 500–501.

35 CCTV (China Central TV), "美军北上继续受阻, 华盛顿加紧调兵" ("U.S. Northbound Troops Continued to Meet Resistance, Washington in a Hurry to Send More Troops"), March 29, 2003.

Chapter 7 Endnotes

36 时寒冰 (Shi Hanbing), "评论: 美军的三点 '小' 失误" ("Commentary: U.S. Troop's Three 'Small' Mistakes"), 华夏时报 (*China Times*), March 26, 2003.

37 王南 (Wang Nan), "人民观察: 美军孤军深入, 命运凶多吉少" ("People's Observation: Isolated U.S. Troops Drove Deep in Iraq, Its Fate Was More Dangerous Than Fortune"), 人民网 (*People's Net*), March 26, 2003. Also by the same reporter, "战术分析: 美地面部队为何急于进攻" ("Analysis of War Tactics: Why Were the U.S. Ground Troops in a Hurry to Make Offensive Advance"), 环球时报 (*Global Times*), March 26, 2003.

38 李成刚 (Li Chenggang), "伊拉克战争综述" ("A Comprehensive Analysis of the Iraq War"), 军事历史 (*Military History*), No. 5, 2007.

39 韩旭东 (Han Xudong), "巴格达之战: 美伊战争的转折点?" ("Battle on Baghdad: the Turning Point of the Iraq War?") 中国青年报 (*China Youth Daily*), April 12, 2003.

40 The Chinese believed that the disappearance of Iraqi troops and lack of resistance were well-planned operations to mislead the U.S. troops.

41 邱永峥 (Qiu Yongzheng), "青年参考特稿: 萨达姆抵抗美军五大战术" ("Special Report by Youth Brief: Saddam's Five Tactics in Resisting the U.S. Military"), 青年参考报 (*Youth Brief Daily*), March 25, 2003. 陈辉 (Chen Hui), "伊拉克战争伊军战法得失大盘点" ("An Overall Assessment of Iraqi Military Tactics in the Iraq War"), 华北民兵 (*North China Militia*), No. 7, 2003. 王明亮 (Wang Mingliang) and 董振山 (Dong Zhenshan), "伊拉克防空四大战法" ("Iraq's Four Main Air Defense Tactics"), 中国青年报 (*China Youth Daily*), March 23, 2003. 倪乐雄 (Ni Lexiong), "伊拉克战争七问之一: 悲情巴格达仗怎打成这样" ("Seven Questions about the Iraq War (I): Sorry for Baghdad How Can the War Be Fought as Such"), 新闻晚报 (*Evening News*), April 15, 2003. 郭斯仁 (Guo Siren), "伊军的五大战术和三大缺陷" ("Iraqi Military's Five Main Tactics and Three Shortcomings"), 环球时报 (*Global Times*), March 31, 2003. 王南 (Wang Nan), "人民观察: 美军孤军深入, 命运凶多吉少" ("People's Observation: Isolated U.S. Troops Drove Deep in Iraq, Its Fate Was More Dangerous Than Fortune"), 人民网 (*People's Net*), March 26, 2003. Also by the same reporter, "战术分析: 美地面部队为何急于进攻" ("Analysis of War Tactics: Why Were the U.S. Ground Troops in a Hurry to Make Offensive Advance"), 环球时报 (*Global Times*), March 26, 2003. 雨生 (Yu Sheng), "萨达姆有意让美军长驱直入, 城市巷战为最后王牌" ("Saddam Let U.S. Troops in on Purpose, City-Street Fight

Chapter 7 Endnotes

as the Last Trump Card"), 国际先驱导报 (*International Herald*), March 24, 2003. 吴苗萱 (Wu Huixuan), "化整为零, 全民上阵, —萨达姆要打'人民战争'" ("Breaking the Troops into Small Units, All People Joined the Fight—Saddam Wanted to Wage 'People's War'"), 法制日报 (*Rule of Law Daily*), March 26, 2003. 北京青年报 (*Beijing Youth Daily*), "吸取教训, 改变抵抗战术, 萨达姆抗敌有高招" ("Learning the Lessons, Changing Resistance Tactics, Saddam Had Smart tricks against the Enemy"), March 27, 2003. See also 刘广聚 (Liu Guangju), "分析: 大仗就要打响, 萨达姆如何应对" ("Analysis: Major Battle about to Start, How Would Saddam React?") 法制日报 (*Rule of Law Daily*), March 28, 2003. 晨晖 (Chen Hui), "美伊对峙: '持久战' 与 '速决战' 的较量" ("U.S.-Iraq Showdown: a Contest between 'Protracted War' and 'Quick Showdown War'"), 国际先驱导报 (*International Herald*), March 24, 2003. 张昭忠 (Zhang Zhaozhong), "军事分析: 伊拉克军队还未完全暴露实力" ("Military Analysis: Iraqi Troops Had Yet Exposed Its Full Power"), 生活时报 (*Daily Life*), March 2003.

42 北京青年报 (*Beijing Youth Daily*), "战事分析: 伊拉克空军哪里去了?" ("War Analysis: Where Did the Iraqi Air Force Go?"), March 28, 2003.

43 京华时报 (*Beijing Times*), "伊拉克 '四大战术' 奏效, 游击战让美军伤亡惨重" ("Iraq 'Four Big Tactics' Making Impact, Guerilla Warfare Inflicted Heavy Casualty on U.S. Troops"), March 25, 2003. 文松辉 (Wen Songhui), "伊战局动态: 伊军以 '游击战' 对付美军进攻" ("Iraq War Update: Iraqi Troops Used 'Guerilla War Tactics' to Deal with U.S. Troop's Attack"), 新华网 (*Xinhua Net*), March 23, 2003. See also 牛道斌 (Niu Daobin), "分析: 美英联军攻伊的 '矛' 与 '盾'" ("Analysis: The 'Spear' and 'Shield' [Contradiction] of the U.S.-U.K. Coalition Attacks on Iraq"), 法制日报 (*Rule of Law Daily*), March 25, 2003. 樊高月 (Fan Gaoyue) "美军最不擅长打巷战, 强攻巴格达损失会很重" ("U.S. Troops Not Good at Street Fight, Forceful Attack on Baghdad Would Inflict Heavy Loss on the U.S. Troops"), 北京青年报 (*Beijing Youth Daily*), March 26, 2003.

44 樊高月 (Fan Gaoyue), 王宝付 (Wang Baofu), 曲星 (Qu Xing), and 张昭忠 (Zhang Zhaozhong), "军事专家: 伊军以 '劣势抗优势' 初见成效" ("Military Commentators: Initial Success of the Iraqi Military on 'the Weak Overcoming the Strong'"), 北京青年报 (*Beijing Youth Daily*), March 25, 2003. See also 王文 (Wang Wen) and 李大军 (Li Dajun), "我国专家评美伊两军攻防的得与失" ("Our Military Experts Analyzing the Gain and Loss on the U.S. and Iraqi Sides during Their Offenses and Defenses"), 新华网 (*Xinhua Net*), March 25, 2003. 萨仁 (Sa Ren), "分析: 透过战争看萨达姆的

Chapter 7 Endnotes

'谋略'" ("Analysis: Saddam's 'Skills in Strategy' through the War"), 新华网 (*Xinhua Net*), March 30, 2003. See also 肖作 (Xiao Zuo), "军事述评: 伊军游击战有多大作用" ("Military Analysis: How Big an Impact Would Guerilla Warfare Be"), 环球时报 (*Global Times*), March 31, 2003. 萨仁 (Sa Ren), "时事分析: 美国的误判与失算" ("News Analysis: U.S. Misjudgments and Miscalculations"), 新华网 (*Xinhua Net*), March 25, 2003.

45 章田 (Zhang Tian), "萨达姆在战争初期的应对之策—'拖'" ("Saddam's Strategy at the Beginning of the War—'Delaying'"), 中国新闻网 (*China News Net*), March 22, 2003. See also 顾德伟 (Gu Dewei), "实力相去甚远, 伊拉克军事上如何应对美国" ("Power Greatly Mismatched, How Would Iraqi Military Deal with the U.S. Counterpart"), 北京青年报 (*Beijing Youth Daily*), March 22, 2003. 刘克 (Liu Ke), "战事分析: 巴格达巷战—美军面临最大挑战" ("War Analysis: Baghdad Street Fight—U.S. Troop's Biggest Challenge"), 北京青年报 (*Beijing Youth Daily*), March 22, 2003. 陈辉 (Chen Hui), "伊战谈兵录: 开战 6 天—以弱抗强地面相持" ("Iraq War Analysis: Day 6 in War—the Weak against the Strong on the Ground"), 新华网 (*Xinhua Net*), March 25, 2003. See also 樊高月 (Fan Gaoyue), "军事述评: 美军三大新战法能否奏效" ("Military Analysis: Can the U.S. Three New Tactics Succeed"), 环球时报 (*Global Times*), March 24, 2003.

46 萨仁 (Sa Ren), "新闻分析: 伊拉克战争中的两大迷信与出乎意料" ("News Analysis: the Two Big Myths in the Iraq War and Surprises"), 新华网 (*Xinhua Net*), March 29, 2003. 林治波 (Lin Zhibo), "人民时评: 伊拉克给美英上了一课" ("People's Daily Analysis: Iraq Taught the U.S. and U.K. a Lesson"), 人民网 (*people.com.cn*), April 1, 2003. See also 韩旭东 (Han Xudong), "伊拉克战争第一阶段述评: 意想不到的开局" ("Iraq War First Phase Analysis: Unexpected Opening"), 中国青年报 (*China Youth Daily*), April 2, 2003. 魏岳江 (Wei Yuejiang), "美英联军攻打伊拉克主要作战特点点评" ("Comments on the Key Tactics of U.S. Troops in the Iraq War"), 人民网 (*people.com.cn*), April 8, 2003.

47 高铁军 (Gao Tiejun), "伊称正 '战略撤退, 诱敌深入, 后发制人': 孤军深入敌后, 美军狂奔巴格达, 是福? 是祸?" (Iraq Claim to Make 'Strategic Retreat, Lure the Enemy Deep in, and Post-emption': Isolated U.S. Troops Advancing Deep into Enemy Territory, U.S. Troops Ran Madly Toward Baghdad, Good? Or Bad?"), 人民网 (*People's Net*), March 25, 2003.

48 李海元 (Li Haiyuan), "伊拉克战局分析: 伊军不会大规模反击?" ("Iraq War Analysis: Would Iraq Troops Make Large-scale Counterattack?") 人民网 (*people.com.cn*), April 1, 2003.

Chapter 7 Endnotes

49 钟和 (Zhong He), "联军心理战全盘告负, 伊拉克军民一致对外" ("Coalition Psycho-warfare Completely Failed; Iraqi Military and People in United Front against Invasion"), 扬子晚报 (*Yangzi Evening News*), April 1, 2003.

50 洪安德 (Hong Ande), "美伊巴格达决战两大悬念: 攻城兵力, 人城作战" ("Two Big Uncertainties in U.S.-Iraq Baghdad Showdown: Forceful Attack and Street Fight"), 京华时报 (*China Capital Times*), April 1, 2003. 杨民青 (Yang Minqing) and 陈辉 (Chen Hui), "伊战谈兵录: 巴格达攻防战八大悬念" ("Iraq War Analysis: Eight Uncertainties in the Attack and Defense of Baghdad"), 新华网 (*Xinhua Net*), April 1, 2003.

51 章田 (Zhang Tian), "美英军队来犯, 巴格达会战斗到底吗?" ("U.S.-U.K. Troops Invading, Would Baghdad Fight to the Last?") 中国新闻网 (*China News Net*), March 27, 2003.

52 周贺 (Zhou He), "伊战谈兵录: 为何未见伊军大规模抵抗" ("Iraq War Analysis: Why We Had Not Seen Iraq Troops Make Large-scale Counterattack"), 新华网 (*Xinhua Net*), April 9, 2003. 韩旭东 (Han Xudong), "伊战启示录: '先发制人' 的理论抢占先机" ("Iraq War Lessons: 'Preemption' Theory Took an Early Start'"), 中国青年报 (*China Youth Daily*), April 19, 2003. 洪德安 (Hong Dean), "焦点将转向提克里特, 萨达姆想在老家打游击" ("Focal Point Switching to Tikrit, Saddam Hoped to Wage Guerilla Warfare at His Hometown"), 新闻晨报 (*Morning News*), April 10, 2003. 萨仁 (Sa Ren), "伊拉克战局的四条关键线索" ("Four Key Hints in the Iraq War"), 新华网 (*Xinhua Net*), April 6, 2003. 郭斯仁 (Guo Siren), "战术分析: 伊拉克常规师为何不动" ("Analysis of Tactics: Why Iraq Troops Did Not Move"), 环球时报 (*Global Times*), April 7, 2003. 吴茴萱 (Wu Huixuan), "巴格达迷雾笼罩, 萨达姆握有 '最后王牌'" ("Fog of War Overshadowing Baghdad, Saddam Still Held 'Last Trump Card'"), 人民网 (*people.com.cn*), April 9, 2003. See also 倪乐雄 (Ni Lexiong), "评论: 萨达姆在以 '游动火力' 抗衡联军" ("Analysis: Saddam Was Using "Moving Target" to Counter the U.S.-U.K. Coalition"), 文汇报 (*Wenhui Daily*), April 9, 2003. 张莉 (Zhang Li), "伊拉克共和国卫队 '消失' 的三种可能性" ("Three Possible Reasons for the 'Disappearing' of the Iraqi Troops"), 中国新闻网 (*China News Net*), April 5, 2003.

53 邱永峥 (Qiu Yongzheng), "青年参考特稿: 萨达姆抵抗美军五大战术" ("Special Report by Youth Brief: Saddam's Five Tactics in Resisting the U.S. Military"), 青年参考报 (*Youth Brief Daily*), March 25, 2003. 倪乐雄 (Ni Lexiong), "伊战攻防战略探究, 美军直取巴格达战略正确" ("An Analysis

Chapter 7 Endnotes

of Offensive and Defensive Strategies in the Iraq War, U.S. Troops Attacking Directly Baghdad Was Correct"), 文汇报 (*Wenhui Daily*), April 18, 2003. 贾小华 (Jia Xiaohua), "评论: 巴格达之役背后的六个问号" ("Analysis: Six Questions Behind the Battle on Baghdad"), 北京晨报 (*Beijing Morning News*), April 11, 2003.

54 韩旭东 (Han Xudong), "巴格达之战, 美易战争的转折点?" ("Battle on Baghdad, the Turning Point in the Iraq War?") 中国青年报 (*China Youth Daily*), April 12, 2003.

55 伏流 (Fu Liu), "表现未有出格, 萨达姆最终选择了放弃" ("No Outstanding Measures, Saddam Finally Gave Up"), 扬子晚报 (*Yangzi Evening News*), April 1, 2003. 郑若麟 (Zheng Ruolin), "分析: 伊战进程出人意料, 一连串问号仍无答案" ("Analysis: Iraq War Development Unexpected; Many Questions Had No Answers"), 文汇报 (*Wenhui Daily*), April 11, 2003.

56 陈辉 (Chen Hui), "伊拉克战争伊军战法得失大盘点" ("An Overall Assessment of Iraqi Military Tactics in the Iraq War"), 华北民兵 (*North China Militia*), No. 7, 2003. 石丁 (Shi Ding), "军事专家分析制约美军速战速决的几大因素" ("Military Expert Comment on the Factors Impacting U.S. Troops Quick and Decisive Victory"), 环球时报 (*Global Times*), March 21, 2003.

57 刘健宇 (Liu Jianyu), "伊拉克战争中伊军为什么迅速溃败" ("Why Iraqi Military Suffered a Quick Collapse in the Iraq War"), 中国-东盟博览 (*China-ASEAN*), No. 5, 2011. 郭斯仁 (Guo Siren), "军事评述: 伊军的五大战术和三大缺陷" ("Military Analysis: Iraqi Troop's Five Tactics and Three Short Comings"), 环球时报 (*Global Times*), March 31, 2003.

58 张勇建 (Zhang Yongjian), "美伊军队实力悬殊过大, 伊不具备打游击基础" ("The Difference in Military Power between the U.S. and Iraqi Troops Was Too Big, Iraq Did Not Have the Basis for Guerilla Warfare"), 新闻晨报 (*Morning News*), April 8, 2003.

59 王如君 (Wang Rujun), "评论: 伊拉克战争更像一场游戏" ("Analysis: Iraq War Is More Like a Show"), 环球时报 (*Global Times*), April 16, 2003. 严国群 (Yan Guoqun) and 陶中华 (Tao Zhonghua), "巷战究竟对谁划算? 萨达姆难 '克敌制胜'" ("Who Had the Advantage on Street War? Saddam May Not Be Able to Win"), 解放日报 (*Liberation Daily*), April 2, 2003. 李海元 (Li Haiyuan), "萨达姆布阵疑有失误, 伊军再难 '咸鱼翻身'" ("Saddam May Have Made Mistake in Strategy, Iraqi Troops Could Not Turn Things Around"), 新闻晚报 (*Evening News*), April 11, 2003.

Chapter 7 Endnotes

60 张荣 (Zhang Rong) and 张兢 (Zhang Jing), "对伊拉克战争中强弱矛盾对抗发展的理性思考" ("Thoughts on the Conflict and Development of the Strong-Weak Contradiction in the Iraq War"), 南京政治学院学报 (*Nanjing College of Politics Journal*), Vol. 20, 2004.

61 樊高月 (Fan Gaoyue), "浅析伊拉克战争的特点" ("An Analysis of the Special Aspects of the Iraq War"), 现代军事 (*Contemporary Military*), No. 7, 2003.

62 赵小卓 (Zhao Xiaozhuo), "冷战后美国对外军事干预分析" ("An Analysis of U.S. Military Interventions Abroad after the Cold War"), 中国军事科学 (*China Military Science*), No. 4, 2007.

63 谭新木 (Tan Xinmu), "伊几十万军队失踪, 美新战争模式能否奏效?" ("Several Hundred Thousand Iraqi Troops Disappeared, Could the U.S. New Way of War Make a Difference?") 新华网 (*Xinhua Net*), April 11, 2003.

64 李德才 (Li Decai) and 徐敏飞 (Xu Minfei), "伊拉克战争的思考与启示: 积极应对新军事变革挑战" ("Reflections and Lessons from the Iraq War: Actively Respond to the Challenges of New Military Transformation"), 国防科技 (*National Defense Science and Technology*), 2003. 熊光楷 (Xiong Guangkai), "论世界新军事变革趋势和中国新军事变革" ("On the Trends in World New Military Transformation and China's New Military Transformation"), 外交学院学报 (*Foreign Affairs College Journal*), No. 76, June 2004. See also 王均伟 (Wang Junwei), "江泽民与中国特色军事变革" ("Jiang Zemin and Military Transformation with Chinese Characteristics"), 中国共产党 90 年研究文集 (中) (Chinese Communist Party 90 Years of History), Beijing, May 2011. 曹智 (Cao Zhi), 徐壮志 (Xu Zhuangzhi), 白瑞雪 (Bai Ruixue), "中国军事改革何处去" ("Where Will China's Military Transformation Go?" 中国新闻网 (*China News Net*), 2003.

65 熊光楷 (Xiong Guangkai), "关于新军事变革问题" ("On New Revolution in Military Affairs"), 解放日报 (*Liberation Daily*), May 30, 2003 and "论世界新军事变革趋势和中国新军事变革" ("On World New Revolution on Military Affairs and China's New Military Transformation"), 外交学院学报 (*Foreign Affairs College Journal*), August 1, 2008. 李建华 (Li Jianhua), "从海湾战争到伊拉克战争—美军是这样改革的" ("From the Gulf War to the Iraq War—The Transformation of the U.S. Military"), 环球军事 (*Global Military*), April 1, 2003. 赵小卓 (Zhao Xiaozhuo), "伊拉克战争中美军的作战特点" ("The Characteristics of U.S. Military Operations in the Iraq War"), 军事历史 (*Military History*), No. 3, 2003.

Chapter 7 Endnotes

66 吕级三 (Lü Jisan), 谷立祥 (Gu Lixiang) and 孟京 (Meng Jing), "伊拉克战争的分析及启示" ("An Analysis and Lessons Learned on the Iraq War"), 导弹与航天运载技术 (*Missiles and Space Vehicles*), No. 5, 2003. 江平 (Jiang Ping), "军事述评: 伊拉克战争三大军事影响; 各国调整军事战略, 突出质量建军, 亚洲更受关注" ("Military Analysis: Iraq War Three Big Military Impact; Nations Adjust Military Strategies, Emphasis on Quality in Military Modernization, Asia Would Draw More Attention"), 环球时报 (*Global Times*), April 21, 2003. 时殷弘 (Shi Yinhong), 陈如为 (Chen Ruwei), 钱文荣 (Qian Wenrong), 彭光谦 (Peng Guangqian), 李荣 (Li Rong), 侯若石 (Hou Ruoshi), et al, "半月谈: 专家谈伊拉克战争冲击波" ("Bi-Weekly: Military Experts on the Impact of Iraq War"), 新华网 (*Xinhua Net*), May 13, 2003. 朱培臣 (Zhu Peichen), 孙大庆 (Sun Daqing), and 曲子 (Qu Zi), "伊拉克战争给予我们什么启示" ("What Are the Lessons of the Iraq War to Us?") 当代海军 (Modern Navy), No. 6, 2003.

67 任天佑 (Ren Tianyou), "未来 20 年中国军事发展将走向何方" ("What Is China's Direction for Its Military Development in the Next 20 Years"), 国防参考 (National Defense Briefing), January 12, 2015. 解放军报 (*PLA Daily*), "紧紧把握新军事变革的走势" ("Hold Correctly the Direction of New Military Transformation"), 解放军报 (*PLA Daily*), September 21, 2011.

68 刘焕松 (Liu Huansong), "美海军陆战队装备伊战测评" ("An Analysis on U.S. Marine Weaponry during the Iraq War"), 轻兵器 (*Small Arms*), No. 1, 2005.

69 李丽娟 (Li Lijuan), 赵志芳 (Zhao Zhifang) and 刁天喜 (Diao Tianxi), "美军 2001–2011 年伊拉克和阿富汗战争医疗后送情况分析" ("An Analysis of U.S. Military Battlefield Medical Treatment and Dispatch during the Iraq War and Afghan War from 2001 to 2011"), 解放军预防医学杂志 (*Journal of Preventive Medicine of Chinese People's Liberation Army*), No. 6, 2013.

70 吴曙霞 (Wu Shuxia), "伊拉克战争战伤救治研究进展" ("A Study on Medical Treatment of Wounded Soldiers during the Iraq War"), 人民军医 (*People's Military Surgeon*), No. 1, 2012.

71 蒋铭敏 (Jiang Mingmin), "美陆军旅在伊拉克战争中疾病与非战斗损伤情况介绍" ("An Introduction to U.S. Military Treatment of Wounded Soldiers and Ailment during the Iraq War"), 人民军医 (*People's Military Surgeon*), No. 7, 2011.

Chapter 7 Endnotes

72 张卫东 (Zhang Weidong), "阿富汗战争后勤保障经验" ("Experience on Logistics Supply during the Afghan War"), 国外坦克 (*Foreign Armors*), No. 4, 2013. 王映红 (Wang Yinghong) and 吕传禄 (Lu Chuanlu), "伊拉克战争中英军后勤保障的经验与不足" ("An Analysis on the Experience and Shortcomings of U.S. and U.K. Military Logistics Supply"), 海军医学杂志 (*Journal of Navy Medicine*), No. 1, 2008.

73 蒲瑶 (Pu Yao), "阿富汗战争中的宣传, 情报战与中国的情报安全未来与发展" ("Propaganda and Intelligence in the Afghan War and China's Intelligence Security and Its Future Development"), Future and Development, No. 6, 2008. 郭戈 (Guo Ge), "浅析美国在伊拉克战争中对传媒的控制和利用" ("A Preliminary Analysis of the U.S. Media Control during the Iraq War"), 解放军外国语学院学报 (*Journal of PLA University of Foreign Languages*), No. 2, 2007.

74 潘志高 (Pan Zhigao), "美陆军工程兵的伊战经历及对我军的启示" ("The Experience of U.S. Army Corps of Engineering during the Iraq War and Lessons for the PLA"), 成都大学学报(社会科学版 (*Journal of Chengdu University (Social Sciences)*), No. 5, 2010.

75 梁百川 (Liang Baichuan), "从阿富汗战争看新的作战概念" ("A View on the New Operational Concepts through the Afghan War"), 航天电子对抗 (*Aerospace Electronic Warfare*), No. 1, 2003.

76 吴颖 (Wu Ying), "美军武器装备在阿富汗战争中的使用及效能" ("The Use and Effect of U.S. Military Weapon and Equipment in the Afghan War"), 现代兵器 (*Modern Weaponry*), No. 7, 2002. 王华 (Wang Hua), "阿富汗战争中美军武器装备运用特点" ("The Characteristics of U.S. Military Weapon and Equipment during the Afghan War"), 现代军事 (*Modern Military*), No. 4, 2002.

77 "从阿富汗战争看信息战技术对传统作战方式的影响" ("Influence of Information War Technology through the Afghan War"), 国际航空 (*International Aviation*), No. 5, 2002.

78 李成刚 (Li Chenggang) and 朱爱民 (Zhu Aimin), "浅析伊拉克战争中美英联军的空袭作战" ("An Analysis of Air Raid by the U.S. and U.K. Coalition Forces during the Iraq War"), 军事历史 (*Military History*), No. 1, 2010.

79 赵汉清 (Zhao Hanqing), 施建安 (Shi Jianan) and 汪卫华 (Wang Weihua), "美军在伊拉克战争中自杀的预防及对我军的启示" ("The Prevention of U.S. Military Soldier Suicide during the Iraq War and Lessons for

Chapter 7 Endnotes

the PLA"),东南国防医药 (*Military Medical Journal of Southeast China*), No. 1, 2010.

80 蔡洋 (Cai Yang), "伊拉克战争中美军心理战谋略的传播学解读" ("An Analysis of U.S. Military Psychological Warfare during the Iraq War"), 西安政治学院学报 (*Journal of Xi'an Politics Institute of PLA*), No. 3, 2008. 吴义龙 (Wu Yilong) and 彭岩 (Peng Yan), "伊拉克战争美军心理战特点及启示" ("The Characteristics of U.S. Military Psychological Warfare during the Iraq War"), 中国国情国力 (*China National Conditions and Strength*), No. 12, 2004.

81 陈松海 (Chen Songhai), "伊拉克战争中美军战场心理疾病对我军的启示" ("An Analysis on U.S. Military Treatment of Psychological Problems during the Iraq War"), 解放军预防医学杂志 (*Journal of Preventive Medicine of Chinese People's Liberation Army*), No. 5, 2007.

82 吴更生 (Wu Gengsheng), "伊拉克战争中美英联军运输保障特点和启示" ("The Characteristics of U.S.-U.K Coalition Transportation and Supply and Lessons for the PLA"), 国防交通工程与技术 (*Transportation Engineering and Technology for National Defense*), No. 4, 2005.

83 高晓颖 (Gao Xiaoying), "从伊拉克战争看制导技术发展历程 航天控制" ("An Analysis of U.S. Space Control and Munition Guidance in the Iraq War"), *Aerospace Control*, No. 5, 2005.

84 王勇 (Wang Yong) and 徐向东 (Xu Xiangdong), "从伊拉克战争看机载武器发展趋势" ("An Analysis on the Trends of Airborne Weapons through the Iraq War"), 飞航导弹 (*Winged Missiles Journal*), No. 11, 2004.

85 肖咏捷 (Xiao Yongjie), "伊拉克战争中初露锋芒的美国陆军 FBCB~2 系统" ("The Emerging Power of U.S. Army FBCB-2 System"), 现代军事 (*Modern Military*), No. 3, 2005.

86 谢朝新 (Xie Chaoxin), 龙腾锐 (Long Tengrui), 方振东 (Fang Zhendong) and 周宁玉 (Zhou Ningyu), "从伊拉克战争看美军的野战供水保障特点给水排水" ("An Analysis of U.S. Military Water Supply during the Iraq War"), Water & Wastewater Engineering, No. 10, 2004.

87 张春润 (Zhang Chunrun), 曲明辉 (Qu Minghui), 曹会智 (Cao Huizhi), 令狐昌应 (Linghu Changyin), 蔡强 (Cai Qiang), "伊拉克战争对车辆装备维修保障力量建设的启示" ("U.S. Military Vehicle Maintenance and Repair during the Iraq War and Lessons for the PLA"), 装备指挥技术学院学报 (*Journal of Institute of Command and Technology*), No. 4, 2004.

Chapter 8 Endnotes

88 程立斌 (Cheng Libin) and 李珊珊 (Li Sansan), "透析伊拉克战争 GPS 干扰与反干扰电光与控制" ("An Analysis of GPS Jamming and Counter-Jamming during the Iraq War"), *Electronics Optics & Control*, No. 1, 2004.

CHAPTER 8
Japan's Lessons in Iraq and Afghanistan

1 White House, Office of the Press Secretary, "U.S.-Japan Joint Vision Statement," April 28, 2015, https://www.whitehouse.gov/the-press-office/2015/04/28/us-japan-joint-vision-statement.

2 Terayuki Aizawa, NIDS Briefing Memo: "The Significance and Lessons of the Dispatch of Minesweepers Units to the Persian Gulf (sic)," December 2014, http://www.nids.go.jp/english/publication/briefing/pdf/2014/briefing_e193.pdf.

3 Ibid., 1.

4 Noboru Yamaguchi, "The Role of the Self Defense Forces in Peace Building: Changes in Policy and the Arguments That Informed Them (sic)," in *The 11th International Symposium on Security Affairs*, ed. (NIDS, February 3, 2009), http://www.nids.go.jp/english/event/symposium/pdf/2008/e_09.pdf, 53–72.

5 "The North Korea Nuclear Crisis February 1993–June 1994," *GlobalSecurity.org*, http://www.globalsecurity.org/military/ops/dprk_nuke.htm (accessed August 3, 2015).

6 Ibid.

7 Note: These are personal observations. The author was a U.S. Army drilling individual mobilization augmentee (DIMA) assigned to US Army Japan Host Nations Affairs/G-5 during this period. He participated in numerous planning sessions as well as negotiations with the Japan Defense Agency during and after the crisis.

8 Jamie McIntyre, "Washington Was on Brink of War with North Korea 5 Years Ago," CNN, October 4, 1999, http://www.cnn.com/US/9910/04/korea.brink/.

9 Japan Ministry of Foreign Affairs. "The Guidelines for Japan-U.S. Defense Cooperation," http://www.mofa.go.jp/region/n-america/us/security/guideline2.html (accessed August 10, 2015).

Chapter 8 Endnotes

10 Ibid., 54.

11 Masanori Yoshida, "Kaijo Jietai ni Yoru Kokusai Katsudo no Jisseki to Kyokun: Perusha-wan ni Okeru Sokai Katsudo to Indo-yo ni Okeru Hokyu Katsudo" [Lessons learned from JMSDF's international operations: focusing on minesweeping activities in the Persian Gulf and replenishment activities in the Indian Ocean], *Kokusai Anzen Hosho* [*Journal of International Security*] 38, no. 4 (March 2011): 5–20.

12 Ibid., 5.

13 Ibid., 8.

14 Ibid., 8.

15 Ibid., 9.

16 Ibid., 11.

17 Yamaguchi, "The Role of the Self Defense Forces in Peace Building," 61.

18 Sebastian Gorka. "Invocation of Article 5: Five Years Later", *NATO Review* (Summer 2006): http://www.nato.int/docu/review/2006/issue2/english/art1.html.

19 Yoshida, "Lessons learned from JMSDF's international operations," 14.

20 Ibid., 15.

21 Ibid., 16.

22 Ibid., 17.

23 Ibid., 19.

24 Yamaguchi, "The Role of the Self Defense Forces in Peace Building," 65.

25 Tim Kelly and Nobuhiro Kubo, "Japan May Give Planes to Manila for South China Sea Patrols: Sources," Reuters, August 6, 2015, http://www.reuters.com/article/2015/08/06/us-japan-philippines-aircraft-idUSKCN0QB06920150806.

26 Ibid.

27 David Fouse. "Japan's Dispatch of the Ground Self Defense Force to Iraq: Lessons Learned," Asia-Pacific Center for Security Studies (July 2007): 2, http://www.apcss.org/wp-content/uploads/2011/03/Japans-Dispatch-of-the-GSDF-to-Iraq.Fouse_.doc.pdf.

28 Ibid., 2.

Chapter 8 Endnotes

29 Kuwait News Agency (KUNA), May 30, 2004, http://www.kuna.net.kw/ArticlePrintPage.aspx?id=1478839&language=en.

30 Fouse, "Japan's Dispatch of the Ground Self Defense Force to Iraq: Lessons Learned," 4.

31 Ibid., 4.

32 Yoshiyuki Sakaemura, "Iraku Fukko Shien ni Okeru Minsei Kyoryoku Katsudo no Jisseki to Kyokun" [Practical activities and lessons learned of the JGSDF's civil-military cooperation on humanitarian and reconstruction assistance in Iraq], *Kokusai Anzen Hosho* [*Journal of International Security*] 38, no. 4 (March 2011): 38–56.

33 Yoshiyuki Sakaemura, "A New Role for Armed Forces in a Non-permissive Environment: On the Coordination Between the Japan Self-Defense Forces' International Peace Cooperation Operations and the Official Developmental Assistance in Iraq", Japan Peacekeeping Training and Research Center, Working Paper No. 201301, July 15, 2013, 10, http://www.mod.go.jp/js/jsc/jpc/research/image/eng04.pdf.

34 Sakaemura, "Practical activities and lessons learned of the JGSDF's Civil-Military Cooperation," 40.

35 Ibid., 42.

36 Ibid., 44.

37 Ibid., 45.

38 Ibid., 47.

39 Ibid., 49.

40 Sakaemura. "A New Role for Armed Forces in a Non-permissive Environment," 13.

41 Fouse, "Japan's Dispatch of the Ground Self Defense Force to Iraq: Lessons Learned," 7.

42 Fouse, "Japan's Dispatch of the Ground Self Defense Force to Iraq: Lessons Learned," 6.

43 Japan Ministry of Defense, http://www.mod.go.jp/e/d_act/anpo/shishin_20150427e.html.

44 "Japan To Allow Military Role Overseas in Historic Move," BBC, September 18, 2015, http://www.bbc.com/news/world-asia-34287362.

Chapter 8 Endnotes

45 Tomonori Yoshizaki. "The Role of the Military in Peace-Building: A Japanese Perspective," in the 11th International Symposium on Security Affairs, ed. (NIDS, February 3, 2009), http://www.nids.go.jp/english/event/symposium/pdf/2008/e_12.pdf.
[NOTE: Yoshizaki is a Professor and Director of Policy Simulation at Japan's National Institute for Defense Studies (NIDS)]

46 Ibid., 116.

47 Ibid., 117.

48 Ibid., 119.

49 JICA Research Institute, "Afghanistan and Japan: Working Together on State-Building and Development," (2012): https://jica-ri.jica.go.jp/publication/assets/file_2881.pdf.

50 Ibid., 25.

51 Japan Ministry of Foreign Affairs, "Japan's Assistance to Afghan Refugees and Displaced Persons," December 2001, http://www.mofa.go.jp/region/middle_e/afghanistan/assist0112.html.

52 Note: The Japan Platform (JPF) is a consortium of NGOs, the business community, and the government designed to respond to emergency humanitarian crises such as a refugee crisis or natural disaster in a more effective and rapid manner than any one party could do on its own. The government (the Ministry of Foreign Affairs) appropriates funds in advance for this purpose. The Standing Committee (comprised of representatives of the NGOs, the business community, the government, and experts), under the mandate of the Board of Directors of the JPF, makes the decisions regarding the implementation of emergency humanitarian aid. In fiscal year 2012, 68 out of the 180 emergency humanitarian aid projects undertaken in 20 countries, including in Asia, Middle East, Africa, Latin America and the Caribbean, and in Japan, were funded by the government. The main activities were distribution of emergency relief supplies and water, as well as providing education and sanitation programs. http://www.mofa.go.jp/files/000024755.pdf, p. 9, (October 4, 2015).

53 JICA Research Institute, "Afghanistan and Japan: Working Together on State-Building and Development," 26.

54 Ibid., 27.

55 Ibid., 32.

Chapter 8 Endnotes

56 Ibid., 54.

57 Ibid., 56.

58 Ibid., 58.

59 Mujib Mashal, Joseph Goldstein, and Jawad Sukhanyar, "Afghans Form Militias and Call on Warlords to Battle Taliban", *New York Times*, May 24, 2015, http://www.nytimes.com/2015/05/25/world/asia/as-taliban-advance-afghanistan-reluctantly-recruits-militias.html?_r=0.

60 JICA Research Institute, "Afghanistan and Japan: Working Together on State-Building and Development," 285.

61 Ibid., 290.

62 Japan Ministry of Foreign Affairs, "Japan's Assistance in Afghanistan: Towards Self-Reliance", p. 2, http://www.mofa.go.jp/files/000019264.pdf, (September 6, 2015).

63 Ibid., 19.

64 Erick Slaven. "Japan enacts major changes to its self-defense laws." September 18, 2015, http://www.stripes.com/news/pacific/japan-enacts-major-changes-to-its-self-defense-laws-1.368783, (September 20, 2015).

65 Wendy Anhika Prajuli and Nur Alia Pariwita. "Between fear and hope on Japan's new defense policy," http://www.eastasiaforum.org/2015/08/08/between-fear-and-hope-on-japans-new-defence-policy/, (September 7, 2015).

66 Sydney Freedberg Jr., "Japan Looks South: China's Rise Drives New Strategy," http://breakingdefense.com/2015/08/japan-looks-south-chinas-rise-drives-new-strategy/, (September 3, 2015).

67 Japan Ministry of Defense, http://www.mod.go.jp/e/publ/w_paper/2015.html, (October 4, 2015).

68 Masaaki Kameda, "Defense white paper stresses threat posed by China," July 21, 2015, http://www.japantimes.co.jp/news/2015/07/21/national/politics-diplomacy/defense-white-paper-stresses-threat-posed-china/, (October 4, 2015)

69 Adam P. Liff, "Japan's Defense Policy: Abe the Evolutionary," *Washington Quarterly* Vol. 38, No. 2 (August 2015): pp. 79–99, http://twq.elliott.gwu.edu/japan%E2%80%99s-defense-policy-abe-evolutionary, (October 12, 2015).

Chapter 9 Endnotes

CHAPTER 9
Perspectives of International Nongovernmental Organizations

1 Most of the statistical data in this section come from two main sources: "Emerging Trends in Humanitarian Action and Professionalization of Humanitarian Workers," produced by the European Universities on Professionalization of Humanitarian Workers (EUPRHA), n.d., and Cynthia Brassard-Boudreau and Don Hubert, "Shrinking Humanitarian Space? Trends and Prospects on Security and Access," *The Journal of Humanitarian Assistance*, November 24, 2010.

2 Ibid.

3 Ibid.

4 Ibid.

5 "Swiss 'Shocked' at Targeting of Hospitals," *SWI*, October 29, 2015, http://www.swissinfo.ch/eng/topic/crime-law-and-justice-02000000/40003776.

6 Although there are contradictory reports of the number of civilian deaths in both wars, one credible estimate calculated that since the start of the Afghan war in 2001, about 26,270 civilians had been killed by direct war-related violence and more than 29,000 injured. It is not clear how many of these deaths were the result of airstrikes by the United States and its allies, and how many were from attacks by the Taliban and other insurgents. Neta C. Crawford, "War-related Deaths, Injury, and Displacement in Afghanistan and Pakistan 2001–2014," *Costs of War*, Watson Institute, Brown University, May 22, 2015, http://watson.brown.edu/costsofwar/files/cow/imce/papers/2015/War%20Related%20Casualties%20Afghanistan%20and%20Pakistan%202001-2014%20FIN.pdf.

7 The IHFFC website describes the commission as follows: "The Commission has a specific profile. It is composed of fifteen personalities elected as individuals by the States having recognized its competence. They are diplomats, military officers, medical doctors, and academic specialists in international humanitarian law from four continents. It is an impartial body which has no political agenda of its own. It is not related to the Security Council with its enforcement powers (unless the Security Council decides to have recourse to the services of the Commission) nor to the International Criminal Court with its powers to initiate a criminal prosecution. Its approach to

Chapter 9 Endnotes

fact-finding is co-operative. It will assist the parties to a conflict to redress a situation where international humanitarian law may have been violated, and thus help to promote the rule of law in international relations and create conditions conducive to peace." http://www.IHFFC.org

8 Eric Schmitt and Matthew Rosenberg, "General Is Said to Think Attack Broke U.S. Rules," *New York Times*, October 7, 2015.

9 Ibid.

10 Ibid.

11 Eric Schmitt and Matthew Rosenberg, "Hospital Strike Fueled by Units New to Kunduz," *New York Times*, October 21, 2015.

12 Editorial Board, "Is the Pentagon Telling the Truth About Afghanistan?" *New York Times*, October 13, 2015.

13 David Herszenhorn, "Senate Passes Military Bill That Bans Transfers of Guantanamo Detainees," *New York Times*, November 10, 2015.

14 Crawford, "War-Related Deaths, Injury, and Displacement in Afghanistan and Pakistan 2001–2014."

15 Joseph Goldstein, "Clues Point to 'Illegal' Strike on Afghan Hospital, Doctors' Group Says," *New York Times*, November 11, 2015.

16 Jason Cone, "Doctors Without Hospitals," *New York Times*, October 24, 2015.

17 Amy Davidson, "Five Questions About the Bombing of a Hospital in Kunduz," blog entry, *newyorker.com*, October 5, 2015, http://www. newyorker.com/news/amy-davidson/five-questions-about-the-bombing-of-a-hospital-in-kunduz.

18 Ibid.

19 Cone, "Doctors Without Hospitals."

20 Cynthia Brassard-Boudreau and Don Huber, "Shrinking Humanitarian Space? Trends and Prospects on Security and Access," *The Journal of Humanitarian Assistance*, November 24, 2010.

21 Richard Read, "Aid Agencies Reject Money Due to Strings," *Oregonian*, June 6, 2003.

22 Ibid.

Chapter 9 Endnotes

23 There is an extensive literature on the issue of shrinking humanitarian space. This description of the various meanings comes from a review of this literature and the ongoing public conversation about the terms and conditions of humanitarian work. In addition, confidential interviews with NGO representatives were conducted. These sources confirm that, while it is a major topic of concern, there is no single definition that is accepted or applied in the field.

24 Sarah Collinson and Samir Elhawary, *Humanitarian Space: A Review of Trends and Issues*, Overseas Development Institute, London, 2015, http://www.odi.org/sites/odi.org.uk/files/odi-assets/publications-opinion-files/7643.pdf.

25 Michael Pugh, "Civil-Military Relations in Peace Support Operations: Hegemony or Emancipation?" London: ODI, February 2001, 2.

26 Stephen Cornish, "There Can Never Be a Humanitarian Component to Military Action," *Huffington Post*, April 14, 2015, updated June 14, 2015, http://www.huffingtonpost.ca/stephen-cornish/humanitarian-aid-military-action_b_7057226.html.

27 Ibid.

28 Lara Olson, Research Fellow, Centre for Military and Strategic Studies, University of Calgary, "Fighting for Humanitarian Space: NGOs in Afghanistan," *Journal of Military and Strategic Studies* 9, issue 1 (Fall 2006).

29 Some of the differences between Afghanistan and Iraq in the early years of intervention are discussed in Eric James, "Two Steps Back: Relearning the Humanitarian-Military Lessons Learned in Afghanistan and Iraq," *The Journal of Humanitarian Assistance*, November 1, 2003.

30 Joel Charny, "The United States in Iraq: An Experiment with Unilateral Humanitarianism," *Foreign Policy in Focus*, June 26, 2003, www.fpif.org/authors/Joel-Charny/.

31 "Iraq: Some International NGOs Downsizing," IRIN NEWS, irinnews.org, UN Office for the Coordination of Humanitarian Affairs (OCHA), August 28, 2003.

32 David Rieff, "How NGOs Became Pawns in the War on Terrorism," *New Republic*, August 3, 2010.

33 IRIN NEWS, "Iraq: Some International NGOs Downsizing."

Chapter 9 Endnotes

34 "Humanitarian Responses: NGOs as Key Actors in the Field," *NCCI*, May 2007,www.NCCIRAQ.org/en/.

35 Ibid.

36 Dr. Edwina Thompson, "Principled Pragmatism: NGO Engagement with Armed Actors," *World Vision International*, 2008, http://documents.tips/documents/thompson-2007-principled-pragmatism-world-vision.html.

37 Ibid.

38 Ibid.

39 Ibid.

40 Michael Ignatieff, "International Committee of the Red Cross (ICRC)," *Crimes of War*, http://www.crimesofwar.org/a-z-guide/international-committee-of-the-red-cross-icrc/.

41 Dahr Jamail and Ali Al-Fadhily, "In Iraq, NGOs Eyed with Mistrust," *Alternet*, July 24, 2008.

42 Abby Stoddard, "Humanitarian NGOs: Challenges and Trends," *Humanitarian Action and the 'Global War on Terror'*, HPG Report, 1998. The term "briefcase NGOs" refers to NGOs that spring up in response to specific emergencies.

43 Ibid.

44 Sarah Collinson and Mark Duffield, "The Paradoxes of Presence: Risk Management and the Aid Culture in Challenging Environments," *Humanitarian Policy Group*, March 2013, www.odi.org/uk/hpg/.

45 The U.S. Department of Treasury designates certain persons and entities as "Specially Designated Nationals" or "SDNs" for narcotics trafficking, weapons proliferation, terrorism, and other reasons. U.S. sanctions are imposed on such individuals and entities, including blocking the transfer of funds.

46 Sara Pantuliano, Kate Mackintosh, and Sami Elhawary, with Victoria Metcalfe, "Counter-terrorism and Humanitarian Action: Tensions, Impact and Ways Forward, *Humanitarian Policy Group*, *Policy Brief* 43, October 2011, 6.

47 Ibid.

Chapter 10 Endnotes

48 Kate Mckintosh and Patrick Duplat, *Study of the Impact of Donor Counter-Terrorism Measures on Principled Humanitarian Action*, Independent Study Commissioned by United Nations Office for the Coordination of Humanitarian Affairs (OCHA) and the Norwegian Refugee Council (NRC), 2013. Also see Hugh Muir, "Counter-terrorism Laws Can Stifle Humanitarian Action, Study Shows," *Guardian*, July 25, 2013.

49 Youngwan Kim and Peter Nunnenkamp, "Does It Pay for US-based NGOs to Go to War? Empirical Evidence of Afghanistan and Iraq," *Kiel Institute for the World Economy, Working Paper* No. 1878, October 2013, https://ideas.repec.org/p/kie/kieliw/1878.html.

50 Velina Stoianova, "Private Funding: An Emerging Trend in Humanitarian Donorship," *Development Initiatives Briefing Paper*, April 2012.

51 Ibid.

52 "Aid Groups Criticize U.S. Plan on Syrian Refugees," *Washington Post*, September 16, 2015.

53 Kim and Nunnenkamp, "Does It Pay for US-based NGOs to Go to War?" The authors are, respectively, associated with Korea University in Seoul, Korea, and the Kiel Institute for the World Economy in Kiel, Germany, though the views are those of the authors themselves.

54 Ibid.

55 Miriam Arghandiwal, "As Foreign Aid Drives Up, Afghan NGOs Fight To Survive," *Reuters*, July 4, 2012.

CHAPTER 10
Learning by Insurgents

1 For a good detailed argument of this approach, see Dominic Johnson, "Darwinian Selection in Asymmetric Warfare: The Natural Advantage of Insurgents and Terrorists," *Journal of the Washington Academy of Sciences* 95 (Fall 2009): 89–112.

2 Cited in Bruce Hoffman, *Insurgency and Counter-Insurgency in Iraq* (Santa Monica, CA: RAND, June 2004), 6.

3 Publicly released segments of the Manchester Manual are at http://cgsc.cdmhost.com/cdm/ref/collection/p15040coll2/id/3642. Available in the Combined Arms Research Library Digital Library, which is provided by the Army Command and General Staff College.

Chapter 10 Endnotes

4 For examinations of earlier insurgent groups as learning organizations, see Brian A. Jackson, John C. Baker, Peter Chalk, Kim Cragin, John V. Parachini, and Horacio R. Trujillo, *Aptitude for Destruction, Volume 1: Organizational Learning in Terrorist Groups and Its Implications for Combating Terrorism* (Santa Monica, CA: RAND Corporation, MG-331-NIJ, 2005); Brian A. Jackson, John C. Baker, Peter Chalk, Kim Cragin, John V. Parachini, and Horacio R. Trujillo, *Aptitude for Destruction, Volume 2: Case Studies of Organizational Learning in Five Terrorist Groups* (Santa Monica, CA: RAND Corporation, MG-332-NIJ, 2005).

5 Ahmed S. Hashim, *Insurgency and Counter-Insurgency in Iraq* (Ithaca, NY: Cornell University Press, 2006), 163.

6 James J. F. Forest, "Introduction," in *Teaching Terror: Strategic and Tactical Learning in the Terrorist World*, ed. James J. F. Forest (Lanham, MD: Rowman & Littlefield, 2006), Kindle edition, location 270. For other cited training materials, see locations 270–300.

7 A note on terminology: Multiple names are used by varying users for this group, including Islamic State, Islamic State in Iraq and Syria, Islamic State in Iraq and al Shams, and al Daish (the Arabic acronym for the last title). In some ways, these represent the group's change of titles over time, but also have political, diplomatic, and ideological connotations. It is probably most accurate to use the group's name for itself, the Islamic State.

8 For example, see Hashim, *Insurgency and Counter-Insurgency in Iraq*, 17; Brian Reed, "A Social Network Approach to Understanding an Insurgency," *Parameters* 37, no. 2 (Summer 2007): 19–30.

9 Thomas X. Hammes, "Insurgency: Modern Warfare Evolves into a Fourth Generation," *Strategic Forum* 214 (Washington: Institute for National Strategic Studies, National Defense University, January 2005): 6.

10 Shiv Malik, Ali Younes, Spencer Ackerman, and Mustafa Khalili, "How Isis Crippled al-Qaida", *Guardian*, June 10, 2015, http://www.theguardian.com/world/2015/jun/10/how-isis-crippled-al-qaida. Abu Muhammad al-Maqdisa has been termed the intellectual "godfather" of jihadist movement. He has written widely and maintains the website the "Pulpit of Monotheism and Jihad." He also was the mentor for Abu Musab al-Zarqawi, the (now deceased) leader of al-Qaida in Iraq, while the two men were jailed together in Jordan in the mid-1990s. Abu Qatada al-Filistini operated out of the United Kingdom for a number of years and became prominent in jihadist circles for his calls for international jihad.

Chapter 10 Endnotes

11 A similar argument is made by Steven Metz, *Rethinking Insurgency* (Carlisle, PA: U.S. Army War College, Strategic Studies Institute, June 2007), 12–14.

12 Samia Nakhoul, "Saddam's Former Army Is Secret of Baghdadi's Success," Reuters, June 16, 2015, http://www.reuters.com/article/2015/06/16/us-mideast-crisis-baghdadi-insight-idUSKBN0OW1VN20150616. This also has been noted by jihadists in other movements. Malik, Younes, Ackerman, and Khalili, "How Isis Crippled al-Qaida."

13 For a good detailed examination of one such group in an earlier period, see Michael Knights, "The JRTN Movement and Iraq's Next Insurgency," *CTC Sentinel* 4, no. 7 (West Point, NY: Combating Terrorism Center at West Point, July 2011): 1–6.

14 Christoph Reuter, "The Terror Strategist: Secret Files Reveal the Structure of Islamic State," *Spiegel Online* International, April 18, 2015, http://www.spiegel.de/international/world/islamic-state-files-show-structure-of-islamist-terror-group-a-1029274.html.

15 Ibid.

16 Major General Michael T. Flynn, Captain Matt Pottinger, and Paul D. Batchelor, *Fixing Intel: A Blueprint for Making Intelligence Relevant in Afghanistan* (Washington: Center for a New American Security, January 2010).

17 Seth G. Jones, *Counterinsurgency in Afghanistan* (Santa Monica, CA: RAND Corporation, 2008), 37. Also see Mallory Sutika Sipus, Peace Brief 186, "Insurgent Alliances in Afghanistan," United States Institute of Peace, June 2015. In fairness, not everyone agrees with this assessment. For example, see Gilles Dorronsoro, *The Taliban's Winning Strategy in Afghanistan* (Washington: Carnegie Endowment for International Peace, 2009). The key issue in this case, however, might be the relative multiplicity of groups in Afghanistan.

18 Harald Håvoll, "COIN Revisited: Lessons of the Classical Literature on Counterinsurgency and its Applicability to the Afghan Hybrid Insurgency," in *The Character of War in the 21st Century*, eds. Caroline Holmqvist-Jonsäter and Christopher Coker (New York: Routledge, 2009), 60.

19 Seán D. Naylor, "The Islamic State's Best Weapon Was Born in the USA," *Foreign Policy*, June 4, 2015, http://foreignpolicy.com/2015/06/04/hell-on-wheels/. Hannah Allam, "In Reversal, U.S. Official Admits Iraq Troops Reeling

Chapter 10 Endnotes

from Islamic State Offensive," *McClatchy Washington Bureau*, May 20, 2015, http://www.mcclatchydc.com/2015/05/20/267354/in-reversal-us-official-admits.html?utm_source=Sailthru&utm_medium=email&utm_term=%2ASituation%20Report&utm_campaign=SitRep0521#storylink=cpy.

20 Gilles Dorronsoro, *The Taliban's Winning Strategy in Afghanistan*, Washington: Carnegie Endowment for International Peace, 2009; Richard Norton-Taylor, "Taliban switch to long-range fire in fight against UK troops," *Guardian*, June 25, 2010 at https://www.theguardian.com/world/2010/jun/25/taliban-long-range-fire-afghanistan. Accessed August 13, 2016.

21 Hashim, *Insurgency and Counter-Insurgency in Iraq*, 161.

22 Phil Williams, *Criminals, Militias, and Insurgents: Organized Crime in Iraq* (Carlisle, PA: Strategic Studies Institute, June 2009), 115–16.

23 For a brief discussion of IED issues, see Hashim, *Insurgency and Counter-Insurgency in Iraq*, 161–62.

24 Army Press Release, cited in John Reed, "Insurgents Used Cell Phone Geotags to Destroy AH-64s in Iraq," *Defense Tech*, March 15, 2012, http://defensetech.org/2012/03/15/insurgents-used-cell-phone-geotags-to-destroy-ah-64s-in-iraq/#ixzz3coHAYvDN. It should also be noted that insurgents can be equally guilty, as noted in a *Military Times* online article whose headline summarizes the event concisely: Brian Everstine, "Carlisle: Air Force Intel Uses ISIS 'Moron's' Social Media Posts to Target Airstrikes," *Military Times*, June 4, 2015, http://www.militarytimes.com/story/military/tech/2015/06/04/air-force-isis-social-media-target/28473723/?utm_source=Sailthru&utm_medium=email&utm_term=%2ASituation%20Report&utm_campaign=SitRep0605.

25 Caleb Weiss, "Islamic State Uses Drones To Coordinate Fighting in Baiji," *Long War Journal*, April 17, 2015, http://www.longwarjournal.org/archives/2015/04/islamic-state-uses-drones-to-coordinate-fighting-in-baiji.php?utm_source=Sailthru&utm_medium=email&utm_term=%2ASituation%20Report&utm_campaign=SitRep0417.

26 James J. F. Forest, "Introduction", in *Teaching Terror: Strategic and Tactical Learning in the Terrorist World*, ed. James J. F. Forest (Lanham, MD: Rowman & Littlefield, 2006) Kindle Edition, location 349.

27 Michael Kenney, "How Terrorists Learn," in *Teaching Terror: Strategic and Tactical Learning in the Terrorist World*, ed. James J. F. Forest (Lanham, MD: Rowman & Littlefield, 2006) Kindle Edition, location 982.

Chapter 10 Endnotes

28 Bill Roggio and Caleb Weiss, "Over 100 Jihadist Training Camps Identified in Iraq and Syria," *Long War Journal*, June 21, 2015, http://www.longwarjournal.org/archives/2015/06/over-100-jihadist-training-camps-identified-in-iraq-and-syria.php?utm_source=feedburner&utm_medium=email&utm_campaign=Feed%3A+LongWarJournalSiteWide+%28The+Long+War+Journal+%28Site-Wide%29%29.

29 Paul Moorcraft and Peter McLaughlin, *The Rhodesian War: A Military History* (London: Pen & Sword Military, 2008), Kindle Edition, location 1976.

30 For details of this debate, see Fawaz A. Gerges, *The Far Enemy: Why Jihad Went Global* (New York: Cambridge University Press, 2005).

31 Ideological splits between AQ Central and its various purported erstwhile affiliates are examined in Tara Ashraf, et al., *The Spring of Al-Qa'ida's Discontent: An Analysis of Terrorist Propaganda 2001–2012* (Washington: American University, December 2012).

32 Hannah Allam, "In Reversal, U.S. Official Admits Iraq Troops Reeling From Islamic State Offensive," *McClatchy Washington Bureau*, May 20, 2015, http://www.mcclatchydc.com/2015/05/20/267354/in-reversal-us-official-admits.html?utm_source=Sailthru&utm_medium=email&utm_term=%2ASituation%20Report&utm_campaign=SitRep0521#storylink=cpy.

33 Christoph Reuter, "The Terror Strategist."

34 For a useful archive of IS local administration documents, see Aymenn Jawad Al-Tamimi, *Archive of Islamic State Administrative Documents*, January 27, 2015, http://www.aymennjawad.org/2015/01/archive-of-islamic-state-administrative-documents.

35 BBC, "Islamic State NHS-style Hospital Video Posted", April 24, 2015, http://www.bbc.com/news/world-middle-east-32456789.

36 For day-to-day IS governance, see Aidan Lewis, "Islamic State: How It Is Run," *BBC News*, May 22, 2015, http://www.bbc.com/news/world-middle-east-32829096.

37 For a propaganda map showing the area that the Islamic State of Iraq claimed, see July 13, 2007 http://mypetjawa.mu.nu/archives/188678.php.

38 For an overall review of recent Taliban operations, see Lauren McNally and Paul Bucala, *The Taliban Resurgent: Threats to Afghanistan's Security* (Washington: Institute for the Study of War, March 2015).

Chapter 10 Endnotes

39 Waliullah Rahmani, "Taliban Devise New Strategy in Afghanistan: Territorial Control and War on Afghan Intelligence Headquarters," *Jamestown Foundation Terrorism Monitor* 12/18, September 26, 2014, http://www.jamestown.org/programs/tm/single/?tx_ttnews%5Btt_news%5D=42881&cHash=90661e082f272f67fbc4cd23402e8ab0#.VYs83_lViko.

40 Rajiv Chandrasekaran, "Taliban's New Strategy Focuses More on High-profile Assaults, Less on Territory," *Washington Post*, September 18, 2012, http://www.washingtonpost.com/world/national-security/talibans-new-strategy-focuses-more-on-high-profile-assaults-less-on-territory/2012/09/18/369f6c7a-01cc-11e2-b260-32f4a8db9b7e_story.html.

41 Ibid.

42 Bill Roggio and Lisa Lundquist, "Green-on-blue Attacks in Afghanistan: the Data," *Long War Journal*, August 23, 2012 (Data last updated on April 8, 2015) at http://www.longwarjournal.org/archives/2012/08/green-on-blue_attack.php.

43 Richard Sisk, "Taliban Infiltrators Blamed For Insider Attacks," *Military Times*, August 17, 2012, http://www.military.com/daily-news/2012/08/17/taliban-infiltrators-blamed-for-insider-attacks.html.

44 Bill Roggio and Lisa Lundquist, "Green-on-blue Attacks in Afghanistan: the Data."

45 Rajiv Chandrasekaran, "Taliban's New Strategy."

46 Neville Bolt, *The Violent Image: Insurgent Propaganda and the New Revolutionaries* (New York: Columbia University Press, 2012), 36.

47 Dauber, *YouTube War*, viii. Italics in original.

48 International Crisis Group, *Taliban Propaganda: Winning the War of Words?* Asia Report N°158, July 24, 2008, 2. For another example of the Taliban's targeting of multiple audiences, Taliban leader Mullah Omar in an Eid communique in 2009 addressed it to nine distinct audiences: "1) 'our Mujahid people'; 2) 'heroic protective mujahideen in the trenches'; 3) 'those working in the cooperative administration in rights institutions'; 4) 'the Islamic conference and what is referred to as human rights institutions'; 5) 'the educated…the writers…the literary'; 6) 'regional and neighboring countries'; 7) 'the rulers of the White House, and the American war supporters'; 8) 'supporters of freedom from the people of Europe and the West in general'; 9) 'the entire Islamic Nation.'" Bolt, *The Violent Image*, 41.

Chapter 10 Endnotes

49 For some details on this era of Taliban propaganda, see International Crisis Group, *Taliban Propaganda*, 4–6.

50 Ibid., 1.

51 Henry Tuck, *How to Win the Battle Against the ISIS Propaganda Machine*, Canadian International Council, April 23, 2015, http://opencanada.org/features/how-to-win-the-battle-against-the-isis-propaganda-machine/.

52 Dauber, *YouTube War*, 11.

53 Amin Tarzi, "*Neo-Taliban Free To Communicate With Media*, Afghan Report: August 15, 2005," Radio Free Europe/Radio Liberty, http://www.rferl.org/content/article/1340551.html.

54 Dauber, *YouTube War*, 43. Dauber goes on to describe specific instances of this.

55 Andrew Exum, "The Spectacle of War: Insurgent Video Propaganda and Western Response, 1990-Present," *Arab Media & Society* (Oxford, UK: The Middle East Centre, St. Anthony's College, May 2008), 6.

56 Seán D. Naylor, "Top U.S. General: Many Iraqis Believe Washington Aiding Islamic State," *Foreign Policy*, May 20, 2015, https://foreignpolicy.com/2015/05/20/top-u-s-general-many-iraqis-believe-washington-aiding-islamic state/.

57 Lieutenant General Thomas F. Metz, U.S. Army, with Lieutenant Colonel Mark W. Garrett, U.S. Army; Lieutenant Colonel James E. Hutton, U.S. Army; and Lieutenant Colonel Timothy W. Bush, U.S. Army, "Massing Effects in the Information Domain: A Case Study in Aggressive Information Operations," *Military Review*, May/June 2006, 103–13.

58 Bradford H. Baylor (Project Lead, USJFCOM Joint Center for Operational Analysis), "Multinational Force-Iraq (MNF-I) Strategic Communication Best Practices 2007-2008," *Joint Center for Operational Analysis Journal*, 11/2 Spring 2009, 15.

59 News Release, Headquarters International Security Assistance Force–Afghanistan, "ISAF Discusses Insurgent Propaganda Messaging," August 8, 2006, 2.

60 80th Congress, 2nd Session, CH. 36, January 21, 1948, PUBLIC LAWS-CBS. 35, 36-JAN. 27, 1948, 6–14. Also see the discussion in Catherine A. Theohary and John Rollins, *Terrorist Use of the Internet: Information Operations in Cyberspace* (Washington DC: Congressional Research Service, March 8, 2011), 12–13.

Chapter 11 Endnotes

61 For some details, see Broadcasting Board of Governors, "Facts About Smith-Mundt Modernization," undated, at http://www.bbg.gov/smith-mundt/.

62 Major General John F. Kelly, "Foreword," to *Al-Anbar Awakening Volume II Iraqi Perspectives From Insurgency to Counterinsurgency in Iraq 2004-2009*, by Colonel Gary W. Montgomery and Chief Warrant Officer 4 Timothy S. McWilliams (Quantico, VA: Marine Corps University Press, 2009), viii.

63 Montgomery and McWilliams, *Al-Anbar Awakening*, 115.

64 Seán D. Naylor, "Top U.S. General: Many Iraqis Believe Washington Aiding Islamic State," *Foreign Policy*, May 20, 2015, at https://foreignpolicy.com/2015/05/20/top-u-s-general-many-iraqis-believe-washington-aiding-islamic-state/.

65 Daniel S. Roper, "Global Counterinsurgency: Strategic Clarity for the Long War," *Parameters* 38, no. 3 (Autumn 2008): 92–108.

CHAPTER 11
U.S. Intelligence Credibility in the Crosshairs: On the Post-War Defensive

1 See President Barack Obama's *National Security Strategy*, May 2010: "Our intelligence and law enforcement agencies must cooperate effectively with foreign governments to anticipate events, respond to crises, and provide safety and security."

2 For added insight into the spectrum of liaison partnering, see also Jennifer Sims, "Foreign Intelligence Sharing: Devils, Deals, and Details," *International Journal of Intelligence and Counterintelligence* 19, no. 2 (2006): 195–217.

3 There is a growing literature on intelligence partnering, often termed liaison, including, among others, the work of Jennifer Sims (supra); Derek Reveron, "Old Allies, New Friends: Intelligence-Sharing in the War on Terror" *Orbis*, Summer 2006, no. 1: 1-15; James Igoe Walsh, *The International Politics of Intelligence Sharing*, (New York: Columbia University Press, 2010); and Stephane Lefebvre, "The Difficulties and Dilemmas of International Intelligence Cooperation," *International Journal of Intelligence and CounterIntelligence* 16, no. 4 (2003): 527–42.

Chapter 11 Endnotes

4 See Jennifer Morgan Jones, "What use can the United Nations and its agencies make of secret intelligence?" University of Aberystwyth, 2007 (unpublished paper). She states: "…any information provided by national intelligence agencies has the potential to be purposefully biased in order to manipulate UN policy in line with national goals."

5 See Gilles Andreani, "The 'War on Terror': Good Cause, Wrong Concept," *Survival* 46, no. 4 (Winter 2004/5): 31–50. (Following the November 13, 2015, attacks by ISIL in Paris, however, French President Hollande has himself declared "war" on terrorism, contrary to Andreani's key argument that waging "war" is inconceivable domestically.)

6 Those attentive to such signals will recall renaming French fries "freedom fries" in Congressional canteens, and, as this author observed personally, the pointed shunning of the October 3, 2003, observance of German national day at the German ambassador's residence in Washington by almost all senior U.S. officials.

7 Key Judgments: Iraq's Continuing Programs for Weapons of Mass Destruction [from October 2002 National Intelligence Estimate], (http://fas.org/irp/cia/product/iraq-wmd.html).

8 See Walsh, *The International Politics of Intelligence Sharing*, Chapter 1, 1–28, re Curveball.

9 These and other euphemisms, to include calling combat "kinetic operations," deserve a study of their own. For a detailed look at how the U.S. Senate examined this issue, in the face of major reluctance from both the CIA and the White House, see Connie Bruck, "The Inside War: To Expose Torture, Dianne Feinstein Fought the C.I.A.—and the White House," *The New Yorker*, June 6, 2015, http://www.newyorker.com/magazine/2015/06/22/the-inside-war.

10 Paul R. Pillar, *Intelligence and U.S. Foreign Policy: Iraq, 9/11, and Misguided Reform* (New York: Columbia University Press, 2011), 32.

11 Ibid., 42.

12 Ibid., 120.

13 Brian Jones, Failing Intelligence: *The True Story of How We Were Fooled Into Going to War in Iraq* (London, Biteback, 2010), 84. See William Shawcross, *Allies: The U.S., Britain, Europe and the War in Iraq* (London: Publicaffairs [sic] Reports, 2005). In Chapter 18 of former JIC Chairman

Chapter 11 Endnotes

Sir Percy Craddock's book, *Know Your Enemy: How the Joint Intelligence Committee Saw the World*, (London: Murray, 2002) Craddock tells readers that the ideal relationship between the worlds of intelligence and policy is like having adjoining rooms in a third rate hotel—close enough to know what is going on on the other side but without being directly a part of it.

14 See also Jonathan Lord, "Under Cover Under Threat: Cover Identity, Clandestine Activity, and Covert Action in the Digital Age," *International Journal of Intelligence and CounterIntelligence* 28, no. 4 (Winter 2015): 666–91.

15 "Italy denies role in CIA extraordinary rendition of imam," *Yahoo News*, October 16, 2015, http://news.yahoo.com/italy-denies-role-cia-extraordinary-rendition-imam-141658573.html.

16 See also Bowman H. Miller, "The Death of Secrecy: Need to Know… With Whom to Share," *Studies in Intelligence* 55, no. 3 (September 2011): 1–6.

17 Ibid.

18 "Edward Snowden Approached Washington Post, Guardian with Caution," (http://www.huffingtonpost.com/2013/06/10/edward-snowden-washington-post-guardian, accessed November 23, 2015). Both papers then printed a range of revelations reportedly provided by Snowden.

19 See, inter alia, Bradley F. Smith, *The Ultra-Magic Deals* (Novato, CA: Presidio Press, 1992) for insights into the rather fitful beginnings of Anglo-American collaboration in intelligence, especially in wartime communications code-breaking directed against Germany and Japan.

20 Jones, *Failing Intelligence*, 82.

21 Ibid., 229.

22 Ibid., 232–33.

23 Ibid., 225–39.

24 Personal experience and recollection of the author.

25 "Kanzleramt fordert Reform des BND," ZEITONLINE, http://www.zeit.de/digital/datenschutz/2015-04/bnd-nsa-spionage-kanzleramt-reacktionen, accessed April 23, 2015.

26 Andreani, "The 'War on Terror': Good Cause, Wrong Concept," 31–50.

Chapter 12 Endnotes

CHAPTER 12
Conclusion: Lessons of the Lessons

1 Richard D. Hooker, Jr. and Joseph J. Collins, *Lessons Encountered: Learning from the Long Wars* (Washington: National Defense University Press, 2015).

2 Michael R. Gordon and Bernard E. Trainor, *Cobra II: The Inside Story of the Invasion and Occupation of Iraq* (New York: Pantheon, 2006); Thomas E. Ricks, *Fiasco: The American Military Adventure in Iraq* (New York: Penguin, 2006), 32–34, 40–43, 68–76.

3 Craig S. Smith and Richard Bernstein, "3 NATO Members and Russia Resist U.S. on Iraq Plans," *New York Times*, February 11, 2003, http://www.nytimes.com/2003/02/11/international/middleeast/11IRAQ.html?pagewanted=all.

4 Andrew Scobell, David Lai, and Roy Kamphausen, eds., *Chinese Lessons from Other Peoples' Wars* (Carlisle, PA: U.S. Army War College Strategic Studies Institute, 2011).

5 For example, Douglas A. Borer and Stephen W. Twing, "Blundering into Baghdad: An Analysis of Strategy, Structure, Principals and Agents," *Cambridge Review of International Affairs* 24, no. 3 (September 2011): 493–512; Holman W. Jenkins, Jr., "The U.S. Has No Global Strategy," *Wall Street Journal*, January 30–31, 2016, A9.

6 For example, many observers view the preventive U.S. invasion of Iraq in 2003 as illegal because it violated the United Nations Charter by using aggressive force without UN Security Council authorization in the absence of an immediate threat.

7 For a good description of how Soviet leaders saw the West and the Cold War through ideological lenses, see Raymond L. Garthoff, *Soviet Leaders and Intelligence: Assessing the American Adversary during the Cold War* (Washington: Georgetown University Press, 2015).

8 Michael T. Flynn, Matt Pottinger, and Paul Batchelor, *Fixing Intel: A Blueprint for Making Intelligence Relevant in Afghanistan* (Washington: Center for a New American Security, 2010).

9 Harry G. Summers, Jr., *On Strategy: A Critical Analysis of the Vietnam War* (New York: Presidio, 1982), 1.

Chapter 12 Endnotes

10 For example, Bret Perry, "Non-Linear Warfare in Ukraine: The Critical Role of Information Operations and Special Operations," *Small Wars Journal*, August 11, 2015, accessed January 26, 2016 at smallwarsjournal.com/printpdf/27014; Kristin Ven Bruusgaard, "Crimea and Russia's Strategic Overhaul," *Parameters* 44, no. 3 (Autumn 2014): 81–90.

11 John A. Gentry, "Norms as Weapons of War," *Defense & Security Analysis* 26, no. 1 (March 2010): 11–30; William S. Riley, Jr., "Deceived to Intervene: Non-State Actors' Use of Deception to Elicit Western Intervention in Libya in 2011," *American Intelligence Journal* 32, no. 2 (2015), 35–46; John A. Gentry, "Warning Analysis: Focusing on Perceptions of Vulnerability," *International Journal of Intelligence and CounterIntelligence* 28, no. 1 (Spring 2015): 64–88.

12 Kelly M. Greenhill, *Weapons of Mass Migration: Forces Displacement, Coercion, and Foreign Policy* (Ithaca: Cornell University Press, 2010), 60–63.

13 Matt Bradley and Ghassan Adnan, "Fleeing Residents Detail Ramadi Horrors," *Wall Street Journal*, January 2–3, 2016, A5.

14 See, for example, Sam C. Sarkesian, John Allen Williams, and Stephen J. Cimbala, *US National Security: Policymakers, Processes & Politics*, 4th ed. (Boulder: Lynne Rienner, 2008).

15 John A. Gentry, "Intelligence Learning and Adaptation: Lessons from Counterinsurgency Wars," *Intelligence and National Security* 25, no. 1 (March 2010): 50–75.

16 Field Manual 3-24 (and MCWP 3-33.5), *Insurgencies and Countering Insurgencies* (U.S. Army, May 2014), accessed January 4, 2016 at http://fas.org/irp/doddir/army/fm3-24.pdf.

17 For example, Robert Jervis, *Why Intelligence Fails: Lessons from the Iranian Revolution and the Iraq War* (Ithaca: Cornell University Press, 2010), especially chapter 3.

18 Mark M. Lowenthal, *Intelligence: From Secrets to Policy*, 5th ed. (Los Angeles: CQ Press, 2012), 60–61, 67, 207, 251.

19 Leo Blanken and Justin Overbaugh, "Looking for Intel? … or Looking for Answers? Reforming Military Intelligence for a Counterinsurgency Environment," *Intelligence and National Security* 27, no. 4 (July 2012): 559–75.

Chapter 12 Endnotes

20 Benjamin B. Fischer, "Anglo-American Intelligence and the Soviet War Scare: The Untold Story," *Intelligence and National Security* 27, no. 1 (February 2012): 75–92; Len Scott, "Intelligence and the Risk of Nuclear War: Able Archer-83 Revisited," *Intelligence and National Security* 26, no. 6 (December 2011): 759–77.

21 Shawn Brimley et al., *Enabling Decision: Shaping the National Security Council for the Next President* (Washington: Center for a New American Security, June 2015). Accessed September 27, 2015 http://www.cnas.org/ shaping-the-national-security-council; Donald R. Drechsler, "Reconstructing the Interagency Process after Iraq," *Journal of Strategic Studies* 28, no. 1 (February 2005): 3–30.

INDEX

A

Abe, Shinzo 152, 163, 214

Abizaid, John 185

Abu Ghraib prison 105, 115, 170

Abu Muhammad al-Maqdisi 187

Abu Qatada 187

Afghanistan

    Bagram Air Base 206

    government of 158, 161, 194

    Taliban regime 5, 32, 33, 37, 52–53, 77, 83–84, 119–127, 130–31, 133, 135–36, 139, 157–59, 168, 170, 173–75, 177, 186, 188–89, 193–97, 199–200, 222, 224–25

Afghan National Army 160

Al-Aqsa Martyrs' Brigades 186

Alawis 110

Al-Hashd al-Shaabi (Popular Mobilization Forces, Iraq) 86

Al-Nusra, Jabhat 107, 109, 111

Al-Qaida 5, 19, 37–38, 41, 76, 107, 109–11, 116, 119–22, 124, 127–28, 130, 133, 135–36, 139, 174, 185–87, 191, 195, 199

    Al Baqaa fi al-Zuraf al-Sa'ba 186

    Al-Qaida in Iraq, relations with 186, 199

    information operations of 185

    Manchester Manual 185

Al-Qaida in Iraq (AQI) 5, 186–88, 191–92, 198–99, 225

Amir-Abdollahian, Hossein 76, 95

Amu Darya 54

Ansar al-Shariah (Libya) 111

Aqakishi, Mohammad 93

Arab Spring 12, 64, 77

Asad, Bashar al- 79, 86, 106–10, 114

Asa'ib al-Haqq 87

I N D E X

INDEX

Ataturk, Mustafa Kemal 100–01, 104, 109–10, 113

Australia 151, 153, 204, 219

Avetisyan, Andrei 52

B

Bahadur, Hafiz Gul 129–31

Bakr, Haji (Samir Abd Muhammad al-Khlifawi) 187

Baluyevsky, Yuri 51

Barazani, Masoud 106, 109

Barzegar, Kayhan 75

Bashkiria 68

Belgium 11, 219

Berlusconi, Silvio 14–15

Bin Ladin, Usama 187

Blair, Tony 211

Bosnia 13, 15, 34, 83, 178

Bush administration policies of 2, 32, 41–42, 116, 134, 139–42, 203, 205, 207, 220, 227

Bush, George W. 2, 32, 41–42, 116, 134, 139–42, 203, 205, 207, 220, 227

C

Cameron, David 13, 16, 19, 22–23

Campbell, John F. 169

Canada 33, 93, 151, 169, 204

CARE 172, 174, 176–77, 182

Carter, Jimmy 149

Catholic Relief Services 165, 182

Chechen fighters 67–70

Chechnya 49, 56, 58–60, 62–63, 65, 67–70, 71, 178, 225–26

Cheng, Dean 68–69

China 5, 133–46, 152, 161–63, 220–21, 223, 225, 228–29

    critiques of Iraqi war strategy 136–37

    critiques of U.S. war strategy 133–37

    Deng-ism 134, 137–38, 222

INDEX

military modernization 134

People's Liberation Army (PLA) 134, 144–46

perceptions of tensions with United States 133–34, 137–41

perceptions of U.S. intelligence 142, 145–46

perception of U.S. "hegemonic drive" 137–41

perceptions of U.S. military "transformation" 145–46

perceptions of U.S. "preemption/prevention" strategy 133, 140–41

PLA Academy of Military Science Department of Foreign Military Studies 145

PLA National Defense University 144

Christian Democratic Union (Germany) 30, 32

Christian Social Union (Germany) 30, 33

Coalition Humanitarian Liaison Cells (Chicklets) 174

Cold War 14, 27, 34, 43–44, 65, 99–100, 116, 138, 145, 149, 152, 171–72, 222

Collective Security Treaty Organization (CSTO) 53–54

Collins, Joseph 175

Commonwealth of Independent States (CIS) 51, 55, 63

Cone, Jason 171

Cornish, Stephen 169

counterinsurgency 3, 5, 30, 36, 49–50, 56, 65, 67–69, 125, 129, 156–57, 166, 176, 183, 185–200, 216, 226

counterintelligence 84, 185, 188, 203

Craddock, Sir Percy 208

Crytzer, Kurt 197–98

D

Dadullah, Mullah 121

Dagestan 69–70

Davutoğlu, Ahmet 104, 106, 117

Da'wa Party (Iraq) 178

de Maizière, Thomas 16, 33–34, 43

de Mello, Sergio Viera 176

Democratic People's Republic of Korea (DPRK). *See* North Korea

INDEX

Dempsey, Martin 217

Deng Xiaoping 138

Denmark 10–11

Deobandi school of thought 124–26

Die Linke (Germany) 36

Doctors Without Borders. *See* Médecines sans Frontières

E

Economic Community of West African States (ECOWAS) 19

Erdogan, Tayyip 101, 104, 106–08, 110–11, 113, 117

Estonia 60, 62–63, 65

European Court of Human Rights 209

European Union 24, 46, 112, 116, 178, 213

F

Fabius, Laurent 22

Fan Gaoyue 145

Farabundo Martí National Liberation Front (FMLN) (El Salvador) 193

Field Manual (FM) 3-24, *Counterinsurgency* 156–57, 199, 226

Fischer, Joschka 16

Five Eyes 151, 204

Flynn, Michael 2, 188, 222

FMLN. *See* Farabundo Martí National Liberation Front

Fourth Generation Warfare 186

France 4, 8–13, 15, 17–22, 25–27, 33, 38, 203, 207, 213, 218–19

    operations against ISIL 21–22

    operations in Afghanistan 7–8, 27–28

    operations in Libya 10–13, 15

    operations in Mali 17–20

    prospects for future use of force by 26

    public opinion in 8, 12, 21–22

    relations with the United States 12, 19, 21–22

Franks, Tommy 141–42

INDEX

Free Democratic (Liberal) Party (FDP) (Germany) 30, 32–33

Free Syrian Army 107, 109

G

Galula, David 199

Gates, Robert 7, 84, 221, 228

Gellman, Barton 211

Gerasimov, Valery 52

Germany 4–5, 8–9, 11, 15–18, 20–21, 24–27, 29–47, 64, 100, 159, 183, 201, 203, 213–14, 218–20, 222–23, 229

  alliance with the United States, importance of 16–17, 24, 26, 41–42

  Bundesnachrichtendienst (Federal Intelligence Service) 213–14

  Bundestag (Federal parliament) 20, 31, 33, 35, 41, 44

  Bundeswehr (military), missions of 29, 33, 35–38, 41–44

  casualty sensitivity 35–37

  civil-military cooperation (CIMIC) and 39, 227

  criticisms of Afghan policies 31–34, 41–42

  concerns about U.S. policies 31–34, 41–42

  foreign aid 16, 29, 39

  Foreign Office 29, 40

  identity of 34–35

  Kunduz incident 32–33

  Libya operation of 2011 15–17

  Ministry of Defense 30

  Ministry of International Development and Cooperation 29

  military doctrine 42–44

  NATO membership 31–34, 39–45

  operations in Afghanistan 31–35

  Petersberg Conference in 31

  political communication of 40

  political strategy of 30

  prospects for future use of force by 26, 35–37

  Provincial Reconstruction Teams (PRTs) 40–41

INDEX

public opinion in 17, 20, 24, 36–37

Red-Green coalition 31

relationship with ISAF 31–32, 34–34, 41–42

security versus defense 42–45

Vernetzte Sicherheit (networked security) policy 32, 39

Ghani, Mohammad Ashraf 46, 122

Golkar, Saeid 74

Gonzales, Alberto 215

Grand, Camille 7

Green Party (Germany) 30–31

Greenwald, Glenn 211

Group of Eight (G8) 159

Guantanamo Bay Naval Base, prison of 170

Gulf War of 1991 68, 102–04, 138, 142, 145, 148–49, 151

H

Hajizadeh, Amir Ali 79

Haji Bakr. *See* Bakr, Haji (Samir Abd Muhammad al-Khlifawi)

Ham, Carter 84

HAMAS 90, 92–93, 111, 186

Hamedani, Hossein 87

Hammes, Thomas X. 186

Han Xudong 144

Haqqani Network 120–24, 127–31, 225

Hizballah 49, 59, 77, 79–80, 83–84, 86–90, 104, 106, 108–09

2006 war with Israel 59, 104

connections with Iran 77, 79–80, 83–84, 86–90, 106, 108–09

Hollande, François 18

Hooker, Richard 217

Humanitarian Study Group 181

Hussein, Saddam 102, 104, 139, 142, 174–75, 179, 203, 205, 207, 212

INDEX

I

Incirlik Air Base 102, 106

India 119–24, 126–27, 129, 130–31, 220, 225

information operations 4, 62, 71, 80, 93, 185, 191, 194–97, 199–200, 223–24

insurgent groups 2, 5, 32–33, 38, 68, 82, 84, 109, 114, 122, 133, 157, 160, 167–69, 171, 173, 175, 185–200, 206, 217, 224–25

    importance of "strategic patience" to 200

    information operations of, compared to U.S. practice 196–200

    "sub-contracting" 189–90

    strategies 190–94

    use of improvised explosive devices (IEDs) 189–90

intelligence 201–16

    counterterrorism and 215–16

    "extraordinary renditions" and 206

    Five Eyes and 204–05

    partnerships among states and agencies of 201–02

    sharing of 201–05

    Snowden revelations and 206–07, 210–11

    U.S. credibility and 202–04, 205–07, 208–09

    U.S. 2002 National Intelligence Estimate on Iraqi WMD 205, 207, 227

    Wikileaks and 206, 209–10

International Committee of the Red Cross (ICRC) 172, 176–78

International Humanitarian Fact-Finding Commission (IHFFC) 168

International Humanitarian Law 171–72, 180

International Rescue Committee 172–76

International Security Assistance Force (ISAF) 31–32, 34–35, 39–46, 151, 193–94, 197, 219

    Coalition Humanitarian Liaison Cells (CHLCs) 174

    Provincial Reconstruction Teams (PRTs) 40, 167, 174

    Regional Command North 34

Internet 70, 91, 115, 190, 196, 211

INDEX

Iran 5, 22, 55, 73–98, 99–100, 102–04, 106–09, 111, 117, 137, 139, 141, 159, 218, 220–26, 228–29
    Ansar Al Mahdi Corps of 84–85
    Artesh, armed forces of 80–83, 85, 93
    asymmetric warfare strategy of 73, 81, 88–89, 92
    Basij of 85, 89, 92
    Civil Defense Organization of 78
    Cyber Army of 91–92
    cyber operations of 91–93
    information operations of 93–97
    Islamic Revolutionary Guards Corps (IRGC) 74, 78–88, 91–92, 97
    IRGC–Qods Force 79–80, 83–87, 89
    IRGC—Command Network 82–83
    mercenary forces of 86–87
    Ministry of Intelligence and Security (MOIS) 85–86
    mosaic defense strategy 89
    operations in Afghanistan 79–81
    operations in Iraq 79–81
    Pasdaran (*see* IRGC)
    Passive Defense Organization of 91–92
    Peoples' Mujahedin of Iran (MKO) 76–77
    perceptions of winner in U.S. wars of 73–76
    propaganda 85, 88
    views of U.S. strategy 73–76
Iran-Iraq War of 1980–88 78
Iraq
    invasion of Kuwait in 1990 102, 148
    weapons of mass destruction (WMD) 136, 203, 205–08, 210, 212–13
ISIL (self-proclaimed Islamic State of Iraq and the Levant) 20–27, 52–53, 76–77, 81, 84, 93, 95–96, 106–16, 131, 186–200
    Al Hayat Media Center of 196
    Free Youth Assembly of 192
    governance of 186–89

INDEX

    information operations of 194–96

    intelligence service of 188

    NATO military operations against 20–25

    recruiting 191

    strategic patience 200

    strategy of 190–92

    sub-organizations of 189–90

    training of 189–90

Islam 76, 94, 96, 99, 102, 139, 195

    Alawi 110

    Deobandi school of thought of 124–26

    Shia 77, 80–81, 83–87, 94, 96, 102–03, 106, 108, 119, 126, 194

    Sunni 76–77, 85, 93–94, 96, 102, 105–06, 109–10, 117, 187, 191, 198

Islamic Justice and Development Party (AKP) (Turkey) 100–05, 107–09, 112–14

Islamic Revolutionary Guards Corps (IRGC). *See* Iran

Islamic Unity Conference 94

Israel 88–90, 92–96, 101, 104, 106, 108–09, 115–17, 140

Issoufou, Mahamadou 19

Italy 8, 9, 11–12, 14–15, 18, 20–21, 23–26, 159, 209, 218, 220

    constitutional restrictions on use of force of 14

    military operations in Afghanistan 14

    military operations in Albania 14

    military operations in Lebanon 14

    military operations in Libya 11, 14–15, 24

    military operations in Mali 18, 20

    Operation MARE NOSTRUM 24

    prospects for future use of force by 26

    public opinion in 14–15

    relationship with the United States 14

Ivanov, Sergei 50, 60, 70

Ivanov, Viktor 53

INDEX

J

Jafari, Mohammad Ali 87

Jaish-e-Mohammad (JEM) 123, 130–31

Jalali, Gholamreza 78, 91–92

Japan 5, 64, 133, 138, 147–63, 201, 214–15, 218–20, 223–24, 226–227, 229
    alliance with United States 147
    Anti-Terrorism Special Measures Law 150
    casualty aversion 156, 163
    constitution 147
    Defense Facilities Administration Agency (DFAA) 153
    Disarmament, Demobilization and Reintegration (DDR)
      work of 158–60
    Ground Self-Defense Forces 153–58, 161–63
    Guidelines for U.S.-Japan Defense Cooperation 147
    Gulf War of 1991 and 148–149
    Intelligence activities of 151, 214–15
    International Peace Cooperation Activities 157
    Japan Defense Agency 153, 158
    Japan International Cooperation Agency 155, 159–60
    Maritime Self-Defense Forces 149–52, 161–63
    Ministry of Defense 153, 158
    Ministry of Foreign Affairs (MoFA) 153–56
    National Institute of Defense Studies of 156
    Official Development Assistance of 153–54
    Overseas Minesweeping Force of 148, 150
    public opinion in 163, 214
    peacekeeping operations of 148

Jihad 17–20, 49, 119, 123–27, 129, 131–32, 187, 191–92, 194–95, 225

Jones, Brian 208, 212

Jones, Seth G. 188

Jung, Franz Josef 32–33

INDEX

K

Kabulov, Zamir 52–54

Karyakin, Vladimir 63

Karzai, Hamad 121, 188

Kashmir 119, 123–24, 126, 130

  insurgent/terrorist activities in 123–24, 126

  Line of Control of 124

Kataib Hizballah 87

Kayani, Ashfaq Parvez 123, 129

Khamenei, Grand Ayatollah Ali 73, 75, 77, 91, 94–95

Khan Said (Sajna) 129

Khatami, Ayatollah Ahmad 94–95

Khlifawi, Samir Abd Muhammad al-. *See* Bakr, Haji

Khyber Pakhtunkhwa 127

Kitson, Frank 199

Klein, Georg 32

Köhler, Horst 37

Koichi, Koizumi 150

Kosovo, 1999 NATO war over 13–15, 26, 34, 49, 59, 173, 175

Kunduz, Afghanistan 32–33, 35, 40, 166–171

  German collateral damage incident, 2009 32–33, 35

  MSF incident, 2015 166–171

Kurdish Democratic Union Party (PYD) 109, 112

Kurdish Peshmerga 25

Kurdish Workers Party (PKK) 76, 102–04, 106, 109, 112–14

Kuwait 13, 84–85, 102, 138, 148–49, 153

Kyrgyzstan 70

L

Lashkar-e-Jhangvi (LeJ) 124, 126–27, 131

Lashkar-e-Tayyiba (LeT) 123–24, 126–27, 130–31

  Mumbai attack (2008) 123–24

INDEX

Leninist theory of political struggle 63–65, 222

Libya 7–11, 13, 15–19, 21–27, 35, 44, 46, 52, 54–56, 105–06, 108, 111, 204, 218, 222

    Benghazi incident and 111

M

Makarov, Nikolai 55–56, 61

Mali 7–8, 10, 17–22, 25–26

Maliki, Nouri al- 178

Manilov, V.L. 50

Manning, Bradley/Chelsea 206, 209, 211

Mansoor, Mullah Akhtar 123

Manwaring, Max 69

Mazar-e Sharif 159

McCain, John 148

Medvedev, Dmitry 62

Mehsud, Baitullah 129–30

Mehsud, Hakimullah 129

Médecines sans Frontières (MSF) 165–73, 177, 180, 182

    Kunduz incident involving 166–71

Mercy Corps 172

Merkel, Angela 16, 32–34, 213–14

Messner, Yevgeny 61

Milan, Italy 206, 209

Musharraf, Pervez 119–20, 122–23, 125

Muslim Brotherhood 99, 110–111

N

Al-Nahda (Tunisia) 111

National Defense Forces (NDF) (Syria) 87

Natsios, Andrew 175

Nazir, Maulvi 129–30

Netherlands 33

New Zealand 151, 204

INDEX

NGO Coordinating Committee in Iraq (NCCI) 176, 179

Niger 19

nongovernmental organizations (NGOs) 4, 40, 64, 158, 165–84, 226–27

    casualties of 166–71

    concerns about governments of 171

    ethical dilemmas of 173, 178, 180–82

    funding of 179–83

    "humanitarian space" 171–79

    operations in Afghanistan 166–71, 173–75, 180, 182–83

    operations in Iraq 170–76, 178–79, 182–83

    policies of 171–83

North Atlantic Treaty Organization (NATO) 7–27, 30–34, 41–45, 52–56, 83–84, 102, 105, 108, 110–17, 135, 150–51, 170, 178, 183, 202, 204, 213, 218–24, 227

North Korea 55, 90, 139, 141, 148–49, 161, 215

    Agreed Framework 149

North Ossetia 69

Norway 11

O

Obama administration 2, 11, 13, 22, 33, 41, 95, 116, 122, 167–68, 170, 202, 220, 222, 227

Obama, Barack 2, 13, 22, 33, 41, 95, 116, 122, 167–68, 170, 202, 220, 222, 227

Ocalan, Abdallah 113

Omar, Mullah Muhammad 123

Operation DESERT STORM (Iraq) 49, 61

Operation ENDURING FREEDOM (Afghanistan) 31, 151

Operation RESOLUTE SUPPORT (Afghanistan) 34, 46

Operation UNIFIED PROTECTOR (Libya) 44

Overseas Development Institute (ODI) 172

Oxfam 165, 176

Ozal, Turgut 100–05

INDEX

P

Pakistan 5, 37, 87, 119–32, 150–51, 159, 176, 181, 209, 220, 222, 225, 228
   Army of 125, 129–30
   Federally Administered Tribal Areas (FATA) 121, 125, 127–31
   Inter-Services Intelligence (ISI) 123–24, 128–31
   Kashmir policy of 119, 123–24
   Lal Masjid (Red Mosque) raid by 125
   North Waziristan Agency 121, 129–31
   nuclear weapons program of 120, 122
   Operation al-Mizan of 121, 124
   Operation Rah-e-Nijat of 126
   Operation Rah-e-Rast of 126
   Operation Zarb-e-Azb of 121
   policy toward insurgent groups of 119–32
   relations with Afghanistan of 119–32
   relations with India 119–20, 122–24, 126–27, 129
   relations with Washington 121, 122, 129–30
   South Waziristan Agency 121, 125–26, 130
   support for Haqqani Network by 120–24, 127–31
   support for Taliban by 119–22, 125, 130, 131
Patrushev, Nikolai 55, 64, 67
Peace Winds Japan 158–59
Peoples' Mujahedin of Iran (MKO) 76
People's Republic of China. *See* China
Pillar, Paul 207
Powell, Colin 173, 175, 203, 205
Provincial Reconstruction Teams (PRTs) 40, 167, 227
Putin, Vladimir 52–53, 59, 63, 65, 67–68, 70–71 110, 211, 223

Q

Qadhafi, Muammar al- 10, 12, 15, 105
Qatar 93, 95, 99, 111
Qods Force. *See* Iran

INDEX

R

RasGas 93

Reagan, Ronald 228

Red Cross and Red Crescent societies 166, 172, 176–78, 181

Republic of Korea. *See* South Korea

"Revolution in Military Affairs" 146

Rieff, David 176

Rouhani, Hassan 96

Rühe, Volker 44

Rumsfeld, Donald 228

Russia 5, 9–10, 22, 24, 27, 43, 47, 49–72, 99–100, 106, 108–09, 113–14, 117, 135, 139, 161, 171, 206, 210–11, 219–21, 223, 225–26, 228–29

    annexation of Crimea by 9, 24

    assessment of U.S. ability to learn of 54, 58

    assessment of U.S. military doctrine of 51–52, 55–56

    assessment of U.S. strategy in Afghanistan of 51–54

    assessment of U.S. strategy in Iraq of 51

    cyber operations of 61–63

    economic warfare theory of 64

    Federal Drug Control Service of 53

    Federal Security Service (FSB) of 56, 207, 211

    Fisheries Inspectorate of 57

    General Staff of 50–52, 55, 61

    information operations (IO) of 62–67

    information warfare (IW) doctrine of 60–67

    information warfare, differences with U.S. doctrine of 60–63

    insurgencies in North Caucasus of 49

    military doctrine of 50–51

    military forces in Tajikistan of 52–54

    military operations in Afghanistan in 1980s of 49

    military operations in Chechnya of 49, 58–59, 67–70

    military operations in Georgia of 58–59

INDEX

military operations in Syria of 52–53

    SU-24 shootdown 114

military operations in Ukraine of 55

Ministry of Defense (MoD) of 51, 56

Ministry of Interior (MVD) of 56–58, 60

Ministry of Interior, armed forces of (VVMVD) 56–58

National Security Strategy of 67

Nizhny Novgorod Oblast of 66

perceptions of U.S. "net-centric warfare" of 60–67

perceptions of vulnerability of 54–58

precision strike weapons doctrine of 59

public opinion in 68–70

"securitization of the media" of 68–71

Special Designation Forces of MoD 56

Special Designation Forces of MVD (OMSN) 57

Special Purpose Police Detachments (OMON) of 57–58

Spetsnaz of 56

terrorism in 50–52, 56–57

U.S. information warfare against Japan and Germany, perceptions of 64

S

Sadr, Muqtada 87, 198

Sands Casino Corporation 93

Sarkozy, Nicolas 12

Sato, Colonel Masahisa 157

Sattar, Abdul 120

Saudi Arabia 95, 99, 111, 138–39

Saudi Aramco 93

Save the Children 165, 172, 176

Schmidt, Eric 92

Schröder, Gerhard 31–32, 41, 213

INDEX

September 11, 2001 (9/11) attacks 1, 30, 37, 45–46, 119, 123–24, 126, 130–31, 135, 138, 140, 149–50, 159, 187, 202–03, 215, 219, 227

Shanghai Cooperation Organization 53

Shawcross, William 212

Shoigu, Sergei 54, 61

Sipah-e-Sahaba Pakistan (SSP) 124, 127

Smith, Leighton 83

Snowden, Edward 206–07, 210–11

South Korea 148, 183

    Combined Forces Command in 148

Soviet Union 9, 50, 101, 119, 138

Steinmeier, Frank-Walter 25

Stepanov, Oleg 60

Stevens, Christopher 111

Struck, Peter 32, 45

Stuxnet 91, 97, 224

Sudan 83, 148, 161, 167

Summers, Harry 222

Swat Taliban. *See* Tehreek-e-Nafaz-e-Shariat-e-Mohammadi

Switzerland 178

Syria 9–10, 19–25, 35, 46, 52–53, 55, 61, 79–88, 90, 95–97, 99, 102, 104–17, 168, 182, 187, 190–92, 196

    civil war in 9–10, 19–25, 35, 46, 52–53, 55, 61, 79–88, 90, 95–97, 99, 102, 104–17, 168, 182, 187, 190–92, 196

T

Tajikistan 52–54

Takei, Admiral Tomohisa 161–62

Taliban 29, 32–33, 52–53, 77, 83, 84, 119–32, 135–36, 158–59, 168–71, 173, 175, 177, 185–200

    information operations of 193, 195–97

    intelligence activities of 193

    learning by 188

INDEX

    regime of 188–89

    strategic patience of 200, 186, 188

    strategy of 121

Tartarstan 68

Tehreek-e-Nafaz-e-Shariat-e-Mohammadi (TNSM) 125

Tehrik-e-Taliban Pakistan (TTP or Pakistani Taliban) 125–31

Thatcher, Margaret 208

Thompson, Robert 199

Tokyo Conference on Afghanistan 160

Turkey 5, 11, 95, 99–117, 139, 141, 219, 226

    "Armenian Problem" of 101, 110

    civil war risk and 103

    economic costs of war in Iraq of 102–06

    Lost Decade of 103–04

    military capabilities of 101

    military doctrine of 100–02

    policy toward Iraq war of 102–06

    public opinion in 101–02, 104–05, 115–16

    relations with Israel 101, 104, 106, 108–09, 115–16

    relations with Libya 105–06, 108

    relations with the United States 115–16

    role in NATO 100, 105, 107–08, 110–14, 116–17

    security threats of 100–02

    shootdown of Russian aircraft by 99, 114

    Syrian refugees in 108, 112–13

    views about U.S. strategy in Iraq in 2003 of 102–106

    views of Gulf War of 1991 of 102–04

    views of 2011 Libya war of 105–06, 108

    views of civil war in Syria of 106–113

Turkmenistan 52–53

INDEX

U

Ukraine 9, 24, 27, 43, 46, 49, 54–56, 60, 62, 70–71, 110, 114, 219, 223

United Arab Emirates 99, 111

United Kingdom 4, 8–13, 15, 18, 20–23, 25–26, 95, 151, 159, 182, 185, 201, 204–06, 211, 218–20

    House of Commons of 22

    Official Secrets Act of 206

    operations against ISIL by 20–23

    operations in Afghanistan of 201

    operations in Iraq of 20–25

    operations in Libya of 11, 13–14

    operations in Mali of 18, 19–20

    prospects for future use of force by 25–27

    public opinion in 9

    Security Service (MI5) of 206

    Special Intelligence Service (MI6) of 206

    special relationship with U.S. of 10, 13, 19, 26

United Nations 4, 10–17, 21, 24, 31, 51, 100, 135, 139, 141, 144, 148, 161, 168, 172–78, 181, 203, 219

    operations in Afghanistan of 31–32, 34–35, 39–46, 151, 193–94, 197, 219

    operations in Iraq of 144, 148, 176

    peacekeeping missions of 148, 153, 156, 159, 173

    Security Council of 56, 148, 203, 205, 212

    Security Council resolutions of 152

United States

    anti-Turkish political constituencies of 101

    Central Intelligence Agency (CIA) 206

    Counterinsurgency doctrine (FM 3-24) of 199, 226

    democracy promotion of 136, 139–41, 165, 172, 215, 222–23

    Department of Defense policy 174–75

    "enhanced interrogation techniques" of 206, 215

    "extraordinary renditions" of 206

INDEX

Field Manual (FM) 3-24, *Counterinsurgency* of 199, 226

Information and Educational Exchange Act of 1948 (Smith-Mundt Act) 197

information operations of 60–64, 71, 194–97, 199–200, 223–24

Intelligence Community (IC) 202–03, 205–12

Joint Chiefs of Staff 149, 217

National Intelligence Estimates (NIEs) of 205, 227

nation-building in Iraq and Afghanistan and 30, 46, 135–36, 219

National Security Agency (NSA) 210, 213

National Security Strategy 202

Operation DESERT STORM (1991) 49, 61

Operation ENDURING FREEDOM 31, 151

Operations Plan (OPLAN) 5027 of 149

public diplomacy of 39, 69, 223–24

Radio Free Europe of 197

"soft power" of 134–35, 139

special operations forces of 168–69, 198, 215

strategy critiqued 31–34, 41–42, 51–58, 73–76, 102–13, 133–37

War on Terrorism 135, 138–39, 176

U.S. Agency for International Development (USAID) 172, 174–75, 179, 181

funding policies of 179–81

Partner Vetting System of 179–80

Specially Designated Nationals list of 179

U.S. Central Command (USCENTCOM) 151, 185

U.S. Navy 149–51, 163

U.S. Pacific Command (USPACOM) 151

unmanned aerial vehicles (UAVs) 59–60

V

von der Leyen, Ursula 43

INDEX

W

weapons of mass destruction (WMD) 136, 139, 203, 205–08, 210, 212–13

Wikileaks 206, 209–10

World Vision 165, 172, 177–78

Y

Yeltsin, Boris 71

Yemen 79, 95, 99, 111, 162, 168

Yoshizaki, Tomonori 156–57

Yugoslavia 219

Z

Zarif, Javad 74–76

Zebari, Hoshyar 74

Zhao Xiaozhuo 145

Zoller, Richard 63

zu Guttenberg, Karl-Theodor 33, 36, 42–43

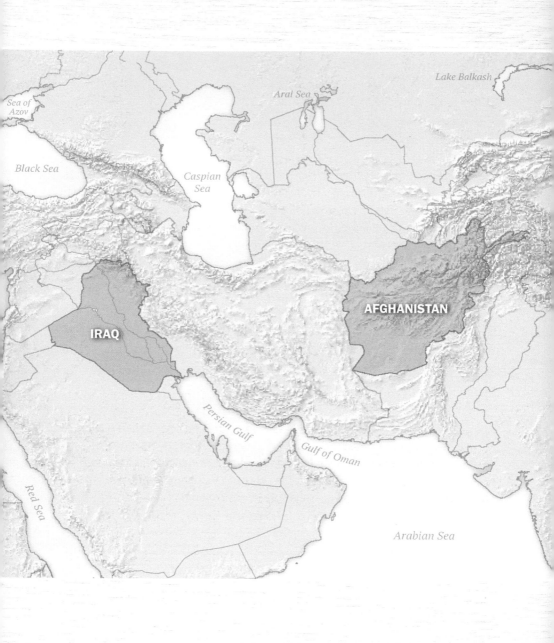

CONTRIBUTORS

Pauline H. Baker, Ph.D., is president emeritus and a trustee of The Fund for Peace, a nongovernmental organization where she initiated several innovative programs, including the *Fragile States Index*, which is published annually in *Foreign Policy* magazine. She also was a professorial lecturer at the Johns Hopkins School of Advanced International Studies, an adjunct professor at Georgetown University, and a lecturer at the University of Lagos, Nigeria, where she lived for 11 years. Dr. Baker received her doctorate with distinction in political science from the University of California, Los Angeles. She is a member of the Council on Foreign Relations, was a Rockefeller Foundation Fellow, and served as a professional staff member on the Senate Foreign Relations Committee. She also worked at the Carnegie Endowment for International Peace, the Aspen Institute, and the Battelle Memorial Institute. Specializing in state fragility and resilience, her most recent work is a series of papers exploring the "Correlates of Economic Development and Inequality in Conflict Affected Environments" for Creative Associates International. She is author of over 100 publications, including "Unraveling Afghanistan," which appeared in *The American Interest* (December 2013).

K.A. Beyoghlow, Ph.D., is adjunct professor of international politics at the Elliott School of International Affairs at the George Washington University and adjunct professor of homeland security and the U.S. Intelligence Community at American University in Washington, DC. He is a former professor of grand strategy and policy and resident scholar on the Middle East, North Africa, and Islamic studies at the National War College and the chair of the Department of Culture and Regional Studies. He completed a 2-year special assignment as the U.S. State Department principal representative to the President's Periodic Review Board, where he and five other senior interagency officers were tasked with reviewing the legal and political status of the remaining detainees at the Guantanamo Naval Facility in Cuba. Dr. Beyoghlow earned his doctorate in political science from the University of California at Berkeley. He is fluent in verbal and written Arabic. Dr. Beyoghlow started his U.S. government career as a political analyst in 1982 with the U.S. Army 4th Psychological Operations Group at Fort Bragg, North Carolina, where he worked on political issues with a focus on the greater Middle East and Iran. He joined the Directorate of Intelligence at the CIA as a political analyst in 1985.

He was later a foreign affairs officer of the U.S. Coordinator for Counterterrorism at the U.S. Department of State, where he was responsible for initiating and implementing U.S. counterterrorism policy for the Middle East and the Eastern Mediterranean, including Turkey, Greece, Malta, and Cyprus. He is the recipient of numerous U.S. government and other awards, including the Director of Central Intelligence Exceptional Intelligence Award in 1983 and 1984.

Stephen Blank, Ph.D., is a senior fellow at the American Foreign Policy Council in Washington, DC. From 1989 to 2013, he was a professor of Russian national security studies at the Strategic Studies Institute of the U.S. Army War College in Pennsylvania. Before these appointments, Dr. Blank was associate professor for Soviet studies at the Center for Aerospace Doctrine, Research, and Education of Air University at Maxwell Air Force Base and assistant professor of Russian history at the University of Texas, San Antonio. Dr. Blank has published over 1,000 articles and monographs, and published or edited 15 books on Soviet/Russian, U.S., Asian, and European military and foreign policies. He has testified frequently before Congress on Russia, China, and Central Asia, consulted for the CIA and major think tanks and foundations, chaired major international conferences, been a commentator on foreign affairs in U.S. and international media, and advised major corporations on investing in Russia. His most recent book is *Russo-Chinese Energy Relations: Politics in Command* (Global Markets Briefing, 2006). He is currently writing a book *Light From the East: Russia's Quest for Great Power Status in Asia*, to be published by Ashgate Publishers. Dr. Blank's M.A. and Ph.D. are in Russian history from the University of Chicago. His B.A is in history from the University of Pennsylvania.

Lawrence E. Cline, Ph.D., is an adjunct professor with Troy University and a contract instructor with the Counterterrorism Fellowship Program, Center for Civil-Military Relations, Naval Postgraduate School. In the latter position, he has worked in over 30 countries. He is a retired U.S. Army military intelligence officer, with assignments as a military observer in southern Lebanon during the Israeli occupation and as an advisor in El Salvador during its civil war. Dr. Cline had intelligence assignments in Operation DESERT STORM, Somalia, and Iraq. He is the author of *Pseudo Operations and Counterinsurgency: Lessons from Other Countries* (Strategic Studies Institute, 2005); *The Lord's Resistance Army* (Praeger, 2013); and co-editor (with Paul Shemella) of *The Future of Counterinsurgency: Contemporary Debates in Internal Security Strategy* (Praeger, 2015). He is also the author of numerous academic articles and book chapters on insurgencies and terrorism.

Michael W. David, Ph.D., is a faculty member at the National Intelligence University's School of Science and Technology Intelligence, where he teaches courses on cyber and geostrategic intelligence. He worked with SAIC/Leidos and the Scitor Corporation from October 2009 to March 2014. Previously, Dr. David worked for the Cubic Corporation of San Diego, California, from March 1982 to September 2009. He served as a vice president in Tokyo, New York City, Singapore, and Brussels. Dr. David served on active duty in the U.S. Army in Korea and Japan from 1971 to 1981, and in the Army Reserve from 1981 to 1999. While on active duty, he served in reconnaissance, special forces, and information warfare units. His last reserve service was at the U.S. Mission to the United Nations in New York at the rank of lieutenant colonel. Dr. David holds an M.S. in system management from the University of Southern California. While serving as an officer in the U.S. Army, he studied at the Defense Language Institute and the Foreign Service Institute, and is fluent in Japanese. Dr. David is a graduate of the Stanford Graduate School of Business Executive Program, and has also studied cryptography at the Massachusetts Institute of Technology and Swiss Federal Institute of Technology Zurich. Dr. David wrote his doctoral thesis on critical infrastructure protection at Kyushu University, Japan. His research has focused on secure identity and access control systems, information analysis systems, security for the electrical power infrastructure, and supervisory control and data acquisition (SCADA) systems.

Thomas E. Dowling is a retired U.S. foreign service officer. Over his 30-year career, he served in Pakistan, Egypt, Iran, Tunisia, the United Arab Emirates, Jerusalem, Switzerland, and Mongolia. From 1987 to 1990, he was State Department representative and deputy head of delegation for the U.S.-Soviet Nuclear Testing Talks and led a U.S.-Soviet working group that produced new protocols to the Peaceful Nuclear Explosions Treaty and Threshold Test Ban Treaty, enabling their ratification by both countries. In the last 6 years of his career, he served as deputy director and acting director of the Office of North African, Near East, and South Asian Affairs in the Department of State's Bureau of Intelligence and Research. After retirement, he was a professional staff member of the Commission on Terrorist Attacks on the United States (9/11 Commission) on the team that analyzed the origins of al-Qaida. Mr. Dowling also was a member of the National Intelligence University faculty. He holds a variety of awards, including the National Intelligence Medal.

John A. Gentry, Ph.D., is adjunct associate professor with the Security Studies Program of Georgetown University's Edmund A. Walsh School of Foreign Service and adjunct associate professor with the School of International and Public Affairs, Columbia University. He was for 12 years an intelligence analyst at CIA, where he worked mainly economic issues associated with the

Soviet Union and Warsaw Pact countries; for two of those years he was senior analyst on the staff of the national intelligence officer for warning. He is a retired U.S. Army Reserve officer, with most assignments in special operations and intelligence arenas. He was mobilized in 1996 and spent much of that year as a civil affairs officer in Bosnia. Dr. Gentry formerly taught at the College of International Security Affairs, National Defense University, and at National Intelligence University. His research interests primarily are in intelligence and security studies. His most recent book is *How Wars are Won and Lost: Vulnerability and Military Power* (Praeger Security International, 2012). He received his Ph.D. in political science from the George Washington University.

Peter Viggo Jakobsen, Ph.D., is associate professor at the Institute for Strategy, Royal Danish Defence College, and professor (part time) at the Center for War Studies, University of Southern Denmark. He is a former head of the Department of Conflict and Security Studies and director of The Defence and Security Studies Research Programme at the Danish Institute for International Studies, and former associate professor in the Department of Political Science, University of Copenhagen. He is a frequent commentator in the Danish and international media on defense and security issues, gives many lectures on these issues, and has acted as an advisor and consultant for several governments and international organizations. He has written extensively on civil-military cooperation and the integrated approach, coercive diplomacy, Danish and Nordic foreign and security policy, NATO, peace and stabilization operations, and use of military force.

David Lai, Ph.D., is research professor of Asian security affairs at the Strategic Studies Institute of the U.S. Army War College. His recent publications are *The PLA in 2025* (U.S. Army War College Press, 2015) and "China's Moves and Countermoves in the Asia-Pacific," which appeared in *Parameters* (Winter 2014/15). This article applies the game of Go to put U.S.-China competition and Asia-Pacific conflicts in perspective. It also introduces a theoretical analysis of the U.S.-China power transition in its second stage. Both are groundbreaking contributions to the study of international relations.

Patrick Keller, Ph.D., is the coordinator of foreign and security policy at the Konrad Adenauer Foundation in Berlin, Germany. He studied international relations at Bonn University, Germany, and Georgetown University, Washington, DC, and holds a Ph.D. in political science from Bonn University, where he was an assistant professor of political science and North American studies from 2003 until 2008. Dr. Keller is a frequent commentator on national radio and TV, and his essays on international security have appeared in numerous newspapers and magazines, including the *Wall Street Journal*, *Survival*, and the *Weekly Standard*. He has published five books.

Bowman H. Miller, Ph.D., teaches graduate courses in globalization and intelligence, conflict analysis, European issues, foreign intelligence partnerships, thesis methodology and design, and all-source analysis at National Intelligence University (NIU). Before joining the NIU faculty in August 2005, he served for 27 years in the U.S. Department of State in intelligence and terrorism analysis positions, the last 18 as director of analysis for Europe in the Bureau of Intelligence and Research. From 1969 to 1978, he was a regular U.S. Air Force officer performing special investigations and counterintelligence analysis in Germany and in Washington. He was educated at the University of Iowa, Cornell University, the University of Tübingen (Germany), and at Georgetown University, where he received his Ph.D. in German in 1983. His research interests, lectures, and publications center on conflict analysis, intelligence challenges, all-source analysis, European and German issues, transatlantic relations, and the role of language in politics and diplomacy.

William M. Nolte, Ph.D., is research professor with the School of Public Policy of the University of Maryland. He is the former director of education and training in the Office of the Director of National Intelligence and chancellor of National Intelligence University, and is a former deputy assistant director of central intelligence, CIA. He was director of training, chief of legislative affairs, and senior intelligence advisor at the National Security Agency. He also served as deputy national intelligence officer for the Near East and South Asia during the first Gulf War. He has taught at several Washington area universities, is on the board of CIA's *Studies in Intelligence*, and directed the CIA Intelligence Fellows Program. He holds a B.A. from La Salle University and a Ph.D. from the University of Maryland.

Stephen Tankel, Ph.D., is an assistant professor in the School of International Service at American University and a non-resident senior fellow at the Center for a New American Security. Professor Tankel specializes in international security with a focus on terrorism and counterterrorism, political and military affairs in South Asia, and U.S. foreign and defense policies related to these issues. He has published widely on these topics and conducted field research on conflicts and militancy in Algeria, Bangladesh, India, Lebanon, Pakistan, and the Balkans. He has also lived and worked in Egypt. Columbia University Press published his first book, *Storming the World Stage: The Story of Lashkar-e-Taiba*, in summer 2011, and will publish his next one exploring how partner nations in the Middle East, North Africa, and South Asia enable and constrain U.S. counterterrorism efforts. In addition to his writing, Professor Tankel is on the editorial board of *Studies in Conflict and Terrorism* and is a senior editor of the web magazine *War on the Rocks*. He is frequently asked to advise U.S. policymakers and practitioners on a range of security issues. Professor Tankel spent 2014 serving as a senior advisor for Asian and Pacific security affairs at the Department of Defense. He received his Ph.D. in War Studies from King's College London, has an M.Sc. from the London School of Economics, and a B.S. from Cornell University.

GPO U.S. GOVERNMENT PUBLISHING OFFICE 2018 – 405-099